THE
SPECTACULAR
PAST

THE SPECTACULAR PAST

Popular History and the Novel in Nineteenth-Century France

MAURICE SAMUELS

CORNELL UNIVERSITY PRESS

ITHACA AND LONDON

Parts of Chapters One and Five appeared in an earlier version as "Realizing the Past: History and Spectacle in Balzac's *Adieu*," in *Representations*, no. 79. © 2002 by the Regents of the University of California. Reprinted from *Representations* by permission of the University of California Press. Part of Chapter Two appeared in an earlier version as "Illustrated Historiography and the Image of the Past in Nineteenth-Century France," in *French Historical Studies*, vol. 26, no. 2. Reprinted from *French Historical Studies* by permission of Duke University Press.

First published 2004 by Cornell University Press
First printing, Cornell Paperbacks, 2004

Printed in the United States of America

Library of Congress Cataloging-in-Publication Data
Samuels, Maurice.
   The speactaclar past : popular history and the novel in nineteenth-century France / Maurice Samuels.
      p. cm.
   Includes bibliographical references and index.
   ISBN 0-8014-4249-4 (colth : alk. paper) — ISBN 0-8014-8965-2 (pbk. : alk. paper)
   1. French fiction—19th century—History and criticism.   2. History in literautre.   I. Title.
   PQ653.S23 2004
   843'.709358—dc22   2004010283

Cloth printing   10   9   8   7   6   5   4   3   2   1
Paperback printing   10   9   8   7   6   5   4   3   2   1

Contents

Illustrations

Acknowledgments

I was able to undertake the initial research for this book in Paris thanks to a Bourse Chateaubriand given by the French government, a Harvard University Term-Time award, and a Krupp Foundation grant given by the Center for European Studies at Harvard University. A Packard Fellowship provided time to begin writing, and research funds given by the University of Pennsylvania allowed me to return to Paris for three additional summers to complete the book. I thank these various institutions for their generous support.

I had the good fortune to work with remarkable scholars in the Department of Romance Languages and Literatures at Harvard University. My thanks go first to the late Naomi Schor, mentor and friend, whose brilliant scholarship has been a continual source of inspiration. I could not have written this book without the help of Jann Matlock, who offered guidance at every stage, from original conception to final revision. Susan Suleiman has provided encouragement since my undergraduate days, and I thank her for her careful reading. Tom Conley was generous with his editing and enthusiasm. I also thank Patrice Higonnet, Alice Jardine, Barbara Johnson, Christie McDonald, and Per Nykrog for their help.

This book benefited enormously from the readings it received at Cornell University Press, especially those by Catherine Nesci and Vanessa Schwartz, whose perceptive criticisms sharpened many of my ideas. I owe a huge debt to Richard Terdiman for providing comments on the entire book, as well as to those colleagues who helped me refine one or more chapters: Diane Brown, Margaret Cohen, Ghita Schwarz, Mary Sheriff,

Daniel Sherman, and Susan Weiner. Frank Bowman kindly proofread the final version and offered many valuable suggestions.

Gerald Prince and Caroline Weber read multiple drafts and have made work a pleasure. I thank my other colleagues in the French section of the Department of Romance Languages at the University of Pennsylvania for their advice and encouragement: Kevin Brownlee, Joan DeJean, Lance Donaldson-Evans, Philippe Met, Lydie Moudileno, Michèle Richman, and my chair, Carlos J. Alonso. I'm also grateful to colleagues in different areas of the university who lent their expertise: Roger Chartier, Barbara Fuchs, Ignacio López, Millicent Marcus, Kevin Platt, Peter Stallybrass, and Emily Steiner. Jerome Singerman and Liliane Weissberg deserve special thanks for their friendship and support.

I learned a great deal from the students in my graduate seminars on Realism and Literature and Spectacle at the University of Pennsylvania, who engaged with the issues in this book in intelligent ways. Many colleagues have provided feedback on papers I have delivered from this material at conferences. I thank especially the participants at the Nineteenth-Century French Studies Colloquium for welcoming me into their ranks. The members of the History of the Material Text seminar at the University of Pennsylvania, as well as the members of the Department of French and Italian at Miami University of Ohio, made very useful comments. Colleagues here and in France have been a wonderful source of research suggestions: Haskell Block, Marshall Brown, Barbara Cooper, Judith Dolkart, Mary Donaldson-Evans, Priscilla Ferguson, Odile Krakovitch, Lawrence Kritzman, Sandy Petrey, Stephen Pinson, Jean-Marie Roulin, Jacob Soll, and Margaret Waller.

I am grateful to Antoine de Baecque for sponsoring my Bourse Chateaubriand. I thank all those who helped me at the Bibliothèque Nationale de France, the Archives Nationales, the Bibliothèque de l'Arsenal, the Bibliothèque Historique de la Ville de Paris, the Bibliothèque de l'Opéra, and the Bibliothèque Marmottan, as well as at the libraries of Harvard University and the University of Pennsylvania. Erin Kearney provided expert research assistance. Bernhard Kendler, my editor at Cornell University Press, has been very supportive throughout the entire publishing process. I also thank Teresa Jesionowski and Julie Nemer for shepherding the book through the final stages of production.

I am very lucky to have so many friends who are great scholars and writers. Margaret Flinn, Seth Graebner, Elisabeth Hodges, and Jenny Lefcourt have been vital interlocutors since I began this project. David Geller, Valerie Steiker, and Elliot Thomson provided editorial advice and moral support all along the way. My other friends helped in ways that cannot be measured. My stepmother, Barbara Samuels, has been a constant inspiration, and my father, Richard Samuels, has made everything possible. I dedicate this book to the memories of my mother, Virginia Samuels; my grandmother, Edith Samuels; and my aunt, Judith Samuels.

M. S.

THE
SPECTACULAR
PAST

Introduction

Honoré de Balzac's *Le Colonel Chabert* (1832) begins with a curious digression. A hero of the Napoleonic Wars has recently returned to Restoration-era Paris only to discover that everyone believes he is dead. Distraught and disheveled, the man attempts to hire a lawyer to prove that he is in fact still alive and to help him recover his name, his fortune, and his wife. His pathetic appearance, however, fails to inspire confidence in the lawyer's clerks. After taunting the would-be hero and sending him on his way, they interrupt the story with a debate over his true identity: "I'll bet everyone tickets to a spectacle that he was not a soldier,"[1] declares one of the clerks, Godeschal. This challenge then provokes a discussion of the stakes of the wager: "What theater will we go to?" one of the clerks asks. "To the Opera!" another responds with glee. Alarmed at the ruinous proposition of taking the whole office to the Opera, Godeschal tries to hedge his bet by defining his terms, pointing out that the word *spectacle* means more than just a theatrical performance: "What is a spectacle?" replies Godeschal. "Let's first establish the *facts of the matter*. What did I bet, gentlemen? a spectacle. What is a spectacle? Something you see" (32).

---

1. "Ah! je parie un spectacle pour tout le monde qu'il n'a pas été soldat." Honoré de Balzac, "Le Colonel Chabert," *Le Colonel Chabert suivi de trois nouvelles* (Paris: Gallimard, 1974), 31. Subsequent quotations are cited in the text. I have elected to use the English word *spectacle* in my translation, rather than the more common *show*, to retain the resonance of the original French. All translations from the French throughout this book are my own unless otherwise specified.

The clerk's parody of a legal inquiry into the nature of spectacle fails to convince his comrades. "But in your system," one of them complains, "you could satisfy the bet in bringing us to see water flow under the Pont-Neuf" (32). Godeschal is then forced to admit that not everything that can be seen constitutes a spectacle, but only things "that one sees for money" (32). A commercial character distinguishes spectacles from sights that are merely visible. As Godeschal points out, however, such a definition includes even an inexpensive form of entertainment such as the Curtius wax display. The other clerks protest, but Godeschal defends his claim: "I'll bet a hundred francs [. . .] that Curtius's display contains all the qualities that constitute a spectacle. It consists of a thing to see at different prices according to the place from which one looks" (33). With no further objections to this definition of the spectacle, the clerks finally return to their jobs and to the story: "To work, gentlemen!" (33) one of them finally declares.

Scholars of literature have ignored this passage in a text that has otherwise been analyzed minutely, both as an exemplar of Balzac's early Realist style and as a commentary on the Restoration's effort to put the Revolutionary and Imperial past behind it, to "turn the page" of history.[2] Godeschal's musings on the spectacle seem to take the reader on a detour, away from the story of a man attempting to recover an identity lost amid the chaos of revolution and war and into the irrelevant realm of nineteenth-century popular culture. This book is located at the intersection where Balzac's text goes astray—or rather at the point where the seemingly diverse threads of the narrative converge. As I show, the search for historical identity and knowledge about the past during and after the French Revolution and the Napoleonic Wars led to precisely such spectacles as the Curtius wax display discussed by Godeschal and his fellow clerks. Far from being a meaningless interruption in the narrative, the question "What is a spectacle?" lies at the heart of Chabert's attempt to recover his former self, as well as at the center of my inquiry into the invention of the modern historical imagination in nineteenth-century France.

I began this book as an attempt to understand the references to history in fictions that have traditionally been called "Realist," such as *Le Colonel Chabert*.[3] Why do certain works by Balzac and Stendhal depict

2. One such analysis can be found in the 1974 preface by Pierre Gascar to Balzac, *Le Colonel Chabert* (7–18). Gascar writes that Balzac, "Like a large part of France in 1830 [. . .] attempts to turn the bloody pages of history" (18).

3. Although I problematize the term *Realism* below, I use its capitalized form to refer to a specific group of French novels of the nineteenth century. English, Russian, and German novels take up the question of history in interesting ways but lie beyond the scope of this book, as do realistic novels from other centuries.

the past as a problem? Whereas Romantic historical novels by Walter Scott, Victor Hugo, and Alexandre Dumas *père* transport the reader back in time, attempting with more or less success to materialize a realistic vision of the past before the reader's eyes, Realist fictions from the 1830s tend to take place in the present (or in the very recent era of the Restoration) and many show characters who come to bad ends as the result of a historical obsession. Like Colonel Chabert, Philippe de Sucy, the hero of Balzac's *Adieu* (1830), remains fixated on the events of the recent past and dies after reenacting a Napoleonic battle scene. In Stendhal's *Le rouge et le noir* (1830), Julien Sorel attempts to copy historical models and ends up on the scaffold, whereas in Stendhal's *La chartreuse de Parme* (1839) the Prince courts disaster by aping Louis XIV.[4] Why, I wanted to know, do these Realist texts show a present in which the past weighs on the characters, corrupting their lives and subverting their destinies? What does this negative view of history signify?[5] And what does it say about French culture in the nineteenth century?

Numerous scholars have described how modernity instituted, and was in turn defined by, a new conception of history. The character of this new relation to the past depends on the way modernity is periodized. Some locate the shift in the era of the Renaissance and Reformation, when medieval notions of the unity and immutability of past and present gave way to a new recognition of change and of time as a dynamic force.[6] Others see a more decisive break with the Revolution[7] and the early nineteenth century.[8] Richard Terdiman has described how the post-Revolutionary period witnessed the loss of an organic connection with the past as traditional forms of government and modes of life were overthrown, forcing a new

---

4. The list does not end here. In Balzac's *Illusions perdues* (1843) and in Gustave Flaubert's *L'éducation sentimentale* (1869) the protagonists dream of becoming historical novelists in the style of Walter Scott and fail to make the most of the present.

5. In general, I take *the past* to refer to the events that form the historical record and *history* to refer to the attempt of consciousness to come to terms with the past, to give it form. Anthony Kemp, in *The Estrangement of the Past: A Study in the Origins of Modern Historical Consciousness* (New York: Oxford University Press, 1991), however, shows how the two entities are intertwined: "The past cannot exist as an object apart from the consciousness of it" (vi). When I refer to *the spectacular past*, therefore, I mean a certain vision of the past engendered by spectacular forms of historical representation.

6. See, for example, Kemp, p. 104.

7. Throughout this book, when unmodified, the term *Revolution* refers to the French Revolution of 1789.

8. Reinhart Koselleck, in *Futures Past: On the Semantics of Historical Time*, trans. Keith Tribe (Cambridge: MIT Press, 1985), observes that the three centuries leading up to the Revolution witnessed a "temporalization of history, at the end of which there is the peculiar form of acceleration which characterizes modernity" (5).

recognition of the past as different and of the present as dislodged from what had gone before. Terdiman refers to this rupture as a "memory crisis" in which "the very coherence of time and of subjectivity seemed disarticulated" and the new notions of identity characteristic of modernity took shape.[9] The new form of historical consciousness, according to Terdiman, developed in the early nineteenth century as a response to this crisis.

Attempting to understand the destructive obsession with history that characterizes the protagonists of certain key Realist fictions, I began to investigate the so-called historical renaissance of early nineteenth-century France.[10] According to most accounts, during the decade prior to the emergence of literary Realism in 1830, the group later known as the Romantic historians began to alter the way the past was represented.[11] In the work of Prosper de Barante, François Guizot, Auguste Mignet, Jules Michelet, Augustin Thierry, and Adolphe Thiers, historiography ceased to be a stale compilation of constantly repeated facts about French monarchs, as it had largely been during the ancien régime, and became instead a site of animation and contention.[12] As many scholars have pointed out, Romantic history writing brought the past to life through renewed attention to archival sources and a highly imagistic writing style, but also explored the previously taboo topic of the Revolution, revealing it to be a necessary and organic force in French cultural life. History became overtly political, as well as increasingly relevant to an understanding of the emergence of the modern world. But if this version of the rise of a new historical consciousness

9. Richard Terdiman, *Present Past: Modernity and the Memory Crisis* (Ithaca: Cornell University Press, 1993), 3–4.

10. I borrow the term *renaissance* to describe the renewed attention to history in the early nineteenth century from Terdiman (ibid., 32). Hayden White employs a similar metaphor of death and regeneration when describing Romantic historiography's renewal of the "moribund" discipline of history in "Romantic Historiography," in *The New History of French Literature*, ed. Denis Hollier et al. (Cambridge: Harvard University Press, 1989), 633.

11. The following studies have been crucial in shaping my understanding of nineteenth-century French historiography: Lionel Gossman, *Between History and Literature* (Cambridge: Harvard University Press, 1990); Georges Lefebvre, *La naissance de l'historiographie moderne* (Paris: Flammarion, 1971); Sophie-Anne Leterrier, *Le XIXe siècle historien* (Paris: Belin, 1997); Linda Orr, *Headless History: Nineteenth-Century French Historiography of the Revolution* (Ithaca: Cornell University Press, 1990); Ann Rigney, *The Rhetoric of Historical Representation: Three Narrative Histories of the French Revolution* (Cambridge: Cambridge University Press, 1990); and Hayden White, *Metahistory: The Historical Imagination in Nineteenth-Century Europe* (Baltimore: Johns Hopkins University Press, 1973).

12. Voltaire's brand of philosophical history writing was an exception to the compilation histories that dominated the ancien régime, and an important, although contested, model for the Romantics.

in nineteenth-century France helps explain the parodic passages in Gustave Flaubert's last novel, *Bouvard et Pécuchet* (1881), in which the ex-clerks endlessly debate the merits of conflicting explanations of the Revolution, each taking sides according to his political persuasion, it failed to illuminate what I saw as the core the Realist attitude toward history—a view of the past as an alienating and destructive force, a false model, leading the plots of the characters awry.[13]

Something seemed to be lacking in accounts of nineteenth-century France's historical renaissance; Romantic historiography alone could not be to blame for the negative representation of history in Realism.[14] As the vast cultural production of the period revealed, however, the Romantic historians did not write in a vacuum. The renewal of interest in history in France in the decades following the Revolution embraced not only the relatively limited production of professional historians, destined to a socially and intellectually elite readership, but also a veritable explosion of popular forms of historical representation.[15] In addition to traditional media—such as painting,[16] historiography, and the novel—a variety of visual entertainments took history as their primary subject during the first half of the nineteenth century. Wax displays (which, like the Curtius wax display mentioned in *Le Colonel Chabert,* predate the Revolution), phantasmagoria shows, panoramas, dioramas, and Boulevard theater all exploited history for profit during this period, luring crowds of paying customers with

13. Sophie-Anne Leterrier uses *Bouvard et Pécuchet* to introduce her account of nineteenth-century French historical developments (*XIXe siècle historien,* 9).

14. I use the term *historiography* throughout this book to designate writing about the past rather than to refer to discourse on the writing of the past.

15. I use the word *popular* to refer to forms of representation that were relatively accessible in terms of both the financial and intellectual investment they required. As I show, such representations were geared toward a largely bourgeois public throughout the first half of the nineteenth century. *Popular* is thus not a synonym of *mass culture,* a phenomenon that began in the second half of the nineteenth century. Vanessa Schwartz offers a similar definition of *popular* in *Spectacular Realities: Early Mass Culture in Fin-de-Siècle Paris* (Berkeley: University of California Press, 1998), 2. In *Popular French Romanticism: Authors, Readers, and Books in the 19th Century* (Syracuse: Syracuse University Press, 1981), James Smith Allen provides a model for looking beyond conventional canonical categories to show how "Romanticism was an enormously popular phenomenon in Paris from 1820 to 1840" (3–4).

16. History painting had a long and well-established tradition in France as the most noble of genres. As nineteenth-century history painting has been the subject of several excellent studies, however, it does not concern me directly in this book. See Stephen Bann, *Paul Delaroche: History Painted* (Princeton: Princeton University Press, 1997); Christopher Prendergast, *Napoleon and History Painting: Antoine-Jean Gros's* La Bataille d'Eylau (Oxford: Clarendon Press, 1997); and Beth S. Wright, *Painting and History during the French Restoration* (Cambridge: Cambridge University Press, 1997).

realistic visual representations of events, particularly those from the recent past of the Revolution and Empire.[17]

I began to understand the innovations of Romantic historiography as part of a widespread effort to envision the past in a new way. The desire to *see* history that new popular forms of history both inspired and gratified defined a radically different experience of the past that took shape in the Romantic period. The transformation of history into what Balzac's clerk refers to as something to be viewed for a price represented a cultural shift with profound—and, according to Realist novels, dangerous—implications for the organization of knowledge and the structuring of the self in the modern world.[18] The clerks' effort to define the spectacle in *Le Colonel Chabert* thus no longer appeared to be a meaningless digression in a work about history and memory but rather represented a particularly apt means of characterizing the material conditions through which the past came to be known in nineteenth-century France. In turning both visual and commodified, history became a spectacle, and Realist fiction diagnosed the alarming symptoms of this transformation.

By examining traditional forms of historical representation, such as historiography, alongside popular spectacles, I seek to redefine the French historical renaissance of the Romantic period. I show how Romantic historiographic innovations formed part of a wider impulse to foreground the image, both as a literal object and as a conceptual tool, in early nineteenth-century historical representation and to market these images to a history-hungry public. In my view of the period's obsession with history, Romantic historians and historical novelists were surrounded by such popular forms of representation as Robertson's phantasmagoria show,

17. Stephen Bann relates Romantic historiography to larger cultural forces and other media, particularly fiction and painting, in *The Clothing of Clio* (Cambridge: Cambridge University Press, 1984). See also Stephen Bann, *The Inventions of History: Essays on the Representation of the Past* (Manchester: Manchester University Press, 1990). Stuart Semmel describes nineteenth-century British practices of memory in "Reading the Tangible Past: British Tourism, Collecting, and Memory after Waterloo," *Representations* 69 (2000): 9–37.

18. In *Les mots et les choses* (Paris: Gallimard, 1966), Michel Foucault locates an epistemic rupture in the conception of history in French culture at the end of the eighteenth century and the beginning of the nineteenth, but characterizes this transformation as a shift away from a "visible" and toward a "philosophical" conception of time. The anatomy lessons of Cuvier at the Muséum d'histoire naturelle, which replaced the (visible) classifications of Buffon with an inquiry into the way species change through time, typify this shift for Foucault (140–44). I would argue that the new conception of history following the French Revolution, although perhaps "philosophical," is all the more "visible." For more on conceptions of natural history and their representation in this period, see Maurice Samuels, "Drôles d'oiseaux: Le Muséum d'histoire naturelle et les langues de l'histoire au XIXᵉ siècle," in *Langues du XIXᵉ siècle*, ed. Graham Falconer, Andrew Oliver, and Dorothy Speirs (Toronto: Centre d'Études Romantiques Joseph Sablé, 1998), 107–21.

historical book illustration, and the twenty-nine new plays about Napoleon that attracted enormous crowds in the 1830–31 theatrical season. I use the term *surrounded* in part literally, because during this period history even became the subject of a new style of panoramic wallpaper design.[19] I should emphasize from the start, however, that this is not another book about the Romantic historians, but rather an effort to contextualize their works by revealing the links between canonical Romanticism and popular forms of historical representation.

In this book, I offer a cultural and material history of a characteristically modern way of seeing the past. Following Roger Chartier and Lynn Hunt, I take cultural history to mean not only a history of culture that looks beyond traditional canonical boundaries to include popular forms of literary and artistic production, but also a method of historical analysis that examines cultural products and their public as part of a complex network of economic exigencies, social anxieties, and political forces.[20] By showing how a spectacular—which is to say visual and commodified—historical imagination took shape through the development of new optical technologies, I emphasize the importance of materiality in tracing a history of mentalities: my history of history in nineteenth-century France documents the evolution of the forms and practices through which the past came to be known in this period. Moreover, by calling attention to the way the new popular representations of history functioned as commodities within the increasingly dominant capitalist order, as well as loci both of ideological manipulation and resistance, I show how the history of history proves central to a more general history of modernity as it took shape in France, and particularly in Paris, during this period.[21]

19. Odile Nouvel-Kammerer, *Papiers peints panoramiques* (Paris: Flammarion, 1990), 288. According to Nouvel-Kammerer, historical wallpaper designs from the period included *Kléber in Egypt* (1818), *The French in Italy* (c. 1830), *The Battle of Austerlitz* (1829–30), and the *July Revolution* (1830–35). Giuliana Bruno discusses panoramic wallpaper as a protofilmic experience in *Atlas of Emotion: Journeys in Art, Architecture, and Film* (New York: Verso, 2002), 165–69.

20. See Roger Chartier, *Cultural History: Between Practices and Representation*, trans. Lydia G. Cochrane (Ithaca: Cornell University Press, 1988); Lynn Hunt, ed., *The New Cultural History* (Berkeley: University of California Press, 1989). More recently, Victoria E. Bonnell and Lynn Hunt have collected essays assessing the impact of the cultural turn in the social sciences in *Beyond the Cultural Turn* (Berkeley: University of California Press, 1999). Their introduction provides a useful account of the rise of cultural history and historical sociology as well as a description of their methodologies (1–32).

21. The spectacles of history that I consider here were largely but not exclusively a Parisian phenomenon. Romantic historical novels and illustrated histories did make their way to the provinces, as did some plays about Napoleon. On the origins of modernity in nineteenth-century Paris, see Marshall Berman, *All That Is Solid Melts into Air: The Experience of Modernity* (New York: Simon and Schuster, 1982); T. J. Clark, *The Painting of Mod-*

My interest lies in detecting the work that the new popular forms of historical representation seemed to perform for a culture emerging, like Chabert, from the chaos of Revolution and war. Why did the French effort to forge new national, class, and individual identities after this period of turmoil, and during a period of continued economic and political upheaval, coincide with the rise of a spectacular historical consciousness?[22] The coincidence is not gratuitous; the demand for visual realism in historical representation—fulfilled by new representational technologies such as the panorama—sprang from a desire to ground Revolutionary and post-Revolutionary identities in a stable vision of the past. By simulating total historical vision, by making details of the past visible with an unimagined degree of specificity, the new spectacles of history purported to reassure spectators that a difficult past could be known and mastered.[23]

Nineteenth-century French Realist novels expose this reassurance as a dangerous illusion. After the first four chapters describing the development of a new form of spectacular history and the emergence of a new kind of historical spectator during and after the Revolution, I show in the final two chapters how certain early Realist fictions by Balzac and Stendhal critique the effects of the spectacular historical consciousness. Instead of providing the ground for a stable set of identities to emerge, the new mode of historical vision subverts the very identities the spectacles had purported to foster. For the heroes of Balzac and Stendhal, spectacular forms of history inhibit the formation of subjectivity and prove alienating or even deadly.

The new popular forms of historical representation that were changing the nature of the past in the early nineteenth century do not necessarily appear explicitly in the novels of Balzac and Stendhal. Realist novels do not

---

ern Life: Paris in the Art of Manet and His Followers (Princeton: Princeton University Press, 1984); David Harvey, *Paris, Capital of Modernity* (New York: Routledge, 2003).

22. I focus on France in this book because of the way historical factors (the need to make sense of the Revolution and Napoleonic Wars as home-grown phenomena) intersected with cultural developments (the rise of Romantic historicism and literary Realism) in the nineteenth-century French context. Historical spectacles were, however, popular in other countries as well during the nineteenth century—indeed, as I show, the panorama and the novels of Scott were British imports.

23. Numerous representational practices posited the detection of visible signs as the key to knowledge in early nineteenth-century France. The pseudoscience of physiognomy purported to read a person's moral character from facial characteristics just as the popular literary genre of *physiologies* made the burgeoning metropolis legible through the classification and decoding of types. On the link between these new modes of vision and popular forms of Realism, see Margaret Cohen, "Panoramic Literature and the Invention of Everyday Genres," in *Cinema and the Invention of Modern Life*, ed. Leo Charney and Vanessa R. Schwartz (Berkeley: University of California Press, 1995), 227–52.

catch the historical spectacles in the act of alienating their protagonists. Although the novels occasionally make reference to spectacular forms of historical representation—as in Stendhal's *Le rouge et le noir,* in which the characters debate the merits of various real Romantic historical dramas— Realist novels generally show the effect rather than the cause of the obsession with history plaguing the nineteenth century.[24] Balzac's characters do not actually look at historical panoramas—although something quite close does occur in *Adieu*—but the spectacular mode of historical vision epitomized by the panorama determines the way Balzacian characters relate to the past. My goal is to describe how French literary Realism emerged in part as a reaction to Romanticism's spectacular mode of viewing history.

Although scholars have long used the term *Realism* to describe a style or genre of nineteenth-century literary production, such a use is problematic.[25] Whereas Romanticism in France repeatedly attempted to define itself through manifestos,[26] Realism did not, at least at first, boast a coherent set of principles or claim followers. Balzac's declaration in *Le père Goriot* (1835) that "All is true"[27] and Stendhal's familiar characterization of the novel in *Le rouge et le noir* as "a mirror moving along a main road"[28] have led to the common misconception that French Realism constituted itself as a school in the 1830s aiming at the objective reproduction of reality. In fact, as Jann Matlock has shown, the first applications in France of the term *Realism* to a set of aesthetic principles were made in the 1840s by critics hostile to Balzac's fiction.[29] During the trial over Flaubert's

24. Modes of spectacular historical representation recur as topoi in Realist fiction throughout the nineteenth century. In Gustave Flaubert's *Madame Bovary* (1857; reprint, Paris: Gallimard, 1972), Emma learns about the past by eating off plates decorated with historical scenes, and comes to see history as a "murky expanse [immensité ténébreuse]" (67). In Flaubert's *Bouvard et Pécuchet* (1881; reprint, Paris: Gallimard, 1970), the clerks find in the novels of Alexandre Dumas *père* all the charms of a "magic lantern" (202).

25. Jann Matlock, in "Censoring the Realist Gaze," in *Spectacles of Realism,* ed. Margaret Cohen and Christopher Prendergast (Minneapolis: University of Minnesota Press, 1995), shows how the label *Realism* was forged through anxieties about looking and was imposed on writers by hostile critics (28–65).

26. The preface to Victor Hugo's historical drama *Hernani* (1830; reprint, Paris: Gallimard, 1995) offers a celebrated definition of Romanticism: "Romanticism, which has so often been wrongly defined, is nothing else but [. . .] liberalism in literature" (32).

27. "Ah! Make no mistake: this drama is neither a fiction nor a novel. *All is true,* it is so truthful that everyone can recognize its elements in themselves, perhaps even in their hearts." Balzac, *Le père Goriot* (1835; reprint, Paris: Gallimard, 1971), 22. Italics indicate English in the original.

28. Stendhal, *Le rouge et le noir* (1830; reprint, Paris: Flammarion, 1964), 398.

29. Matlock, "Censoring the Realist Gaze," 28–65. Bernard Weinberg provides a valuable survey of nineteenth-century criticism in *French Realism: The Critical Reaction, 1830–1870* (New York: Modern Language Association, 1937).

Madame Bovary in 1857, the attorney for the prosecution railed against "realist literature" as an art that attacks moral decency, and the judgment of the court, which exonerated Flaubert, described "realism" as "the negation of the beautiful and the good."[30] Flaubert, however, never called himself a *Realist*. To speak of Realism in regard to Balzac and Stendhal, then, is to accept anachronism in exchange for a convenient designation. I hope to endow the term with a more historically accurate set of associations.

As Christopher Prendergast states, "Realism" as a "developed concept [. . .] belongs rather to the twentieth century" than to the nineteenth.[31] Although authors who would later be called *Realist* did not, at least at first, see themselves as forming a coherent literary movement in the nineteenth century, the various critical movements of the twentieth century, from Marxism to structuralism to feminism, all defined themselves in part by offering definitions of what they designated as Realist literary practice. Each of these critical movements has helped to problematize or nuance the primitive conception of Realism as an objective reproduction of reality that developed from the pronouncements of Balzac and Stendhal. For Marxists such as Georg Lukács, Realism grew out of a particular world-historical moment and represents the attempt to expose the ideological effects of historical change, particularly the encroachments of capitalism, on individual consciousness.[32] Roland Barthes sees Realism as a construction rather than a reflection of reality and emphasizes the way writers such as Balzac generated a "reality effect" through manipulations of language aimed at naturalizing ideological perspectives, endowing them with the appearance of objectivity.[33] Feminists such as Naomi Schor underscore the investment of these ideological perspectives in the reproduction of patriarchy.[34]

The conception of Realism advanced in this book borrows from these recent approaches, but situates the novels that scholars refer to as Realist in relation to other discourses of their time. Following the lead of cultural historians and scholars of literature who have revealed the connection be-

30. "Le procès de *Madame Bovary*" in Flaubert, *Madame Bovary*, 491.

31. Christopher Prendergast, "Introduction: Realism, God's Secret, and the Body," in *Spectacles of Realism*, ed. Margaret Cohen and Christopher Prendergast (Minneapolis: University of Minnesota Press, 1995), 2.

32. See Georg Lukács, *The Historical Novel*, trans. Hannah Mitchell and Stanley Mitchell (1937; Lincoln: University of Nebraska Press, 1983); and *Studies in European Realism*, trans. Edith Bone (1948; New York: Grosset and Dunlap, 1964).

33. See Roland Barthes, "L'effet de réel," *Communications II* (Paris: Seuil, 1968), 84–89.

34. See Naomi Schor, *Breaking the Chain: Women, Theory, and French Realist Fiction* (New York: Columbia University Press, 1985).

tween literary Realism and such diverse contemporary phenomena as world's fairs, collections and museums, medical treatises on hysteria, and the morgue, I highlight the aesthetic and ideological overlapping between Realist fictions and the various ways that nineteenth-century French culture viewed the past.[35] In my study of the early Realist fictions of Balzac and Stendhal, history not only emerges as a privileged theme but is also shown to determine elements of style and structure.

At first glance, such a foregrounding of history may seem like a return to the concerns of an earlier Marxist criticism. In *The Historical Novel* (1937), Georg Lukács argues that Realism applies the techniques of the Romantic historical novel (as inherited from Walter Scott) to the world of the present. Balzac, he writes, "passes from the portrayal of *past history* to the portrayal of the *present as history*."[36] What gets left out of Lukács's formulation of the smooth transition between Romanticism and Realism, however, is a recognition of the way the past is problematized within the early Realist fictions of Balzac and Stendhal. Lukács overlooks all the terrible fates that befall Realist protagonists because of their fixation on a spectacularized past.

As I show, Romantic historicism reveals a complicity with the spectacular historical entertainments of the early nineteenth century. Like the panorama, Romantic forms of historical representation (in historiography, drama, and the novel) generally evoke a realistic vision of a past world and offer this illusion to the reader/viewer as a ground for the formation of identity.[37] Realist fiction, in contrast, shows the negative effects of a spectacular historical vision. Realist protagonists such as Philippe de Sucy and Julien Sorel may act like Romantic historians (or historical novelists or actors in Romantic dramas) in their attempts to resurrect the past according to the logic of the spectacle, but the texts that contain them

35. Recent works that approach nineteenth-century Realism in relation to the cultural history of the time include Jann Matlock, *Scenes of Seduction: Prostitution, Hysteria, and Reading Difference in Nineteenth-Century France* (New York: Columbia University Press, 1994); Schwartz, *Spectacular Realities.*

36. Lukács, *Historical Novel,* 83.

37. French Romantic historians writing in the 1820s include Prosper de Barante, François Guizot, Jules Michelet, Auguste Mignet, Augustin Thiers, and Adolphe Thierry. French Romantic historical novelists writing in the wake of Walter Scott include Alfred de Vigny, Prosper Mérimée, Victor Hugo, and Alexandre Dumas *père.* Romantic historical dramatists include Hugo and Dumas *père.* As I show in the chapters that follow, these writers kept producing Romantic texts even after Balzac and Stendhal began to critique the spectacular approach to the past in 1830. For a discussion of nineteenth-century technologies of visuality, including such contemporary spectacles as the panorama, in relation to British Romanticism, see William Galperin, *The Return of the Visible in British Romanticism* (Baltimore: Johns Hopkins University Press, 1993).

point to the futility and danger of such historical gestures. In this book, I present Realism less as a poetics than as a theory of history, one that diagnoses the dangers of a certain way of looking at the past.

But if I read literature as theory, what place does this leave for theory as such? As the preceding discussion of twentieth-century theories of Realism indicates, there are limits to applying recent theories to earlier historical periods. The theory of spectacle provides a case in point. The Situationist movement of the late 1950s and 1960s used the concept of spectacle to designate—and critique—modern capitalism's extension of control over individual and social consciousness. In *The Society of the Spectacle* (1967) Guy Debord offers an analysis of the way modern Western society deploys images to destroy the unity of life and the reality of lived experience, leading to the pervasive alienation that he took to be characteristic of modern subjectivity.

Although Debord himself is vague about the precise dates of the emergence of the society of the spectacle, he does indicate that he sees it as an essentially twentieth-century phenomenon.[38] Debord's reticence has not, however, prevented historians from backdating the spectacle to the mid- to late nineteenth century to explain such phenomena as the emergence of modernist artistic representation and the rise of mass culture.[39] In what follows, I look even farther back in time, to the early nineteenth century, for indications of the spectacle's emergence, but not without reconfiguring, which is to say historicizing, Debord's theory.

History is crucial for Debord, but his view of the spectacle's relation to the past differs in significant ways from my own. As Jonathan Crary observes, "As much as any single feature, Debord sees the core of the spectacle as the annihilation of historical knowledge—in particular the destruction of the recent past."[40] For Debord, the spectacular organization of society prevents subjects from perceiving time as anything other than a commodity, parceled out like a vacation and divorced from nature's cycli-

---

38. In *La société du spectacle* (Paris: Gallimard, 1992), Guy Debord does not periodize his concept. In his later *Commentaires sur la société du spectacle* (Paris: Gérard Lebovici, 1988), however, he specifies that the origins of spectacular culture date to the 1920s. Jonathan Crary suggests that this date corresponds to the first experiments leading to television or, more probably, the development of synchronized sound in cinema, in "Spectacle, Attention, Counter-Memory" *October* 50 (1989): 97–107.

39. In *Painting of Modern Life,* Clark associates the rise of the spectacle with such earlier phenomena as Haussmann's reconstruction of Paris in the 1850s and 1860s and sees the art of Manet and his followers as inextricably linked to these developments. In *Spectacular Realities,* Vanessa Schwartz describes how modernity involves the transformation of consumers into spectators and locates the origin of this process in *fin-de-siècle* Paris.

40. Crary, "Spectacle, Attention, Counter-Memory," 106.

cal rhythms. "The spectacle, as the current social organization of the paralysis of history and memory, of the abandonment of history based on historical time, is a *false consciousness of time*."[41] The erasure of what Debord calls "historical time" proves essential to the maintenance of the spectacular regime because it prevents the kind of awareness (of the possibility of change, of the dialectic) that could lead to revolution. In place of historical time, Debord explains, the spectacle imposes an eternal present.

In the account I provide of the nineteenth century's view of the past, the spectacle does not so much abandon history as fixate on it obsessively. The spectacle acts on history by rendering it as a static image that is then offered for consumption as entertainment. My focus on the early nineteenth century as a key moment in the formation of the spectacular historical imagination allows us to see how the rise of new forms of popular representation goes hand in hand with the need to assimilate, or in the words of Debord to "abandon," the Revolution. I argue that the emergence of such technologies as the panorama and the diorama, precursors to television and cinema, at precisely the moment that the French public was struggling with the effects of the Revolution, is not a random conjunction, but a vital link in the "progress" to modernity.

Rather than simply apply Debord's theory of the spectacle to the nineteenth century, I examine how the nineteenth century theorized the spectacles of its own era. Debord certainly did not coin the term *spectacle*. According to the *Trésor de la langue française,* by the early nineteenth-century *spectacle* not only referred to various forms of public entertainment but had also acquired a figurative definition as that which attracts attention, as in "servir de spectacle, faire spectacle," and that which presents itself for observation or study.[42] One look at a nineteenth-century newspaper confirms the prevalence of the term in the period: daily listings of all sorts of entertainments, from theater and Opera to the panorama and wax display, often appeared under the rubric "Les Spectacles." Yet, as indicated by the passage from Balzac's *Le Colonel Chabert* with which I began, the term possessed a semantic indeterminacy that demanded clarification and necessitated debate. Indeed, a debate over the nature of the spectacle, although not always designated as explicitly as in *Le Colonel Chabert,* runs through both the popular press and the novelistic production of the period.

41. Debord, *La Société du spectacle,* 114, emphasis in original.
42. Tellingly, perhaps, the dictionary cites a letter by that famous observer of the French Revolution, Joseph de Maistre, from 1808: "Mon fils me dévore, malgré une sagesse qui fait spectacle ici." *Trésor de la langue française. Dictionnaire de la langue du XIXᵉ et du XXᵉ siècles (1789-1960)* (1971; reprint, Paris: Gallimard, 1992), 855.

Each of the first four chapters of this book explores a facet of this debate in relation to a different medium or genre that took history as its subject—popular entertainments (such as the wax display, the phantasmagoria, and the panorama), historiography, Boulevard theater, and the historical novel. In addition to describing how a specific historical genre or medium became visual and commodified during the Romantic period, each of these chapters also focuses on an aspect or effect of history's spectacularization that, while central to the genre or medium in question, also sheds light on the larger phenomenon of the spectacular past. Chapter 1, on popular entertainments, takes up the question of visual realism and its appeal to viewers. Chapter 2, on historiography, focuses on the epistemological claims of visual forms of history and their political ramifications. Chapter 3, on theater, centers on the problem of historical identification and the development of individual and national identities based on a vision of the past. Chapter 4, on the historical novels of Scott and his French imitators, describes the dynamics of popularity and the commodification of history. Taken together, these chapters build toward a general theory of the spectacular past.

Each of the first four chapters also describes how critics of the particular genre or medium in question resisted the spectacularization of the past in explicit or covert ways. These chapters thus develop simultaneously a theory of the historical spectacle and its critique. In the final two chapters on Balzac and Stendhal, I show how literary Realism emerged in France both as a product of this debate over the spectacularization of history and as a contributor to it. I show how early Realist texts reflect many of the critiques of the historical spectacle formulated previously in the popular press while foreshadowing the critiques of later theorists from Karl Marx to Debord. I focus on early Realist texts by Balzac and Stendhal from the 1830s because even though the negative effects of the spectacular past can still be felt in their later novels, as well as in the novels of Flaubert, history ceases to be the defining theme in these works.

Following the definition set down in *Le Colonel Chabert,* my own response to the question "What is a spectacle?" is likewise: something to be seen for a price. But if my definition emphasizes the visuality and commodification of the spectacle, I understand these categories, particularly that of the visual, in broad ways. Whereas the visual nature of such forms of historical representation as the panorama, the wax display, the theater, and book illustration is self-evident, the visuality of an unillustrated novel or history can only be understood metaphorically. Yet this metaphor is essential to understanding the ekphrastic efforts of such Romantic writers as Scott and Michelet, who attempted to transfer the properties of one medium into another, to generate the effects of visual representation in their writing.[43] Even an unillustrated text becomes spectacular through the use of verbal images that materialize an object before the mind's eye. Indeed, the originality of Scott, and of the Romantic historians who looked to Scott as a model, lies precisely in the adaptation of the form of fiction or historiography to the spectacular conventions of nineteenth-century historical culture. I argue that Romantic historiography and historical novels function, in telling and important ways, like panoramas.

Although this book offers a cultural history of a certain way of viewing the past, it does not unfold in a strictly chronological fashion. I have organized the chapters according to genre or medium rather than date. Chapter 1, on popular historical entertainments, does begin at the beginning, with the introduction of wax displays in pre-Revolutionary Paris and of phantasmagoria shows and panoramas at the end of the eighteenth century. But it also describes how these and similar forms of historical entertainment continued to seduce audiences into the nineteenth century. Chapter 2 traces the rise of illustrated historiography and focuses on the introduction of a new technique of wood engraving in the 1830s and 1840s. Chapter 3 recounts how the most significant form of spectacle in the nineteenth century, the theater, changed its mode of historical representation in the Romantic period and focuses on the explosion of plays about Napoleon following the July Revolution of 1830. Chapter 4 then reaches back to 1816, when the first translation of Walter Scott appeared in French, to describe how the historical novel became a spectacle. As I show, Scott had an enormous influence on all the spectacular forms of historical representation in nineteenth-century France, including Romantic historiography and the Romantic historical drama of the 1820s and 1830s. I have chosen to discuss his impact after these other genres so as to keep the three chapters on the novel together.

The last two chapters on the fiction of Balzac and Stendhal reveal how the transition in the work of both these writers from Romanticism to Realism around 1830 involved a rejection of the historical spectacle. These chapters provide a logical end point for what has come before and make reference to many different forms of historical representation, but I have not attempted to show how Balzac and Stendhal critiqued each and every aspect of the spectacular past mentioned in the preceding chapters; rather, I read these Realist novels as a general diagnosis of the dangers of a certain way of looking at history epitomized by historical spectacles. Specific features of the spectacle's infiltration of each genre, although not always re-

43. I take up the issue of ekphrasis in relation to Scott's visual poetics in Chapter 4.

ferred to again in my readings of Balzac and Stendhal, are illustrative of a general mind-set that comes under fire in the Realist novel.

Whereas the first four chapters cast a wide net, reading a number of forgotten works in order to provide a picture of the broad range of historical representation during the period, the last two chapters provide detailed analysis of a few well-known novels that epitomize what I define as Realism's reaction to Romanticism's spectacular form of historical representation. If I reproduce conventional canonical categories by privileging Realist fiction in the final section of the book, it is not out of an allegiance to a transcendent notion of its aesthetic merit but rather because of the way certain Realist novels buck historical trends. My claims for Realism's exceptional status depend on seeing it in relation to—and, indeed, in dialogue with—a range of historical discourses from the time.

Much of my discussion in this book centers on the year 1830. A significant year in French political history, marking the transition from the conservative constitutional monarchy of the Bourbon Restoration to the liberal bourgeois monarchy of the citizen-king Louis-Philippe, 1830 also marks the moment at which the trend toward spectacular historical representation reached a climax and a crisis. Many scholars, from Georg Lukács to Peter Brooks, have commented on the relation between the political revolution of 1830 and the momentous literary development of the same year, namely the rise of Realism in the fiction of Balzac and Stendhal.[44] In this book, I argue that Realism emerged not only from political but also from cultural upheaval and that Realism's representation of the past as a problem responds to debates over the nature of history that dominated the intellectual landscape of the moment. As I show, the spectacular model of historical representation continued to develop and expand in the nineteenth century despite Realism's warnings. Indeed, it continues to determine how we view the past today.

Although the scope of this book does not extend beyond the boundaries of nineteenth-century France, the issues it raises have relevance for our own time and place. Just as nineteenth-century media such as the panorama and the Boulevard theater depended on history for their primary subject matter and received from history the justification for their technological developments, so too do our own modern technologies of mass communication—cinema, television, and virtual reality—engage in a symbiotic relation with the past. Hollywood looks to history and history looks to Hollywood; each year sees the production of more historical films

---

44. See Lukács, *Historical Novel,* 84; Peter Brooks, *Reading for the Plot* (Cambridge: Harvard University Press, 1984), 62–66.

whose techniques of verisimilitude perpetually astound. The result is a continued spectacularization of the historical imagination—a relation to the past both visual and commodified, dominated by images and subject to the laws of the marketplace. Whereas some delight in these spectacles, praising their technical virtuosity and their ability to make history accessible to the masses, others denounce the way audiences now derive their understanding of the past from the most recent Hollywood blockbuster.[45] But this is not a new phenomenon. Rather, it represents the latest manifestation of a mode of historical vision that already both thrilled and troubled observers in 1830. By exploring how history became a spectacle in the nineteenth century and how certain writers at the time articulated an opposition to this process, this book provides a perspective on modernity's relation to the past.

45. Ann Rigney, for example, remarks, "The interest in the boundaries between fiction and history is a response, on the one hand, to the proliferation of mediatized images of the past in contemporary culture, where the public at large are arguably as dependent on filmmakers and novelists for their views of history as they are on professional historians," *Imperfect Histories: The Elusive Past and the Legacy of Romantic Historicism* (Ithaca: Cornell University Press, 2001), 4–5. The historical epics of Steven Spielberg (*Schindler's List, Amistad,* and *Saving Private Ryan*) are mentioned frequently in debates on the subject, including in Simon Schama's "Clio at the Multiplex," *New Yorker* January 19, 1998, 38–43. For an anthology of the reactions of historians to historical cinema, see Mark Carnes, ed., *Past Imperfect: History according to the Movies* (New York: Henry Holt, 1995). Jacques Rancière theorizes the relation of cinema to history in "L'historicité du cinéma," in *De l'histoire au cinéma,* ed. Antoine de Baecque and Christian Delage (Paris: Éditions Complexe, 1998), 45–60.

Chapter One

Showing the Past

On July 6, 1810, the *Panorama de Wagram* opened its doors on the boulevard des Capucines, offering a representation of Napoleon's great victory to commemorate the one-year anniversary of the battle. An enormous circular canvas displayed in a giant rotunda, the *Panorama de Wagram* excited the admiration of both average citizens and cultural connoisseurs. "Crowds flock there to enjoy the imposing view offered by the picture," declared a review of the panorama in the highbrow *Journal des Arts*. Enthusing over the "perfect expression" of the panorama's depiction of burned Prussian villages, of cannons exploding, and of Napoleon himself serenely surveying the battlefield, the critic marveled at the "striking truth" of the "vast and ingenious" spectacle, so lifelike as to make observers feel they were witnessing the event. "The illusion is total," the reviewer declared; "you think you've been transported to the scene."[1] To the Parisian public of the Empire, the panorama seemed to have brought the past to life.

The panorama represents one of a host of spectacles popular in France during and after the Revolution that turned history into a form of public entertainment. These shows, including the wax display, the phantasmagoria, and the diorama, drew crowds of spectators eager to pay to see images of the past, and particularly of the recent past of the Revolution and Empire, represented with an unprecedented visual realism. Exploiting the latest optical technologies, the historical spectacles of the early nineteenth

---

1. "Variétés," review of *Panorama de Wagram,* by Pierre Prévost, *Journal des Arts, des sciences, de littérature et de politique,* August 5, 1810, 179.

century aimed at surpassing the illusionistic effects of conventional painting to startle and seduce viewers with representations of famous men and great battles. The press accounts of the time, along with the spectacles' receipts, bear witness to their remarkable success.

Most studies of nineteenth-century France's historical renaissance, however, ignore popular entertainments such as the panorama and give the impression that the change in historical representation during this period was an exclusively literary affair. According to such accounts, it was the Romantic novelists and historians who, beginning in the 1810s and 1820s, transformed the nature of historical writing. One of the principal arguments of this book is that the Romantic historical writing of Walter Scott and Jules Michelet can be seen as participating, along with spectacles such as the panorama, in a widespread movement to envision history in a new way. Indeed, the highly visual style of these Romantic authors has more in common with the popular spectacles than with the late nineteenth-century scientific histories that are commonly seen as their legacy.

By transforming history into an object to be viewed and into a popular entertainment responsive to and dependent on the marketplace, shows like the wax display, the phantasmagoria, and the panorama provided a model not just for historiography, but for a range of historical discourses in the nineteenth century. Subsequent chapters in this book explore how more traditional media and genres of historical representation—including historiography—came to resemble the spectacles of popular culture. This chapter describes how popular entertainments redefined the way the past was seen and known, as well as the kind of ideological work that history performed, during the Revolutionary and post-Revolutionary periods. Offering up images of the nation's history in a public forum in as visually realistic a manner as possible, historical spectacles such as the panorama provided perspectives through which new individual and national identities could take shape through the consumption of a vision of the past. To trace this process is to witness the formation of one of modernity's founding illusions.

Waxing Historical

No trip to Paris was complete in the last decades of the eighteenth century or in the first decades of the nineteenth without a visit to Philippe Curtius's wax display. Opened in the 1770s as a fairground attraction, the wax *salon* eventually found its permanent home on the boulevard du Temple and for a while also at the Palais-Royal. "The exhibition room of the honorable Curtius is a spectacle worthy of the curiosity of respectable people," reports Jacques-Antoine Dulaure's *Nouvelle description des curiosités de Paris,* a guidebook from 1791, in its list of the capital's attractions. "One sees there colored wax figures that imitate nature in a most striking manner. One sees the faces of all sorts of famous people from all walks of life."[2] Although the use of wax sculpture dates back to ancient times and wax was used for a range of purposes in the late eighteenth century, including in medical anatomy collections, Dulaure's guidebook legitimates the wax display as a means of acquiring knowledge about history—about famous people both living and dead.[3]

In Curtius's *cabinet,* wax busts, attached to costumed mannequins and displayed in naturalistic settings, offered spectators a view of history's leading actors.[4] In the decade preceding the Revolution, Curtius regaled visitors to his display with a depiction of "the royal family at dinner at Versailles," which featured the effigies of the king and his family seated around a large table laden with wax food.[5] To compete with rival wax displays that sprang up around Paris in the years preceding the Revolution, Curtius began to add other celebrities to his collection.[6] Voltaire, Benjamin

2. Jacques-Antoine Dulaure, *Nouvelle description des curiosités de Paris,* 3rd ed., vol. 2 (1785; updated reprint, Paris: Le Jay, 1791), 404.

3. Two recent books offer histories of the use of wax sculpture: Michelle E. Bloom, *Waxworks: A Cultural Obsession* (Minneapolis: University of Minnesota Press, 2003); and Pamela Pilbeam, *Madame Tussaud and the History of the Waxworks* (London: Hambledon and London, 2003). Jean Adhémar describes how wax was used in medical anatomy collections in "Les musées de cire en France, Curtius, le 'Banquet royal,' les têtes coupées," *Gazette des Beaux-Arts,* 92 (July–December 1978): 202–3. Jann Matlock shows how wax was linked to "fascinations with the physiology of the female body" thanks to displays depicting women's internal organs in "Censoring the Realist Gaze," in *Spectacles of Realism,* ed. Margaret Cohen and Christopher Prendergast (Minneapolis: University of Minnesota Press, 1995), 49. My account of wax displays has been informed by these works as well as by Marie-Hélène Huet, *Monstrous Imagination* (Cambridge: Harvard University Press, 1993), 188–218; Michel Lemire, *Artistes et Mortels* (Paris: Chabaud, 1990), 88–101; and Vanessa Schwartz, *Spectacular Realities: Early Mass Culture in Fin-de-Siècle Paris* (Berkeley: University of California Press, 1998), 89–148.

4. According to Pilbeam, in *Madame Tussaud,* for the relatively high price of 12 sous, privileged visitors to Curtius's *salon* in the pre-Revolutionary period could stroll among the wax sculptures; for 2 sous they could peer at them from a distance. For an additional 24 sous visitors to the Curtius display could watch a ventriloquist in the basement, and they could gape at natural history exhibits for a mere additional 2 sous. In the late eighteenth century, nearby theaters on the boulevard du Temple charged between 6 and 24 sous a ticket (26).

5. Curtius was not the first to use wax to depict historical figures in France. In the seventeenth century, Antoine Benoist displayed his famous royal circle, which included full-size likenesses of the royal court of France. Adhémar, "Musées de cire," 204–6. As Pilbeam shows, similar displays were popular in seventeenth- and eighteenth-century London (*Madame Tussaud,* 11–16).

6. Claude-François-Xavier Mercier de Compiègne's *Manuel du voyageur à Paris* (Paris: Favre, Year VII) describes the various competing wax establishments: "The first and the oldest is that of Citizen Curtius, boulevard du Temple [. . . .] The second is that of Citizen Orsy,

Franklin, and Jacques Necker joined the royals at Curtius's display, providing an eclectic representation of the people who were in the process of changing the course of French history.

During the Revolution, Curtius took an active role in politics.[7] He participated in the storming of the Bastille and sent his niece and associate, Marie Grosholtz, the future Madame Tussaud, to make sculptures of the prisoners there for display in the exhibition.[8] Following the fall of the Bastille, Curtius substituted revolutionaries for the royals at his wax banquet; Roland, Thomas Paine, Georges-Jacques Danton, Maximilien Robespierre, Jean-Paul Marat, and many others whom Curtius's prodigious niece had modeled, many from life, could be seen by visitors to the *cabinet*. Madame Tussaud later claimed that the Revolutionary Convention commissioned her to make wax busts of the decapitated heads of Louis XVI and Marie-Antoinette, which, once completed, she displayed in Curtius's *cabinet* alongside a model of the guillotined remains of Philippe-Egalité.[9]

Curtius's constantly changing displays evolved along with events. According to Victor Fournel, writing later in the century, "Each revolutionary event was reflected in [Curtius's] salon."[10] Curtius considered removing the bust of Lafayette in August of 1792 following his *accusation;* after Thermidor, the busts of the Revolutionaries gave way to representations of the Revolution's victims—Charlotte Corday, Camille Desmoulins, Cécile Renault (guillotined for having attempted to kill Robespierre), and Madame Elisabeth (the sister of Louis XVI). The executioner Sanson even put in an appearance.[11] As Fournel recounts, "The victors of one day were exhibited the next day as victims [. . .]. The virtuous Maximilien, the incorruptible, could still serve after the 9th of Thermidor under the guise of the infamous Robespierre."[12] Curtius had only to change the labels that accompanied his mannequins to keep up with the times.

---

sculptor, whose display is situated near the gate on the Boulevard St. Martin, in the old Opera auditorium [. . . .] His figures stand out through the truth of their depiction and the naturalness of their attitudes. The other displays of this type that may exist in Paris are imitations of these two, and thus cannot interest the *amateur*," (139–140).

7. Curtius became a member of the Club des Jacobins, joined the National Guard, and participated in the siege of Mayence in 1793. Adhémar, "Musées de cire," 207.

8. As Pilbeam points out, although Marie referred to Curtius as her uncle, her ancestry is ambiguous: her mother was Curtius's housekeeper, and it is possible that Curtius was Marie's father (*Madame Tussaud*, 32).

9. Adhémar, "Musées de cire," 208. Huet notes that Madame Tussaud's claim to having moulded severed heads cannot be confirmed (*Monstrous Imagination*, 198).

10. Victor Fournel, *Le vieux Paris: Fêtes, jeux et spectacles* (Tours: Alfred Mame et fils, 1887), 330.

11. Adhémar, "Musées de cire," 208, and Lemire, *Artistes et mortels*, 100.

12. Fournel, *Vieux Paris*, 332.

Although Curtius died in 1794, his display lived on into the nineteenth century, run by Madame Tussaud until she moved to England in 1802.[13] During the Consulate, the display featured a bust of Napoleon, commissioned by the great man himself, as well as an assortment of other historical figures. "Among the curiosities of the display, where the truth of the colors and of the faces and their expressions leaves nothing to be desired, one admires the portraits of the consuls, of the kings and princes of Europe, a superb mummy, and the shirt that Henri IV was wearing when he was assassinated," advertised the *Manuel du voyageur à Paris* for the Year XI.[14] When the Bourbons eventually ousted Napoleon from power, their effigies returned to Curtius's banquet table, occupying the seats vacated by Napoleon and his retinue, until they too were replaced by Louis-Philippe and his family after the July Revolution. Fournel describes how although the wax figures at the banquet changed with the times, the plates of fake fruit remained the same into the 1830s, becoming "incrusted with sixty years' worth of dust."[15]

At its origin the Curtius wax display offered representations of contemporary figures and served as a means of acquainting subjects with the likenesses of their rulers and other celebrities, but over the course of the Revolution it increasingly focused on dead rather than living figures. The past rather than the present became the focus of the spectacle. This represents an important shift, one that marks the beginning of the new mode of historical representation instituted in France during the Revolutionary period. In the wax display, the Revolutionary public first came face to face with the actors who had changed the course of their nation's history. Decades before the Romantic historians turned their sights on the history of the Revolution, showing it to be an organic part of the nation's past, Curtius's *salon* integrated Revolutionary and Imperial figures into a vision of French history, placing Robespierre and Napoleon alongside Henri IV and Marie-Antoinette. "Ancient history and modern history, sacred history and profane history, were all elbow-to-elbow in this simple museum," writes Fournel. "The death of Holophernes could be admired next to the coronation of Napoleon."[16] Curtius's *cabinet* provided a place where different periods of history could be joined together and frozen in time, suspended in an eternal present.

13. Adhémar describes how Curtius left his entire collection to Madame Tussaud and provides a description of the inventory ("Musées de cire," 208).

14. Mercier de Compiègne, *Manuel du voyageur à Paris* (1798; updated reprint, Paris: Favre, Year XI), 261.

15. Fournel, *Vieux Paris,* 330.

16. Ibid., 332.

The purpose of the wax display was to amuse and edify. Like all the spectacles of the era, it provided a form of entertainment, a distraction from the political and economic crises of everyday life in Revolutionary Paris. But the wax display also served a pedagogical function that links it to larger Enlightenment concerns.[17] Like the pseudoscience of physiognomy, which would have remarkable success in the nineteenth century, wax exhibitions allowed visitors to glean insight into the great men and women of the age through study of their facial features. As one guidebook described the process of looking at wax figures in Curtius's display: "one recognizes their features, their bearing, and one delights in comparing their physical presence with their spiritual qualities."[18] Meant to appeal to those who had some prior knowledge of the characters represented, of their actions or reputations, the wax display offered a new kind of information that was specifically visual in nature. Spectators could examine the faces of Revolutionary leaders, as well as their style of dress and hair, for clues to their personalities, to their real selves.

All forms of the plastic arts, including conventional portraiture, convey a similar sort of visual information. But the pedagogical authority of Curtius's *cabinet* relied on the claims of wax to supersede painting and conventional sculpture as forms of naturalistic historical representation. The primary illusionistic effect of wax derived from its simulation of the texture and color of human flesh, made even more "realistic" with the application of actual human hair. Painting cannot hope to imitate the uncanny way in which wax absorbs light like the surface of the body—the skin, that most perishable of elements, the first thing to decompose when a human enters the realm of history.[19]

For some artists and observers at the end of the eighteenth century, wax sculpture and historical painting seemed to complement and supplement each other, both aiming for illusionistic effects.[20] For certain Enlightenment

17. In *Artful Science: Enlightenment Entertainment and the Eclipse of Visual Education* (Cambridge: MIT Press, 1994), Barbara Maria Stafford analyzes how many popular visual demonstrations in the eighteenth century exemplified the Enlightenment "principle of educating while entertaining" (29) and how "rational education was visual education" for Enlightenment pedagogues (73).

18. *Le Pariséum moderne* (1816; updated reprint, Paris: J. Moronval, 1817), 35.

19. In "The 'Uncanny'" (1919), Sigmund Freud describes how wax figures provoke uneasiness in the viewer because they seem indeterminately animate. "The 'Uncanny,'" in *The Standard Edition of the Complete Psychological Words of Sigmund Freud,* ed. James Strachey et al., vol. 17 (London: Hogarth Press, 1953–1974), 226.

20. Several scholars have relied on Madame Tussaud's *Memoirs and Reminiscences of the French Revolution,* ed. Francis Hervé (Philadelphia: Lea and Blanchard, 1839) to recount how Jacques-Louis David, the leading history painter of the neo-Classical school, visited the Curtius display and used Tussaud's mortuary modeling of Marat as a model for his famous

art critics, however, wax represented the example *not to follow:* wax's claim to represent nature with an illusionistic finality seemed to plunge viewers into a coarse materialism, away from the contemplation of a classical ideal of beauty.[21] Yet the desire for such a material treatment of history was enthusiastically affirmed by the Revolutionary public—a need that painting could not satisfy to the same degree as the wax display. Wax, which made use of technologies and materials that were considered foreign to the artistic process, clearly fulfilled a need to see something beyond *le beau.*

This something was the material reality of history. As I show in this and later chapters, all the historical spectacles of the early nineteenth century employed new optical technologies to depict the past in a visually realistic manner.[22] Along with commodification, this is what defines the mode of historical representation I call the spectacular past. Wax's particular claim to realism lay in its ability to make history come alive, or at least seem freshly dead—the rigid poses of the figures in Curtius's *cabinet* resembled those of a corpse suffering from rigor mortis.[23] The wax display also relied on supposedly authentic costumes and props to bolster its historical illusion. Henri IV's "actual" shirt or stones and chains recovered from the Bastille acted metonymically to endow the wax sculptures with a veridical aura.[24] Just as a new generation of historical painters began depicting garments and architectural settings in their historical paintings with a lavish attention to detail and sumptuous material specificity, the sculptures in the Curtius *cabinet* trumped painting's illusionistic renderings with three-dimensional objects.[25]

---

canvas depicting the Revolutionary leader's death. David's composition was then reproduced with three-dimensional figures for display at the wax gallery in a fruitful interchange among media. Fournel, *Vieux Paris,* 333; Adhémar, "Musées de cire," 207–8; and Pilbeam, *Madame Tussaud,* 50.

21. According to Julius von Schlosser, to some critics at the time wax represented "that vile and repulsive body, which reveals the difference between art and non-art." *Histoire du portrait en cire,* trans. Valérie Le Vot (1910; Paris: Macula, 1997), 165.

22. Huet writes in *Monstrous Imagination* that the waxwork's "claim to life is its true lie, part of its monstrosity" (188).

23. According to von Schlosser, the introduction of paraffin as an embalming technique in the nineteenth century further increased the resemblance of the wax figure to the cadaver. *Histoire du portrait en cire,* 209.

24. Bloom comments, in *Waxworks,* that the "authenticity" of historical wax displays "takes the form of effigies wearing the clothes (or using the props) actually worn (or used) by the historical figures" (160). According to Bloom, wax exhibitions "imaginatively re-present historical reality" through their hybrid visual-verbal displays and invite the visitor to "assume the role of a revisionist historian" by strolling at will through the exhibition (173). Bloom calls attention to a text by Charles Dickens entitled "History in Wax" (1854), in which he meditates on the historical lessons offered at Madame Tussaud's (172–74).

25. Nicolas-Guy Brenet's *Mort de Du Guesclin* (1777, Louvre) represents historical figures, their physiognomies, and their costumes with a material specificity that the Troubadour painters of the early nineteenth century would take to even greater extremes. Troubadour

If Curtius's goal was to transcend the traditional boundaries between art and life, to cross the line between historical reality and its representation, he seems to have succeeded. Not only did contemporary observers repeatedly pay tribute to the naturalness of his sculptures, but Revolutionaries looked to his lifelike representations as substitutions for the real thing. After the incendiary speech of Camille Desmoulins at the Palais-Royal, on July 12, 1789, following Necker's dismissal as finance minister by Louis XVI, a crowd of angry revolutionaries stormed Curtius's *cabinet,* took Necker's bust, and paraded it through the streets of Paris.[26] The wax sculptures in Curtius's exhibition not only represented history—they made it.

Although Curtius's display remained open into the 1840s,[27] it lost the heart of its collection when Madame Tussaud relocated to England, taking with her the figures she had helped create during the Revolution.[28] Her permanent display on Baker Street in London, opened in 1830, continued to focus on history, particularly French history, and included a veritable shrine to Napoleon featuring the emperor's carriage used at Waterloo, the clothes he wore in exile, and even one of his teeth along with the instrument used to extract it.[29] As Vanessa Schwartz recounts, Paris was without a permanent wax display in the middle years of the nineteenth century until the opening of the Musée Grévin, which still welcomes huge crowds of visitors today on the boulevard Montmartre. Focusing at first on the representation of current events, the proprietors of the Musée Grévin eventually found it easier to rely on historical scenes that did not need to be changed as frequently to maintain the interest of the public.[30] In this

---

painters included Fleury Richard, Pierre Révoil, Charles Bouton, and Marie-Phillipe Coupin de la Couperie. In *Painting and History during the French Restoration* (Cambridge: Cambridge University Press, 1997), Beth S. Wright describes their attention to detail and local color as a spectacle: "There, narrative explanation was cut apart into spectacles [. . .] each inviting the optical and emotional investment of the audience" (35).

26. Schwartz provides a fuller account of this episode (*Spectacular Realities,* 95), as does Pilbeam (*Madame Tussaud,* 38).

27. Adhémar describes how the Curtius display finally closed around 1847 ("Musées de cire," 210). An English-language guidebook to Paris from 1842 still mentions the Curtius *cabinet:* "Salon de Figures, 54, Boulevard du Temple,—This is an exhibition of wax-work representations of celebrated characters, some of which are executed with excellent effect." *Galignani's New Paris Guide* (1824; updated reprint, Paris: A. and W. Galignani and Co., 1842) 475.

28. After Madame Tussaud moved to England, her husband François ran the Curtius display in Paris.

29. Robert Altick, *The Shows of London* (Cambridge: Belknap Press, Harvard University Press, 1978), 335.

30. According to Schwartz, the Musée Grévin opened a display of Marat's assassination featuring the actual bathtub in which he was killed, along with copies of his newspaper, *L'Ami du Peuple,* in 1886. This was followed by a gallery of the French Revolution in 1889 to commemorate the one-hundredth anniversary of the storming of the Bastille (*Spectacular Realities,* 120–46).

new wax museum, the realistic re-creation of the past continued to prove a powerful attraction.

Spectral Spectacles

Whereas the wax display's appeal lay in its re-creation of the "flesh" of the past, Étienne-Gaspard Robertson's phantasmagoria show entertained audiences with a far less corporeal spectacle. "The devil, spectres, and ghosts being very fashionable in France today," advised a guidebook from the Year VII, "foreigners, go see the apparitions, phantoms, and ghosts [*revenans*] at Robertson's."[31] First opened in 1798, Robertson's phantasmagoria show delighted and terrified audiences during the Consulate and into the early years of the nineteenth century.[32] At 6:30 in the evening, as darkness was falling, visitors would gather at the Pavillon de l'Échiquier to watch Robertson—like Curtius, a larger-than-life showman—conjure images of the dead, which would hover in mid-air or move out toward the frightened audience and then retreat back and disappear.[33] Robertson's

31. Mercier de Compiègne, *Manuel* (Year VII), 101. Seminal discussions of the phantasmagoria show occur in Max Milner, *La fantasmagorie: Essai sur l'optique fantastique* (Paris: Presses Universitaires de France, 1982); Terry Castle, *The Female Thermometer: Eighteenth-Century Culture and the Invention of the Uncanny* (Oxford: Oxford University Press, 1995); Françoise Levie, *Étienne-Gaspard Robertson: La vie d'un fantasmagore* (Paris: Éditions du Préambule, 1990); and in three articles by Jann Matlock: "Voir aux limites du corps: Fantasmagories et femmes invisibles dans les spectacles de Robertson," in *Lanternes magiques, tableaux transparents,* Exhibition Catalogue, Musée d'Orsay, ed. Ségolène Le Men et al. (Paris: Réunion des Musées nationaux, 1995), 83–100; "The Invisible Woman and Her Secrets Unveiled," *Yale Journal of Criticism* 9, no. 2 (1996): 175–221; "Reading Invisibility" in *Field Work: Sites in Literary and Cultural Studies,* ed. Marjorie Garber, Paul B. Franklin, and Rebecca L. Walkowitz (New York: Routledge, 1996). Laurent Mannoni discusses the representation of Napoleon in Robertson's phantasmagoria, as well as in panoramas and nineteenth-century optical toys, in " 'Son ombre descend parmi nous . . . ': Napoléon et la Grande Armée des jeux d'optique," in *Napoléon et le cinéma,* ed. Jean-Pierre Mattei (Ajaccio: Alain Piazzola, 1998), 15–29.

32. According to Levie, Robertson closed his Paris phantasmagoria in 1802 and took his show on the road, displaying his ghosts in Berlin, Vienna, and Saint Petersburg. He then reopened on the boulevard Montmartre in Paris from 1814 to 1818, before journeying to Portugal and Spain. He opened a last Parisian phantasmagoria in the Tivoli gardens in 1827, which he operated until shortly after the Revolution of 1830. Levie reconstructs the repertories of these various shows in *Étienne-Gaspard Robertson,* 292–309. As Levie points out, the phantasmagoria quickly gave rise to many imitators at the beginning of the century, prompting Robertson to engage in an unsuccessful lawsuit to protect the rights to his spectacle (96). F.-M. Marchant's guidebook, *Le conducteur de l'étranger à Paris* (1811; updated reprint, Paris: Moronval, 1814) does not list Robertson's spectacle among the capital's attractions but does list a rival phantasmagoria: "M. Le Breton, rue Bonaparte. One sees there all the marvels of optics, of perspective, of physics and of the apparitions of phantoms" (89).

33. According to Levie, the phantasmagoria remained open at the Pavillon de l'Échiquier for three months, from January 23 to April 25, 1798. *Étienne-Gaspard Robertson,* 90.

phantasmagoria attracted *le tout Paris* despite the relatively high price of a seat (3 to 6 *livres*).[34]

Improving on the common magic lantern technology that projected images painted on glass slides onto a screen or smoke, Robertson placed the lantern on wheels and rolled it back and forth behind the screen to give the impression that the images were alive and capable of movement.[35] His other innovation lay in capitalizing on the gothic taste for horror by choosing subjects calculated to delight and terrify the public. Although some audience members were drawn to Robertson's show in the hope of seeing deceased loved ones, the bulk of the phantasmagoria's repertoire consisted of literary and historical subjects.[36] Fictional characters, often those associated with the macabre, such as Shakespeare's Macbeth, joined recently departed Revolutionary figures on Robertson's phantasmagoric stage.

Like the wax display, the phantasmagoria show presented a visual representation of the leading figures of the recent Revolutionary past. At the phantasmagoria, however, history was interactive, the repertoire changing depending on the tastes of the audience. In his entertaining autobiography, *Mémoires récréatifs, scientifiques et anecdotiques d'un physicien-aéronaute*, Robertson describes one particularly heated show during the Directory. Asked by an unkempt member of the audience to conjure the ghost of Marat, who had been assassinated by Charlotte Corday in 1793, the *physicien-aéronaute* complied by mixing together two glasses of blood, a bottle of vitriol, some alcohol, and two copies of the Revolutionary journal *Les Hommes Libres*. Suddenly there appeared "a ghastly, hideous little phantom, armed with a dagger, and wearing a red cap."[37]

34. Ibid., 79.

35. Robertson called his invention the fantoscope. Ségolène Le Men provides a history of magic lantern technology in "Monsieur le soleil et Madame la lune . . . ," in *Lanternes magiques, tableaux transparents,* Exhibition Catalogue, Musée d'Orsay, ed. Ségolène le Men et al. (Paris : Réunion des Musées nationaux, 1995), 17–80.

36. Spectators wishing to see dead relatives or friends had to give Robertson a portrait ahead of time so that he could have it copied onto a glass slide. A guidebook from the period signals this proviso, but does so rather ambiguously, without revealing the "secret," allowing viewers to maintain the illusion of Robertson's resurrective powers should they so desire: "It is false that we can make appear, at our will, the shade of a person we have lost unless the inventor has first been given a portrait of the dead person." Mercier de Compiègne, *Manuel du voyageur à Paris,* 101). In *Atlas of Emotion: Journeys in Art, Architecture, and Film* (New York: Verso, 2002), Giuliana Bruno describes Robertson's phantasmagoria as a "spectacle of death" (146).

37. Étienne-Gaspard Robertson, *Mémoires récréatifs, scientifiques et anecdotiques d'un physicien-aéronaute* (1831 ; reprint, Langres: Café Clima, 1985), 131. Robertson takes this description of the episode from an article by Poultier, "Fantasmagorie," *L'Ami des Lois,* 8 germinal (Year VI): 1.

Delighted, the audience member recognized the ghost as Marat, but when he tried to embrace it, the image disappeared.

According to Robertson's own account, the business of reviving ghosts during the Directory required a great deal of political savvy, along with skills in necromancy. The same evening that Marat's ghost appeared to the delight of the disheveled radical, another audience member, from the opposite side of the political spectrum, requested the ghost of Louis XVI.[38] This time Robertson sagely refused the request: "I used to have a recipe for that, before the 18th Fructidor," he replied; "I have since lost it: it is likely that I will never find it again, and it will henceforth be impossible to make the kings of France return."[39] Like Curtius and Madame Tussaud, who altered the subject matter of their wax displays to stay on the right side of prevailing popular opinion, Robertson's ghosts kept up with the times.

Despite his ingenious escape from what he claimed was a trap laid by a secret agent—the "physician" apparently had enemies—Robertson was driven from Paris for a few months by the Revolutionary authorities. Upon his return from exile in Bordeaux, he set up shop near the Place Vendôme, in the former convent of the Capucines, emptied during the Revolution of all but the spirits of its former occupants. Here Robertson continued to conjure up the ghosts of the recent past.[40] In one display, the ghost of Robespierre attempted to rise from his tomb, but was pulverized by a flash of lightning. Less horrifying spectres then appeared in order to "lighten the picture," including Voltaire, Antoine-Laurent Lavoisier, and Jean-Jacques Rousseau.

Like the wax display, the phantasmagoria turned Bonapartist during the Consulate. According to Françoise Levie, Robertson showed the ghosts of generals of the Grande Armée just days after they had died gloriously on the battlefield.[41] In his memoirs, Robertson describes a spectacle from this period in which thunder and lightning cleared to reveal a bright star with the words "18 brumaire" emblazoned on it. The ghost of Napoleon, "the peace-maker," then appeared (despite the fact that he was still very much alive) to be crowned with an olive branch by Minerva. "It is unnecessary,"

38. He is described as a *Chouan*. The Chouans were counter-Revolutionary guerrilla warriors in the western provinces, eventually pacified by the Republican armies.

39. Robertson, *Mémoires récréatifs*, 133. Matlock also mentions this episode in "The Invisible Woman," 213n12.

40. The phantasmagoria at the Capucines convent remained open from January 10, 1799, to October 8, 1802. Levie, *Étienne-Gaspard Robertson*, 292.

41. Françoise Levie, *Lanterne magique et fantasmagorie* (Paris: Musée national des techniques, 1990), 20.

one observer commented, "to say how that ingenious allegory is always welcomed with enthusiasm."[42]

At first glance, the effect produced by the phantasmagoria show seems quite different from that of the wax display. Whereas wax endowed the past with flesh, creating a simulacrum of the bodies of historical figures, the phantasmagoria show relied on immaterial, diaphanous images that could float through the air and disappear at the command of the animator. Whereas the wax display's representations were created on a human scale, the phantasmagoria shrunk historical figures to the size of miniature demons or expanded them to horrific proportions. The immobility of the wax sculpture allowed for prolonged contemplation; wax figures could be observed and studied. The phantasmagoria's images were less pedagogical; they provoked feelings of fear or admiration, provided viewers did not look too closely or carefully. The wax display offered insights into the correlation between the physical and moral attributes of its subjects; the phantasmagoria show played on preconceived historical ideas and prejudices.[43]

On closer inspection, however, the two spectacles can be seen to share certain fundamental goals. Like the wax display, the phantasmagoria show employed new representational strategies and optical technologies to show the past with a startling realism.[44] Viewers at the time reacted similarly to the images produced by the different entertainments, delighting in the verisimilitude of the spectacles. "It is impossible for the illusion to be any greater," enthused the *Nouveau guide du voyageur à Paris* of 1802 in a review of Robertson's ghosts, echoing the kinds of plaudits heaped on Curtius's lifelike figures.[45] Just as Curtius updated a preexisting technology (the ability to mould wax into human shape) with new devices (the addi-

---

42. Anonymous review cited in Robertson, *Mémoires récréatifs,* 165.

43. Stafford describes how Robertson took pains to distinguish himself from the deluding conjurors denounced by Englightenment pedagogues (and associated with the Jesuits) by unmasking the mechanism of the illusion of his phantasmagoria. Robertson thus capitalized on popular superstitions and fears of ghosts while at the same time turning his spectres into what Stafford calls "pedagogical weapons in the arsenal of the Enlightenment," (*Artful Science,* 46). My point is that even while the phantasmagoria purported to teach audiences about such lying appearances, it offered fewer lessons about history than the wax display or the panorama.

44. In *Female Thermometer,* Castle argues that the phantasmagoria show reflects changing post-Enlightenment images of the imagination itself. She shows how, as the move toward rationalism eroded belief in the supernatural, thought itself was increasingly conceived as a "spectral" process. The phantasmagoria becomes a favorite symbol for the mind's spectralization in authors from the Romantics to Proust.

45. *Paris et ses curiosités ou Nouveau guide du voyageur à Paris* (Paris: Marchand, 1802), 103.

tion of "real" costumes and innovative staging) to create a realistic effect, Robertson improved on the old-fashioned magic lantern. Formerly employed by evangelists to inspire religious dread in superstitious subjects by convincing them they were seeing the face of the devil, the magic lantern became, in Robertson's hands, a far more convincing delusion through the addition of mobility (the apparatus was mounted on wheels) and sound effects (the thunder that accompanied Robespierre's rise from the tomb), foreshadowing the technology of cinema.

Like the wax display, the phantasmagoria show beckoned the observer into the space of the past. Just as Curtius invited visitors to circulate among his historical figures, the illusion of the phantasmagoria was increased by the incorporation of the spectator's body into the spectacle. The disheveled *maratiste's* attempted embrace of his elusive idol helped convince other viewers of the spectacle's reality. But what aligns the two spectacles more than any technical analogy is their choice of subject matter. Both Curtius and Robertson turned to the recent events of the Revolution and Napoleonic Wars for their primary source of inspiration, heralding what was, by the early years of the nineteenth century, fast becoming a popular obsession.

Histo-rama

Nineteenth-century guidebooks recommended the wax display and the phantasmagoria show as worthy stops on a visit to Paris, but they positively raved about the panorama. "It is impossible to imagine and to describe all the excitement and curiosity of this spectacle," declared one guide to "Paris and its curiosities" from 1802.[46] To its first viewers, the panorama seemed fabulous and otherworldly, its mystery increased by its foreign name, derived from two Greek words meaning "view of the whole." A circular painted canvas, which could measure up to 15 by 120 meters, viewed from a central platform in a building designed especially for it, the panorama achieved its effect by erasing all points of comparison between the horizon and the representation. Lit only from above by windows placed just below the circular roof, so that the light shone only on the canvas and not on the viewer, the picture took on the scale and depth of a "real" landscape. "Our senses are easy to fool, vision especially," stated a report made to the *Institut national des sciences et des arts* shortly after the panorama's invention, "size and distance can only be gauged through comparison [. . .]. Therefore in depriving the eye of all points of

46. Ibid., 104.

comparison, it is possible to fool it into confusing art and nature."[47] In the panorama, as in its sister spectacles, the goal was to cross the boundary between the reality of the past and its representation.

The panorama was invented in England by a Scotsman named Robert Barker, who received a patent on June 19, 1787.[48] In 1799, Robert Fulton, the American who later invented the steamboat, brought the panorama to Paris, displaying a view of the French capital painted by Constant Bourgeois, Jean-Michel-Denis Fontaine, Jean Mouchet, and Pierre Prévost, who went on to become the great *panoramiste* of his generation. Fulton eventually sold his import permit to an American couple, James Thayer and his wife, Henriette Beck, who partnered with Prévost to create a series of panoramas displayed first in a rotunda on the boulevard Montmartre and, after 1808, in a new and much bigger building on the boulevard des Capucines.[49] The price for a ticket to one of these early panoramas ranged from about 1.30 to 2 francs.[50]

For their first panoramic venture, the partners chose another cityscape, but endowed it with a patriotic and historical allure. The panorama depicting the port of Toulon (displayed 1800–1802) showed the moment "at which the English were compelled, in 1793, to evacuate the scene because

47. Léon Dufourny, *Rapport fait à l'Institut national des sciences et des arts, sur l'origine, les effets et les progrès du panorama. Classe de Littérature et Beaux-Arts, séance du 28 fructidor, an VIII.* N.p., Year VIII, 3.

48. Barker displayed his first circular canvas, a view of Edinburgh, in London in 1789 and followed it up with a panorama depicting the Lord Mayor's procession along the Thames to Westminster. His special rotunda, designed for the panorama, opened on Leicester Square in 1794 and experienced immediate success. Altick, *Shows of London*, 133; "The Panorama: With Memoires of Its Inventor, Robert Barker, and His Son, the Late Henry Aston Barker," *Art Journal* 3 (1857): 46–47.

49. The most comprehensive study of the panorama in France is François Robichon, "Les panoramas en France au XIXe siècle," Ph.D. diss., University of Paris X, Nanterre, 1982. Other studies of the panorama that have informed my account include: Altick, *Shows of London;* Bernard Comment, *The Painted Panorama*, trans. Anne-Marie Glasheen (1993; New York: H. N. Abrams, 2000); Jonathan Crary, *Techniques of the Observer: On Vision and Modernity in the Nineteenth Century* (Cambridge: M.I.T. Press, 1992); Stephen Oettermann, *The Panorama: History of a Mass Medium*, trans. Deborah Lucas Schneider (1980; New York: Zone Books, 1997); Schwartz, *Spectacular Realities.* In *Panoramas du XIXe siècle*, trans. Jean-François Boutout (1938; Paris: Gallimard, 1996), Dolf Sternberger furnishes an interesting meditation on the ways in which the panoramic mode of vision came to occupy the cultural imaginary of the nineteenth century. For an earlier account of the panorama phenomenon, see Germain Bapst, *Essai sur l'histoire des panoramas et des dioramas* (Paris: G. Masson, 1891).

50. According to Robichon, prices ranged from 1.50 to 2 francs for a ticket, and older panoramas could be seen for less until they were destroyed ("Panoramas en France," 159). The lowest price I have found in a guidebook from the period for Prévost's panoramas was 1.30 francs for the *Panorama d'Anvers* in 1814 (Marchant, *Conducteur de l'étranger à Paris,* 188–89).

of the approach of the French army."[51] Several of the subsequent panoramas executed by Prévost over the following years continued to combine landscape and history painting, depicting places with a connection to recent historical events. Another view of Paris, as seen from the Tuileries palace (1803) showed Napoleon bestowing honors on his soldiers at the *fête nationale* of the preceding year.[52] A panorama of Boulogne (1806–9, 1811–15) showed the French fleet waiting to attack England, a plan that was abandoned in 1805, following the battle of Trafalgar. For the first spectacle in the new rotunda on the Boulevard des Capucines, Prévost painted the *Panorama de Tilsit* (1808–9), which depicted the historic meeting in 1807 between Napoleon and the Russian emperor Alexander.[53]

The following year, Prévost painted the *Panorama de Wagram,* which drew visitors to the boulevard des Capucines from 1810 to 1811.[54] Although the Wagram panorama was Prévost's only actual battle scene, history dominated the panorama throughout the Consulate and Empire; even the landscapes contained a historical component, offering views of "the great cities of Europe to which the French are attached either through personal memories or diplomatic relations."[55] Indeed, the cities chosen as subjects during the Empire all had some relation to the Napoleonic Wars: the *Panorama de Londres* depicted the capital of the enemy, while the panoramas of Naples, Rome, Amsterdam, Antwerp, and Vienna represented cities occupied by the French army.[56]

In the panorama, as in the wax display and the phantasmagoria show, the events of the recent past became the object of the public's gaze. Like these other spectacles, the panorama relied for its effects primarily on optical illusion (although visitors could sometimes benefit from the explana-

51. Dufourny, *Rapport,* 7. Friderich Johann Lorenz Meyer, a church official, described the historical action in the panorama of Toulon: "one sees the enemy retreating in haste, with the victors in hot pursuit and the fleet leaving the harbor with sails billowing." Cited in Oettermann, *Panorama,* 145.

52. See "Panorama," *Le Courrier des Spectacles,* 5 floréal, Year XI, 2–3, for a review of this spectacle.

53. See M. B., "Beaux-Arts," *Le Journal de l'Empire,* October 4, 1808, 3–4, for a review of this spectacle.

54. Robichon comments that this panorama took in only 13,835 francs the first month, compared to 39,120 francs for the *Panorama d'Anvers,* Prévost's next canvas ("Panoramas en France," 377). This seems to contradict the less quantitative description of the "crowds" drawn to the spectacle in the *Journal des Arts* ("Variétés," 179), which I quote at the start of this chapter.

55. "L'abus des mots ou les panoramas," *Journal des Arts, des Sciences, de Littérature et de Politique,* February 22, 1809, 409.

56. None of Prévost's panoramas survives, although some of his preparatory sketches for a panorama of Paris still remain, including one at the Musée Carnavalet. Comment reproduces images of these studies in *Painted Panorama,* 31–43, 46–47.

tions of a guide or purchase a written description). In the panorama, visitors found themselves in the center of a historical scene. Surrounded on all sides by the painted canvas, with no external objects or points of reference (except the bodies of other spectators on the platform), the panorama promised a total immersion in history. As in the wax display and the phantasmagoria, but to an even greater degree, the panorama sought to transport the viewer backward in time or to make the past come alive in the present.

The wax display, the phantasmagoria show, and the panorama shared certain fundamental features. All three spectacles took up the subject of the recent past, its actors or its events. All three charged money for the privilege of witnessing this representation. And despite differences in media, all three used new optical technologies to depict the past visually, to present its visible, surface aspect. It is this visual aspect that links the historical spectacles of the Revolutionary period; it is their common effort to transcend conventional forms of painting and sculpture to generate a new kind of historical illusion that defines the new spectacular mode of historical representation that becomes characteristic of modernity.

But what did this desire for illusion signify? What purpose did it fulfill for a public in the midst of Revolutionary upheaval? And why did this new form of historical representation continue to appeal to audiences throughout the nineteenth century? The answers, I argue, lie in the discourse surrounding these spectacles, embedded in the way observers at the time described what they saw. To understand the significance of this new form of spectacular historical representation, it is necessary to look through the eyes of contemporary viewers in both senses of the preposition: looking *along with* those who recorded their responses, but also looking *past* these responses, attempting to decipher the fears, longings, or desires they betray.

The Role of the Real

Revolutionary audiences—and indeed audiences throughout the nineteenth century—were eager to be fooled.[57] Over and over again, observers testify to the startling realism of the spectacles. Just as visitors to

57. Neil Harris details how nineteenth-century American audiences responded to trickery in *Humbug: The Art of P. T. Barnum* (Boston: Little, Brown, 1973); see especially chap, 8, "The Man of Confidence," 207–31. In *The Arts of Deception: Playing with Fraud in the Age of Barnum* (Cambridge: Harvard University Press, 2001), James W. Cook describes how the "artful deception" of Barnum and other antebellum entertainers relied on a "calculated intermixing of the genuine and the fake" (16–17).

Curtius's wax display enthused over the "truth" and "naturalness" of the historical sculptures displayed there and guidebooks commented on the illusion of the images in the phantasmagoria show, observers likewise celebrated the overwhelming veracity of Prévost's panoramas. "A man who found himself transported to the platform in his sleep, and without knowing it, would have a hard time telling whether the images before him were real or not," posited one guidebook to "Paris and its fashions" from 1803, describing the experience of visiting Prévost's second panorama of Paris.[58]

The endlessly repeated praise of the realism of the historical spectacles represents more, however, than just a critical commonplace; it provides insight into the stakes of the spectacular mode of historical representation for the Revolutionary public. To understand these stakes, references to the spectacle's realism must be situated at the juncture where certain traditions and trends in aesthetic discourse meet a set of social and political factors at a particular historical moment. Three questions arise at this juncture: What does it mean to see a representation as real? What, furthermore, does it mean to see a representation of history as real? And why, around the time of the Revolution, did realistic visions of the past suddenly become so pervasive?

The idea that representation, particularly painting, provides a window onto the real has a long history in the tradition of Western art theory. In *Vision and Painting,* Norman Bryson describes the assumptions governing what he calls "the generally held, vague, common-sense conception of the image as the resurrection of Life,"[59] which has determined notions of art from the Greeks onward. Bryson recounts the famous episode of the competition between Zeuxis and Timanthes from Book XXXV of Pliny's *Natural History,* in which two painters vied to create the most exact copy of nature: whereas Zeuxis painted an image of grapes so realistic that some birds attempted to eat them, Timanthes eventually won the contest with a representation of a curtain that fooled even Zeuxis. It is one thing to dupe nature, Zeuxis conceded, but to fool an artist requires real skill. The responses of nineteenth-century observers to the panorama and other historical spectacles provide a modern version of this legend. One commentator on Prévost's *Panorama d'Anvers* from 1812, in fact, made reference to Zeuxis' grapes when describing the panorama's stunning effect.[60] Other

58. *Le Pariséum* (Paris: Michelet, 1803), 325.

59. Norman Bryson, *Vision and Painting: The Logic of the Gaze* (London: Macmillan, 1983), 3.

60. "If we believe the historians, the Greeks carried painting to such a high degree of perfection that they had perfected illusion. We will not cite to this effect the grapes of Zeuxis

viewers at the time told similar stories of mistaking reality for its representation. One woman reportedly complained of feeling seasick while looking
at a naval panorama; another spectator claimed to have smelled tar.[61]

As Bryson explains, the image's power to reproduce reality depends on
an idealized viewing process in which the image's actual material existence
is reduced to the point that it becomes an "essential copy" of nature while
simultaneously the historical and physiological conditions governing the
viewer's act of perception are minimized to the point that he or she becomes a universal viewing subject. Of course, as Bryson demonstrates, no
such idealized viewing instance is possible because perception is a socially
and materially determined act. A representation's illusionistic effect, moreover, is always relative and usually temporary; what one culture or period
sees as realistic may not seem at all so at a different time or place. Twenty-
first-century viewers, accustomed to the technologies of photography and
cinema, would surely fail to find the panorama or the phantasmagoria
show remotely convincing as an illusion of reality.

What needs to be explained is not why early nineteenth-century viewers
found the panorama realistic; each new technological advance has the
temporary ability to impress spectators with its illusionistic capabilities. A
more important question is what purpose this experience of realistic historical representation served in the psychic and social lives of the Revolutionary public. Why did the Revolutionary period in France give rise to
such a diversity of new realistic representational technologies? Why did
the representation of recent historical events (the Revolution and the
Napoleonic Wars) suddenly necessitate the transcendence of the conventional techniques of history painting?

The answer has to do with the way historical events themselves were
perceived. If a certain segment of the public needed to see the representations provided by the historical spectacles as real, it was because the events
depicted there—the Revolution and the Napoleonic Wars—had come to
seem *unreal*. Beginning with the storming of the Bastille, the pace of political and social change in France accelerated at an unprecedented rate. The
relatively stable Bourbon monarchy, which had governed France for hundreds of years, was succeeded by a prolonged period of political upheaval:
France experienced four different forms of government in the last decade

---

that birds came to peck." A. L. Castellan, "Sur les panoramas," *Le Moniteur Universel*, May
20, 1812, 552.
    61. The critic for the *Cabinet de Lecture* noted that on seeing the *Panorama de Navarin*,
"an odor of tar wafted toward me" "Panorama de Navarin," *Cabinet de Lecture*, February
4, 1831, 74. Comment cites this review as well as reports of seasickness (*Painted Panorama*,
102–3).

of the eighteenth century alone, as Constitutional Monarchy was replaced by a Republic and then by the Directory and the Consulate. The wars of the Revolution and later of the Empire, meanwhile, mobilized vast numbers of men and women, scattering people who knew nothing beyond their villages to the farthest corners of Europe.

Pierre Nora and Richard Terdiman have both described how the French experienced these changes as a radical rupture with the traditional past, as a severing from the age-old rituals performed by successive generations, linking individuals to a particular place and way of life.[62] Terdiman refers to this lost link with the past as a "memory crisis" and explains how the renewed interest in all forms of history during the post-Revolutionary period became a substitute for memory's loss: whereas memory is organic, the product of centuries of tradition, history is constructed, imposed on events to explain changes that can no longer be assimilated by a culture in transition. The rise of a particular type of history, specifically one that emphasizes a naturalistic representation of people and events from the past, thus fulfills a need to "realize"—both making real and making sense of— events that had happened out of sight but whose effects had nevertheless been felt.

The popular entertainments of the Revolutionary period enabled the realization of history by making the recent past visible. The nineteenth century saw the creation of a number of representational practices that relied on visibility to make sense of the complex world of modernity.[63] It is important to recognize, however, that the epistemological claims of the visual, and the uses of the image as a tool for the dissemination of knowledge, stretch back long before the nineteenth century. The *Encyclopédistes* of the eighteenth century made elaborate use of engravings to explain technological and scientific developments, thus linking the Enlightenment ideal of rationality with visuality. The historical entertainments of the Revolutionary period grew out of this tradition and helped lay the groundwork for the proliferation of visual practices in such diverse venues as the

62. See Pierre Nora, "Between Memory and History: *Lieux de mémoire*," trans. Marc Roudebush, *Representations* 26 (Spring 1989): 7–24; and Richard Terdiman, *Present Past: Modernity and the Memory Crisis* (Ithaca: Cornell University Press, 1993).

63. Jonathan Crary describes the visual technologies of modernity in *Techniques of the Observer*. On the uses of photography after mid-century to provide visual knowledge in a number of domains, from criminality to history, see Tom Gunning, "Tracing the Individual Body: Photography, Detectives, and Early Cinema"; Jeannene M. Przyblyski, "Moving Pictures: Photography, Narrative, and the Paris Commune of 1871." Both appear in *Cinema and the Invention of Modern Life*, ed. Leo Charney and Vanessa R. Schwartz (Berkeley: University of California Press, 1995), 15–45 and 253–78.

illustrated press and the *physiologies* of the nineteenth century.[64] The wax display, the phantasmagoria show, and the panorama took shape in a culture that placed an increasingly large amount of faith in the image's ability to access hidden realms of truth.

Visitors to the wax display or to the phantasmagoria show came face to face with the Revolutionary leaders whose actions and decisions had such an impact on their lives, but who remained in a distant realm, unknowable. These spectacles likewise allowed visitors to see the image of Napoleon and the other generals who had brought glory to the nation or who had been responsible for the death of their child, husband, or friend. The wax display and the phantasmagoria offered a visual supplement to the printed or oral descriptions that formerly had formed the basis of most people's familiarity with historical personages. The panorama provided the same kind of information, but focused more on events than people. These spectacles materialized the past, depriving it of its mysterious otherness. They allowed the Revolutionary and Imperial public to make sense of historical change by allowing it to be perceived by the senses.

That these spectacles represented a moment in the recent rather than distant past also signified a change in notions of time and history during the Revolutionary period. Stephen Kern has located a shift in perceptions of time, and hence of historical change, in the second half of the nineteenth century, with the development of new technologies of communication.[65] Mary Ann Doane also argues that time began to be felt as a distinct entity in this later period. She links time's reification in capitalist modernity with such late nineteenth-century social and economic phenomena as the assembly line, which demanded that time be rationalized and standardized. As Doane emphasizes, the obsessive effort to visualize the passing of time in early cinema comes in response—and at times in resistance—to the new demands of capitalism.[66] Leo Charney has likewise

---

64. On the use of images in the popular press during the 1830s, see Richard Terdiman, *Discourse/Counter-Discourse* (Ithaca: Cornell University Press, 1985), 149–97. On images in the physiologies, see Margaret Cohen, "Panoramic Literature and the Invention of Everyday Genres," in *Cinema and the Invention of Modern Life,* ed. Leo Charney and Vanessa R. Schwartz, 227–52 (Berkeley: University of California Press, 1995).

65. Stephen Kern describes how the telegraph expanded the boundaries of the present by linking people in diverse localities, allowing for events in one place to be related almost simultaneously to those in another, whereas previously they had become "past" before they were known. Similarly, the phonograph and the cinema endowed the past with a new kind of presence in the later part of the century. *The Culture of Time and Space, 1880–1918* (Cambridge: Harvard University Press, 1983), 67–68.

66. Mary Ann Doane, *The Emergence of Cinematic Time: Modernity, Contingency, the Archive* (Cambridge: Harvard University Press, 2002).

analyzed a certain preoccupation with the "moment" in such philosophers of modernity as Martin Heidegger and Walter Benjamin, emphasizing the way that their philosophies reflect an anxiety over the possibility of isolating a present in a world in which time has begun to flow increasingly quickly.[67]

Indeed, the roots of time's acceleration, and of modernity's preoccupation with it, reach back to the Revolutionary period when historical events began to succeed one another at a fast and furious pace. New communication technologies such as the telegraph eventually expanded the boundaries of the present, allowing an event to be perceived simultaneously in multiple locations; a rather different result of the rapid shift in political as well as social and economic realities during the Revolution made the present increasingly ephemeral. Current events did not stay current for long, but rather came to seem quickly historical. The historical spectacles allowed their patrons to come to terms with the abruptness of a present made suddenly past and to confront the shock that resulted from this abrupt transition.

For a culture in which history had become unstable, in which a constantly changing past made for a disruptive present, these spectacles isolated particular moments and events. They overcame the shock of the new by fixing a certain vision of the past and making it available for contemplation. Spectacles of history such as the panorama, the phantasmagoria, and the wax display made the past *present* and hence capable of being experienced by spectators. In a sense, however, the present of the past on display at the panorama, the phantasmagoria, and the wax display was not really a present at all, but rather a spectacular realm outside of time, in which past and present confronted each other in a moment of pure contemplation that allowed for the full play of fantasy and longing necessary for the construction of new forms of identity.[68] This was especially true of the panorama and the wax display, which allowed viewers to take their time looking, whereas the more programmed phantasmagoria show controlled the spectator's temporal experience. In all three spectacles, however, the distance separating past and present was

67. Charney discusses Heidegger's notion of the "Moment of Vision" and Benjamin's "shock" of the moment in "In a Moment: Film and the Philosophy of Modernity," in *Cinema and the Invention of Modern Life,* ed. Leo Charney and Vanessa R. Schwartz, 279–94 (Berkeley: University of California Press, 1995).

68. Doane describes how moments of "spectacle" in film, as opposed to moments of "event," halt narrative progression and function to localize desire, fantasy, and longing in a timeless time (*Emergence of Cinematic Time,* 170). I emphasize that event and spectacle coexist in historical panoramas, phantasmagorias, and wax displays.

erased, and viewers were provided with the ability to visualize a historical moment.[69]

Given the inability of the panorama to show time passing or events unfolding, its creators took care to locate the meaning of the past not in a sequence of events, but in isolated fragments of time. Thus the majority of
panoramas depicted the moment that supposedly determined the outcome
of events, the causes that produced the effects felt by the French public.
This isolated moment was thus given prominence but was always recuper-
ated by a larger historical narrative. According to Doane, one of the functions of narrative cinema is to control and stabilize the contingency of the
moment, to assert that time is rational and irreversible, that events had to
happen in a certain way. Such an approach to the representation of time,
for Doane, allies itself with the demands of capitalist modernity: the assembly line likewise reifies time and rationalizes it.[70] The panorama, another characteristically modern technology, also worked to control or
structure time by acknowledging the singularity of the moment and then
denying its contingency.

The booklet accompanying a Napoleonic panorama from later in the
century, presumably distributed to visitors at the entrance and meant to
serve as a guide to the spectacle, assured visitors that what they were seeing represented not so much the climax of the battle depicted, as the moment that made the climax a foregone conclusion, the crucial minute that
led to important results. "It's nine o'clock," states the guide to this
Panorama de la bataille de la Moscowa.[71] Just as the French commander
gives orders to cross the Semenowska river with his mounted troops, as-
suring victory for the French, he is struck by a Russian bullet, "and the
body of the army remains without direction or guide" (21). This bullet begins "that series of cruel losses" that nearly cost the French the battle.
"Such is the moment represented by the Panorama," the booklet proclaims, "the moment at which the outcome of the battle, which before had
seemed unsure, will now be determined by the emperor" (31). The guidebook assures viewers that time is irreversible, that history could not have
happened differently. The context provided by the booklet proves essential
to the panorama's effect; by incorporating the frozen moment of the

69. Describing the Panorama of Sedan, Doane argues that it allowed spectators to experience a "certain presence in relation to the event." Doane then makes a link with the semiotics
of the "pan" in early cinema, especially in the genre of cinematic reenactments of historical
events, which likewise signified a form of historical presence (ibid., 154).

70. Ibid., 138.

71. Charles Langlois, *Panorama de la bataille de la Moskowa* (Paris: Imprimerie de
Ducessois, 1834), 21. Subsequent quotations are cited in the text.

panorama into a narrative that acknowledges that moment as its source, the booklet helps produce the illusion that the meaning of history can be grasped in a single *coup d'oeil*. By showing the moment that caused all subsequent effects, moreover, the panorama provides viewers with the feeling of witnessing history in the making.

The spectacles of the early nineteenth century also offered spectators the illusion of having participated in historical events. Whether approaching wax sculptures of historical actors, grasping at the phantasmagoric image of a revolutionary, or standing surrounded by a circular canvas of a battle, visitors paid for the privilege of projecting themselves into the space of the past. One reviewer of a panorama of a naval battle from the 1830s registers just such a fantasy of historical participation: "There I am on the forward deck at the foot of the mast, the lieutenant in charge of making a report on the battle and of transmitting to my commander the signals from the admiral's frigate, the outline of which is just visible in the distance, slender and fiery red."[72] Projecting himself into the scene, the critic *becomes* a naval officer. Instead of feeling that the past has merely happened to him, he imagines that he has played a role in bringing history about. As this testimony suggests, the spectacle functioned by providing viewers with a supposedly more active relation to historical events, convincing them of the reality of the event in question while allowing them to feel as if they contributed to its realization.

To some extent, the French public felt that such a proximity to events was their right; as Marie-Hélène Huet and Mona Ozouf have shown, historical spectatorship took on a new significance during the Revolution as crowds gathered to watch the guillotine and popular demonstrations and festivals came to resemble theatrical performances.[73] The historical spectacles of the Revolutionary period provided much of this same Parisian public with the opportunity to see the historical figures of the era up close and to experience events that happened behind closed doors. This kind of substitute spectatorship became increasingly important during the Consulate and the Empire, when important events no longer played out on the Parisian stage. The popularity of the panorama during the first decade of the nineteenth century, just as the locus of history was shifting to remote battlefields, testifies to the desire to bring distant historical events closer to

72. Ch. L., "Le combat de nuit," review of *Panorama de Navarin* by Charles L'Anglois [*sic*], *Le Cabinet de lecture*, February 4, 1832, 13.

73. See Marie-Hélène Huet, *Rehearsing the Revolution: The Staging of Marat's Death, 1793–1797*, trans. Robert Hurley (Berkeley: University of California Press, 1982); Mona Ozouf, *La fête révolutionnaire, 1789–1799* (Paris: Gallimard, 1976).

home. The panorama allowed the Parisian public of the immediate post-Revolutionary period to see what they were missing.

Class Pictures

This sense of historical spectatorship was intended for a specific segment of the population—those who could afford to pay for it. Few workers could afford the price of a ticket to the panorama (1.30 francs for the cheapest seat), much less the more expensive phantasmagoria show.[74] According to François Robichon, who estimates that about 36,000 people visited the *Panorama de Wagram* in 1810, the "middle bourgeoisie" constituted the majority of the panorama's clientele.[75] This class remained the prime audience for the historical spectacles until the 1830s, when prices began to be lowered.[76]

If the panorama and the other historical spectacles appealed primarily to a bourgeois public, however, it was not only because ticket prices were on a scale with their budgets. The bourgeoisie of the early nineteenth century was a heterogeneous class, marked by a varying degree of economic as well as educational advantage. Whereas traditional forms of *ancien régime* historiography were read by a restricted and elite clientele—those who could afford to buy books and those with the time and ability to read them—the new spectacles made far fewer demands on the public's financial and intellectual resources. These spectacles appealed to the broad class of the semiliterate that was beginning to make its presence felt and contin-

74. Jacques Rougerie stresses that the wages (for male workers) even in most specialist trades, such as clockmaking and printing, remained stable at between 3 and 4.50 francs a day during the first half of the nineteenth century and that many workers made much less than this. "Remarques sur l'histoire des salaires à Paris au XIXe siècle," *Le Mouvement Social* 63 (1968) : 74–75. John McCormick adopts the lower figure of 2 francs a day as the average wage against which to set the cost of going to the theater for the popular classes. *Popular Theatres of Nineteenth-Century France* (New York: Routledge, 1993), 78. Jann Matlock notes that the average wage for a female worker in 1840 was only 0.81 francs and rose by 1850 to 2.41 francs. *Scenes of Seduction: Prostitution, Hysteria, and Reading Difference in Nineteenth-Century France* (New York: Columbia University Press, 1994), 321n54.

75. Robichon, "Panoramas en France," 160. He derives his figures by taking the total receipts and dividing by the entry price, adjusting for the amount they were taxed by the government to support hospices and the poor. The middle bourgeoisie includes office holders, large-scale tradesmen, and investors (*rentiers*).

76. According to Robichon, with *The Battle of the Moskowa* (1835) prices went down to 1.25 francs (ibid., 160). With the panorama depicting the burning of Moscow (1839), 1-franc tickets became available to army officers, and lower-ranking soliders and groups of workers could purchase tickets for as little as 50 centimes. Robichon calculates that this allowed roughly 25 percent of the population to become panorama spectators. By the end of the century, he calculates that this figure had risen to 50 percent (204).

ued to grow tremendously as the rise of industrial capitalism in the nineteenth century generated wealth faster than it produced a cultivated elite. These audiences responded eagerly to visual forms of historical representation.

The historical spectacles also appealed to the bourgeoisie for less material reasons. It is no coincidence that a handful of popular entertainments depicting history emerged at the moment that the bourgeoisie asserted its new political role; these spectacles provided an image of bourgeois power and authority.[77] In both of Prévost's panoramas of Paris (1799 and 1803), the viewer looked out at the city from the palace of the Tuileries. Choosing the Tuileries as the point from which to view a panorama of Paris made spatial sense because the palace represented nearly the geographic center of the city, the place from which viewers could take in the most of the urban landscape and surrounding countryside. But it also served a political function: by placing the viewer at the seat of historic and contemporary power—the Tuileries palace served as the residence for French monarchs before the construction of Versailles and had become the center of the new Consular government—the panoramas allowed spectators to assume an authoritative subject position in relation to the nation's past and present history. Robichon has pointed out that while depicting the city, these two canvases actually represented the Revolution, enacting the transfer of power that turned subjects into citizens.[78] As the report to the *Institut* described the authority of the panorama's elevated point of view: "it dominates, it glides over all these objects [beneath it]."[79] Prévost's canvases thus offered bourgeois viewers not only a view of the city as seen from on high, but a representation of the historical shift that had made this perspective possible.

The other spectacles offered viewers a similar subject position. Just as in the panorama, where spectators could move about the platform looking at the canvas from any number of different positions, in the wax display the historical representations remained stationary, allowing visitors to see them from a variety of perspectives. The viewer thus gained a multiplicity

77. Robichon makes a similar argument in relation to Langlois's historical panoramas: "The vogue for historical subject matter is closely linked to the rise of new social strata to power; 1830 and 1880 are there to prove it" (ibid., 166). I point out that the dynamic begins earlier, after the first Revolution, with the historical panoramas of Prévost as well as the other historical spectacles.

78. "If the Tuileries are a central point, they are also the former residence of the kings of France. A new vision forms in which all citizens can literally dominate the city." François Robichon, "Le panorama, spectacle de l'histoire," *Le Mouvement Social* 131 (1985): 83.

79. Dufourny, *Rapport,* 7.

of viewpoints on the past and the power to choose among them.[80] Like the legendary urban *flâneur,* who has been taken by scholars since Walter Benjamin as an emblem of the nineteenth-century's emerging modern vision, the spectator of these entertainments adopted a mobile perspective on the past, along with the ability to remain in control—aloof and superior to its concerns.[81] In relation to the wax display and the panorama, the spectator became a *historical flâneur.*[82]

In the phantasmagoria, the *animateur* furnished by other means the illusion of the spectator's power over the past. Robertson took requests from his audience, summoning the ghosts they desired to see (with the exception of Louis XVI) and enacting elaborate otherworldly dramas that rendered historical figures subservient to the will of the spectator. By conjuring the ghost of Robespierre and then driving him back into the tomb with bolts of thunder, Robertson provided viewers with the comforting illusion that the dangers of history could be controlled.

Significantly, this view of the past made itself available to women as well as men. After a brief period in the spotlight during the early events of the Revolution, women became increasingly marginalized during the Revolution's later phases and especially under the Empire. The exclusion of women from the center of political life, intensified by the mobilization of the Imperial nation around a seemingly endless series of wars, became formalized in the Napoleonic Code of 1804, which officially deprived them of civic rights.[83] The new popular entertainments that came into existence

80. Oettermann refers to the possibility of multiple perspectives offered by the panorama (in contrast to conventional perspectival painting in which the eye is assumed to be a fixed point) as inherently, if unintentionally, "democratic" (*Panorama,* 31).

81. On the *flâneur* as an emblem of modernity, see Charles Baudelaire, "Le peintre de la vie moderne," in *Oeuvres complètes,* ed. Claude Pichois, vol. 2 (1863; Paris: Gallimard, 1976), 687–94; Walter Benjamin, "Paris, Capital of the Nineteenth Century," in *Reflections,* trans. Peter Demetz (1935; New York: Shocken Books, 1986), 146–62. Benjamin makes the connection between the *flâneur* and the spectacles I am discussing explicit: "The crowd is the veil through which the familiar city lures the *flâneur* like a phantasmagoria" (156). My understanding of the *flâneur* has been informed by Priscilla Ferguson, "The Flâneur: The City and Its Discontents," in *Paris as Revolution* (Berkeley: University of California Press, 1994), 80–114; and Jann Matlock's forthcoming book, *Desires to Censor: Spectacles of the Body, Vision, and Aesthetics in Nineteenth-Century France.*

82. Nineteenth-century critics liked to cast themselves as *flâneurs* who had happened upon the spectacles they described. In an article by E. de Lachaux, the *Panorama d'Eylau* becomes but one more stop on an aimless stroll through Paris. "My life as a *flâneur* offers many adventures," the critic writes before confiding how he could not pass up "this picture of our glory and our miseries." Review of *Panorama d'Eylau* by Langlois, *L'Illustration,* April 19, 1845, 116.

83. Accounts of the social and political position of women during the Revolution and Empire can be found in Claire Goldberg Moses, *French Feminism in the 19th Century* (Al-

at just this time allowed women to witness history and to do so from the same perspective as male spectators.[84]

As discussions of these spectacles in the popular press of the day indicate, women not only attended popular spectacles such as the panorama, but were seen as taking full advantage of their empowering perspective. The leading women's magazine in the early nineteenth century, the *Journal des Dames et des Modes,* touted the panorama as offering "all the charm of truth and all the seductions of optics."[85] Female readers were encouraged to imagine that the spectacle provided something more than mere historical knowledge; a later article in the same journal followed its enthusiastic review of the first panorama of Paris with a spicy vaudeville song in which a hapless husband is so taken in by the canvas that he loses his balance and falls off the balustrade, thus offering his wife a chance to be alone with her lover.[86] If the author of this song fantasized that women had liberties under the cover provided by the spectacles, it was because these public entertainments placed men and women on equal footing.

National Vistas

The historical spectacles of the Revolutionary period promoted the formation of personal and class identities for newly empowered bourgeois subjects, but they also interpellated viewers as part of a nation, helping to draw the boundaries around an emerging collective identity. As Benedict Anderson and, more recently, David A. Bell have shown, modern nationalism came into existence during the eighteenth century, replacing the religious and dynastic affiliations inherited from the Middle Ages. Nowhere was this process more explicit than in France, where the Revolution invented a new form of collective social identity binding individuals to-

---

bany: State University of New York Press, 1984); Joan B. Landes, *Women and the Public Sphere in the Age of the French Revolution* (Ithaca: Cornell University Press, 1988).

84. Whereas feminist historians have argued that women were in theory excluded from the public sphere in the post-Revolutionary period, Jann Matlock uses female attendance at the popular spectacles of the era to show that this was not the case in practice ("Invisible Woman," 182). Elizabeth Wilson provides an account of the relation of women to spectatorship in "The Invisible Flâneur," *New Left Review* 191 (1992): 90–110.

85. C. J. B. Lucas Rochemont, "Panorama," review of *Panorama de Paris* by Prévost, *Journal des Dames et des Modes,* 20 Thermidor, Year VII, 349–350.

86. In the song, the husband falls off the platform while looking at the panorama: "Pour mieux voir cet objet mignon, / Je me baissai . . . J'étois bien libre; / Mais par suite de mon guignon, / Zeste, je perdis l'équilibre." Levrier Champrion, "Panorama," review of *Panorama de Paris* by Prévost, *Journal des Dames et des Modes,* 20 Vendémiaire, Year 8, 28–29. A translation reads: "In order to see that delightful object better, / I bent over . . . I was free to do so; / But my luck was such, / That I lost my balance."

gether, no longer as subjects of a king, as members of the Church, or as residents of a particular region, but as citizens of a new nation founded on a set of universal political ideals. But although the *Déclaration des droits de l'homme et du citoyen* may have constituted the new nation in theory, more concrete material practices were required to help the nation gain purchase in the popular imagination.

According to Anderson, the nation exists as an "imagined community," in which members "will never know most of their fellow-members, meet them, or even hear of them, yet in the minds of each lives the image of their communion."[87] Like the map and the museum, two visual modes of discourse discussed by Anderson, historical spectacles provide an important weapon in the new nation's arsenal of image-promoting practices, furnishing a myth through which the past comes to justify or legitimize the present.[88] It follows from Anderson's theory that the modern nation exists as an image in the minds of its citizens that a new mode of visual history should emerge at the same time as this new mode of nationalism.[89] By turning the past into a series of images, the spectacles developed during and just after the Revolution gave form to the idea of France in the popular imagination.

In a remarkable lecture delivered at the Sorbonne in 1882, Ernest Renan described how the nation is a "spiritual principle" formed not through racial, linguistic, religious, geographic, or strategic affiliations but rather through identification with more intangible qualities.[90] One of these qualities resides in the present, in the collective desire to live together and to share a common destiny. The other resides in the past, in the common heritage that the nation affirms: "A heroic past, great men, glory (and I mean of the true sort), this is the spiritual capital on which the idea of a nation rests."[91] The historical spectacles of the early nineteenth century, particularly the panorama, provided a vision of the heroic past that the French

87. Benedict Anderson, *Imagined Communities: Reflections on the Origin and Spread of Nationalism* (1983; reprint, London: Verso Books, 1991), 6. For an account of the rise of nationalism focusing on eighteenth-century France, see David A. Bell, *The Cult of the Nation in France: Inventing Nationalism, 1680–1800* (Cambridge: Harvard University Press, 2001).

88. On the role of museums in fostering spectacularized national identities, see the articles in *Museum Culture: Histories, Discourses, Spectacles,* ed. Daniel J. Sherman and Irit Rogoff (Minneapolis: University of Minnesota Press, 1994), especially Detlef Hoffmann, "The German Art Museum and the History of the Nation," 3–21. Hoffmann associates the rise of the German art museum with the French Revolution (3).

89. Anderson describes how paintings of episodes in the national past were used for ideological purposes in Indonesia in the 1950s (*Imagined Communities,* 183).

90. Ernest Renan, "Qu'est-ce qu'une nation?" in *Qu'est-ce qu'une nation? et autres écrits politiques* (1882; reprint, Paris: Imprimerie nationale, 1996), 223–43.

91. Ibid., 240.

public could consume collectively, in group settings that fostered the kind of imaginary bonds the representation was intended to foster.

James Thayer, the American businessman who partnered with Prévost to create panoramas during the first decade of the nineteenth century, clearly saw the power of his spectacle as a tool for promoting a sense of pride in the French nation. He did not hesitate, moreover, to offer this tool to the Imperial state. "The government protects and encourages the Arts principally when their work has as its goal the propagation of its glory and the progress toward their perfection," he wrote in a letter dated February 7, 1809, to the Minister of the Interior requesting a prolongation of the import permit he had purchased from Robert Fulton, which was set to expire in April of that year. In his effort to market his product, Thayer outlined a strategy whereby the panorama became a form of nationalistic, and hence Napoleonic, propaganda:

> I have long had the project of placing before the eyes of the inhabitants of Paris, by means of that process that alone can rival the color and the exactitude of nature, the battles and other memorable events that have taken place since the accession to the throne of the hero who has dedicated himself to our glory and our happiness, as well as views of the principal cities of the globe. The execution of this project, that at once fulfills the desires of the capital and renders homage to the glory of our homeland [*notre Patrie*], has only been delayed by the labors that I deemed necessary to the perfection of the Panoramas.[92]

Thayer's plea for state support of his enterprise links the popular desire for historical images with an emerging national consciousness. But his letter operates on another level as well, enacting the very process of ideological identification it describes and proposes. Professing a filial devotion to "notre Patrie," the American stakes his claim to participation in the imagined community of Napoleonic France, an identity that he shows to be less a contingency of birth than an act of vision, a willingness to look at history collectively ("*our* glory and *our* happiness"), the opportunity for which his spectacle provides. Thayer thus demonstrated through his own example the efficacy of his enterprise.

To Empire-era observers, the patriotic function of the panorama was unmistakable. Even the critic for the aesthetically minded *Journal des Arts* praised the patriotism of the panorama's creators who "are on the lookout for periods that are glorious and dear to the homeland." The critic goes on to call for a proliferation of panoramas devoted to Napoleon's glory,

92. Cited in Robichon, "Panoramas en France," 22.

echoing the proposal put forth by Thayer: "We have begun to suspect that the executors of the Panoramas, after having painted one after the other all the pages of our history, will soon make appear in separate frames, the battlefields of Millesimo, Lodi, Arcole, of the Pyramides and of Aboukir, Ulm, Austerlitz, of Jéna, Eylau, Friedland, etc." Given Napoleon's prodigious exploits, if this dream were made reality, the Parisian landscape would soon have been spotted with panoramic rotundas, as the critic from the *Journal des Arts* deliriously forecasts: "these rotundas will be constructed one after the other on the boulevard, and soon Paris will see itself framed by objects richer and more brilliant than the rarest metals and the most precious stones."[93] In this panoramic fantasy, Paris becomes one large collection of historical spectacles.

Despite such compelling elaborations of the panorama's potential as a tool for promoting Imperial ideology, Napoleon appears to have refrained from making popular entertainments an official part of his propaganda machine.[94] Whereas the Empire aggressively cultivated more traditional forms of historical representation, acting as patron to both painters and historians, it left the spectacles with a relative degree of autonomy. Thayer did receive some state subsidies for his *Panorama de Wagram,* but by and large Napoleon restricted himself to more subtle means of encouraging this new medium.

Post-Revolutionary Spectacles

The historical spectacles that became popular during the Revolution and its imperial aftermath allowed the bourgeoisie to assume their new political and social ascendancy through the consumption of visually realistic representations. These spectacles provided for the processing of the rapid progress of history and offered perspectives through which new individual and national identities could take shape. The historical spectacle did not fade out, however, with the end of the Empire. On the contrary, the spectacular mode of historical representation continued to animate a variety of popular entertainments throughout the nineteenth century.

Versions of Robertson's phantasmagoria periodically reappeared during the first three decades of the century. Despite the death of its founder and

93. "L'abus des mots ou les panoramas," *Journal des Arts,* February 22, 1809, 409.
94. Following Bapst, Oettermann claims that Napoleon, after seeing the *Panorama de Wagram,* hired the architect Jacques Cellerier to design seven great rotundas to be built on the Champs-Elysées to commemorate his victories (*Panorama,* 152). Robichon suggests that this story is apocryphal, having found no mention of it in the archives ("Panoramas en France," 22).

the exportation of much of its contents to England with Madame Tussaud, the Curtius wax display remained open well into the July Monarchy, continuing to depict actors from the Revolutionary and Imperial periods. No new panorama appeared in Paris for several years after the death of the great *panoramiste* Prévost in 1823, although a series of similar spectacles—such as the cosmorama[95] and the géorama,[96] and, most famous, the diorama—entertained the Restoration public with technologically enhanced images throughout the 1820s.

Opened on the rue Sanson in 1822 by Louis-Jacques-Mandé Daguerre,[97] a theatrical set designer who later went on to invent one of the early photographic processes, the diorama attempted to solve what critics perceived as one of the major shortcomings of the panorama—its inability to depict movement or change in a landscape. It aimed for an even greater realism than the panorama by depicting "light, mist, and their modifications."[98] Daguerre's solution to the problem of depicting changes in atmospheric conditions and time consisted in altering the lighting on the canvas, giving the impression, for example, of day passing into night. He also placed spectators on a platform that shifted to provide views of different canvases. As opposed to the circular panorama, the diorama's canvas was flat, like a film screen.[99] Daguerre's simulation of the moving image, if not its actual technology, foreshadowed cinema, and he took an even greater step in this direction by introducing the "double effect diorama," which featured a canvas painted on both sides; lit first from the front to reveal one scene and then from the back to reveal the other, the spectacle gave the impression of change without shifting the position of the spectator.

The diorama tended to provide views of landscapes and monuments, as opposed to the scenes of battles and cities favored by the panorama, in order best to display its primary effect, the change of atmospheric condi-

95. Several of the subjects of the Cosmorama (located in the Palais-Royal), such as the views of the islands where Napoleon was exiled, had historical significance. Edward Planta, *A New Picture of Paris* (London: Samuel Leigh, 1832), 387.

96. "Géorama: 7, Blvd. des Capucines, Spectacle of the entire globe, whose surface is seen from the interior of a sphere of 120 feet in circumference," A. Person de Teyssèdre, *Conducteur général de l'étranger à Paris* (Paris: Constant-Chantpie, 1833), 281.

97. The painter Charles Bouton aided Daguerre in the creation of the early dioramas.

98. *Notice explicative des tableaux exposés au diorama* (N.p., n.d.), Bibliothèque de l'Opéra, Paris, B277, 3. Studies of the diorama that have informed my account include Altick, *Shows of London*, 163–70; Comment, *Painted Panorama*, 57–65; Robichon, "Panoramas en France," 107–10, 159. An early description of the diorama can be found in Étienne-Jean Delécluze, *Précis d'un traité de peinture* (Paris: Bureau de l'Encyclopédie portative, 1828), 232.

99. A notice accompanying the diorama explained that the circular form used by the panorama was only necessary for "the representation of a considerable spread of landscape, especially when one wants to depict the full extent of the horizon in every direction." *Notice explicative*, 4.

tions in a single location. But Daguerre did not choose his subjects at random. The frequent views of churches presented at the Diorama, such as Saint Peter's in Rome and Canterbury Cathedral, no doubt resonated with the renewed religiosity of certain conservative elements of the Restoration governing class. As an explanatory pamphlet that accompanied the spectacle made clear, the Diorama's "project has not been to reproduce ordinary views, but only those views that hold a particular interest, either for the memory of historical facts or for the picturesque qualities of particular locales."[100] Like the wax display, the panorama, and the phantasmagoria show (which its use of lighting effects resembled), the diorama was billed as a new form of historical representation. Brochures that accompanied the spectacle mentioned all points of historical interest in the *tableau*.

Like the other spectacle entrepreneurs of the period, Daguerre and his rivals attempted to blow with the political winds. On January 22, 1831, Daguerre, now installed in a new amphitheater on the boulevard du Temple, unveiled a canvas depicting the July Revolution entitled, *Le 28 juillet 1830 à l'Hôtel-de-Ville*. He was beaten to the punch, however, by a rival *dioramiste* named A. Colin, who displayed a tableau representing the same event.[101] In Colin's diorama, spectators found themselves transported to the place de Grève, in the middle of a revolutionary crowd. "It's a barricade!" reported one reviewer; "Behind you, all around you, tranquil spectator! Men, children, women draped in rags [. . .] at the foot of the Hôtel-de-Ville, red uniforms [. . .] furiously charge the proletarian masses [. . . .] It's a page of history written with a brush dipped heartily in powder, blood, and dust."[102] Shortly after the opening of Daguerre's diorama, the newly enthroned Louis-Philippe visited the representation of the event that had brought him to power.[103]

Later that same year, Daguerre offered another spectacle of profound historical interest, this time with a Bonapartist slant—a view of Napoleon's tomb on Saint Helena.[104] Critics at the time praised Daguerre's canvas not only for its serene beauty but also for the accuracy of its represen-

---

100. Ibid., 3.

101. An article reviewing Colin's spectacle points out that his diorama does not really merit the name because it lacks the key features invented by Daguerre: the moving stage and the double effect achieved by painting the canvas on both sides. "Diorama Montesquieu," review of diorama by A. Colin, *Journal des Artistes et des Amateurs,* January 16, 1831, 48–49.

102. "Diorama Montesquieu," review of diorama by A. Colin, *Le Cabinet de Lecture,* January 19, 1831, 3.

103. "Their majesties, after having examined with a great deal of attention this new canvas, conveyed their admiration to M. Daguerre in the most flattering terms; the king wanted to see it again several times." "Nouvelles des arts," *Journal des Artistes et des Amateurs,* January 24, 1831, 72.

104. One can still see a full-scale re-creation of the tomb at the Musée de l'armée in Paris.

tation of this important landmark. "As for the exactitude of the portrait, you can count on it," assured an article in *L'Artiste*, "M. Daguerre used a great many documents whose authenticity is incontrovertible. This certitude adds a great deal of charm to the work."[105] Visitors, it seems, went to this diorama not only to admire a picturesque setting, but to see for themselves the final resting place of Napoleon—depicted in as realistic a manner as possible.[106]

The July Monarchy saw a rebirth of interest in the panorama. The artist and entrepreneur who led this new wave of "panoramania"[107] was Charles Langlois, a former military officer. Langlois had fought in the Napoleonic Wars and later trained with such noted history painters as Horace Vernet, Anne-Louis Girodet, and Antoine-Jean Gros. In 1826, he saw his first panorama, a depiction of Athens that was Prévost's final work and dedicated the rest of his life to celebrating France's military history through the aid of this large-scale spectacle.[108] Using his first-hand knowledge of military combat, Langlois undertook for his first panoramic subject a naval battle—the *Panorama de Navarin* depicted a recent joint Anglo-French military endeavor, a victory still fresh enough in the public's mind to excite patriotic enthusiasm and bring in the public in droves.[109]

After a *Panorama d'Alger,* depicting the recently colonized capital of Algeria, Langlois focused on the Napoleonic epic for his next panoramas. Sent as a military attaché to Russia in 1833, Langlois spent a large portion of the next year surveying the battlefield for a panorama of the Battle of

105. "Diorama," review of *Le tombeau de Napoléon à Sainte-Hélène* by Daguerre, *L'Artiste* 1 (1831): 138.

106. According to Altick, Daguerre's diorama operated on the rue Sanson from 1822 until it was destroyed by fire in 1839. The new building on the boulevard Bonne-Nouvelle burned nine years later (*Shows of London*, 170).

107. I borrow the coinage from Ralph Hyde, *Panoramania: The Art and Entertainment of "All-Embracing" View* (London: Trefoil Publications, 1988).

108. Étienne-Charles Bourseul, *Biographie du Colonel Langlois* (Paris: Paul Dupont, 1874), 11. According to Bourseul, Langlois was born in 1789, attended the École polytechnique, and fought at Wagram in 1809. He entered Napoleon's *Vieille Garde* as a captain in 1814 and later fought in Spain and in the Battle of France. He was wounded at Waterloo and took up painting in 1817. He won a gold medal at the Salon of 1822 for his rendering of the Battle of Sedim and went on to do conventionally sized paintings of the Passage of the Beresina, the Battles of Smolensk and the Moskowa, and the naval combat of Navarino. He rejoined the military in 1823 and was present at the conquest of Algiers in 1830. He continued painting panoramas until his death at age 80.

109. The battle of Navarino, part of an allied English, Russian, and French effort to help Greece secure independence from Turkey, took place on October 20, 1827. Lord Byron died in this campaign, which became something of a Romantic cause célèbre. One reviewer commented, "Of all the feats of arms of the Restoration, the Battle of Navarino is the only one that was truly popular." "Beaux-Arts," review of *Panorama de Navarin* by Langlois, *Le Temps*, February 9, 1831, 4.

the Moskowa, which he showed in Paris from 1835 to 1839. "For nearly a month," he wrote in the booklet that accompanied the spectacle, "I traveled all over that plain in every direction, observing and drawing every detail in order later to reproduce them with a religious exactitude."[110] Langlois brought a historian's accuracy to bear on his panorama, and observers at the time acknowledged its pedagogic value.[111] In his next canvas, which depicted the burning of Moscow (1839–42), Langlois represented the following stage in the Russian campaign of 1812, when the victorious French soldiers entered the Russian capital to find it deserted, its buildings set afire by the departing inhabitants. After this foray into one of the more picturesque but dark moments of the wars of the Empire, Langlois turned once again to Napoleon's victories, journeying to Germany and Egypt to do research for his *Panorama d'Eylau* (1843–51) and *Panorama des Pyramides* (1853–55). These canvases were displayed in a grand new building, designed by Jacques-Ignace Hittorff and constructed in 1839 on the Champs-Elysées.[112]

During the Second Empire, Langlois turned temporarily to more contemporary history, glorifying the military victories not of Napoleon but of his nephew, Napoleon III. In 1855 he traveled to see the theater of the Crimean War up close and (with an assistant, Léon Méhédin) took photographs of the battlefields shortly after the fighting ended, which he used to paint his *Panorama de Sébastopol* (1860–64).[113] The first major innovation in the technique of painting panoramas since Barker, photography also helped Langlois in the creation of his final panorama, of the Battle of Solferino, a French victory of 1859, which was exposed from 1865 to 1870.[114] Langlois died while at work on yet another commemoration of the First Empire, a panorama of the Battle of Marengo.[115]

110. Langlois, *Panorama de la bataille de la Moskowa*, 3–4. The Musée de l'armée possesses a study by Langlois for this panorama. Comment reproduces this image in color, in *Painted Panorama*, 9–16.

111. See F., review of *Panorama de la bataille de la Moskowa* by Langlois, *Journal des Artistes et des Amateurs*, July 26, 1835, 60, for an appreciation of the panorama's historical accuracy.

112. The building, which cost 330,000 francs, was demolished in 1855, following the Universal Exposition. Oettermann, *Panorama*, 163.

113. Some of these photos can be seen at the Musée de l'Armée in Paris.

114. François Robichon describes Langlois's use of photography to paint the *Panorama de Sébastopol* in "Langlois, photographe et panoramiste," in *Jean-Charles Langlois: La Photographie, La Peinture, La Guerre*, ed. François Robichon and André Rouillé (Paris: Jacqueline Chambon, 1992), 20–33.

115. During the Third Republic, panoramas continued to draw large crowds and continued to look to history for their subject matter. Langlois's *Bataille de Solferino* was replaced in 1872 by a panorama showing the bombardment of the Fort of Issy (where the Parisians fought the invading Prussians in 1870), executed by the noted history painter Félix Philip-

Technically and artistically, the panoramas of Langlois departed only slightly from the formula established by Prévost. Like his predecessor, Langlois relied for his primary visual effect on the optical trick produced by removing all points of comparison between the viewer and the horizon. Like Prévost, he lit his canvases only from above and had viewers pass through a darkened staircase in order to increase their sense of spatial disjuncture. Before using photography as an aid in sketching the panorama, Langlois's only major improvements to panoramic technology consisted in the placement of actual three-dimensional figures or props in front of the image and in altering the central platform from which viewers looked at the canvas. In the *Panorama de Navarin,* Langlois's first undertaking, spectators viewed the panorama from the deck of a real battleship, the *Scipion,* purchased by Langlois after the battle and refitted by him to make visitors believe they were actually at sea.[116]

To mid-century viewers, the panorama looked just as real as it had to their turn-of-the-century counterparts. Praise of the panorama's illusion remains a commonplace in the discourse surrounding the panorama throughout the nineteenth century. "I forgot I was in front of a canvas," wrote one reviewer of Langlois's *Panorama de la bataille de la Moskowa.*[117] And no less of an observer than Théophile Gautier remarked of the *Panorama de Sébastopol* that "the appearance of reality would certainly not produce a different impression."[118] As during the Empire, viewers of Langlois's canvases paid tribute to the panorama's power to substitute representation for reality, and to transport them to the scene of history. "Soon the illustration takes hold of the spectator who, after a few minutes of silent contemplation, is ready to imagine that it is no longer the picture of the battlefield but the battlefield itself that he has before his eyes," wrote Langlois's biogra-

---

poteaux. This panorama remained open to the public until 1883. Spectators at the end of the century could also view episodes from Revolutionary history in *La prise de la Bastille* (1882–1890) and *Le tableau du siècle,* which was painted by Alfred Stevens and Henri Gervex and which depicted important historical personages such as Louis XVI, Marie Antoinette, and Camille Desmoulins. Robichon, "Panoramas en France," 28, 204; Schwartz, *Spectacular Realities,* 157–76.

116. Schwartz discusses the technical innovations of this panorama in *Spectacular Realities,* 154.

117. F., review of *Panorama de la bataille de la Moskowa* by Langlois [2nd article], *Journal des Artistes et des Amateurs,* August 30, 1835, 140.

118. Théophile Gautier, review of *Panorama de Sébastopol* by Langlois, *Le Moniteur Universel,* January 10, 1861, 47. Although so widespread as to become the single dominant trope in the critical discourse surrounding the panorama, the recognition of the spectacle's realism was not made without reservation. Certain commentators pointed to defects in the panorama's execution that detracted from the illusion, particularly the lack of movement and sound that cinema would later provide.

pher of the artist's first Napoleonic panoramas.[119] Like Prévost, Langlois made his viewers into eyewitnesses of the past.

For Langlois's spectators, however, the history of the Napoleonic Wars was more distant than it had been for Prévost's viewers. Whereas the historical spectacles of the Revolutionary and Imperial periods had provided Parisians with a sense of control over events that were affecting their lives but happening out of sight, in distant locations or behind closed doors, the representation of the Napoleonic epic in Langlois's panoramas during the 1830s, 1840s and 1850s and the continued depiction of Revolutionary and Imperial figures in the wax display and the phantasmagoria show now served a primarily nostalgic function. Nostalgia, however, can carry a political force, especially when it takes as its object contested historical events.[120]

During the July Monarchy, partisans of the three main parties that opposed Louis-Philippe each looked backward with longing to a particular moment in the recent past: Legitimists (who sought the reestablishment of the Bourbon monarchy) were nostalgic for the ancien régime or for the Restoration, Republicans (who sought the overthrow of the monarchy and the establishment of democracy) looked to the days of the First Republic during the Revolution, and Bonapartists (who sought a reestablishment of the Napoleonic dynasty) longed for the days of the Empire. Langlois's panoramas devoted to the Napoleonic epic, like the forms of Napoleonic representation that I discuss in later chapters, helped advance the Bonapartist political platform by feeding into the great man's cult.

The militaristic panoramas of Langlois, including those that depicted exploits of the Restoration government (Navarino and Algiers), also had a more specific political thrust. From the very beginning of his career as a history painter, Langlois sought to use his art as a patriotic tool by building a sense of national identity on a bedrock of pride in military triumph. During the 1830s and 1840s, this militaristic vision of the nation implied a critique of the July Monarchy government. The soldier-artist looked to the wars of the past as a means of combating what he saw as a decline in nationalistic sentiment due to Louis-Philippe's policy of avoiding conflict with France's European neighbors. According to Langlois's biographer,

---

119. E. C. Bourseul, *Biographie du Colonel Langlois* (Paris: Paul Dupont, 1874), 4.

120. In *The Future of Nostalgia* (New York: Basic Books, 2001), Svetlana Boym notes that the term *nostalgia* was coined in the late seventeenth century by Johannes Hofer, a Swiss doctor, and referred originally to a sad mood originating from a desire to return to one's native land (3). Boym describes how it became associated with a "changing conception of time" (7) in the post-Revolutionary period (9), and was one of the "side effects of a teleology of progress" (10).

"Colonel Langlois knew that when the military spirit of once mighty nations dries up, these nations fall into decadence, as the history books teach."[121] Representing France's great military moments—and her defeats as well—thus served for Langlois as a means to combat the moral decline into which Louis-Philippe had led the country.

The Napoleonic cult, however, was not purely militaristic. The brochure accompanying Langlois's *Panorama d'Eylau,* apparently written by Langlois himself, draws a connection between Napoleon's military triumphs and the ideals of the Revolution which, according to Langlois, Napoleon had fought to protect:

> How could historians of despotism recognize that their slavish nations, fighting without any hope but to perpetuate their miseries, to fasten their chains, and to increase through their victory the power and the privileges of their oppressors, would be beaten by a brave and enlightened people who had regained their independence, their liberty, their equality before justice and the laws, as there exists before God and religion, and that he, the apostle of this new belief, carried it so far, fighting off insults with victory and filling the world with his bravery and his great deeds![122]

By casting Napoleon as the Revolution's savior, as the defender of the poor and as a supporter of democratic ideals, Langlois's brochure idealizes the great man in a manner meant to appeal not only to the Bonapartists but also to that other oppositional faction, the Republicans.

The vision of Napoleon as the people's hero, a vision popularized in engravings and literature of the 1820s and 1830s, served as an important point of reference for opponents of the bourgeois, pro-business, and pacifistic policies of Louis-Philippe during the July Monarchy.[123] A review of Langlois's *Panorama d'Eylau* in the left-leaning newspaper *La Réforme* makes this critique explicit by pleading for the government to purchase Langlois's old Napoleonic panoramas in order to prevent their destruction, a plea the critic knows will fall on deaf ears. "What becomes of princely glory," the reviewer asks, "if one treads over the glory of the people?" To bury Napoleon's legend by allowing the destruction of Langlois's panoramas is to silence the people's will, according to this article. The review ends with a blatant appeal to the frustrations of veterans and the lower classes, those who posed the most significant threat to Louis-

121. Bourseul, *Biographie du Colonel Langlois,* 5.

122. Charles Langlois, *Relation du combat et de la bataille d'Eylau* (Paris: Panorama des Champs-Elysées, 1844), 2.

123. For more on the formation of the Napoleon myth in the July Monarchy, see Jean Lucas-Dubreton, *Le culte de Napoléon* (Paris: Albin Michel, 1960).

Philippe's bourgeois monarchy: "Soldiers, make sure to obey, that's all that is demanded of you!—And as for the common man, they hide from him his paternal glory, like the son of the great man, because the *entente cordiale* prevents us from getting revenge for Waterloo."[124] Napoleon's son, supposedly kept in ignorance of his father's greatness, serves as a symbol for the nation as a whole, deprived of knowledge of the great man's glory and hence reduced to a tragic ineffectuality. More particularly, Napoleon's son represents the lower classes and former soldiers, who remained most attached to the Napoleonic legend. Historical spectacles such as the panorama thus become a vehicle not only for the resurgence of national pride that would seek revenge for Waterloo, but also for the registering of a more general sense of oppression and dissatisfaction with the bourgeois monarchy.

Not all apologists for the panorama, however, affirmed this populist message. The reviewer for the Legitimist daily *Gazette de France,* which opposed the government of Louis-Philippe from the right of the political spectrum, praised the patriotic and militaristic aspects of the *Panorama d'Eylau,* but saw this nationalism as free of class interests: "All of Paris [*Tout Paris*] will come to see that artistic marvel created by one of the emperor's brave soldiers, who shed his blood for the homeland," the conservative reviewer declared, "and will come to learn to what prodigious feats disinterestedness, love of country, glory and the most astonishing valor, can give rise."[125] As I have indicated, representations of Napoleon's military exploits were anything but "disinterested" in the political climate of the July Monarchy. As Michael Marrinan has shown, moreover, Louis-Philippe realized the danger that Napoleon's image posed to his regime and attempted to co-opt its energy in the historical museum he opened in 1836 at Versailles, which contained hundreds of paintings devoted to the emperor's exploits, as well as in the elaborate spectacle he staged for the return of Napoleon's remains in 1840.[126]

---

124. Camille Duteil, "Le panorama national," *La Réforme,* June 14, 1844, 4. I discuss the popular belief that Napoleon's son was kept in ignorance of his august lineage and the way this legend was manipulated for political ends during the Revolution of 1830 in Chapter 3.

125. "Panorama de la bataille d'Eylau," review of panorama by Langlois, *Gazette de France,* July 20, 1843, 7.

126. See Michael Marrinan, *Painting Politics for Louis-Philippe: Art and Ideology in Orleanist France, 1830–1848* (New Haven: Yale University Press, 1988); Marrinan, "Historical Vision and the Writing of History at *Louis-Philippe's Versailles,*" in *The Popularization of Images: Visual Culture under the July Monarchy,* ed. Petra Ten-Doesschate Chu and Gabriel P. Weisberg (Princeton: Princeton University Press, 1994), 113–43. I discuss the historical museum at Versailles in Chapter 2.

The connotations of the history offered by the panorama changed again with the fall of Louis-Philippe in 1848. Representations of Napoleonic grandeur served to advance the hopes of various factions of the opposition during the July Monarchy, but this ceased to be the case after Louis-Napoléon's coup-d'état, when the Bonapartist political threat became a reality. For the ruler whom Victor Hugo dubbed "Napoleon the little," references to his uncle's glory reflected back on himself, providing a semblance of substance to a figure who had few accomplishments of his own. During the Second Empire, the goals of the panorama and the regime in power thus coincided, and Langlois put his spectacle in service of the state, continuing to produce spectacles that celebrated the First Empire before turning finally to the Second. The two panoramas executed to commemorate Napoleon III's military triumphs at Solferino and Sebastopol received significant government funding for the first time.[127]

The significance of the various historical spectacles, however, did not lie solely in their link to explicit political programs. From their origin, the wax display, the phantasmagoria show, and the panorama offered more intangible benefits to their spectators, serving to bolster imaginary forms of identification, such as nationalism, that depended on images for their realization. During the Revolution and Imperial periods, as I have shown, the spectacles of history helped (bourgeois) viewers take control of historical events and assert their power over the past. Later in the nineteenth century, as the Revolution and the Empire became more distant memories, the spectacles that continued to depict them offered a different kind of reassurance. For the bourgeois customers of Langlois's panoramas in the 1830s and 1840s, the gains of the Revolution no longer seemed precarious; the July Revolution had consolidated their political, as well as economic, power. The spectacles depicting the Revolution and Imperial periods thus appealed to this entrenched bourgeoisie as a sign that the kind of upheaval that had brought them to power, and that might now threaten their power, would never return. Visitors to the diorama of Napoleon's tomb in 1831 paid homage to the great man, but also satisfied themselves that he was really dead.

In *L'écriture de l'histoire*, Michel de Certeau describes the process whereby the historian—and especially the Romantic historian of the nineteenth century epitomized by Michelet—sought to calm the spirits of the

---

127. According to Robichon, the Second Empire subsidized Langlois out of the budget for the fine arts (providing 15,000 francs a year), in exchange for which Langlois agreed to submit his subjects to the Ministry of State and to produce new panoramas every five years. The commission for the *Bataille de Solferino* came directly from Napoleon III. Robichon, "Langlois, photographe et panoramiste," 15–17.

dead through writing. Historiography, according to de Certeau, separates the present from the "otherness" of the past by constructing "scriptural tombs," in which the ghosts of all those who perished on the guillotine or in Napoleon's wars could once and for all be silenced.[128] The spectacular forms of historical entertainment that continued to proliferate in the 1830s, 1840s, and 1850s, at the same time as the emergence of Romantic historiography, responded to a similar set of historical imperatives. Constructing visual rather than scriptural tombs, the historical spectacles allowed visitors not only to see events that had profoundly shaped their lives but that had happened out of sight, but also to put these events behind them once and for all.

Toward a Critique of the Historical Spectacle

Historical spectacles of the first half of the nineteenth century, I have argued, provided visitors a view of themselves, their class, and their country in line with the imperatives of the historical moment. By furnishing a sense of control over history, the spectacles seemed to allow bourgeois spectators, both male and female, to experience historical agency as a class prerogative and to imagine the links binding them to the collection of invisible souls making up the new French nation, forms of illusory identification requiring all the reinforcement the spectacles could muster. The historical spectacles, in other words, offered the image of a new identity for a bourgeoisie struggling to realize the gains of the Revolution.

Such at least was their promise. That the spectacles came through on their promise and delivered an illusion of identity seems to be confirmed by testimonials in the popular press of the period. Whether they generated other effects in the process is another, more difficult question. Although the incorporation of spectacularizing techniques into more traditional genres and media produced negative critical responses that I read in later chapters as constituting a nineteenth-century critique of the spectacular past, the historical entertainments I have discussed in this chapter met with very little contemporary bad press. Even critics who denounced the way historiography was beginning to resemble a panorama did not necessarily object to the panorama itself. But the absence of negative reactions at the time does not mean that the popular historical entertainments cannot be interrogated for the consequences of their spectacular approach to the past.

128. Michel de Certeau, *L'écriture de l'histoire* (Paris: Gallimard, 1975), 8.

In the absence of skeptical voices from the nineteenth century, twentieth-century critical theory, which has varied greatly in its attitude toward popular culture, offers a useful perspective for evaluating the effects of these spectacles. In Theodor Adorno and Max Horkheimer's *Dialectic of Enlightenment,* popular forms of entertainment—or what these critics would label the products of the "culture industry" to underscore the extent to which such forms are imposed from above and do not truly serve the interests of the public—are shown to be mere commodities that reduce art to exchange value.[129] The fetishization of products of the culture industry by the public, according to these critics, only exacerbates the reification of consciousness characteristic of life under capitalism. "The entire practice of the culture industry transfers the profit motive naked onto cultural forms," Adorno writes.[130]

Like their twentieth-century counterparts, the nineteenth-century historical spectacles were aggressively commercial in nature. Capitalizing on the past, they drew crowds willing to pay nearly the equivalent of a male worker's daily wage to see historical figures and episodes depicted with a realism superior to that found in less expensive forms of representation at the time, such as paintings on display at the *salon*. In these spectacles, public taste determined which figures and episodes were represented—history became a commodity. Traded like shares on the stock exchange, certain episodes or figures from the past rose and fell according to the whims of the marketplace. The panoramic painter Prévost learned this lesson the hard way during the brief return to power of Napoleon during the Hundred Days in 1815, when shares in the Bourbon monarchy bottomed out, forcing him to paint over Louis XVIII in a panorama he was creating to celebrate the return of the Bourbons to power. Langlois and Daguerre (and, as I show in Chapter 3, nearly all the theatrical producers of Paris) speculated on a boom in Bonapartiana following the Revolution of 1830 and made a mint—at least until the public's interest waned. By the Second Empire, the receipts at Langlois's panoramas of Napoleonic battles had fallen to such an extent that he needed governmental subsidies to break even.[131]

The commodification of history in the nineteenth-century spectacles coincided with the invasion of the marketplace into other previously uncommercial sectors of experience. As capitalism's mode of production shifted to rely more on the consumption of goods and services, a process linked to

---

129. Max Horkheimer and Theodor W. Adorno, *The Dialectic of Enlightenment,* trans. John Cumming (1944; New York: Continuum, 2002).

130. Theodor Adorno, "Culture Industry Reconsidered," trans. Anson G. Rabinbach, in *The Adorno Reader,* ed. Brian O'Connor (Oxford: Blackwell, 2000), 232.

131. Robichon notes that, "The attendance of the public constantly declines and Langlois will need state subsidies to survive during the Second Empire" ("Panoramas en France," 42).

the rising tide of industrialism and growing urbanization in the nineteenth century, everyday life became saturated with possibilities for the marketing of commodities. The popular historical entertainments of the period represent a part of the expanding leisure industry, a corollary of the new industrial modes of production that were forming a class of people with an increasing amount of free time and disposable income. The explosion of the press, the popularity of shopping arcades, as well as the rise of tourism (often associated, like the spectacles, with an exploitation of history) all figure as part of the consumer nexus during the nineteenth century in France.[132]

The consequences of the commercialization of the past are manifold. Certain periods or subjects receive attention because they appeal to the crowd, whereas others are ignored because of their perceived lack of drawing power. As I show in this and following chapters, Napoleon is the big winner throughout most of the first half of the century. But it is a certain vision of Napoleon that takes center stage, a vision calculated to please the public by emphasizing the heroic, patriotic dimension of his reign. What gets left out? Explicit political opinions or arguments find no place in the popular spectacles. Nor does the darker side of history; Napoleon's weaknesses, defects, mistakes, and betrayals are conspicuously absent from these historical entertainments.

Popular spectacles such as the panorama had other potentially problematic features as well, related to their representational strategies. Although the focus on external, visual aspects of history—on history's surface—provided certain new insights into the past, it obscured others. Critics of Romantic historiography and theater, who are discussed in the next two chapters, pointed out the inability of these representations to portray history as process, as movement (or as dialectic). By freezing the past into a single moment that could be perceived in the blink of an eye, popular entertainments such as the wax display, the phantasmagoria, and the panorama rob history of its narrative force. In this, they are quite different from the Romantic historians, although, as I show in the next chapter, critics at the time worried that Romantic historiography was moving in this direction because of its visual mode of representing the past.

The historical spectacles changed the nature of the history, some would say for the worse, but they also changed the spectator. The Situationist critic Guy Debord denounced the passivity of the twentieth-century

---

132. On the spectacle and the leisure activity of the bourgeoisie in the nineteenth century, see T. J. Clark, *The Painting of Modern Life* (Princeton: Princeton University Press, 1984); Nicholas Green, *The Spectacle of Nature* (Manchester: Manchester University Press, 1990). On the sociology of tourism, see Dean MacCannell, *The Tourist* (New York: Schocken Books, 1976).

spectating subjects as well as their alienation—from others, but also from themselves, from their own thoughts and desires—"the more he looks," Debord writes of the modern observer, "the less he lives."[133] I do not want to imply, following Debord, that all viewers of nineteenth-century histori-cal entertainments were passive, alienated victims, but as I show in Chap-ters 5 and 6, the novels of Balzac and Stendhal do prefigure elements of Debord's critique in their diagnoses of the dangers inherent in looking at spectacles of the past.

Debord published his critique of the society of the spectacle in 1967, a year before a new revolution broke out in Paris. Clearly, the passivity sup-posedly engendered by the spectacle did not completely foreclose the idea of revolt, even if the spectacle did, arguably, recuperate much of the 1968 revolution in the form of a commodified counterculture. In a similar man-ner, the spectacles of history I am discussing here did not prevent the out-break of revolution in the nineteenth century by lulling their consumers into complacency. But, as I show, critical observers such as Karl Marx wondered whether the revolutions of nineteenth-century France were pre-vented from attaining their aim, from turning toward the future, because the public was fixated on spectacles of the past.

Debord's theory, like the critique of Adorno and Horkheimer, can itself be critiqued for its ideologically loaded pessimism. Indeed, Martin Jay has convincingly unmasked the stakes of such an antivisual stance, which he shows to be characteristic of much twentieth-century French theory. His signaling of the dangers of an uncritical acceptance of such discourse ne-cessitates taking a second look before condemning the historical spectacles of the nineteenth century.[134] Jay describes how the antivisual stance of De-bord, like Adorno's attack on the culture industry, smacks of a "Man-darin" or snobbish attitude toward popular culture.[135] Is there not some-thing puritanical and ascetic, he asks, about the distrust of visual pleasure? "Only those who think themselves above the lust of the eyes resist the de-lights of the spectacle," Jay warns.[136]

Jay also points out how antiocularcentrism aligns itself with a privileged relation to literacy. Such an antivisual stance is especially problematic when applied to the nineteenth century, a period of rising literacy rates, to be sure, but also a period in which a vast number of poorly educated

133. Guy Debord, *La société du spectacle* (1967; reprint, Paris: Gallimard, 1992), 31.

134. Martin Jay, *Downcast Eyes: The Denigration of Vision in Twentieth-Century French Thought* (Berkeley: University of California Press, 1993).

135. In *Adorno* (Cambridge: Harvard University Press, 1984), Martin Jay describes how Adorno's attack on the culture industry has been seen as "Mandarin," elitist, and even, when he attacks jazz, racist (119).

136. Jay, *Downcast Eyes*, 590.

people made use of the visual as a comprehension aid or supplement to text-based forms. As I have shown, the spectacular past reached a new kind of public because of its visuality. Critics who relentlessly fault the cultural products of modernity for their imbrication in the dangerous web of capitalism often overlook the fact that these products represented a democratizing liberation of culture from ancien régime elitism. To fault nineteenth-century spectacles for pandering to popular tastes risks denying wide segments of the population forms of historical representation they could afford and understand. This was especially true after the mid-nineteenth century, when the prices of popular spectacles fell and thus they became available to a broader spectrum of audiences.

But is the spectacular past only a debased form of historical representation? Is it, at best, a crutch for the illiterate? Or might it be possible to perceive in it something positive?[137] The writings of two other critics associated with the Frankfurt School point in that direction: in opposition to the dire pronouncements of Adorno, Siegfried Kracauer and Walter Benjamin were far more hopeful about what Miriam Bratu Hansen has called the "liberatory appeal" of modern mass culture.[138] Both Kracauer and Benjamin saw such forms of mass culture as cinema as potentially capable of freeing their public from the hold of bourgeois individualism by encouraging the public to think—and perhaps to act—as a mass.[139] Such mass action could have dangerous effects, as the Nazi manipulation of mass spectacle proved. For Kracauer and Benjamin, however, ignoring or denying the power of popular culture to provide the crowd with an image of itself left a powerful tool in the hands of the enemy.[140]

137. Recently, Susan Sontag, whose *On Photography* (New York: Farrar, Straus and Giroux, 1973) critiqued the visual in a manner akin to Debord ("images consume reality," 179), has revised her position on the visual approach to the past. In *Regarding the Pain of Others* (New York: Farrar, Straus and Giroux, 2003), Sontag offers a defense of photographic images of war and locates such images in the tradition I call the spectacular past, referring to "forms of history-as-spectacle that emerged in the late eighteenth and early nineteenth centuries" (123).

138. Miriam Bratu Hansen, "America, Paris, the Alps: Kracauer (and Benjamin) on Cinema and Modernity," in *Cinema and the Invention of Modern Life,* ed. Leo Charney and Vanessa R. Schwartz (Berkeley: University of California Press, 1995), 365. In *Weimar Surfaces: Urban Visual Culture in 1920s Germany* (Berkeley: University of California Press, 2001), Janet Ward cites Hansen in her critique of the antivisual stance of the Frankfurt School and of Debord (7).

139. See Siegfried Kracauer, *The Mass Ornament: Weimar Essays,* trans. Thomas Y. Levin (Cambridge: Harvard University Press, 1995); and Walter Benjamin, "The Work of Art in the Age of Mechanical Reproduction," in *Illuminations,* trans. Harry Zohn (New York: Schocken Books, 1968), 217–51.

140. On the debates over mass culture among members of the Frankfurt School, see Hansen, "America, Paris, and the Alps"; Ward, *Weimar Surfaces;* Susan Buck-Morss, *The Origin of Negative Dialectics: Theodor W. Adorno, Walter Benjamin, and the Frankfurt Institute* (Sussex: Harvester Press, 1977); and Eugene Lunn, *Marxism and Modernism: An His-*

The forms of the spectacular past I have considered in this chapter, such as the panorama, preceded the age of mechanical reproduction. As I have shown, moreover, at least through the middle of the nineteenth century, the historical spectacles addressed themselves primarily to a bourgeois, rather than truly mass, public. But by asserting the rights of this newly empowered class to the representation of history, these entertainments might be seen to begin a process that could free culture for progressive uses. These spectacles, at least in theory, offered a democratic form of historical representation. They encouraged a collective experience of the past and, in the process, provided crowds with a vision of themselves as historical agents. That such forms of culture might have promoted passivity and alienation, or could be used as tools of propaganda, does not necessarily negate their promise and potential. As I turn now to what was in fact a mechanically reproduced spectacle—the illustrated history—and to the harsh critiques it and other forms of historical spectacle engendered in the nineteenth century, it is important to keep both sides of this debate in mind.

---

torical Study of Lukács, Brecht, Benjamin, and Adorno (Berkeley: University of California Press, 1982).

Chapter Two

Spectacular Histories

In 1836, the right-wing critic Alfred Nettement launched a series of articles attacking new trends in historical writing in the legitimist *Gazette de France*.[1] Although one could imagine a great deal that would displease a reactionary such as Nettement in the writing of the left-leaning Romantic historians, Nettement's reviews cast the question not in terms of politics, but in terms of vision.[2] The problem with the historiography of Prosper de Barante and Jules Michelet was not that it spoke out in favor of the Revolution or that it lent support to the July Monarchy regime, but that it transformed the past into what he called, in a review of the recently released fifth edition of Barante's *Histoire des ducs de Bourgogne de la maison de Valois*, "a series of pictures."[3]

In the eyes of the critic, historiography had come to look dangerously like the kinds of popular entertainment that were turning the past into a spectacle. History, Nettement warned in a review of Michelet's *Histoire de*

---

1. During the Restoration, the *Gazette de France* had strongly supported the Bourbon monarchy. Under the July Monarchy, it opposed the government from the right. From 12,400 subscribers at the beginning of the July Monarchy, its readership declined to 5,500 by 1837. The rise of various *gazettes* in the provinces during this period may have contributed to this decline. Claude Bellanger et al., eds. *Histoire générale de la presse française*, vol. 2 (Paris: Presses Universitaires de France, 1969), 127.

2. In *Between History and Literature* (Cambridge: Harvard University Press, 1990), Lionel Gossman observes that "Romantic historiography was intimately associated with the moderately liberal and nationalist aspirations of the period immediately following the French Revolution and the Napoleonic wars" (153).

3. Alfred Nettement, "Études littéraires," review of *Histoire des ducs de Bourgogne de la maison de Valois* by Prosper de Barante, *Gazette de France*, January 3, 1837, 4.

France, should only give way "with great reserve to that passion for the picturesque that threatens to change literature into a vast panorama."[4] Nettement's fears of the panoramization of the past articulated one side of a debate that raged through the historiographic discourse of the time, opposing the picturesque school of Romantic historiography, epitomized by Barante and Michelet, to the philosophic school that looked to Voltaire as a model. As Nettement's reviews make clear, this debate turned on the question of the visual. For the picturesque historians, visual description through verbal imagery offered new insight into the material world of the past, replacing dry argument with a re-creation of the reality of the past. For Nettement and the "philosophic" historians, such a visual approach abdicated moral responsibility and could too easily lend itself to populist passion.

This debate was more, however, than a war of words. At the same time that the verbal descriptions of the Romantic historians were turning historical texts into a "series of pictures," actual images began to occupy an increasingly large place on the French historiographic horizon. Fueled by developments in printing and engraving technology, new forms of historical illustration brought the image from the margin to the center of the historiographic experience during the 1830s and 1840s. Indeed, the fifth edition of Barante's *Histoire des ducs de Bourgogne,* which occasioned Nettement's vituperative review, was illustrated by such leading artists of the era as Eugène Delacroix, Paul Delaroche, and Alfred and Tony Johannot.

Illustration served as the primary means through which a great deal of the historiographic production of the nineteenth century, including that of the Romantic historians, became known to the public.[5] Aggressively marketed, illustrated editions offered publishers the chance to repackage existing texts as well as the opportunity to reach new markets. To study the

4. Alfred Nettement, "Études littéraires," review of *Histoire de France* by Jules Michelet, *Gazette de France,* October 12, 1836, 1.

5. Studies of illustrated historiography that have informed my understanding include Stephen Bann, *The Clothing of Clio* (Cambridge: Cambridge University Press, 1984), 32–53; Marie-Claude Chaudonneret, "Les représentations des événements et des hommes illustres de la Révolution française de 1830 à 1848," in *Les images de la Révolution française,* ed. Michel Vovelle (Paris, 1988), 329–37; Rémi Mallet, "L'iconographie de la Révolution française dans les livres d'histoire du XIXᵉ siècle," in *Les images de la Révolution française,* ed. Michel Vovelle (Paris, 1988), 339–61; Madeleine Rebérioux, "L'illustration des histoires de la Révolution française au XIXᵉ siècle: Esquisse d'une problématique," in *Usages de l'image,* ed. Stéphane Michaud, Jean-Yves Mollier, and Nicole Savy (Paris, 1992), 15–23; Beth S. Wright, "'That Other Historian, the Illustrator': Voices and Vignettes in Mid-Nineteenth Century France," *Oxford Art Journal* 23.1 (2000): 113–36.

history of nineteenth-century French historical illustration is thus to understand how historiography became a spectacle in the post-Revolutionary
period—something to be seen for a price. As I show, however, the spectacular theory and practice of the illustrated histories provide a vital context
for understanding the figurative spectacle of the Romantic historians; the
Romantics' deployment of verbal images shares key epistemological and
ideological features with the visual images of the illustrators. And as the
condemnation of critics such as Nettement reveals, both types of images
offer a view into the conflict surrounding the legacy of the past in post-
Revolutionary France.

Picturing the Past

The increased importance of historical illustration during the July
Monarchy resulted in part from innovations in printing and engraving
technology, but a general shift in attitudes toward the image as a pedagogical tool also contributed to its triumph in France during the early
nineteenth century. As in the eighteenth-century *Encyclopédie,* which
made use of illustrations to diffuse technological and philosophical knowledge, nineteenth-century newspapers, school textbooks, travel guides, and
social commentaries employed visual representations to disseminate ideas
necessary for the economic and social development of the new century.[6]
History represents only one of many genres to employ illustration during
this period.

The nineteenth century, of course, did not inaugurate the use of visual
imagery in historiography. As Francis Haskell has shown, the Bayeux Tapestry elaborated a visual vocabulary for historical representation in the
Middle Ages.[7] Renaissance and Neoclassical printed histories in Italy and
France, moreover, incorporated portraits of famous monarchs from the

6. Michel Melot describes the use of images in various nineteenth-century French texts in
"Le texte et l'image," in *Histoire de l'édition française: Le temps des éditeurs,* ed. Roger
Chartier and Henri-Jean Martin (1985; reprint, Paris: Fayard/Promodis, 1990), 329–500.
Other important general studies of illustrated books include Henri Girard, "Le livre, l'illus-
tration et la reliure à l'époque romantique," in *Le romantisme et l'art,* ed. Louis Hautecoeur
(Paris: Henri Laurens, 1928), 288–317; Gordon N. Ray, *The Art of the French Illustrated
Book, 1700 to 1914* (New York: Pierpont Morgan Library, 1982); Philip Stewart, *Engraven
Desire: Eros, Image, and Text in the French Eighteenth Century* (Durham: Duke University
Press, 1992); Christian Michel, *Charles-Nicolas Cochin et l'art des lumières* (Rome: École
française de Rome, 1993).

7. In *History and Its Images* (New Haven: Yale University Press, 1993), Francis Haskell
provides a magisterial overview of the use of visual imagery in the representation of the past
from the Middle Ages to the present.

sixteenth century onward.[8] And as Maurice Agulhon, Lynn Hunt, and Ronald Paulson have demonstrated, images played an important role in reflecting shifts in popular sentiment toward political change during the French Revolution.[9]

But if historical illustration was hardly new in the 1830s, it was radically transformed. Ancien régime illustrated historiography had incorporated almost exclusively iconography produced during the period being represented—primarily portraits of monarchs. François de Mézéray's luxuriously illustrated *Histoire de France,* published between 1643 and 1651, featured 800 portraits of France's kings and queens. In the eighteenth century, illustrated histories such as the abbé Bernard de Montfauçon's *L'antiquité expliquée et représentée en figures* (the first of ten volumes appeared in 1719) expanded beyond the portrait to provide a visual record of such material aspects of the ancient world as dress, weaponry, and modes of transport, but these images were still drawn primarily from coins and other "authentic" sources.[10] Nineteenth-century illustrated historiography, on the other hand, favored the use of retrospective images, newly created representations offering an imaginative vision of the past.[11] The shift away from the exclusive use of authentic iconography freed the nineteenth-century illustrated editions to explore a wide range of subject matter. The new illustrations tended to focus on historical events, much like history painting, which also offered imaginative or retrospective representations of the past.

The work of the Romantic historians produced during the 1820s and 1830s proved ideal for this kind of illustration because of its emphasis on material description. As I have noted, the celebrated (and reviled) fifth edi-

---

8. Jean Adhémar, "L'enseignement par l'image," *Gazette des Beaux-Arts* 97 (1981): 53–60; and, "L'éducation visuelle des fils de France et l'origine du Musée de Versailles," *La Revue des Arts,* 6 (March 1956): 29.

9. Maurice Agulhon, Lynn Hunt, and Ronald Paulson have focused on the allegorical representation of political or historical events, whereas I am interested in representations that treat the historical referent in a more literal manner. See Maurice Agulhon, *Marianne au combat: L'imagerie et la symbolique républicaines de 1789 à 1880* (Paris: Flammarion, 1979); Lynn Hunt, "Engraving the Republic," *History Today,* 30 (1980): 11–17; Ronald Paulson, *Representations of Revolution (1789–1820)* (New Haven: Yale University Press, 1983). In *The Family Romance of the French Revolution* (Berkeley: University of California Press, 1992) Hunt discusses the role of popular engravings (especially of the royal family) during the Revolution.

10. Haskell, *History and Its Images,* 131.

11. Whereas some of the events depicted in the new histories, such as the Napoleonic Wars, belonged to a quite recent past, these new images maintained a different ontological relation to their subject from contemporary or "authentic" illustrations—they no longer purported to be eyewitness representations, produced from a living model. Haskell dismisses such "retrospective" images as "fanciful and romantic drawings" Ibid., 288.

tion of Prosper de Barante's *Histoire des ducs de Bourgogne,* which appeared in 1838, was illustrated by the leading artists of the era. "Recently there has developed a trend, as we know, to adorn reprinted works with drawings, *vignettes,* maps and plans," commented Nettement in his review of this edition, quick to draw a parallel between the types of verbal images employed by the Romantics and the graphic images that "show, so to speak, what the text tells."[12] Adolphe Thiers's enormously influential *Histoire de la Révolution française,* first published in 1823, was reissued in illustrated editions in 1834, 1836, 1837, and 1838.[13] And Augustin Thierry's *Histoire de la conquête d'Angleterre par les Normands,* another celebrated work of Romantic historiography, first published in 1825, provided the subject for a set of illustrations in 1838. Like the Barante illustrations, the drawings for this edition of Thierry featured imaginative reconstructions of history, renderings of the past in the Romantic style of the early nineteenth century.

Although artists such as Tony Johannot often went to great lengths to portray details of architecture and costume with accuracy, these images bear a strong resemblance to the vignettes he created for contemporary novelists such as Balzac.[14] The Thierry volume also included four maps, fourteen *planches* representing the Bayeux tapestry in outline form, as well as steel-plate engravings of "various Anglo-Norman antiquities (seals, money, armour, architecture, etc.)." Readers thus benefited from these authentic images, copied from period sources, in addition to the retrospective vision of Johannot and other Romantic artists. Whereas the text itself was published in-octavo, the atlas containing the thirty-six engravings on *papier de Chine* was published in a larger, in-folio volume. Readers could also choose to have the images bound together with the text, but they appeared on separate unnumbered pages, printed vertically so that readers were forced to turn the book sideways to read the image.

Like the images in most eighteenth-century illustrated editions, the reproductions of the Bayeux tapestry and of the "various anglo-norman antiquities" in the Thierry volume were metal engravings. First drawn on paper, they were then engraved (by a separate hand) onto copper (or in the case of the Thierry illustrations, onto steel) plates, which were then inked and used for printing. Unlike traditional woodcuts, which were popular during the Renaissance but had fallen out of favor by the eighteenth

---

12. Nettement, "Études littéraires," January 3, 1837, 4.

13. On the illustrated editions of Thiers, see Rebérioux, "Illustration des histories," 16.

14. For more on the career of Tony Johannot, see Jean-François Champfleury, *Les vignettes romantiques: Histoire de la littérature et de l'art (1825–1840)* (Paris: E. Dentu, 1883), 11.

century, metal engraving allowed for multiple impressions without loss of detail. But metal engravings, unlike woodcuts, could not be printed on the same press as typographical characters. Expensive to produce, metal engravings had to appear on separate pages from printed text (*hors texte*) and were often shrouded by a thin layer of tissue paper. Intended to prevent the illustration from staining the facing page with its ink, this "veil" also served to shield the image from what Madeleine Rebérioux has called "[the] reader's brutal gaze."[15]

Invented in Germany at the end of the eighteenth century and brought to France between 1809 and 1816, lithography was frequently used in high-end illustrated historiography during the 1820s. This new process, in which artists drew images directly onto a stone that was then used for printing, eliminated the need for engraving, thus providing a more direct link between artist and viewer.[16] A. V. Arnault's *Vie politique et militaire de Napoléon,* first published in 1822, provides a stunning example of the use of lithography by enterprising historiographic editors. Capitalizing on the interest in the emperor following his death in 1821, this edition of two luxuriously leather-bound in-folio volumes contained 120 full-page lithographs. The cost of this collector's edition, however, was as monumental as its format: 12 francs for each of the thirty parts (*livraisons*), each containing four images, which made up the completed volume. Like metal engravings, lithographic images also had to be printed separately from type and thus also appeared *hors texte*.

In the 1830s, the perfection of a new technique of wood engraving radically changed the nature of book illustration by bringing image and text closer together. Unlike traditional woodcuts, in which an image was carved on a plank with the grain running horizontal to the surface (*bois de fil*), the new technique, pioneered in England in the eighteenth century, used a harder wood (boxwood), cut the engraving into the end of the wood (*bois de bout*), with the grain perpendicular to the surface, and used a burin instead of a knife.[17] This process allowed for greater precision than

15. Rebérioux, "Illustration des histories," 21.

16. Girard, "Livre," 301–3.

17. Thomas Bewick (1753–1826) was responsible for reviving wood engraving during this period in England. On the "modern" technique of wood engraving, see William Andrew Chatto, *A Treatise on Wood Engraving* (London: Chatto and Windus, 1861). Much of my understanding of nineteenth-century wood engraving derives from Henri Zerner, "La gravure sur bois romantique," *Médecine de France,* no. 150 (1964): 17–32; Charles Rosen and Henri Zerner, *Romanticism and Realism* (London: Faber and Faber, 1984), 71–96. Other classic studies of wood engraving include Pierre Gusman, *La Gravure sur bois en France au XIXe siècle* (Paris: Albert Morance, 1929); Champfleury, "Vignettes romantiques." Girard provides the only discussion I have found of wood-engraved historiography ("Livre," 303–14).

the traditional woodcut and for a greater number of impressions without the loss of detail. And unlike metal engraving or lithography, wood engravings could be printed along with typographical characters, allowing for the first time a high-quality image to appear on the same page as the text. It also allowed for lower production costs and hence less expensive editions that could reach a broader market, because an entire stage of the printing process was eliminated. By rendering it more visual and more commercial, wood engraving helped make nineteenth-century historiography spectacular.[18]

The Spectacular Text

Among the first historiographic works to incorporate wood engravings, the most celebrated was Théodose Burette's *Histoire de France* (1840), which contained five hundred illustrations by Jules David of all periods of French history. "The text of the book is elegant and colorful; its form is brilliant, flattering at once the eye and the mind," enthused the Romantic journal *L'Artiste* in a review that reproduced examples of the remarkable illustrations.[19] Unsurprisingly, given the cult that had grown up around Napoleon since his death in 1821, a host of historical texts marshaled wood engraving in worship of the fallen hero.[20] The discussion that follows focuses on two works bearing an initial publication date of 1839: a reprint of Jacques de Norvins's *Histoire de Napoléon,* with illustrations by the celebrated military artist Denis-Auguste-Marie Raffet,[21] and Paul-Mathieu Laurent de l'Ardèche's new *Histoire de l'empereur Napoléon,*

18. Michel Melot makes a similar point without mentioning historical texts specifically. He describes how the new technique of wood engraving "permitted the image to infiltrate the text, to put down roots there and to transform the space of reading into a space of *spectacle.*" "Texte et l'image," 338, emphasis added.

19. D. Ladet, review of *Histoire de France* by Théodose Burette, *L'Artiste* 6 (1840): 138–44. Beth S. Wright discusses this edition of Burette and its review in *L'Artiste* in "'That Other Historian, the Illustrator.'" She argues for the primacy of the "aural metaphor" over the spectacular in these works, suggesting that the text-image relationships in Burette's history "engaged reader-viewers more actively, enabling them to 'hear' rather than see the past" (117).

20. Frédéric Soulié's *La lanterne magique: Histoire de Napoléon racontée par deux soldats,* featuring wood engravings by Charles-Émile Jacque, appeared in 1838. I discuss this illustrated historical novel in detail at the end of chapter 4. A reprint of Count Emmanuel de Las Cases's *Mémorial de Sainte-Hélène* with illustrations by Nicolas-Toussaint Charlet was published in 1842. A collection of historical poems by Auguste Barthélemy and Joseph Méry, entitled *Napoléon en Égypte,* with wood-engraved illustrations by Horace Vernet, also appeared in 1842, and a *Histoire populaire, anecdotique et pittoresque de Napoléon et de la grande armée,* by Émile Marco de Saint-Hilaire, with illustrations by Jules David, appeared in 1843. Girard points to the Napoleonic affinity of these texts ("Livre," 313).

21. For more on Raffet, see the catalog for the exhibition of his work held at the Bibliothèque Marmottan in Paris in 1999, *Raffet (1804–1860)* (Éditions Herscher, 1999).

illustrated by another renowned military artist, Horace Vernet.[22] Through their literary and pictorial strategies, as well as their subject matter, these two works typify the transformation of the historical text into a spectacle.

The two histories of Napoleon are remarkably alike in appearance and format. Both are in-octavo volumes and both run over six hundred pages—quite substantial for the time, although commonplace by today's standards for biography. Several kinds of images adorn these volumes.[23] In addition to the hundreds of wood-engraved illustrations found alongside the text, the books feature wood-engraved still-life images at the start of chapters (*tête de page*) and at the end (*cul-de-lampe*) showing various Napoleonic accoutrements, as well as decorated first letters likewise adorned with Imperial symbols, including eagles, crowns, and mantles (*see* fig. 2.1).[24]

Just as the form of these two books is quite similar, so too is their content. Following an introduction or preface announcing the works' more or less hagiographic intentions, both books divide Napoleon's life into chapters, beginning with his birth on the island of Corsica and ending with his death in exile on the island of Saint-Helena. The history by Laurent, written expressly for this illustrated edition, tends to highlight the mythic moments of Napoleon's life and quotes liberally from other sources, including the official accounts of Napoleon's battles, the *Bulletins de la Grande Armée;* Napoleon's own memoirs; and especially the account of Napoleon's life in exile, Count Emmanuel de Las Cases's *Mémorial de Sainte-Hélène.* Famous anecdotes or sayings associated with the great man structure the narrative, with Laurent confining himself to commentary on the authenticity or significance of the event or *bon mot.*

The Norvins biography, which was first published in 1827, and which went through twenty-two editions by 1854, some illustrated, some not, is perhaps the more serious historical work, featuring more original source material and more subtle analyses of events, their causes and effects.[25] As

22. For more on Horace Vernet, see the catalogue for the exhibition of his works held at the Académie de France à Rome in 1980, *Horace Vernet (1789–1863)* (Rome: De Luca, 1980).

23. One difference between the two editions is that the Norvins volume also contains metal engravings of drawings by Raffet, along with the wood-engraved vignettes. The metal engravings appear *hors texte* and are covered by tissue paper.

24. Such an arrangement of small images was typical of illustrated editions at the time. See Margaret Cohen, "Panoramic Literature and the Invention of Everyday Genres," in *Cinema and the Invention of Modern Life,* ed. Leo Charney and Vanessa Schwartz (Berkeley: University of California Press, 1995), 240, for a description of such images in the contemporary *physiologies.*

25. According to James Smith Allen, production runs of this work numbered in the tens of thousands. *Popular French Romanticism: Authors, Readers, and Books in the 19th Century* (Syracuse: Syracuse University Press, 1981), 4–6.

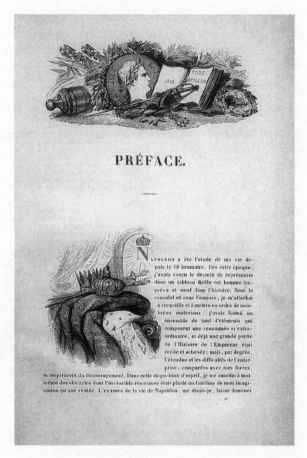

FIGURE 2.1 Engraving after Denis-Auguste-Marie Raffet in J. de Norvins, *Histoire de Napoléon* (1839), p. i. Image courtesy of the President and Fellows of Harvard College.

the prospectus advertising the wood-engraved illustrated edition admits, however, the analyses in this edition have been shortened to make room for more familiar anecdotes.[26] By focusing on specific historical moments—often those that had already attained legendary status—and by describing these in vivid and colorful detail, the texts facilitated the task of the illustrator.

The wood-engraved images relate to the narrative both metaphorically and metonymically.[27] A metaphoric illustration presents a direct visual

---

26. "The author felt that, without making any major changes to his work, he could suppress some of the long passages that slowed down the march of the narrative, and that he could intersperse some facts of great importance, as well as some characteristic anecdotes to complete the portrait of the great man he wished to paint." Jacques de Norvins, prospectus to *Histoire de Napoléon* (1827; reprint, Paris: Furne, 1839), 1.

27. In *The Clothing of Clio*, Bann makes a similar distinction between metaphoric and metonymic illustrations in comparing metal-engraved illustrated editions of Barante and

FIGURE 2.2   Engraving after Horace Vernet in P.-M. Laurent de l'Ardèche, *Histoire de L'Empereur Napoléon* (1839), p 496. Image courtesy of the President and Fellows of Harvard College.

equivalent of the anecdote recounted by the narrative. The description of the emperor's marriage to Marie-Louise in the Laurent volume, for example, is accompanied by a picture of the ceremony, which translates the written content into a parallel visual form (fig. 2.2). Mirroring the economy of the narrative, the image focuses on the event of the marriage in a relatively simplified and pared-down manner, without a great deal of extraneous detail to distract the viewer's eye.

Immediately after the narrative of the ceremony, however, the text produces a close-up image of Napoleon's hand placing the ring on his bride's finger, an action not specifically mentioned by the written text (fig. 2.3). As in the classic example of the metonymical device of synecdoche, "I'll

---

Thierry (45). Bann focuses on the different narrative strategies of the authors, rather than on developments in engraving technology.

Au milieu de ces transports universels et de ces réjouissances splen-
dides, l'ambassadeur d'Autriche devait avoir son jour pour étaler sa
joie officielle et son faste diplomatique. Il choisit le 1er juillet, et la fête
fut marquée par un sinistre événement. Le feu prit à la salle du bal;
la femme du ministre autrichien et plusieurs autres personnes périrent
dans l'incendie. Napoléon ne laissa pas à une main étrangère le soin et
l'honneur de sauver son épouse; il la saisit vivement et l'emporta lui-
même hors des pièces embrasées. On se rappela alors que les fêtes pour
le mariage de Louis XVI et de Marie-Antoinette avaient été troublées
aussi par de graves accidents.

Figure 2.3   Engraving after Horace Vernet, illustration for P.-M. Laurent de l'Ardèche, *Histoire de L'Empereur Napoléon* (1839), p. 498. Image courtesy of the President and Fellows
of Harvard College.

take her hand in marriage," here the part stands for the whole, allowing for a kind of visual abbreviation, summarizing the action by showing its (unrecounted) climactic moment. This visual insert at the conclusion of the description of the wedding thus goes beyond the narrative, directing the reader/viewer's attention to a detail that the written text could not summon without sagging under the weight of excessive specificity. The function of this image as a decorative *cul-de-lampe,* moreover, allows it to disrupt the forward progression of the narrative, providing a space outside the strict chronology in which the history unfolds for contemplation of this sentimental and symbolic moment. The illustration thus allows for multiple and simultaneous levels of discourse, in which the visual relates to but does not entirely mirror the verbal.

Such uses of the historical image were not, strictly speaking, new in the nineteenth century. The real innovation of these wood-engraved works lay in their spatial conjunction of image and text. Prior illustrated historiographies had confined their images to separate pages or separate volumes, forcing readers to pause and turn their heads, sometimes even to turn the whole book when the image was printed horizontally, as was usually the case, causing an interruption in the flow of the narrative. In such works, there was no way to determine at what point the reader would choose to look at the image, and these images seldom referenced specific anecdotes recounted by the text. Instead, they often merely reproduced preexisting images (other engravings or famous paintings) of battles, people, or places.[28] The wood engravings in the new illustrated editions, on the other hand, were always created expressly for the text and appear together, on the same page, with the narrative they accompany.

Perfectly suited to the anecdotal character of these works, the images focus on particularities in the narrative, picking out telling or colorful details. In the Laurent volume, for example, a description of Napoleon's notorious retreat from Moscow through the freezing Russian winter focuses on a picturesque, though gory, aspect of the scene: "the horses of the cavalry, of the artillery, perished every night." In the middle of the word *artillerie,* the text cuts away to an image of a dead horse (fig. 2.4). Indeed, the word itself is not completely uttered before the image intrudes. The layout of the page thus forces the reader to encounter word and picture simultaneously, offering a visual representation of the events before a mental picture can be formed. In this case, the page is dominated by image

28. Rebérioux describes how Charles Furne, who published illustrated histories of the Revolution by Thiers, Lamartine, and Louis Blanc, reprinted many of the same images from one work to the next. This "reuse of graphic material" was typical in illustrated editions ("Illustration des histoires," 18).

si cruelle saison, le nouvel état des choses le nécessitait, il espérait arriver à Minsk, ou du moins sur la Bérésina, avant l'ennemi; il partit le 13 de Smolensk; le 16, il coucha à Krasnoë. Le froid, qui avait commencé le 7, s'accrut subitement, et, du 14 au 15 et au 16, le thermomètre marqua seize et dix-huit degrés au-dessous de glace. Les chemins furent couverts de verglas; les chevaux de cavalerie, d'artil-

lerie, périssaient toutes les nuits, non par centaines, mais par milliers, surtout les chevaux de France et d'Allemagne : plus de trente mille chevaux périrent en peu de jours; notre cavalerie se trouva toute à pied; notre artillerie et nos transports se trouvaient sans attelage : il fallut abandonner et détruire une bonne partie de nos pièces et de nos munitions de guerre et de bouche.

» Cette armée, si belle le 6, était bien différente dès le 14, presque sans cavalerie, sans artillerie, sans transports. Sans cavalerie, nous ne pouvions pas nous éclairer à un quart de lieue; cependant, sans artillerie, nous ne pouvions pas risquer une bataille et attendre de pied ferme; il fallait marcher pour ne pas être contraint à une bataille, que le défaut de munitions nous empêchait de désirer; il fallait occuper un certain espace pour n'être pas tournés, et cela sans cavalerie qui éclairât et qui liât les colonnes. Cette difficulté, jointe à un froid excessif

FIGURE 2.4   Engraving after Horace Vernet in P.-M. Laurent de l'Ardèche, *Histoire de L'Empereur Napoléon* (1839), p. 604. Image courtesy of the President and Fellows of Harvard College.

FIGURE 2.5   Engraving after Denis-Auguste-Marie Raffet in J. de Norvins, *Histoire de Napoléon* (1839), p. 447. Image courtesy of the President and Fellows of Harvard College.

rather than written text, and the words seem almost to intrude on the flow of images.

The Norvins volume employs similar graphic techniques. Describing the same episode of the Russian debacle, the text reads: "The unhappy ones, surprised on all sides by the Cossacks, perished by blows of lances, pikes, and axes, or remained exposed on the snow, waiting to be killed by the cannibals." An image dividing the word *Cosaques* shows French soldiers and their horses lying dying in the snow alongside an exposed naked female body (fig. 2.5). The written text does not specify the sex of the "exposed" bodies—indeed there is no specific mention of women or children accompanying the soldiers at all. The image thus illustrates the specific anecdote while adding its own layer of meaning—and in this case prurient interest.[29] While earlier *hors texte* illustrated editions also juxtaposed image and text to produce meaning, wood-engraved histories achieve their effect through the new proximity of the two levels of discourse. The remarkable page layout breaks down the barrier between the visual and the

29. Michel Melot highlights the way image and text also could contradict one another in these editions ("Texte et l'image," 338).

posé sur son lit de parade; le manteau de Marengo lui servait de drap mortuaire.

Le captif des rois allait descendre dans la tombe avec toutes les décorations
de la royauté européenne ; et la couche de fer où il se reposait après les qua-

FIGURE 2.6   Engraving after Denis-Auguste-Marie Raffet in J. de Norvins, *Histoire de Napoléon* (1839), p. 629. Image courtesy of the President and Fellows of Harvard College.

verbal, creating a mode of symphonic signification in which parallels—
and disjunctures—between image and text register simultaneously.

The images blend into the text visually as well as narratively. As I have
shown, the traditional *hors texte* image remains, structurally at least, marginal to the history, a supplement whose status as luxury object is signaled
by the fetishistic accoutrements, such as the tissue-paper veil. Unlike metal
engravings, which leave a plate mark around the image, wood engravings
are not set off by a border of any kind. The wood-engraved image thus
fuses with the text surrounding it, aided by the centrifugal mode of composition in which the most intense contrasts of light and dark appear in
the center of the image and tend to fade out toward the edges (Fig. 2.6).[30]
The effect is an almost seamless transition from text to image and back
again to text, allowing the reader to assimilate both levels of content, the
graphic and the scriptural, simultaneously and, as it were, effortlessly. In
these editions, the image moves—literally—to the center of the historiographic experience.

30. Rosen and Zerner point out that the same was true of lithography, which also did not
leave a plate mark (*Romanticism and Realism*, 78).

These works came to resemble such spectacular forms of historical representation as the phantasmagoria show and the panorama not only because they accorded primacy to visually realistic images in the representation of the past, but also because of the way they deployed these images commercially. Illustration served not only as a new means of historical representation, but also as a marketing tool, helping to promote reprints of existing texts (such as the Norvins biography) as well as new works (such as the text by Laurent). Identical in price (20 francs), the two biographies of Napoleon were vigorously advertised in the press of the period and vied with one another for readership. They were aggressively advertised in all the major Parisian daily newspapers as ideal presents for the New Year (*étrennes*) and took their place alongside other illustrated editions, including novels, that made innovative use of wood engraving. In these ads, the illustrator's name figures in as large (or larger) typeface than that of the author, suggesting the degree to which the image was essential in the transformation of historiography into a commodity during this period.[31]

Illustration also gave rise to intense competition among publishers, with each new edition attempting to provide the most images for the lowest price. The relative ease and lower cost of image reproduction that wood engraving made possible meant a vast expansion in the number of images these histories contained. Whereas the fourth edition of Adolphe Thiers's *Histoire de la Révolution française,* published by Lecointe in 1834, contained one hundred metal engravings, the illustrated histories of Napoleon by Norvins and Laurent de l'Ardèche each contained over five hundred wood-engraved vignettes. And whereas the Thiers volume cost 50 francs (60 francs if printed on *papier de Chine),* the much more profusely illustrated histories by Norvins and Laurent cost less than half as much.

Like the popular entertainments of the period that represented history in visual form, the format of these editions appealed to a broader segment of the population than had read history during the ancien régime. The conjunction of image and text in the wood-engraved editions, in which the visual acts as a comprehension aid by immediately translating the text into a more accessible form, made these works ideal reading for the growing ranks of the semiliterate—poorly educated, but newly affluent subjects beginning to be produced by the rise of industrial capitalism. Although as many as 85 percent of men and 60 percent of women could at least sign their names in this period,[32] many fewer had the intellectual ability to sustain the reading of a historical work without the visual supplement.

31. These illustrated histories of Napoleon are mentioned in advertisements appearing in both the left-leaning *Le National* (November 29, 1840, 4) and the right-leaning *Gazette de France* (April 14, 1842, 3).

32. Allen, *Popular French Romanticism,* 155.

Pictures also made history accessible to that other segment of the population, children, who continue today to make up a large segment of the readership of illustrated historiography. The wood-engraved illustrated editions most likely did not, however, include the working classes among their readers, just as the lower classes were largely absent from the audiences of the popular spectacles throughout the first half of the nineteenth century. For even if wood engraving had brought the price of illustrated historiography down to 20 francs, in 1830 the wages of even male workers in the specialty trades ranged only from about 3 to 4.50 francs a day. Many male workers made far less, and the average wage for a female worker in 1840 had attained only about 0.81 francs a day.[33] On such salaries, the purchase of one of these moderately luxurious editions was clearly an impossibility. Public reading rooms, *cabinets de lecture,* provided access to books through relatively inexpensive subscriptions, but reading (or looking at) such long works still required the kind of leisure generally unavailable to most workers in the period. Like the popular entertainments that were their analogs, the illustrated editions, overwhelmingly devoted to the recent history of the Revolution and Napoleonic Wars, might thus be said to reproduce on a material level the revolution they depicted on a narrative level: they represented the bourgeoisie's rise to power both in the past and over the past.

Visualizing Romantic Historiography

The rise of the wood-engraved editions marks a crucial, and hitherto little explored, moment in the process of history's spectacularization; the new wood-engraved histories of the 1830s and 1840s gave the image a central place in the discourse of historiography. The transformation of illustrated historiography was not an autonomous development, however, but rather part of a much larger shift in historical writing in the early nineteenth century. To explain the nature of this shift, I turn now from literal images to figurative ones, to the way Romantic historians such as Barante and Michelet used the verbal image as a rhetorical tool in their written histories of the same period. I suggest that their new visual style of historiography signaled an affinity with the spectacular past and, in the process, aroused the ire of critics from both the left and the right of the political spectrum. Reconstructing this debate over the historical image in early-

33. Jacques Rougerie, "Remarques sur l'histoire des salaires à Paris au XIXe siècle," *Le Mouvement Social* 63 (1968): 74–75, 78; Jann Matlock, *Scenes of Seduction: Prostitution, Hysteria, and Reading Difference in Nineteenth-Century France* (New York: Columbia University Press, 1994), 321 n. 54.

nineteenth-century France reveals how the new spectacular form of historiography intersected with the political issues of the post-Revolutionary era.

"I tried to paint [. . .] the XVth century," writes Prosper de Barante in his memoirs; "I wanted to see its face instead of hearing its description."[34] Although Barante is talking about figurative rather than actual images, illustration serves as a dominant metaphor for his historiographic practice. Barante had already developed his theory of historiography as a visual medium in a preface to his *Histoire des ducs de Bourgogne de la maison de Valois,* in which he took issue with the tradition of history writing inherited from the *philosophes* of the eighteenth century. "We are tired," he writes, "of seeing history, like a meek two-bit philosopher, lend itself to all the proofs that anyone can deduce from it."[35] Arguing against the dryness of philosophical history that used the past to draw moral or political lessons, Barante calls for a new style of historical writing that will "picture" rather than analyze.

Whereas philosophical historians saw in the past the proof for their theories about the present, Barante declares an interest in historical details for their own sake. "What we want [from history] are facts. Just as we observe in all its details, in all its movements, this great drama of which we are both actors and witnesses, so too do we want to know about the lives of peoples and individuals before us" (35). For Barante, and for the picturesque school of Romantic historiography that his work exemplified,[36] the hidden causes behind the important events of history inspire less interest than the surfaces and the outer forms—the look of the past. History, he argues, had a visual dimension that historical writing must attempt to capture. The historian must become a painter or risk draining the life from his subject: "The historian must delight in painting rather than analyzing; otherwise, facts will dry out beneath his pen" (14). By analogizing the historian to the visual artist, Barante's preface conjures a new kind of historical imagination, in which history detaches itself from opinion and argument and exists solely as an object of contemplation: "Because there is nothing so impartial as the imagination: it has no need of concluding; all that is necessary is that a picture of the truth be placed before it" (35). For

34. Prosper de Barante, *Souvenirs,* vol. 3 (Paris: C. Lévy, 1890–1901), 215, cited in Sophie-Anne Leterrier, *Le XIXe siècle historien* (Paris: Belin, 1997), 39.

35. Prosper de Barante, preface to *Histoire des ducs de Bourgogne de la maison de Valois* (1824; reprint, Paris: Delloye, 1834), 35. Subsequent quotations are cited in the text.

36. In the introduction to *Extraits des historiens français du XIXe siècle* (1897; reprint, Paris: Hachette, 1913), Camille Jullian provides a helpful breakdown of the various schools of nineteenth-century historiography. On the picturesque school, see Leterrier, *XIXe siècle historien,* 39.

Barante and the historians who followed in his wake, truth emerges only when the past becomes a *tableau*.

In his *Histoire des ducs de Bourgogne,* first published from 1824 to 1826, Barante returned to the sources of French historical narration, purportedly stitching together contemporary chronicles of past events, the "simple accounts of past times" (2), and expressly retaining their archaic turns of phrase. In these supposedly simple accounts that document the sights and sounds of the age they describe, the historian found the kind of visual program for historical studies that became his model. "The native and particular character of French narrators provides a kind of unobstructed allure, a tone both naive and penetrating, that endows their story, in all its colors, with a sort of judgment that makes the author seem above what he's describing and as if amused by the spectacle he is seeing" (2). According to Barante, the superiority of the ancient chroniclers lies in their ability to render judgment without appearing to do so. The critical distance of the historian, which Barante labels "a sort of judgment," emerges not from dry argument but from the "spectacle," which is to say the visual element, of the past. Barante's new brand of historiography thus allies itself epistemologically with the new forms of spectacular entertainment such as the panorama and the wax display, as well as with the new types of historical illustration, which likewise looked to the visual as the primary source of historical knowledge.

Barante's description of the charm of the old chronicles points to the concept of local color which, according to Stephen Bann, Barante was the first to introduce into French critical discourse in a series of articles on theater submitted to *Le Publiciste* in 1806.[37] In painting, the term *local color* signifies the color that is specific to each object in a painting, regardless of the general distribution of light and shade over the whole pictorial field. Barante adapted the visual term to historiography by using it to describe textual details, both turns of phrase and descriptions of costume, buildings, or customs, that are specific to a certain time and place. As I show in chapter 4, the term *local color* became identified, for nineteenth-century novelists and literary critics with the historical fiction of Walter Scott, which began to be translated into French in 1816 and which had a profound influence on the Romantic historians. As opposed to the disregard for anachronism that led seventeenth-century actors at the Comédie-Française to play Romans while dressed like courtiers at Versailles, authors of the new picturesque historiography and historical fiction strove to

37. Bann, *Clothing of Clio,* 38.

capture those local aspects of costume that made a certain historical time or place unique and recognizable.

Although considered the chief of the picturesque or narrative school of Romantic historiography, Barante was hardly the sole practitioner of visual history writing in the first half of the century. To a greater or lesser degree, the other Romantic historians all depicted the local color of the past ages they were describing and paid varying degrees of attention to visual description. Taking their lead from Scott, as well as from François-René de Chateaubriand's *Génie du christianisme* (1802); Joseph-François Michaud's *Histoire des croisades* (1808), which delighted readers with its vivid narrative and its attempt to show what Camille Jullian has called "the poetic color of times past";[38] and Jean-Charles-Léonard Simonde de Sismondi's *Histoire des français* (1821), the young Romantic historians who came of age during the 1820s made use of visual detail as a vital tool for historical understanding.

Augustin Thierry, Adolphe Thiers, François Guizot, and Jules Michelet all incorporated narrative strategies borrowed from the Romantic historical novelists Scott and James Fenimore Cooper, presenting dramatic scenes from the past as a series of visual descriptions.[39] "With the appearance of each new novel by Walter Scott, I hear regrets that nobody has presented the customs [*moeurs*] of Old France in as picturesque a light," wrote Thierry in his enormously influential manifesto for his brand of Romantic historiography, titled *Lettres sur l'histoire de France*.[40] Jullian describes how, in the new Romantic history writing, "the novelistic tastes of the period called especially for battle narratives, touching scenes, picturesque descriptions."[41] These were provided in abundance, even by such historians known for their adherence to the philosophical school, the branch of Romantic historiography that opposed the narrative or picturesque school by seeking not only to describe the past but to offer theories for understanding it and that numbered both Thierry and Guizot among its ranks. Thierry's *Histoire de la conquête d'Angleterre*, first published in 1825, explained the Norman invasion by means of a theory of conflict between competing races, but also abounded in vividly rendered battle scenes.

The partisans of the picturesque mode of historical narration were not, however, necessarily in favor of actual illustration. In the first of his *Lettres sur l'histoire de France,* Thierry complained about the anachronisms

38. Jullian, *Extraits*, xii.
39. In chapter 4, I describe the influence of Scott and Cooper on the French novel.
40. Augustin Thierry, *Lettres sur l'histoire de France* (Paris: Ponthieu, 1827), 111.
41. Jullian, *Extraits*, xxiv.

perpetrated by modern illustrators who portray Charlemagne adorned with such later symbols of the monarchy as the fleur de lys.[42] Michelet likewise complained about the retrospective mode of historical illustration, favoring instead authentic images created at the time of the events depicted. By linking the illustrated editions with the picturesque theories of the Romantic historians, my point therefore is not to suggest that the Romantics consciously made illustration a part of their historical project but rather that certain common assumptions about the nature of the historical image as a conceptual tool underlay forms of historical expression in a variety of different media at the time. When certain critics saw the work of the Romantic historians as somehow analogous to forms of popular entertainment such as the panorama, this was not only because of their verbal images, but also because of what their visual poetics said about their politics.

The Image and its Discontents

For critics in the 1830s and 1840s on both the left and the right of the political spectrum, the Romantic valorization of the visual in historical discourse seemed dangerous both for the discipline of history and for the construction of post-Revolutionary subjectivity. To better understand the stakes of this debate over the visual, I return to the series of reviews published by Alfred Nettement, the critic from the extreme right in the *Gazette de France* in the late 1830s, in which he decried the tendency of Romantic historiography to reduce the past to "a series of pictures."[43] Nettement was not complaining about actual pictures in these reviews, much less about wood engravings. Indeed, he offered nothing but praise for the actual images accompanying the volume by Barante that he lambastes.[44] His critique of the verbal imagery of Romantic historiography nevertheless raises questions about the role of the image as a tool for comprehending the past and thus provides a vital context for understanding the function of the historical spectacle.

42. "Many engravings provide the most bizarre travesties of the principal scenes of our history. Flick through the most popular of those little works, which are so dear to mothers concerned for the education of their children, and you will see [. . .] Charlemagne covered in fleurs de lys, and Philippe-Auguste, in steel armour after the fashion of the sixteenth century." Translated and cited in Haskell, *History and Its Images*, 287–88. When Thierry's *Histoire de la conquête de l'Angleterre par les Normands* became the subject of just such a set of retrospective illustrations in 1838, he had already gone blind (Haskell, 278).

43. Nettement, "Études littéraires," January 3, 1837, 4.

44. Nettement praises the artistic skill of the artists and engravers who worked on the illustrated fifth edition of Barante's *Histoire des ducs de Bourgogne de la maison de Valois, 1364–1477* (1837), and applauds them for depicting with care the historical monuments that the Revolutionaries had attempted to destroy as hated symbols of the ancien régime. Ibid.

"The subject gives way before the pen of the historian," comments Nettement in one of his articles on Jules Michelet's monumental *Histoire de
France* in 1836. "The lines cross and tangle, and the colors of the picture
are so bright and varied that the painter at times seems dazzled by them."[45]
For Nettement, the work of Jules Michelet embodied the best and worst of
the Romantic school; through his critique of Michelet, he aims at the entire generation of Romantic historians who came of age during the 1820s
and whose work was characterized by a taste for the picturesque.[46] Nettement's use of the painting metaphor to describe the new Romantic historiography is, as I have shown, not without precedent; by comparing
Michelet's work to a painter's canvas, the critic implicitly responded to the
rhetoric initiated by Barante in the preface to his *Histoire des ducs de
Bourgogne*.

But whereas for Barante the transformation of the past into a "picture"
makes history vivid and alive, for Nettement, the result is a dangerous—if
entertaining—confusion:

> There is even a certain charm in this motley confusion of a thousand colors,
> this shock of ideas, this complication of images; but the severity of history is
> not well suited either to such impetuous appearances or to such a frenzied
> style, if I can be allowed to use such an expression. History should dominate
> the eras it recounts instead of being dominated by them, it should point out
> the causes and the consequences of events, indicate the political and social
> movements of each people, and the general movement of humanity, and
> only give way with a great reserve to that passion for the picturesque which
> threatens to change literature into a vast panorama.[47]

Nettement implies that history should serve as a model for the present,
rather than dazzle the reader/viewer with an accumulation of "colors." Although visual representations of the past, such as the panorama, may have
their charm, their "impetuous" images complicate the historian's task of
pointing toward examples of proper conduct and signaling errors to be
avoided. Such a "severe" conception of history's purpose derives from the
Greeks, but finds its more immediate precursor in Voltaire, who lost few
opportunities to praise the progress toward reason and to denounce the
follies into which religion and superstition led men and women from past

45. Nettement, "Études littéraires," October 12, 1836, 1.
46. "M. Michelet, we have said, is one of his generation's most serious and reflective representatives. In studying him, one takes account of the state of historical science in our era.
He possesses to a very great degree the qualities that characterize the present generation; the
faults of his era are reflected in his talent in such a manner that the reflections he inspires lose
their individual character and take on a more general cast." Ibid.
47. Ibid.

ages.[48] But whereas Voltaire's condemnations of the irrationality of the institutions of the past foreshadowed Revolutionary ideals, conservatives (or reactionaries) in the early nineteenth century such as Nettement sought to appropriate his philosophical method to mobilize indignation against the Revolution and what they saw as its logical outcome, the Terror.[49]

According to Nettement, the nineteenth-century historian should invoke dangerous periods such as the Revolution only in order to condemn them. Any description of Revolutionary or Napoleonic history that does not denounce these periods risks promoting Revolutionary or Imperial sentiments by enflaming the imaginations of readers/viewers. And the visual historiography of the Romantics abounded in such descriptions, as did, of course, the illustrated histories of Napoleon and such contemporary spectacular entertainments as the panorama. For Nettement, visual forms of historical representation, by divorcing description from judgment, by shifting responsibility for deciphering the meaning of the past from the historian to the viewer, offers a dangerous kind of spectacle.

Nettement articulates similar fears in the entire series of articles dedicated to Romantic historiography that he penned for the *Gazette de France* in the late 1830s and early 1840s. "To envision history in that manner," he writes of Barante's pictorial tendencies, "is to misunderstand his mission, to rob it of its dignity and deprive it of the most beautiful of its attributes." Referring to Barante's writings as "his historical landscapes," Nettement denounces the immorality of the visual approach to the past: "We pity M. de Barante for having seen in such events only the subject of a picture. The colors of this picture are brilliant, the resemblance of the characters is well observed, the tale is interesting; but the work lacks that moral beauty that nothing can replace and that is the seal of perfection on works of the imagination." When Nettement accuses Romantic historiography of reducing the past to a mere picture, of misunderstanding its mission to serve as a model of action, he implies action of a conservative kind, which he labels "good" or "moral."[50]

Nettement opposes historiography that functions as a picture and that provokes viewers to imitate the wrong kind of action, namely the Revolutionary or Imperial scenes depicted on the historians' canvases: "The historian is not only a narrator, he is a judge. [. . .] His mission is not only to color the past in the pages of a book, mixing the good and the bad, glory and shame, as in a certain famous museum, his mission is also to in-

48. Voltaire's *Essai sur les moeurs et l'esprit des nations* was published in 1765.
49. Philosophical history was also written by left-leaning Romantic historians, such as Auguste Mignet, who defended the Revolution.
50. Nettement, "Études littéraires," January 3, 1837, 4.

struct the present."[51] By the "famous museum," Nettement means the Galeries historiques at Versailles, which Louis-Philippe had nearly finished constructing at the time Nettement published this review, transforming a large part of the old chateau into what was essentially a series of pictures. On June 10, 1837, the Citizen King opened the doors to the project that had taken him nearly six years to complete—a giant museum in which all the major periods of French history were represented in painting. Hundreds of newly commissioned canvases supplemented paintings made at the time of the events they depicted. By 1848, the museum contained over 3,000 paintings and sculptures, at the center of which was the enormous Gallery of Battles, featuring key moments of French military triumph from Tolbiac to Wagram.[52]

Given its scale and significance, it is unsurprising that the Versailles museum becomes a key point of reference in the critical discourse of the time—or that it provided the pretext for an illustrated history of France featuring wood-engraved vignettes.[53] For its creators and defenders, Versailles's transformation from the Sun King's palace into a museum open to the general public epitomized the July Monarchy's adherence to democratic and Republican ideals. But inherent in these claims lay a thinly veiled ideological program to use history as a means of cementing a collective national identity in the wake of the Revolution of 1830 and, in the process, to promote loyalty to the state and to the regime. "The Museum of Versailles is the most important and complete monument that has ever been erected to our national glory; the Museum of Versailles is the royal masterpiece of the King of the French, Louis-Philippe the First," announced the prospectus to one of the official guidebooks to the museum published at the time of its opening, with "an explanatory text" by the prominent writer and critic, Jules Janin. "It's the general meeting place of our national history," declared this favorably disposed observer.[54]

For its detractors, however, Versailles represented the epitome of the

51. Ibid.

52. Michael Marrinan describes the nationalistic function of the historical representation at the Versailles museum in "Historical Vision and the Writing of History at Louis-Philippe's Versailles," in *The Popularization of Images: Visual Culture under the July Monarchy,* ed. Petra Ten-Doesschate Chu and Gabriel P. Weisberg (Princeton: Princeton University Press, 1994), 113–43. For a discussion of the transformation of Versailles by Louis-Philippe, see Thomas W. Gaehtgens, *Versailles: De la résidence royale au musée historique. La Galerie des Batailles dans le musée historique de Louis-Philippe,* trans. Patrick Poirot (Paris: Albin Michel, 1984).

53. Count Alexandre de Laborde's *Versailles ancien et moderne* (Paris: Gavard, 1841), featuring eight hundred engravings, served as a guide to the museum as well as a general history of France.

54. Jules Janin, prospectus to *Galeries historiques de Versailles* (Paris: Ernest Bourden et Proust, 1837), 1. In this text, Janin serves as the official mouthpiece for the regime.

dangers of the new spectacular historical imagination—the tendency to depict the past as a series of pictures without the kind of commentary necessary to restrain the dangerous enthusiasms such pictures might provoke. Shortly after the opening of the museum, the *Gazette de France* published an extremely harsh review, signed "A.D.L.," that decried the "degradation" of the former royal residence into a warehouse, an "immense bric-à-brac shop." The reviewer denounced the "jumble of picturesque daubs" in terms similar to those Nettement had used to describe the Romantic historiography of Barante and Michelet: "What is the Chateau of Versailles now? Like everything in this era, it is a thing without a name, a confusion, a mess of paintings."[55] Aside from the insult to the legitimist past that the hijacking of Versailles embodied, the museum's visual approach to history, its representation of the past as a series of pictures, threatened to glorify periods (such as the Revolution and the Napoleonic Wars) that, according to the right-wing critic, should be condemned. At Versailles, as in the panorama, historical illustration, and Romantic historiography, viewers were confronted with "mere images" and were expected to draw their own conclusions—conclusions that would inevitably celebrate rather than condemn the events depicted.

This excursion through the diatribes of right-wing critics helps us see the way the historical image had become a contested site in post-Revolutionary France, fraught with anxieties about how the past was supposed to look and about how viewers were supposed to look at the past. But the reactionary critics were not alone in their anxieties over the historical spectacle. Contemporary observers on the left of the political spectrum also saw certain dangers in the attempt to turn the past into a picture. An example of this anxiety emerges in the criticism directed against the large-scale historical canvases painted by Paul Delaroche in the 1830s.

Delaroche was one of the most popular painters of the period, and his representations of English history—of Lady Jane Grey moments before her execution, and of the children of King Edward awaiting death in the Tower of London—fascinated French spectators in the July Monarchy with their illusionistic representation of emotionally laden moments from the past.[56] As Beth S. Wright points out, these paintings present history as a dramatic scene; frozen in a moment of maximum pathos, Delaroche's

---

55. A.D.L., "Beaux-Arts," *Gazette de France*, August 2, 1837, 1.

56. Frequently discussed in reviews of the *salon* from the 1830s, Delaroche contributed images to several of the period's most significant illustrated histories. In "Delaroche par Goupil: Portrait du peintre en artiste populaire," in *Paul Delaroche: Un peintre dans l'histoire*, eds. Claude Allemand-Cosneau and Isabelle Julia (Paris: Éditions de la Réunion des musées nationaux, 1999), Pierre-Lin Renié notes that Delaroche was "the painter most reproduced by engraving in his time" (173).

historical characters arouse the pity of viewers, especially those inclined to sympathize with suffering and soon-to-be-murdered monarchs.[57] But for certain contemporary left-leaning commentators, such representations denied the complexity of history.[58] These critics felt that by reducing the past to a single moment, Delaroche's paintings prevented viewers from understanding the social and political causes underlying the historical event they depicted. They encouraged viewers to thrill in the moment and perhaps to identify with the beautiful victims, but they did not provide a complete picture of the past.

The left-leaning critique of Delaroche mirrors the right-wing critique of Michelet and Barante. Critics from both sides of the political spectrum attacked the historical image for reducing the past to a mere picture, for depriving it of the accompanying narrative that would have helped viewers make the correct historical or political inferences. In fact, the anonymous reviewer for the right-wing *Gazette* criticizes Delaroche in similar terms:

> By producing Cromwell, Edward's Children, Jane Grey, M. Delaroche perhaps thought he was painting history, but has only made genre pictures [. . .]. What was the artist's idea in showing a young woman, blindfolded, on the scaffold, groping for the block on which to place her head? This is the final scene of a drama, a terrible scene filled with emotions; he has rendered it admirably; but what is the moral of this representation? [. . .] What is M. Delaroche thinking? Is he for Jane Grey, or is he for Mary?[59]

Apparently the conservative reviewer had difficulty detecting a political viewpoint in the picture. Although even the Neoclassical historical canvases of David might be said to freeze history in a single "scene," Delaroche's pictures seemed to the critic to be mere genre paintings because they failed to take sides, because they shirked the responsibility of the historian to think for the viewer, to judge rather than describe.

For this conservative critic, even a judgment in favor of the opposing side would have been preferable to the kind of confusing image that Delaroche provides:

57. Beth S. Wright, *Painting and History during the French Restoration* (Cambridge: Cambridge University Press, 1997), 78–82.

58. Wright discusses an 1837 *salon* review by the Saint-Simonian Louis-Alexandre Piel in which he criticizes Delaroche for failing to depict the monarchy's struggle with Parliament in his paintings of English royalty. According to Piel, these historical events "furnished him with poses, costumes, and furniture, but nothing more." Piel, "Salon de 1837," review of paintings by Paul Delaroche, *L'Européen* (2nd ser.) 2 (July 1837): 29–30, Cited in Wright, "'That Other Historian, the Illustrator,'" 224, n. 108.

59. "Le salon de 1834," review of paintings by Jean-Dominique Ingres, Delaroche, and François-Marius Granet, *Gazette de France*, March 10, 1834, 2.

When David depicted Brutus sentencing his sons to death, the Oath of the Horatii, the Death of Marat, he endowed his paintings with a republican idea. When Gérard showed the entry of Henri IV into Paris, he made him a royalist and not a *ligueur*. David and Gérard are history painters; Gros also, M. Ingres also. But to concentrate the philosophical and moral part of a picture in an almost material and purely external effect, this is genre painting if there ever was such a thing, just as the dramas at the Porte-Saint-Martin, which only show the surface of facts, are genre scenes.[60]

Likening Delaroche's paintings to the historical dramas I discuss in the next chapter, this critic attacks the painter for presenting only the outward surface of history, an "almost material and purely external effect." His critique echoes Nettement's denunciation of the way that Romantic history writing attempts to present a picture of the past. For critics on both sides of the political spectrum, Delaroche's paintings turned the past into an image divorced from judgment and therefore difficult to read from a clear partisan political standpoint.[61] Although, until recently, art historians have tended to dismiss Delaroche's images for their penetrability, for their too easily read political program that allegedly detracts from their pictorial quality, such a view was not held by viewers in the 1830s and 1840s.[62] For contemporary viewers, Delaroche's historical paintings were confusing precisely because they substituted an image for politics. Critics from both ends of the political spectrum saw such a visual approach to the past as dangerous because it could so easily lead to a covert form of ideological manipulation.

The debate over the historical image that opposed picturesque historians such as Barante to critics from both sides of the political spectrum reveals the stakes of the controversy surrounding the past in post-Revolutionary France. For another perspective on this debate, I return now to the illustrated editions—not to the illustrations themselves but rather to the paratextual material that surrounds them. As I show, the prefaces that accompany these editions and the prospectuses[63] used to

60. Ibid.

61. What both the booklet accompanying the exhibit and the painting fail to narrate, according to the monarchist critic, is the calm and courage with which Jane faced her death, the true "moral" (i.e., pro-royalist) lesson to be drawn from this tragic episode. "These circumstances, which are so little evident in the painting, make me think that M. Delaroche merely wanted to paint a tragic scene." Ibid.

62. In *Paul Delaroche: History Painted* (Princeton: Princeton University Press, 1997), Stephen Bann argues against the narrow (and ahistorical) critical focus on the avant-garde tradition in nineteenth-century France and for Delaroche's important place in a more broadly conceived history of nineteenth-century visual culture.

63. The prospectus was a marketing tool. Between two and four pages in length, it usually combined passages from the prefaces with glowing descriptions of the work, and furnished such practical information as the cost for purchase, instructions for subscription and delivery, and an indication of the quality of the paper, the typography, the engraving, and the printing.

market them elaborate an historical epistemology centered on the image that takes Barante's defense of the visual in a more literal direction. These arguments point to the ideological effects of this mode of viewing the past.

Speaking to the Eyes

One of the major claims made by illustrated editions is that illustration offers access to a level of history that unadorned written histories exclude. "The new *Histoire de France* that we are publishing has been carefully conceived and carefully executed," boasts the prospectus to the illustrated edition of Henri Martin's *Histoire de France depuis les temps les plus reculés jusqu'en juillet 1830,* published by Mame in 1833 and made immensely popular through an aggressive marketing campaign and a moderate price. Martin's prospectus, like the preface to Barante's *Histoire des ducs de Bourgogne,* stakes its claim to historiographic superiority on its accessibility to a wide readership, which it in turn ascribes to its images, both verbal and visual: "it was a question of making available to all intelligences and all ages a method that rendered history's true character; in making it local, descriptive, dramatic, we showed that side of history that our forerunners most disdained."[64]

The notion that pictures say something that words cannot was central to the project of the illustrated editions, as well as to the spectacular past more generally. Authors and editors present the illustrations as a kind of parallel history that reveals insights hidden by conventional prose narrative: "Our goal was above all to speak to the eyes," states the prospectus to the illustrated edition of Martin's history; "skilled artists were charged with completing our descriptions according to the most authentic monuments: this series of engravings will itself form a picturesque history."[65] In the details of costume and architecture, this argument goes, lie truths about past generations. Hence the parallel with the illustrated *physiologies* of the period that described social types through reference to (and images of) clothing, as well as with such forms of spectacular entertainment as the wax display and the panorama. In illustrated historiography, just as in the panorama or the wax museum, outward appearances are revelatory of deeper truths. Inherent in both popular entertainments and spectacular historiography is a confidence in the visual as a source of knowledge, as a means of accessing truths that are normally hidden.

64. Henri Martin, prospectus to *Histoire de France depuis les temps les plus reculés jusqu'en juillet 1830* (Paris: L. Mame, 1833), 4.
    65. Ibid.

The 1833 prospectus to Antony Béraud's never-completed *Histoire pittoresque de la Révolution française avec cent dessins des artistes les plus distingués* makes a similar case for the power of the visual, of local color, to penetrate to the very soul of the past: "During periods of popular upheaval, the form of a hairstyle becomes a deep thought, the cut of a suit a venerated symbol."[66] Appearances always carry meaning; choices in personal style always say something about the person who makes them. I point to similar claims made by guidebooks to the visitors of the Curtius wax display, who sought information about the souls of historical actors through the observation of their clothes, hair, and face. But Béraud carries this logic to the next level. Not merely the *reflection* of political ideas and events, hairstyles and costumes become actors on the stage of history: "Each act of this extraordinary drama has its own physiognomy, its own fashions, costumes, language, dress [. . .] effects of great causes that bring with them new causes" (3). According to this prospectus, the historical image functions at the same time as a reflection of an event and as its catalyst; it serves as both effect and cause.

A history that ignores the look of the past risks missing whole strata of meaning. According to Béraud's prospectus, the truth of history inheres in the specificity of its material, visual legacy: "I only understand a man fully by seeing his portrait; in order for me to comprehend fully the importance of a scene, show it to me in its true locality [. . .]. Show me [. . .] that Temple, that Bastille with its enormous towers crumbling along with the monarchy [. . .]. Who could deny the interest that such a series of pictures would add to the story?" (3) As I show in chapter 3, this is the same logic that Victor Hugo and Stendhal mobilized in favor of the Romantic historical drama during the 1820s: historical representation cannot be undertaken in an abstract space; it requires the aura that only authentic locations and props can provide. In the never-completed work fantasized by Béraud's prospectus, words and pictures join together to form an organic whole that transcends the sum of its parts: "It is thus that in our work, the brush and the pen serve one another [. . .] everything, in such a narrative, seems to be alive, everything helps give the impression of vigor, power, life to that imposing lesson from the past" (4). By showing where history took place, by describing how people looked, Béraud's illustrated history promises to make the past come alive for a reader who otherwise would be left cold by the mere record of past events.

66. Antony Béraud, prospectus to *Histoire pittoresque de la Révolution française avec cent dessins des artistes les plus distingués* (Paris: Mesnier, 1833), 3. Subsequent quotations are cited in the text.

These histories take the logic of illustration one step further by suggesting that the power of the image resides less in its content than in the medium itself. Rather than merely providing additional kinds of historical information about the appearances of costumes or buildings, the image captivates by addressing different faculties in the viewer. "There are several kinds of memory," writes L. S. Colart in the preface to his *Histoire de France representée par des tableaux synoptiques et par soixante-dix gravures* of 1825; "the most ordinary, especially in children, is that local memory we refer to as that of the eyes."[67] One of the first nineteenth-century histories to expound a pedagogical program for historical education based around the image, Colart's preface draws on classroom experience to argue that memory is linked to visual stimuli. The eyes become the all important conduit to historical comprehension: "The teacher who knows how to captivate them is sure of success. His lessons will surely be remembered by students [. . .] if they enter their minds through the eyes."[68] Colart's preface claims to provide a physiological basis for the image's power to act on the historical imagination.

Laure de Saint-Ouën, the best-selling historical author of the July Monarchy,[69] expounds a similar theory of the role of the visual in fixing attention on the facts of history: "*To speak to the eyes,* to produce a lasting impression on the mind, such is the goal of these mnemonic pictures."[70] As she explains in the preface to her *Histoire de Napoléon* of 1833, her task in recounting the history of the emperor consisted in inventing a new set of visual signs to supplement the traditional narrative form of conventional histories: "I had to create a new language, to endow ideas with a new form that would render them *apparent*" (2, emphasis in original). She finds her solution in what she labels the "mnemonic picture"—an enormous, foldout, engraved chart that represents historical facts with graphic

67. L. S. Colart, *Histoire de France representée par des tableaux synoptiques et par soixante-dix gravures* (Paris: Ambroise Tardieu, 1825), 1. Colart was the student of the abbé Gaultier, an eighteenth-century pedagogue, who argued for the importance of the visual in a series of writings dedicated to educational theory, including a *Leçons de chronologie et d'histoire*. Gaehtgens describes Gaultier's influence on Restoration and July Monarchy historical pedagogy (*Versailles*, 72).

68. Colart, *Histoire*, 2.

69. Saint-Ouën's *Histoire de France* was not only the best-selling historical work between 1831 and 1845, but ranks among the top five best-selling books in all genres during the period. Martyn Lyons, "Les best-sellers," in *Histoire de l'édition française: Le temps des éditeurs*, ed. Roger Chartier and Henri-Jean Martin (1985; reprint, Paris: Fayard/Promodis, 1990), 419–22.

70. Laure de Saint-Ouën, *Histoire de Napoléon, accompagnée d'un tableau mnémonique des principaux événemens de sa vie* (Paris: A. J. Dénain, 1833), 2, emphasis in original. Subsequent quotations are cited in the text.

emblems. Like Colart, she argues for the special power of the eyes to convey what is important about the past directly to that part of the brain devoted to historical understanding.

In Saint-Ouën's picture, Napoleon's biography is summarized visually by ten medallions, each containing a series of small pictures that are explained in an accompanying legend, although their transparency as communicators of information, she argues, renders such explanation unnecessary. An overturned carriage, for example, represents a defeat and two joined hands designate a peace treaty. As she explains in the preface to the *Histoire de Napoléon,* this picture is indispensable to the narrative and must be referred to constantly while reading. In a sense, the written text exists only to supplement the picture: "the object of this text is to establish links among facts, to provide them with sufficient development so as to fix them in the memory. Indeed, by tying the text to the figures, the memory receives a kind of double impression, since at the same instant that the eyes are struck by an object the mind is struck by a narrative" (7). The efficacy of the illustrated histories, and by extension the power of all forms of spectacular historical representation, lies in their vaunted ability to engage two faculties at once, the eyes and the mind; this double action supposedly has twice the power to imprint historical facts on memory.

Images provide the reader with more than just mnemonic associations. For Saint-Ouën, the visual image is at once more direct and more reliable, more likely to help readers seize the true meaning of an event than its written analog because of its capacity to direct attention to an event's meaning: "thus, when looking at the first medallion, which contains General Bonaparte's Italian campaign, a single glance suffices to determine that that period is a glorious period. A multitude of carts, accompanied by flags and laurel leaves, characterizes at first sight the innumerable and marvelous successes of that admirable campaign" (3–4). Unlike written histories, which she suggests may complicate historical understanding with needless nuance, the *tableau* is said to provide all the information necessary in a single glance. The illustrated history achieves a higher level of truth, according to Saint-Ouën, because it simplifies the historical record, reducing it to unique moments and single ideas that can be apprehended instantly. If the sole historical meaning of Napoleon's Italian campaign consists in seeing it as a "glorious period," then this information can indeed be gleaned in "a single glance." A key advantage of the visual, for Saint-Ouën, lies in its power to assimilate information about the past without hesitation and without the kinds of secondary reflection that accompany the ordinary reading process. This monumentalizing view of the past posits vision as self-evident and the image as an unclouded conveyor of truth.

In the prefaces to these illustrated histories, the visual is equated with a lack of mediation, with an immediate and unbiased form of representation. Here, then, is the other side of the debate—a response to the critiques made by both Nettement and observers on the left that visual forms of historiography are inherently biased. In his preface to the illustrated edition of his history of Napoleon, Norvins responds to potential criticism that his acquaintance with the emperor has distorted his vision. His self-justification takes the form of a meditation on the role of the historian whom he analogizes to a visual artist: "As a painter, he knows the true physiognomy of men and things; and, as a historian, his role is limited to exact reporting, when he seems only to be giving his personal opinion."[71] In contrast to Scott, whose own very critical history of Napoleon was denounced by certain elements in the French press as a calumnious product of English chauvinism, Norvins vaunts his own clear-sightedness.[72]

The visual image provides Norvins with a metaphor for truth, and the illustrations that accompany his text become the extension of this absolute transparency of representation. The prospectus for Henri Martin's *Histoire de France* likewise advertises the objectivity of the narrative in visual terms: "History, in our opinion, should be an optical mirror, which reflects men and things both at a distance and up close; the historian's task is limited to making that painting as exact, lifelike, and animated as possible. It is poor form to erect a tribunal instead of naively presenting the documents of the past."[73] For the promoters of illustrated histories, the image functions not as a window onto the world, not as a mediating force, however transparent, but rather as a mirror, reflecting the truth of history with absolute fidelity.

This desire to revive the past through realistic images defines the spec-

---

71. Norvins, prospectus to *Histoire de Napoléon*, ii.

72. Upon its publication in France in 1827, Scott's biography of the emperor became the subject of a heated debate in the French press. In a series of articles, the critic for the *Journal des Débats* called it the worst thing that Scott had ever written (F., "Variétés," review of *Vie de Napoléon Bonaparte* by Walter Scott, August 9, 1827, 4), faulting it for distorting the truth, for using bad sources, and for turning history into a novel (F., "Variétés," review of *Vie de Napoléon Bonaparte* by Walter Scott, August 18, 1827, 4), but crediting it for awakening French patriotism in response: "at this moment, from all sides, unanimous complaints pour forth; from all sides awakes the sentiment of the national ego [*le moi national*]. I heartily thank Sir Walter for this great service" (F., "Variétés," review of *Vie de Napoléon Bonaparte* by Walter Scott, September 19, 1827, 4). The complaints were not, however, as unanimous as the *Débat's* critic let on; the critic for the *Gazette de France* came to Scott's defense by attacking an anonymous refutation of Scott's work. S., "Variétés," review of *Réfutation de la vie de Napoléon par Sir Walter-Scott* by "M.," *Gazette de France*, November 28, 1827, pp. 3–4.

73. Martin, prospectus to *Histoire de France*, 3.

tacular historical imagination of the post-Revolutionary period, motivating the new popular entertainments as well as the novels, theater, and historiography of the Romantic movement. As I show in chapter 1, the impulse behind this effort to revive the past visually was linked to the search for a new national identity in the early nineteenth century. Although a desire to arouse love for the *patrie* through representations of past glories underpins all forms of history in the period, from the panoramas of Langlois to the historiography of fourteenth-century Burgundy by Barante, the illustrated histories tend to be more explicit than other forms of discourse about their ideological motivations and thus provide a useful lens through which to examine the political ideology of the historical spectacle.

These historiographic works see no contradiction between their supposedly objective view into the reality of the past and their explicitly nationalistic and even propagandistic motives. In numerous prospectuses and prefaces, history in general is offered as a foundation for a new national identity and the historical image in particular is seen as promoting a unique sort of national pride. In the preface to her *Histoire de Napoléon,* Saint-Ouën describes the fascination that the military victories of the past, and particularly those of the Empire, continue to exert on the July Monarchy public: "They exert a powerful attraction and make us contemplate with pride that [. . .] glory whose brilliance shines on us."[74] Basking in the reflected lustre of the past, nineteenth-century spectators could find in visual historical representations a key to the national regeneration that Saint-Ouën felt they needed: "Actors or witnesses of the great drama, of which all of Europe was the theater, we search daily, with constantly renewed vigor, to see those different scenes again. An intimate knowledge of that period of marvels is a historical necessity."[75] The historical spectacle thus purports to serve a patriotic function for the disaffected July Monarchy public through the immediacy—and accessibility—of its images.

The prospectus to the new 1842 edition of Laurent de l'Ardèche's *Histoire de l'empereur Napoléon,* which added illustrations of military uniforms by Hippolyte Bellangé to the five hundred original wood engravings from the original edition, vaunts the patriotic sentiments that its images would provoke in viewers: "Costumes are also a part of history, and we thought the public would welcome a series of watercolored engravings of the uniforms of the Republic and the Empire, of those uniforms that make the hearts of theatergoers beat faster because they recall the national pride associated with those most magnificent triumphs and most noble satisfac-

74. Saint-Ouën, *Histoire de Napoléon,* 1–2.
75. Ibid., emphasis added.

tions."[76] The prospectus goes so far as to suggest that its images will promote a renewed bellicosity and perhaps even a return to France's former tendency to domination, repressed under the relatively pacifistic July Monarchy regime. With its depiction of military uniforms, this text explicitly calls to mind the plays about Napoleon that enflamed viewers in the 1830s (discussed in chap. 3): "Seeing those old uniforms that the memories of the Republic and of the Empire made heroic and reading the narratives to which those pictures act as commentaries and enactments, people will be filled with the desire to equal their ancestor's valor and to show of what stuff French soldiers are made."[77] The visual re-creation of the past, and particularly a certain vision of the past that focuses on periods of glory, supposedly furnished a ground for the July Monarchy public to establish new structures of individual and collective identity.

In their elaboration of the ideological stakes underpinning illustrated historiography, these prefaces and prospectuses offered a theoretical justification not only for the illustrated texts they accompanied, but also for the spectacular past more generally. Like Romantic historiography and the plays about Napoleon, the illustrated histories attributed to the image a superior potential for conveying truth, a capacity for transmitting the reality of the past more directly to the reader-viewer than mere words. The illustrated editions, moreover, vocalized how this illusionistic representation could be used to renew national pride and coherence in the post-Revolutionary context. By making explicit what their contemporaries left unsaid, these long-forgotten texts proved central to understanding the historical processes of the era.

Monumental Vision

Louis Michelant's illustrated *Faits mémorables de l'histoire de France*, first published by Didier in 1844 and republished in updated editions in 1858 and 1871, offers a particularly telling case study of the way nineteenth-century spectacular historiography served not only aesthetic or pedagogical but also ideological ends. Like the panorama, Michelant's text uses the historical image as a ground for the elaboration of a stable national identity amid the turbulence of nineteenth-century war and revolution. Subtitled "Illustrations de l'histoire de France" [Illustrations of French History], Michelant's text, adorned with wood-engraved images by Victor Adam, represents an important moment in the history of the illus-

76. Laurent de l'Ardèche, prospectus to *Histoire de l'empereur Napoléon* (1839; reprint, Paris: J. J. Dubochet, 1842), 2.
77. Ibid.

trated edition, as much for its innovative use of graphic material as for its unabashed embrace of the genre's monumentalizing vision of the past.[78]

Like Barante and the other partisans of picturesque history, Michelant rejects the dry moralistic commentaries of the philosophical school of historiography, calling for a vision of the past that will appeal to the least educated of publics: "History, which of all the subjects of study should be the most attractive, is often, especially for young minds, little more than a dry and tedious exercise."[79] A new kind of history will reach out not to the critical or intellectual faculties but to the imagination and especially to the eyes. History must entertain, especially in order to reach a youthful audience, and the surest way to interest readers is to focus on the main events, on the big, striking, glorious moments in the past that have the power to capture the imagination: "Because isolated facts, forming if I may say, the *summits* of the narrative, strike our intelligence most strongly" (1, emphasis added). This monumental vision of French history puts the big events of the past into relief, emphasizing the traits that make them stand out against the dull background of the rest of the historical continuum. This vision of history leads, inevitably, to the image: "Thus we feel that it is through a series of pictures forming a historical representation that we think we can penetrate most surely into the domain of history" (1).

The series of pictures in Michelant's text begins with the frontispiece (Fig. 2.7). In this image, a winged female figure, representing Clio, the Greek muse of History, holds a sign announcing the book's title, *Faits mémorables de l'histoire de France* [Memorable Facts of French History]. Two historical figures stand in front of the woman: on the muse's right, Louis XIV, and on her left, Napoleon, at whom she directs her gaze. Un-

78. Like nearly all illustrated editions of the time, Michelant's text was sold by subscription in installments or *livraisons*. The prospectus spelled out the terms of the subscription: "Each installment will contain two pictures, and along with them, two historical accounts, with a cover. Price: 25 cent. The volume will contain 60 installments. Price, for Paris, 15 francs, Departments, 18 francs." Louis Michelant, prospectus to *Faits mémorables de l'histoire de France* (Paris: Didier, 1844), 1. Michelant's history cost slightly less than two similar illustrated editions of the period: Jacques-Antoine Dulaure's *Histoire de Paris et de ses monuments,* published by Furne in 1846 at 20 francs (80 installments at 25 centimes each); and Théodose Burette's *Histoire de France,* published by Benoist in 1859 at 18 francs (360 installments at 5 centimes each). As new techniques of production and an enlarged market developed over the course of the century, book prices, including those of illustrated editions, dropped significantly. The 1871 edition of Michelant's text cost only 12 francs. On the economy of book production in the nineteenth century, see Frédéric Barbier, "Une production multipliée," in *Histoire de l'édition française: Le temps des éditeurs,* ed. Roger Chartier and Henri-Jean Martin (1985; reprint, Paris: Fayard/Promodis, 1990), 105–36.

79. Michelant, prospectus to *Faits mémorables,* 1. Subsequent quotations are cited in the text.

FIGURE 2.7 Engraving after Vivant Beaucé, frontispiece for L. Michelant, *Faits mémorables de l'histoire de France*, 3rd ed. (1871). Image courtesy of the Bibliothèque nationale de France, Paris.

like Michelet's brand of Romantic historiography, which focuses on *le peuple* rather than the king, Michelant's text is concerned primarily with sovereigns. Louis XIV and Napoleon, moreover, stand in for the dozens of other kings represented in the text, who themselves stand in for millions of their less memorable historical subjects in the narrative. The frontispiece image thus signals a key representational strategy employed by the narrative, replicating the metonymical process whereby the monarch serves as a historical marker for all those who lived during his reign. But here the substitutive principle is not temporal contiguity; Louis XIV and Napoleon share with the other rulers a common function or quality rather than a convergence of historical dates.

In this frontispiece, Louis XIV and Napoleon stand parallel to one another, occupying the same plane in the fictive space generated by the image. This equating of monarchs from different periods is part of the text's strategy of historical representation. "We have especially abstained from all partiality, from all preference for any particular period," Michelant writes; "we took whatever seemed to us grand and national, whatever had the greatest impact on the destiny of France" (1).[80] Just as conservative critics feared, this new form of spectacular history avoids rendering a judgment on the past: it collapses distinctions, erasing the difference between a "legitimate" monarch and a "usurper." Like the wax display, it places all periods of *grandeur* on an equal footing.

The image on the title page, which faces the frontispiece, reinforces the sense of balance that this strategy implies. In this image, a woman, an allegory of the nation, holds in one hand an orb topped by a crown, symbol of monarchy, and in the other the *Charte,* the document that limited the monarchy's powers during the Restoration and July Monarchy (fig. 2.8). Equal positions are accorded to an Imperial eagle, symbol of Napoleon, and a crown atop a tablet imprinted with the fleur de lys, another symbol of the Bourbon monarchy. On the woman's left stands a Napoleonic officer and on her right a medieval crusader. By placing these historical epochs side by side, in the same plane of the picture, the image appears to avoid the reproach of partisanship. But what impression does such a level-

80. The Versailles museum employed a similar strategy of combining monumental moments from French history in its collection of canvases. As the prospectus to Janin's guide to the museum put it, "In these walls that have been abandoned for so long [. . .] you will find without confusion all the eras, all the places, all the ages, all the great events, all the dynasties, all the periods of France. Clovis and Charlemagne, Saint Louis and François I, Louis XIV and Louis XVI, the French Revolution and the Empire, the Restoration and the July Monarchy, all the great kings and all the great periods [. . .] come together in the palace of Versailles." Janin, prospectus to *Galeries historiques de Versailles,* 1–2.

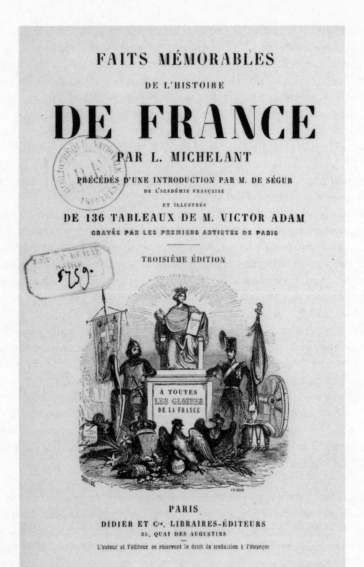

FIGURE 2.8   Engraving after Louis-Pierre-René de Moraine, title page for L. Michelant, *Faits mémorables de l'histoire de France*, 3rd ed. (1871). Image courtesy of the Bibliothèque nationale de France, Paris.

ing of the past leave on the historical imagination of the viewer? By equating such diverse periods and rulers, the image invites the kinds of objections
raised by reactionaries against Michelet's picturesque style. It also invites the
objection that critics from both sides of the political spectrum made to the
paintings of Delaroche, works they accused of refusing to take sides, of reducing the past to "an almost material and purely exterior effect."

The *Faits mémorables de l'histoire de France* divides French history into
120 chapters,[81] each of which contains a wood engraving (8 cm by 15 cm)
on the top of the first page, followed by a short (3.5 page) narrative. (Unlike the biographies of Napoleon described earlier in this chapter, in which
images are sandwiched between text, Michelant's history does not take
full advantage of the possibilities of wood-engraving for its page layout;
image and text here remain spatially distinct.) At the start of each chapter
appears the name of a monarch and the date of a significant event from
that monarch's reign. This event then forms the subject of the narrative
and of the image that illustrates it: the reign of Clovis, for example, is
summarized by the Battle of Tolbiac (fig. 2.9).

The written narrative elaborates on the images, placing the event depicted in the image in the context of the larger history by showing its
causes and effects. This "series of different pictures" summarizes the past,
compacting its lessons into single moments that together form "the complete narrative of our glorious annals." Condensed into isolated illustrations, France's "glorious annals" are meant to act all the more powerfully
and lastingly on the viewer: "Represented in such a manner," the prospectus tells us, "history immediately grabs the mind and engraves itself in the
memory in an indelible way" (1). The engravings in Michelant's text thus
serve as metaphors for the process of imprinting historical images on the
minds of readers/viewers.

Like Colart and Saint-Ouën, Michelant advances a quasi-physiological
theory of the role of the image in the formation of the historical imagination. The images may strike a chord in viewers because they call to mind
historical information garnered previously, perhaps from paintings or
other illustrated histories, and stored in the memory in visual form. "Who
doesn't remember the conquest of the Francs and their conversion upon
seeing Clovis at the feet of Saint Remi?" the prospectus asks. "Who
doesn't rediscover the crusades, the whole struggle between West and East,
on the soil of the Holy Land, by seeing the council of Clermont and the
capture of Jerusalem?" (2) As becomes clear from these examples, the

81. Later editions in 1858 and 1871 added more chapters to bring the text up to date.

BATAILLE DE TOLBIAC.

Le grand mouvement des invasions qui changea si souvent la face de l'Europe s'était arrêté, et les peuples longtemps errants commençaient à former des établissements stables. Les tribus franques qui s'étaient fixées au nord de la Somme avaient, sous la conduite de Clovis, étendu leur domination jusqu'à la Loire. Dirigées par ce prince jeune, actif, audacieux, elles avaient défait une armée romaine; mais, malgré ces succès, malgré les insignes consulaires que l'empereur d'Orient envoyait au chef des Francs, il y avait loin de cette réunion confuse de soldats sous les drapeaux de Clovis à l'unité qui fait les nations. Les guerres, ou plutôt les violentes incursions inspirées par le besoin du pillage, formaient les seules ressources des Francs; leurs mœurs et leur religion, composée de croyances superstitieuses, étaient également barbares. Vainement le christianisme avait déjà fondé d'illustres églises dans les Gaules, les Francs persistaient dans leur idolâtrie.

Clovis cependant avait épousé une princesse chrétienne, la nièce du roi de Bourgogne, Clotilde, dont les écrivains contemporains vantent

FIGURE 2.9   Engraving after Victor Adam, "Bataille de Tolbiac," in L. Michelant, *Faits mémorables de l'histoire de France*, 3rd ed. (1871), p. 9. Image courtesty of the Bibliothèque nationale de France, Paris.

events that Michelant's text promises to invoke lend themselves to visualization because of their picturesque and dramatic qualities. But what also becomes clear is the degree to which these visual qualities function ideologically and are put in service of a nationalistic enterprise that, as I show, becomes increasingly overt with each reprinting of the text.

The events depicted in the original 1844 edition of Michelant's history tend to reflect a patriotic ideal. "We took what seemed to us great and national," the prospectus states, "and we have recounted the facts in all their truth, all their exactitude, only giving space in the *Illustrations de l'histoire de France* to what we thought would truthfully illustrate France in all her national glory" (2). Military triumphs, especially the conquest by the French of foreign lands, occupy pride of place. The first several installments of the original edition included chapters devoted to the "Battle of the Pyramids," "Napoleon Crossing the Alps," and "Jerusalem Taken by the Crusaders."[82] Indeed, whereas most monarchs find their reigns reduced to a single event, Napoleon figures in no less than twenty-two chapters.[83]

The second (1858) reprinting of the work, which added several chapters to cover more recent history, proves even more strongly militaristic than the original 1844 edition. Unsurprisingly, the controversial domestic politics of Charles X is overlooked in favor of France's overseas victories during the period, the Battle of Navarino and the Conquest of Algiers. But while France's drive to conquest receives its due, so too does the heroic defense of the *patrie*—the reign of Childéric is emblematized here by Saint Geneviève stopping Attila the Hun before the walls of Paris in 451 and the reign of Louis XI by the Defense of Beauvais in 1472, in which the women of the city participated in the military effort, giving "the example of courage which was hardly expected of their sex" and recalling the times in which the citizens, both male and female, of France were called on to do the same.

The celebration of military triumphs in all the editions forms part of an ideological program that mobilizes a certain vision of history to aid in the creation of national identity. The pride inspired by identification with the glorious periods of the past translates, for the ideal reader/viewer, into a devotion to the present nation, whether the regime of the July Monarchy or of the Second Empire. The preface to the original 1844 edition, written by the Count Paul-Philippe de Ségur, a noted historian of the Empire, lays bare this project: "Let this vast picture of ancient and modern France in-

---

82. Although the installments were not published in chronological order, subscribers were invited to arrange the individual sections by date before having them bound.

83. This includes chapters in which he figures as General Bonaparte. Louis XIV is the second most represented monarch, with eighteen chapters. Other monarchs with more than a single chapter include: Louis XVI (nine chapters), François I (seven), and, in the third edition from 1871, Napoléon III (seven).

spire respect for our laws, attachment to liberty, and especially love for the sacred homeland!"[84] The inspirational effect of the historical *tableau* is calculated by Ségur (and Michelant) to appeal to a July Monarchy audience for whom the memory of France's recent world domination under Napoleon and humbling defeat at Waterloo still occupies a large psychic space. "Let the aged take pride in their memories at the very mention of the name France!" intones Ségur. "Let ripe hearts follow with pride the progress of grandeur, growing always greater over the course of fifteen centuries, of the empire that has still not shown signs of decadence! Let youth study with ardor the annals of a country of which it is the hope!"[85] Published after a decade in which the bourgeois government of Louis-Philippe largely avoided foreign conflict, the *Faits mémorables* articulates a desire for glory supposedly smoldering beneath the surface of the French nation.

This desire, transformed into bitter regret, occasioned the reprinting of an updated third edition of the text in 1871, following the humiliating French defeat by the Prussians at Sedan that brought down the Second Empire government of Napoleon III. Dedicated to Michelant's son who was killed in the war, the third edition reproduces the inspirational preface by Ségur, but with an appended note alerting readers to the tragic irony that history has imposed on the nation's hopes: "These words, filled with confidence in the grandeur of France, formed the introduction to the *Faits mémorables de l'histoire de France* when it was first published. We are keeping them at the beginning of the third edition to the book, despite the cruel contrast that they create with the events that have darkened our nation's history."[86] Whereas the first edition acts ideologically to promote national pride through a simple strategy of patriotic identification, depicting only moments of military victory, the third edition employs more subtle means toward the same end, appealing to the nation's feelings of shame and disgust aroused by defeat. This later edition features a chapter devoted to Waterloo, "A terrible name indeed for any patriotic soul,"[87] as well as a concluding chapter devoted to the debacle of the Franco-Prussian War of 1870 and the Commune.[88] The engraving for this last chapter, entitled "Guerre de 1870, Révolution du 4 septembre," shows a soldier sitting and contemplating his misfortune (fig. 2.10). This depressing scene of

84. Comte Paul-Philippe de Ségur, preface to Michelant, *Faits mémorables de l'histoire de France* (Paris: Didier, 1844), iv.

85. Ibid.

86. Louis Michelant, *Faits mémorables de l'histoire de France,* 3rd ed. (1844; updated reprint, Paris: Didier, 1871), ii.

87. Ibid., 479.

88. There is no image of the Commune, a period that Michelant condemns: "A civil war broke out [. . .]. For almost three months Paris was abandoned to a ferocious dictatorship that destroyed itself in the ruins it had made, in the fires it had set." (Ibid., 544).

GUERRE DE 1870.
RÉVOLUTION DU 4 SEPTEMBRE.

Il y a pour un pays des malheurs dont le récit doit être laissé à l'avenir; le temps seul peut rendre à l'histoire le calme nécessaire pour en parler avec impartialité. Lorsqu'on sent encore pour ainsi dire le contact de si terribles événements, on ne saurait en porter un jugement complétement équitable. Aussi nous bornerons-nous à esquisser les traits principaux de cette crise nationale, en évitant tout développement, toute appréciation prématurée.

Disons seulement qu'il n'est pas un jour de cette année funeste qui n'ait été marqué par un revers ou par des tentatives d'autant plus coupables qu'elles se produisaient en face de la guerre étrangère. Si quelque chance favorable fut entrevue, toujours elle nous échappa par des négligences et des fautes inexcusables. Un aveuglement fatal obscurcissait toutes les intelligences, et la France, envahie, outragée, épuisée de violences et de pillages, parut sur le point de se dissoudre dans l'étreinte d'un ennemi impitoyable.

Parfois la guerre a des alternatives; la victoire y est assez disputée

FIGURE 2.10   Engraving after Victor Adam, "Guerre de 1870, Révolution du 4 septembre," in L. Michelant, *Faits mémorables de l'histoire de France*, 3rd ed. (1871), p. 541. Image courtesy of the Bibliothèque nationale de France, Paris.

passivity and regret is then followed by a conclusion that places responsibility for the future on the young and on their relation to history: "If they don't know how to learn from the heavy heritage of our faults, if the sad examples of civil discord, in the last fifty years, don't teach them anything, then we can only fear for the future of France."[89] The text offers the promise of national rebirth as a reward to its readers/viewers for learning from the past, as well as the threat of further disaster as the price of ignoring the lessons history has to offer.

In the three editions of Michelant's *Faits mémorables de l'histoire de France,* the image provides a conduit for the comprehension of the past and a catalyst for the process by which history transforms itself into an appreciation of and devotion to the *patrie*. But as I have shown, not all contemporary readers/viewers saw the historical image in the same way. For critics on both the right and left of the political spectrum, the historical tableau distorts the past—while it may contain the power to influence subjectivity, it misguides the viewer with dangerous simplifications. Instead of revealing the complexity of history, the image presents only its monumental aspects, collapsing all meaning into an endlessly repeated celebration of the nation. Michelant's text carries the tendency toward reduction and homogenization to an extreme and thus fulfills the worst fears of Nettement and other critics hostile to the historical image. The "series of pictures" in the *Faits mémorables* are all the same size and are all executed with the same Romantic flousrishes by the hand of Victor Adam. Despite the effort to distinguish the distinct features of different periods by rendering various details of architecture or costume, the overall effect is one of uniformity. Rendered in the same style, with the same manner of shading and modeling, Napoleon and Louis XIV take on a curious resemblance.

In the hands of Michelant, as in the hands of his more canonical contemporary Michelet, the historical text becomes spectacular. In Michelant, however, the ideological and pictorial strategies of the spectacular approach to the past are laid bare: historical illustration functions explicitly as a vehicle for the promotion of nationalistic sentiment. The political implications of such nationalism, and its links with the Bonapartist political platform, are the subject of the next chapter, as I explore what was perhaps the most extreme form of the spectacular past in nineteenth-century France—the outpouring of plays about Napoleon after the July Revolution.

89. Ibid.

Chapter Three

Napoleon Takes the Stage

On August 31, 1830, the Cirque-Olympique theater raised the curtain on a new play, *La prise de la Bastille et le passage du Mont Saint-Bernard*, in which the figure of Napoleon made a silent entrance late in the second act to inspire his troops across an icy Alpine pass. Banished from the French stage throughout the Restoration by government censors afraid of reviving popular support for the Empire, Napoleon aroused enthusiasm that night not only in the soldiers on stage, but also in the audience. "*La prise de la Bastille et le passage du Mont Saint-Bernard* garnered the applause of an astonished and amazed public," gushed *Le Corsaire* in its review of the spectacle. "The periods crowd together. We see everything. We witness everything. This is history in action."[1] Thrilled by this brief glimpse of the "man of destiny," just a month after the July Revolution had toppled the Bourbon monarchy once again, and this time for good, spectators in August of 1830 could little have imagined the number of Napoleons waiting in the wings, ready to reenact the Empire's rise and fall on a nightly basis in theaters all across France.

Taking advantage of the relaxation of governmental control over theatrical subject matter following the Revolution of 1830, nearly every theater in Paris put Napoleon on stage in the course of the next year (see Appendix).[2] As *Le Corsaire* accurately predicted on October 10, 1830, "It's going to rain [. . .] Napoleon Bonapartes." Indeed, that paper's daily list-

---

1. "Butin," *Le Corsaire*, September 2, 1830, 3.
2. A notable exception is the Comédie Française, which resisted Napoleon, but not, as I will show, the spectacular mode of historical representation.

ing of spectacles for January 1, 1831, reads like a biography of the emperor: *Joséphine, ou le retour de Wagram* at the Opéra-Comique, *Napoléon, ou Schoenbrunn et Sainte-Hélène* at the Porte Saint-Martin, *L'empereur* at the Cirque-Olympique, *Napoléon à Berlin* at the Montparnasse, *Napoléon* at the Théâtre d'Élèves, *Quatorze ans de la vie de Napoléon* at the Luxembourg, and *Le fils de l'homme* (a play about Napoleon's son) at the Nouveautés. By the end of 1831, no fewer than twenty-nine new plays about Napoleon and the Empire had opened in France. By 1848, that number rose to over one hundred and twenty.[3]

This chapter shows how yet another genre of historical representation—and the most prominent and public one in the nineteenth century, the theater—turned the past into a spectacle. As in the panorama, or the illustrated histories of the 1830s and 1840s, the plays about Napoleon offered a radically heightened form of visual realism in their historical representation. Like the panorama—and indeed, variations on the panorama were used in certain productions by innovative set designers—these plays simulated the appearance of the past with a remarkable attention to detail.[4] Like the wax display, they re-created the materiality of the past, the textures of costume and prop, with a fidelity that stunned observers at the time. In the Napoleon plays, both the visual and commercial aspects of the historical spectacle reached a frenzied height, provoking the delight of viewers but also the wrath of critics, whose analyses of the dangers of these productions provide a vital framework for elaborating a nineteenth-century critique of the spectacular past.

Along with tracing the ways in which the Napoleon plays marked a significant change in the way the French theater represented the past, this chapter analyzes the phenomenon to explore certain general features of

3. In *Napoléon et l'Empire racontés par le théâtre, 1797–1899* (Paris: Jules Raux, 1900), Louis-Henry Lecomte provides a short description of every play about Napoleon produced during the nineteenth century in France, including many that were never published. Martin Meisel describes nineteenth-century English plays about Napoleon and relates them to their French counterparts in *Realizations: Narrative, Pictorial, and Theatrical Arts in Nineteenth-Century England* (Princeton: Princeton University Press, 1983), 201–28. More recently, Angela C. Pao, in *The Orient of the Boulevards: Exoticism, Empire, and Nineteenth-Century French Theater* (Philadelphia: University of Pennsylvania Press, 1998), discusses plays about Napoleon set in Egypt (117–23).

4. One of several plays to celebrate the return of Napoleon's remains to France in 1840, *Le dernier voeu de l'empereur,* by Ferdinand Laloue and Fabrice Labrousse, incorporated a moving panorama into the stage décor to show Napoleon's coffin traveling from Saint Helena to Paris. In a review of a later play by the same authors at the Cirque-Olympique, a critic explicitly compared the production to a Napoleonic panorama: "It is terrible and true like a panorama by M. Langlois." Alfred Brisbane, "Revue dramatique," review of *L'Empire* by Laloue and Labrousse, *La Démocratie Pacifique,* February 19, 1845, 1.

historical spectacle. Whereas chapter 1 examines the realism central to the functioning of the spectacular past and chapter 2 investigates the epistemological claims made on behalf of historical images, this chapter focuses on the way the spectacle promoted historical identification as a means of identity formation for a nation divided by politics in the post-Revolutionary era. As in the panorama and the illustrated histories, Napoleon emerges once again as the privileged object of historical vision in these large-scale spectacles. It is the goal of this chapter to explain the link between the spectacular past and the politics of Imperial nostalgia. Napoleon's conquest of the Boulevard in 1830 represents an extreme instance of the spectacular past but one, I argue, that brings its inner workings to light.[5]

Le drame national and the Scandal of Romanticism

Because the theater is inherently spectacular and history had long been a major topic on the French stage, to speak of the nineteenth-century theater's spectacularization of the past might seem redundant or inevitable. But this is not the case—the type of history depicted in the theater of the ancien régime and the manner of its representation were far removed from the mode of historical representation that I call the spectacular past. Something changed radically during the early nineteenth century that made it possible—desirable even—to stage French history with the kind of visual realism found in the Napoleon plays. This change did not occur suddenly in 1830, however, but rather emerged as part of a process that links this story to larger trends in French theatrical history.

Napoleon's entrance onto the theatrical scene coincided with another, rather more celebrated theatrical event—the advent of the Romantic drama. Victor Hugo's *Hernani* opened at the Comédie-Française six months before *La prise de la Bastille et le passage du Mont Saint-Bernard* at the Cirque-Olympique, and Hugo's *Marion de Lorme* played at the Porte Saint-Martin the same summer that *Le grenadier de Wagram* played at the Ambigu-Comique. Although the cannons and horses of the Napo-

---

5. Boulevard theater derived its name from the grouping of many of its houses (such as the Gaîté, the Ambigu-Comique, and the Cirque-Olympique) on the boulevard du Temple. This street was also known as the boulevard du Crime because of the lurid subject matter of the plays performed in its theaters. On the origins of popular theater in Paris, see Martine de Rougemont, *La vie théâtrale en France au XVIIIe siècle* (1982; reprint, Geneva: Champion-Slatkine, 1988). In *Les théâtres du boulevard du Crime* (1905; reprint, Geneva: Slatkine, 1977), Henri Beaulieu describes the changes in these theaters from the Old Regime to the nineteenth century.

leon plays made a good deal of noise in the press at the time, subsequent theatrical historians devoted significantly more attention to the battle of *Hernani* than to the Battle of Wagram. The popular success of the Napoleon plays, however, was intertwined with the triumph of the Romantic drama. The two forms of theatrical expression, although different in their cultural ambitions, shared a fundamentally similar outlook on French history, its modes of representation, and its uses in the formation of a post-Revolutionary national identity. Indeed, the seemingly endless—and endlessly repetitive—reenactments of the Empire's glory, although mired in a now unappreciated melodramatic aesthetic, offer a key to understanding how Romanticism's revolution in the literary landscape was bound up with a change in the way post-Revolutionary French culture viewed the past.[6]

Scholars have long seen the triumph of the Romantic drama as a victory for stylistic innovations, such as the *enjambement,* and as a declaration of independence from Aristotle—a loosening of the grip of the Classical unities of time, place, and action. These formal considerations have tended to obscure the fundamental shift in *content* undertaken by the early nineteenth-century theater—a move away from the use of ancient Greek or Roman subject matter to a preoccupation with more modern history and particularly with the French national past. This shift was long in coming. In a review of a new French translation of Shakespeare in 1781, Gabriel-Henri Gaillard lamented that "an old prejudice has long prevented our theaters from representing if not history in general, at least that of our own country."[7] Indeed, the Classical French theater, dominated by Jean Racine and Pierre Corneille, looked almost exclusively to ancient history for its sources and subjects—to the Bible, to Greece, and to Rome. While for the English spectator, the theater meant heavy doses of Shakespeare, and hence of such national figures as Richard III and Henry V, the spectator of the French Classical drama could be excused for thinking that history had come to a stop sometime after the Trojan War.

The French Classical theater's use of history, however, differed from the Shakespearean model in more than just its choice of time periods. In the tragedies of Racine and Corneille, the historical setting serves only as what

6. In *Le Romantisme aux enchères: Ducange, Pixerécourt, Hugo* (Amsterdam: John Benjamins, 1992), Marie-Pierre Le Hir underscores the links between the Romantic drama and the historical melodrama (especially 33–49). In *The French Stage in the Nineteenth Century* (Metuchen, N.J.: Scarecrow Press, 1972), Marvin Carlson calls the Romantic drama "melodrama elevated to the status of literature" (4).

7. Cited in Anne Boës, *La lanterne magique de l'histoire: Essai sur le théâtre historique en France de 1750 à 1789* (Oxford: Voltaire Foundation, 1982), 1. Christopher Prendergast discusses the debate over the use of national rather than ancient history as a subject for painting in *Napoleon and History Painting* (Oxford: Clarendon Press, 1997), 62–65.

the early twentieth-century critic Jules Marsan called "a frame" to the "heroic or romantic adventure" at the center of the intrigue.[8] These plays do not evoke the past in a material sense, they show little concern with the details of speech or costume that defined a particular historical moment or with the depiction of local manners and customs, especially if these could be considered improper, against the rules of *les bienséances.* Indeed, the goal of Classical tragedy might be seen as the denial of the difference of the past or as the affirmation of a universal human subject transcending time and space. The effect of Racine's *Andromaque,* for instance, hinges on the spectator's ability to abstract the heroine's dilemma from the specificity of Pyrrhus's court. The ancient Greek setting functions merely to make the play more believable; it serves as an anchor for the play's evocation of the extremes of human passion, but not as a point of interest in itself.[9]

The period leading up to the French Revolution witnessed a change in the theater's treatment of history. Eighteenth-century playwrights and theorists began to call for a *drame national,* a new kind of play that would draw its subject matter from modern French history and that would serve as a means of reflection on the French national character.[10] Advocates of the *drame national* saw in "modern" French historical subjects, even those from as relatively a remote period as the Middle Ages, a weapon to combat the degeneration of contemporary morals by reminding the French of their ancestors' valor.[11] Voltaire had already innovated in this area, providing several examples of a theater based on narratives of French history.[12] The public's failure to welcome his *Adélaïde de Guesclin* of 1734, however, discouraged the development of the *drame national* for the next several decades.[13] It was not until the Revolution that the theater looked

8. Jules Marsan, "Le théâtre historique et le romantisme," *Revue d'Histoire Littéraire de la France* 17 (1910): 1–33.

9. The rules of classical theater were codified at the start of the nineteenth century by Jean-François de La Harpe's influential *Lycée,* which appeared in 1799.

10. In the preface to his drama *François II* (1747), Président Jean-François Hénault called for a new kind of French tragedy that looks to more recent history for its subject matter. Marsan argues for seeing Hénault as a forerunner of the Romantics ("Théâtre historique et le romantisme," 1–3).

11. Boës, *Lanterne magique de l'histoire,* 9.

12. Voltaire's *Zaïre,* first performed at the Comédie-Française on August 13, 1732, although abounding in historical errors, takes place in a recognizable and specific "modern" historical setting, the seventh crusade in 1249, under the reign of Louis IX. Voltaire's *Adélaïde du Guesclin* (1734), set in fourteenth-century Brittany, likewise employs a French historical episode as its subject and contains such radical departures from the classical *bienséances* as a *coup de canon* and the duc de Vendôme's arm in a sling. Ibid., 53.

13. According to Boës, of the thirty-six new plays performed at the Comédie-Française between 1734 and 1750, only five treated French historical subjects, although seventeen treated historical subjects in general. The Comédie produced several French historical dra-

again to the national past, turning it into a political weapon. Marie-Joseph Chénier's *Charles IX, ou l'école des rois,* banned by the royal censors for its depiction of a weak and evil French king, stirred up controversy when Danton and his followers called for it at the Comédie-Française on August 19, 1789, shortly after the storming of the Bastille. Marvin Carlson shows that this was the first time a play was demanded by a political rather than a literary faction.[14]

As France emerged from the turmoil of Revolution, the movement for the *drame national* gained momentum. For the generation that had witnessed Revolutionary events, the tragedies of Corneille and Racine became even more remote, even less relevant to contemporary political concerns.[15] Although Napoleon favored classical subjects that drew parallels between his Empire and that of Rome, playwrights in the first years of the century turned increasingly to the modern French past to lure audiences back to the major theaters. Thanks to François-René de Chateaubriand's *Génie du christianisme* (1802), as well as to Joseph-François Michaud's *Histoire des croisades* (1811), the French Middle Ages had come into vogue, not just as a subject for theater and the historical novel, but also for architecture, fashion, and interior decoration.[16] By setting their plays in the still relatively distant past of the Middle Ages, moreover, writers and producers could hope to get their plays past Napoleon's police, since any subject that directly or indirectly implied criticism of the Napoleonic regime was forbidden.[17]

"The nation craves historical tragedy," Stendhal writes in his first Romantic manifesto, the *Racine et Shakespeare* of 1823, describing the

mas between 1757 and 1778, but then stopped again until Marie-Joseph Chénier's *Charles IX, ou l'école des rois* in 1789. Ibid., 50.

14. The Comédie-Française tried to placate audiences with another *drame national,* Barthélemy Imbert's *Marie de Brabant,* which can rightfully claim to be the first new tragedy of the Revolutionary period, but the play met with little success. Another attempt, Sedaine's *Raymond V* was hissed off the stage. Finally, the Comédie approved Chénier's drama and it was performed on November 4, 1789. Marvin Carlson, *The Theatre of the French Revolution* (Ithaca: Cornell University Press, 1966), 17–23.

15. Michèle Jones makes a similar point in *Le théâtre national en France de 1800 à 1830* (Paris: Klincksieck, 1975): "To pretend to touch the new classes that had emerged from the revolutionary torment through the spectacle of unhappy Greek or Roman princes now seemed pure heresy" (7).

16. The Middle Ages proved central to the elaboration of the Romantic historical vision: the climax of Hugo's *Hernani* (1830) takes place at Charlemagne's tomb and his novel *Notre-Dame de Paris* (1831) is set in the fifteenth century.

17. Although the Legislative Assembly officially ended theatrical censorship in 1791, Napoleon reimposed it, first surreptitiously, with a letter circulated to the theaters by the head of the police, Fouché, on 28 Brumaire (in 1799) right after the *coup d'état,* and then, officially, on June 8, 1806. Carlson, *French Stage,* 28.

Restoration's desire for historical representation as a thirst that the dry productions of the Empire had failed to quench.[18] For Stendhal and the Romantic dramatists he inspired, the past served as a means of reflecting on the present, as a tool for forcing the nineteenth-century French public to confront their present-day dilemmas. Stendhal argues that the Restoration public needed above all to see scenes of *conflict:* "The reigns of Charles VI, of Charles VII, of the noble François Ier, will provide us with ample national tragedies of a deep and abiding interest" he writes in *Racine et Shakespeare.*[19] Stendhal demands theatrical representations of the bloody civil war that pitted Burgundians against Armagnacs at a time when France was still recovering from the effects of the civil war of the Revolutionary period. Implicit in Stendhal's theory of theatrical historical representation is a notion of identification, in which viewers in the present project themselves onto historical figures from the past who share their basic concerns. By identifying with heroes from the past, audience members are supposed to experience the emotions acted out on stage and then translate these feelings into lessons for the present. Identity is thereby formed in relation to an image from the past. This notion of identification with a visual representation becomes central to the project of the Napoleon plays and to the workings of the spectacular past more generally.

For the Romantics, the historical image had to be as realistic as possible for the process of identification to work. Inspired by the Shakespearean model, as well as by the new mode of historical representation epitomized by the wax display and the panorama, Romantics such as Stendhal and Hugo called for theatrical productions that attempted to re-create the past with the kind of material specificity and heightened attention to detail that could not be contained within the confines of Classicism. In *Racine et Shakespeare,* Stendhal castigated the earlier attempts at a *drame national* by Chénier and his followers for obeying Classical strictures rather than following the lead of the English master. In contrast to the classical theater of Racine, which Stendhal thought evoked the ancient past in a stylized, abstract manner, the new theater of the nineteenth century should seek what Stendhal called the "perfect illusion" of reality through historical specificity.[20] For Stendhal, this meant purging theatrical language of the beauties of Classical verse that might provoke admiration in the viewer, thus disrupting the historical illusion. It also meant ac-

18. Stendhal, *Racine et Shakespeare* (1823; reprint, Paris: L'Harmattan, 1993), 127, cited in Jones, *Théâtre national,* 87.
19. Stendhal, *Racine et Shakespeare,* 2.
20. In the first *Racine et Shakespeare* (1823), Stendhal imagines a dialogue between an Academician and a Romantic. The Romantic declares: "I say that these short moments of

curacy in the depiction of manners and language, a more naturalistic acting style, and elaborate sets and costumes to evoke the past visually and
materially.[21]

During the late 1820s, a group of writers, including Ludovic Vitet and
Prosper Mérimée, in close contact with Stendhal, began experimenting
with *les scènes historiques,* plays that sought an extreme form of historical
realism. Intended to be read but not staged, these plays, often extremely
long and written in prose, mined the new memoirs and chronicles being
published at the time. In Mérimée's group of plays published as *Le théâtre
de Clara Gazul* (1825), the author disregarded not only Classical unities,
but also the rhetorical devices associated with Classical verse. Reading the
play out loud to Stendhal's *cénacle,* the young Mérimée both shocked and
pleased his auditors by his deliberate monotone. These plays paved the
way for the Romantic drama by helping to overthrow Classicism's strictures.[22]

In the preface to his own reading-drama, *Cromwell,* Hugo presented another manifesto calling for a new type of *drame national.* Although he dis-
agreed with Stendhal on some particulars, such as the use of alexandrine
verse, Hugo similarly argues for visual realism in the staging of the past:
"The drama should be radically impregnated with the color of past ages; it
should permeate the atmosphere in such a way that we only realize that
we have changed centuries when we enter or leave the theater. If this requires a certain amount of work and study, so much the better."[23] Like
Stendhal, Hugo emphasizes the importance of settings that reflect a specific time and place: "We are just now beginning to understand that a precise locality is one of the prime elements of reality." Hugo goes on to elaborate the specific settings that the new historical drama demands, the
multiplicity of which contradict the Classical unity of place: "Would the
poet dare to assassinate Rizzio anywhere but in the chamber of Marie Stuart? To stab Henri IV anywhere but in the rue de la Ferronnerie, all
clogged with wheel-barrows and carriages? To burn Jeanne d'Arc any-

---

perfect illusion are more often to be found in the tragedies of Shakespeare than in the
tragedies of Racine" (16, emphasis added).

21. Michel Crouzet points to the centrality of the issue of illusion in Stendhal's manifesto
in "À propos de *Racine et Shakespeare:* Tradition, réforme, et révolution dans le Romantisme," *Nineteenth-Century French Studies* 12, nos. 1–2 (Fall–Winter 1983-1984): 17–24.

22. Jones, *Théâtre national,* 79–83. Barbara T. Cooper, "Toward a Semiotic Description
of French Historical Dramas of the Early Nineteenth Century." *Nineteenth-Century French
Studies* 13, nos. 2–3 (Winter–Spring 1985): 74–85.

23. Hugo, preface to *Cromwell* (Paris: Gallimard, 1963), 437.

where but in the Old Market?"[24] Each of these locations, moreover, must be made to look the part, and set designers were mobilized by Hugo and his fellow Romantics in service of this new historical ideal.

The Boulevard theaters had already experimented with illusionistic techniques of set design and Hugo and Alexandre Dumas *père* did not hesitate to borrow from them in the staging of their Romantic historical dramas.[25] Dumas hired Eugène Cicéri, the famous set designer from the Opéra, to create six gigantic sets for his play *Christine,* based on the life of the queen of Sweden, which featured historically accurate costumes by Louis Boulanger. The cost of the production reportedly exceeded 30,000 francs.[26] For Hugo's *Hernani,* which premiered in February of 1830, Baron Justin Taylor, the director of the Comédie-Française, likewise hired Cicéri to create elaborate sets that Hugo himself had sketched.[27]

By 1830, then, the Romantics had created a new way of staging the past. Their revolution involved not only a rupture with Classical verse structure, but also a radical departure from Classicism's subject matter and visual style. By turning to the national past rather than ancient Greece and Rome and by seeking to depict this history with a new degree of visual realism, the Romantics promoted a new kind of identification with the subject matter of history. In this context, the spectacular staging of Napoleon in 1830 can be seen as the logical culmination of Romantic theatrical trends. Indeed, Stendhal ended his second *Racine et Shakespeare* of 1825 with a project for the ultimate Romantic historical spectacle—a play about Napoleon, *Le retour de l'Île d'Elbe, tragedie en cinq actes et en prose* [The return from the island of Elba, a tragedy in five acts and in prose]. Stendhal predicted that such a play would arouse audiences by encouraging identification with the great man but that the authorities would

24. Ibid., 429.

25. Daguerre, the future inventor both of the diorama and an early photographic technique, created several spectacular sets for the Ambigu-Comique beginning in 1818 and later for the Panorama Dramatique, where the stage was much bigger. René-Charles Guilbert de Pixerécourt, the legendary melodramatist, sought to combine spectacular scenic design with historical accuracy. In *Tékéli* (1814), set in the seventeenth century, he insisted on a realistic river; and the staging of his *Christophe Colomb* (1815) included an extremely detailed reconstruction of a two-story ship, anticipating Langlois's *Panorama de Navarin* by fifteen years (Carlson, *French Stage,* 45). Hassan El Nouty studies spectacular set design in *Théâtre et pré-cinéma* (Paris: Nizet, 1978).

26. Cicéri's diorama of "Vésuve en fureur" for Eugène Scribe's *La muette de Portici* caused a sensation in 1828, as did his introduction of an unfurling moving panorama as a backdrop for a production of *La belle au bois dormant* in 1829, which anticipated the traveling shot of cinema. El Nouty, *Théâtre et pré-cinéma,* 62–63.

27. Carlson, *French Stage,* 29–30.

not allow it to be performed until far into the future. As I show, the Revolution of 1830 caused his vision to be realized much sooner than expected.

The Shadow of Napoleon

Stendhal and Hugo had called for the theatrical representation of the national past as a means of reflecting on historical dilemmas in the present, and the Napoleon plays took them at their word. Whereas other forms of spectacular historical representation, such as panoramas and illustrated histories, had also taken up the period of the recent past of the Revolution and Empire, the theater provided a uniquely powerful form of representation because of its collective, public format and its cultural prestige.[28] The relatively low price of tickets at certain theaters, such as the Porte Saint-Martin and the Cirque-Olympique, also meant that the theater was one of the few forms of historical representation available to a relatively broad segment of the public, in both Paris and the provinces.[29]

28. A number of recent works have focused on the political ramifications of theatrical trends in the period. Paul Friedland, in *Political Actors: Representative Bodies and Theatricality in the Age of the French Revolution* (Ithaca: Cornell University Press, 2002), describes the confluence of theater and politics during the French Revolution resulting from their shared investment in a new conception of representation. Sheryl Kroen, in *Politics and Theater: The Crisis of Legitimacy in Restoration France, 1815–1830* (Berkeley: University of California Press, 2000), argues that the theater provided the Restoration public with a means of making sense of recent history. Odile Krakovitch describes the importance of the theater as a "carrier of myths" during the Restoration in "Les mythes du bon et du mauvais roi: Henri IV et François Ier dans le théâtre de la première moitié du XIXème siècle," in *La légende d'Henri IV, colloque, Palais du Luxembourg, 25 november 1994*, ed. Pierre Tucoo-Chala and Paul Mironneau (Paris: J & D Éditions, 1995), 215. Alain Corbin shows how theaters in the provinces became a locus of political protest in "L'agitation dans les théâtres de province sous la Restauration," in *Popular Traditions and Learned Culture in France*, ed. Marc Bertrand (Saratoga, Calif.: ANMA Libri, 1985), 93–114. Jeffrey S. Ravel examines spectator behavior in three Parisian theaters (the Comédie-Française, the Comédie-Italienne, and the Opéra) as a key to understanding public political culture prior to the nineteenth century in *The Contested Parterre: Public Theater and French Political Culture, 1680–1791* (Ithaca: Cornell University Press, 1999).

29. Whereas the Comédie-Française, at the top of the scale, charged between 1.80 and 6.60 francs for a ticket, the cheap seats at popular theaters cost between 50 centimes and 1 franc. The least expensive tickets at popular theaters such as the Porte Saint-Martin and the Gaîté thus cost substantially less than spectacles such as the panorama (for which the cheapest tickets cost about 1.30 francs in the 1820s). Nevertheless, in *The Theatre Industry in Nineteenth-Century France* (Cambridge: Cambridge University Press, 1993), F. W. J. Hemmings points out that although the upper levels of the working class ("skilled artisans") could afford theater tickets during this period, in general most workers could not, except at the occasional free performances given by the major theaters (122). For a list of ticket prices at Parisian theaters during the nineteenth century, see Maurice Descotes, *Le drame romantique et ses grands créateurs (1827–1839)* (Paris: Presses Universitaires de France, 1955), 9. Also see John McCormick, *Popular Theatres of Nineteenth-Century France* (New York: Routledge, 1993), 78–79.

As a result, the theater deeply threatened the regime in power. Although in the years leading up to the Revolution of 1830 the Restoration's theatrical censors aided the expansion of the *drame national* by permitting the depiction of modern French history, including periods as recent as the Revolution, the representation of Napoleon on stage remained strictly forbidden. Given the longing that certain Restoration subjects—including the large number of ex-soldiers—continued to associate with the memory of Napoleon, any allusion to the emperor was grounds for preventing the performance of a play if the offending passages could not be eliminated. As Odile Krakovitch recounts, Eugène Scribe's *Les moralistes,* which had nothing to do with the emperor, was censored for the line "tonight, the napoleons fall to the cards," despite the fact that the reference was to the coin, not to the man.[30]

The Franconi family's Cirque-Olympique theater, which constantly pushed the limits of the Restoration censors' tolerance by staging Napoleonic battle scenes, even while keeping the emperor himself offstage, became the object not only of censorship but of actual police intervention during the Restoration.[31] In a report to the Ministry of State from 1823, following the performance of a play at the Cirque about the death of one of Napoleon's generals, the police prefect described his effort to contain the threat of such a spectacle: "*La mort de Kléber* was performed yesterday, and according to the instructions that you gave me, my lord, I had the surveillance doubled near the Franconi theater."[32] The intensified surveillance of the Cirque functioned to eliminate its potential dangers. The prefect proudly reported that the "spectacle was peaceful" at subsequent performances: "I have complained several times about the bad effect produced by the military scenes performed at the Cirque-Olympique the-

---

30. Odile Krakovitch, *Hugo censuré: La liberté du théâtre au XIXe siècle* (Paris: Calmann-Lévy, 1985), 36. Krakovitch offers a detailed account of Restoration censorship, as does Victor Hallays-Dabot in *Histoire de la censure théâtrale en France* (Paris: Dentu, 1862).

31. The origins of the Cirque-Olympique date back to 1774 when Philip Astley opened an equestrian spectacle on the rue des Vieilles-Tuileries. Antonio Franconi took the reins in 1793, founding a dynasty that became increasingly associated with the representation of Napoleonic spectacles. In 1817 the Cirque-Olympique moved to the boulevard du Temple, where it remained into the July Monarchy. In her *Dictionnaire des théâtres parisiens au XIXe siècle* (Paris: Aux Amateurs de Livres, 1989), Nicole Wild traces the Cirque's repertory as it evolved from mere equestrian displays to more fully realized plays, always under the watchful eye of the government authorities (79). For more on the history of the Cirque, see Frédéric Hillemacher, *Le Cirque Franconi: Détails historiques sur cet établissment hippique et sur ses principaux écuyers recueillis par une chambrière en retraite* (Lyon: Alf. Louis Perrin & Marinet, 1875), as well as articles by Tristan Rémy: "Ferdinand Laloue et le IIIe Cirque-Olympique," *Le Cirque dans L'Univers,* no. 61 (2nd Trimester, 1966): 7–13; and "La 'Dynastie' des Franconi," *Le Cirque dans l'Univers,* no. 76 (1st Trimester, 1970): 3–8.

32. Archives Nationales F^21 1142.

ater; but I should also acknowledge that the directors of this theater have become much more circumspect recently, and I don't think they any longer wish to incur the disapproval of the authorities now that they have solemnly sworn to use their spectacle for the betterment of the public."[33] The subjection of the Cirque's military repertoire to police scrutiny illustrates the extent to which the historical spectacle became the locus for conservative political anxieties in the years leading up to 1830. Thought capable of producing a bad effect on audiences who might identify with the actions depicted on stage, these plays did much more than show the glories of the Empire: to the Restoration authorities, they offered a space in which Restoration audiences could project fantasies of future revolution.

Indeed, despite its willingness to keep the emperor himself offstage, the Cirque constantly risked having its *privilège* altered or revoked during the 1820s because of its partiality for Imperial spectacles.[34] The archives for the period following the performance of *La mort de Kléber* in 1823 contain numerous requests for a prolongation of the theater's *privilège,* which the government authorities continued to grant only for short periods and with multiple restrictions. By tightening the reins on the Cirque, the government no doubt hoped to discourage the performance of the kind of large-scale historical spectacles that could inflame nostalgic and patriotic crowds. In 1828, despite a temporary loosening of the censorship controls under Martignac's ministry, the authorities debated allowing the Cirque's production of *Le général,* a play about the Italian campaign in which the emperor once again did not figure directly. As the censor's official report admitted, the play did not even contain any direct allusions to Napoleon: "Only a shadow of Napoleon, that's the play." The projection of the government's anxieties, this "shadow" cast a pall over the production; "given the dangerous exultation that seems to dominate the public at this moment," the censors concluded, "perhaps it would be prudent to put an end to the enthusiasm inspired by this melodrama." It was forbidden by decree on February 9, 1828.[35]

33. Ibid.
34. The *privilège* was a permit accorded by the government to the theater allowing it to operate and determining what kinds of plays it could perform. According to Wild, during the Empire, the Cirque was restricted to "pantomimes with horses," but the renewed *privilège* of March 16, 1826, allowed it to perform one-act plays as long as equestrian exercises remained part of the action (*Dictionnaire,* 79). Horses were easily integrated into the Cirque's specialty—military history plays.
35. The censors' reports pertaining to productions at the Cirque-Olympique can be found in Archives Nationales F[21]991.

This degree of governmental interference was unique to the theater. In 1821, the year of Napoleon's death, references to the emperor abounded in engravings and printed matter, which were not subject to the same type of censorship; 108 books about Napoleon and the Empire were published in 1821 alone, over half of all historical titles published that year.[36] Dramatists, meanwhile, were forced to seek out ingenious substitutes to cater to the popular demand to see the great man. Some six months after Napoleon's death, François-Joseph Talma, the tragic actor whom Napoleon had encouraged and supported, copied the emperor's distinctive hairstyle for a performance of Étienne de Jouy's *Sylla* at the Théâtre-Français. The public recognized and responded enthusiastically to the subterfuge; as Louis-Henry LeComte put it, "despite its very real beauties, *Sylla* was above all a triumph of the wig [*un succès de perruque*]."[37]

With the fall of the Restoration monarchy and the suppression of its censorship restrictions in July of 1830, the directors of Paris's theaters, attuned to the desires of the public, lost little time serving up a batch of often hastily composed plays featuring Napoleon as a character. "All the makers of dramas [...] are mad for the *Victoires et conquêtes des Français*,"[38] announced *Le Corsaire* in October 1830, as the various Parisian theaters hurried to get their Napoleon plays up and running. "Now that liberty has removed the restriction, and that we can remember out loud without being suspect," commented the left-leaning journal *Le National*, "it seems only fair that the victor of Austerlitz and of Marengo should receive the first homage of a free theater. Our dramatic authors thought so, at least, and they hurried to respond to the public's curiosity, excited to a feverish pitch by the hope of a new kind of spectacle and by the magic of a famous name."[39] By freeing the theaters from the Napoleonic interdiction, the Revolution of 1830 gave enormous impetus to the spectacularization of the past. Although the French continued to produce plays about Napoleon throughout the nineteenth century, the years between 1815 and 1848 witnessed their greatest concentration and the period between August, 1830 and August, 1831 was without doubt

36. I derive this figure from publication statistics in the *Bibliographie de la France* (Paris: Cercle de la librairie, 1814–1971).

37. Lecomte, *Napoléon*, 279.

38. "Butin," *Le Corsaire*, October 8, 1830, 4. *Les victoires, conquêtes, revers et guerres civiles des Français de 1792 à 1815*, published by Pankoucke in 29 volumes from 1817 to 1823, detailed the military history of the Revolution and Empire.

39. A.R., "Théâtre de la Porte Saint-Martin," review of *Napoléon, ou Schoenbrunn et Sainte-Hélène* by Hippolyte-François Régnier[-Destourbet], and Charles Dupeuty, *Le National*, October 22, 1830, 1.

the theater's single most Napoleonic year. Because this year was remarkable both for the founding of a new political regime and for the emergence of literary Realism, it is the principal focus of the discussion that follows.

Reviving Napoleon

The Napoleon plays of 1830–31 did not just represent the history of the Empire; they offered up incredibly elaborate spectacles aimed at producing a realistic image of the past. The Napoleon plays made use of all of the theater's tricks to conjure Stendhal's "perfect illusion" of history. One of the theater's principal advantages over other forms of spectacle was the vitality of its actors. Whereas the figures in the panorama, the wax display, and the illustrated history were static, inanimate representations, in the theater the historical figures quite literally came to life through movement. The incorporation of live horses into the Cirque-Olympique's re-creations of Napoleonic battles during the Empire and Restoration had already made the spectacle seem more real through the addition of movement. But a live Napoleon made the illusion seem more real still; the success of a Napoleon play often hinged on the extent to which the leading actor could imitate the emperor, copying both his physical appearance and his gestures.

Frédérick Lemaître, later to become one of the most famous French actors of the nineteenth century, played Napoleon in the Odéon's production of Dumas's *Napoléon Bonaparte,* although the author at first disapproved of this choice because the actor looked nothing at all like the emperor.[40] The producers of the Nouveauté's *Bonaparte à l'école de Brienne,* meanwhile, scored a coup by engaging a woman, Virginie Déjazet, another leading light of the French stage, to travesty (literally) Napoleon as a schoolboy, but her performance was quickly eclipsed by her many rivals. "[Nicolas-Joseph] Cazot is currently the actor who best represents the Man of Destiny, the illusion is almost perfect," declared *Le Corsaire* on October 17, 1830, but a few weeks later the young Auguste Berger playing in *Napoléon à Brienne* at the Théâtre de Comte, "whose gestures, walk, and even face call to mind the victor of Austerlitz and of Iéna,"[41] gave him a run for his money. The reviewer for *Le National,* however, preferred Gobert at the Porte Saint-Martin: "This role serves him well; at

---

40. Fernande Bassan, preface to Alexandre Dumas, *Théâtre complet,* vol. 8 (Paris, Minard, 1989), 306. Lemaître went on to star in several historical plays, including Hugo's *Lucrèce Borgia* in 1833.

41. "Butin," *Le Corsaire,* October 27, 1830, 4.

many moments he produced a great illusion."[42] The reviewer for *Le Constitutionnel* agreed: "Gobert bears a striking resemblance to Napoleon."[43]

In order to bring the past to life, actors sought to imitate Napoleon's distinctive tics—the way he took his tobacco, the way he placed his hand in his vest, the way he paced. Each of these gestures was judged by the audience, often composed of veterans who had seen the emperor up close, and then debated in the press. "All the marshals still living in Paris went to see the *Napoléon* at the Odéon yesterday," noted *Le Corsaire* in the column devoted to theatrical gossip on January 15, 1831, a few days after the opening of Dumas's play, while the jury was still out as to whether Frédérick Lemaître could pull off his act. "The painful agony of Napoleon is perfectly rendered in the expressions of the Odéon's Frédérick," the same paper enthused two weeks later. "Each night that actor moves a huge assembly to tears as Napoleon, dying at Saint Helena, calls Larrey, the brave surgeon who followed him on all his victories, to his bedside."[44]

Although actors at the Boulevard theaters had pioneered a more expressive style of acting in the melodramas of the preceding decades—a style that deliberately rejected the restrained stylistics of the Classical theater—in the Napoleon plays, the emotional impact derived not from interpretation but from *impersonation.* This new style of hyperrealism succeeded so well, in fact, that audience members had difficulty leaving the illusion behind when they exited the theater; Jean-Alexandre-François Delaistre, the unfortunate actor playing Hudson Lowe, Napoleon's jailor on Saint Helena, was jeered by patriotic patrons at the stage door after performances of Dumas's play.[45] Indeed, savvy producers encouraged this slippage between art and life for publicity purposes by having their actors walk the streets of Paris in their Napoleon costumes. As Carlson describes it, "for some time Napoleons were a common sight on the streets of Paris, stalking alone, scowling, hair combed forward, and hand thrust in coat."[46]

The competition among theaters to produce the most realistic recreation of the Napoleonic legend led to increasingly elaborate spectacles.

42. A. R., "Théâtre de la Porte Saint-Martin," 2.

43. "Théâtre de la Porte Saint-Martin," review of *Napoléon, ou Schoenbrunn et Sainte-Hélène* by Hippolyte-François Régnier[-Destourbet] and Charles Dupeuty, *Le Constitutionnel,* October 22, 1830, 3. Gobert's real name was Mongobert. According to Henry Lyonnet, his immense success as Napoleon "rather harmed his artistic career" because future audiences could only see him as the emperor. His performance in Hugo's *Marion de Lorme,* also at the Porte Saint-Martin, in 1831, was not a success. *Dictionnaire des comédiens français* (Paris: Librairie de l'art du théâtre, 1904), 142.

44. "Butin," *Le Corsaire,* January 27, 1831, 3.

45. Bassan, "Preface," 306.

46. Carlson, *French Stage,* 82.

Indeed, the effort by producers to engage huge numbers of extras to play soldiers in the battle scenes caught the attention of contemporary satirists. In a text by Eugène Morisseau accompanying a lithograph by Nicolas-Toussaint Charlet in the illustrated satirical journal *La Caricature,* two soldiers contemplate a poster for the Cirque-Olympique's production of *L'empereur* (figure 3.1). When a younger soldier asks an older one if his name appears among the characters in the production at the "Circumference [*sic*] Olympique" the older soldier responds, "Oh Pacot! what an idea! But why not actually, since I was there with *him* [Napoleon]. Oh! virtuous Pacot!," the veteran asks his young comrade, "you who know how to write, see if in the 5th regiment, 3rd battalion, 6th company, you don't read the name of Jean-François Brutignon, called The Skull."[47] Unable to see because the cast list contains so many names (and also, possibly, because he cannot really read), the young solider mounts on his superior's shoulders to get a closer look. While gently mocking the ignorance of the soldiers who form part of the audience of such a "military and historical spectacle,"[48] *La Caricature* also satirizes the blurring of the line between reality and representation that such spectacles attempted to produce.

In order to compete with the realism of the other Napoleon plays that arrived earlier on the scene, François-Antoine Harel, the director of the Odéon, spent enormous sums on sets, costumes, and the cast of Dumas's *Napoléon.* Publicity announcements in the major newspapers and literary journals boasted of the production's expenditures, which supposedly topped 80,000 francs. On November 7, 1830, almost two months before the curtain went up, one such announcement in the highbrow *Revue de Paris* announced "a new drama" by the author of *Christine,* "written in verse" (although it would be written in prose): "It is said that there will be one hundred and fifty historical characters featured in these memoirs brought to life. M. Harel, we are told, is leaving no stone unturned in his efforts to fill his gigantic cast. Actors from the Bobino theater, actors from the provinces, actors from the suburban theaters, have already, we are told, been engaged. No expense will be spared for the costumes, the décor, the truth of the production."[49] Harel extended his production design to the

47. Eugène Morisseau, "Of dramatic liberty—Of poster laws—Of Romanticism in the streets—Seeing as how Pacot not being big enough to understand was reduced to standing on the shoulder pads [*épaulettes*] of his corporal," *La Caricature,* February 8, 1831, 109. The lithograph (no. 29) by Nicolas-Toussaint Charlet follows.

48. The soldiers discuss how they are sent to such spectacles to "applaud for free" and refer to this work as forced labor [*une corvée*].

49. "Album," *Revue de Paris,* November 7, 1830, 63.

FIGURE 3.1 Nicolas-Toussaint Charlet, "Lecture de l'affiche," lithograph from *La Caricature*, no. 14 (February 3, 1831). Image courtesy of the Bibliothèque nationale de France, Paris.

audience as well. Former members of the National Guard were invited to wear their uniforms to the opening night performance, and the orchestra played military music during the many intermissions required to change the scenery. By the time of the premiere, the fantasy had taken hold: each of the twenty-three sets was enthusiastically applauded by the audience, with the scene depicting the Crossing of the Beresina receiving the most adulation because of its incorporation of real horses, borrowed for the production from the Cirque-Olympique.[50]

50. My description of this première derives from Carlson, *French Stage*, 82, and Bassan, "Preface," 306; and contemporary newspaper accounts.

The Napoleon plays attempted to represent the reality of the past through animation and movement, but also relied on an opposite technique—the *tableau*—in which action comes to a halt and actors freeze in a pose, to achieve a similar end. The Napoleon plays, like many theatrical productions from the period, enacted *tableaux* that mimicked the gestural configurations of paintings and engravings that were familiar to audiences at the time.[51] At the end of the production of *Quatorze ans de la vie de Napoleon, ou Berlin, Potsdam, Paris, Waterloo et Sainte-Hélène* at the Luxembourg, the description of the climactic deathbed scene instructed directors to re-create a famous painting of Napoleon's death by Charles Steuben.[52] Auguste Jouhaud's *Les cendres de Napoléon ou le retour en France* at the Théâtre Saint-Marcel, another of the plays from 1841 that celebrated Napoleon's post-mortem return from Saint Helena, ended with an "apotheosis," which the printed version indicated should depict Napoleon rising out of the clouds and pointing toward the Arc de Triomphe and his funeral procession. A note at the bottom of the page, however, instructed future directors (no doubt at less technically sophisticated or well-funded theaters in the provinces) that "the apotheosis can be staged in different ways; if the procession under the Arc de Triomphe presents too many problems, it can be replaced by a reproduction of the painting by Horace Vernet ('Napoleon leaving his tomb')."[53]

Although such artificial disruptions of the action in the play might seem to detract from the realism of the production rather than enhance it, theorists at the time saw things quite differently. According to the eighteenth-century theory of Denis Diderot, the *tableau* increases the illusion of a theatrical production by providing a moment outside of time and the exigencies of plot in which spectators can project themselves onto the scene. The frozen picture on stage allows the viewer to enter the world of the play, whereas action (particularly *les coups de théâtre,* the sudden twists and turns of the plot typical of Classical theater and later of melodrama) prevents the kind of fantasizing that makes a play come to life.[54] As Michael Fried has emphasized, moreover, the Diderotian *tableau* helps convince the spectator of the reality of the events onstage precisely be-

51. Meisel describes how the theatrical *tableau*, like the related *tableau vivant*, "mediates between the picture, painted or engraved, and the nineteenth century's pictorial dramaturgy" (*Realizations*, 49).

52. Louis-François-Nicolaïe Clairville aîné, *Quatorze ans de la vie de Napoleon, ou Berlin, Potsdam, Paris, Waterloo et Sainte-Hélène* (Paris: Barbier, 1830), 59.

53. Auguste Jouhaud, *Les cendres de Napoléon ou le retour en France* (N.p., n.d.), 10

54. Denis Diderot, "Entretiens sur le fils naturel," in *Oeuvres completes,* ed. Jacques Chouillet et Anne-Marie Chouillet (Paris: Hermann, 1980), 133.

cause the actors appear fully engrossed in their actions and unaware of the spectator's presence. This mode of theatricality must be seen as a departure from the prior Classical model in which actors directly faced the audience while speaking their lines "and in general performed in a manner that at every moment addressed the audience as if seeking its approval."[55] As in the frozen pictures of the panorama, which the *tableaux* of the Napoleon plays simulated, these productions allowed spectators to lose themselves in a picture from the past.

The fact that these images were often recognizable works of art also increased, rather than detracted from, the reality of the productions. Indeed, the image of Napoleon in 1830 might be said to be a creation of secondary representations. With the exception of the tiny element of the public that had seen Napoleon up close, viewers in 1830 expected the Napoleons on stage to look like familiar portraits they had seen. Thanks to the trade in popular engravings during the preceding decade and to the outpouring of illustrated histories, the emperor's image had been reduced to two main sartorial features—the *redingote grise* (the gray frock coat) and the *petit chapeau* (the bicorne hat).[56] The published plays that specify what the actors wore (most likely intended for productions in the provinces) inevitably return to these two symbols that were instantly recognizable to the French public at the time. In *Bonaparte, lieutenant d'artillerie, ou 1789 et 1800*, which depicted Napoleon as a young officer and emphasized his Republican sentiments, the costumer sought to integrate the trappings of Revolutionary sentiment with the familiar icons of the future emperor: "Bonaparte: cavalry uniform, white vest [. . .] *gray frock coat* over the uniform, yellow gloves, hair long in back, *bicorne hat* without a braid and with a very small red, white, and blue cockade."[57] The repetition of these iconic elements focused attention away from the distinctive features of the actor, which most likely did not resemble those of the historical Napoleon, thus minimizing disruptions of the historical illusion.

The Napoleon plays thus used a variety of techniques to generate an illusion of the past, implicitly following the Romantics' guidelines. But how

55. Michael Fried, "Salons," in *A New History of French Literature,* ed Denis Hollier (Cambridge: Harvard University Press, 1989), 478. On Diderot and the *tableau,* see also Michael Fried, *Absorption and Theatricality: Painting and Beholder in the Age of Diderot* (Berkeley: University of California Press, 1980), 91, 93, 104.

56. Michael Marrinan refers to the use of such "iconic aspects" of Napoleon in popular imagery as well as *salon* painting of the period in *Painting Politics for Louis-Philippe: Art and Ideology in Orleanist France, 1830–1848* (New Haven: Yale University Press, 1988), 168–70.

57. Xavier [Boniface], Félix-Auguste Duvert, and Nombret St.-Laurent, *Bonaparte, lieutenant d'artillerie, ou 1789 et 1800* (Paris: Bezou, 1830), 59, emphasis added.

exactly did the process of theatrical identification imagined by Stendhal work in the case of Napoleon? If critics, playwrights, and public in 1830 believed in the power of historical theater to shape the national character, what kind of character was shaped by the Napoleon plays? And how was this character similar to or different from the kind of identities fostered by other spectacles at the time?

Napoleon and the Post-Revolutionary Politics of Identification

The answer is bound up with the complex political situation of 1830. Like the panoramas of Langlois and the wood-engraved illustrated histories of the 1830s and 1840s, the Napoleon plays offered an illusion of the Empire in the very real context of the July Monarchy. And just as those other instances of the spectacular past served strategic political ends, so too did the plays about Napoleon. Unlike the panoramas and illustrated histories, however, which required long periods of time to paint or write, the plays were written and staged quickly—often in a matter of a few weeks or less, as many critics lamented—and thus responded to the changing political attitudes in much more specific and immediate ways than other forms of spectacle. As a result, not all the plays of the 1830–31 season presented the same image of Napoleon. To explain the specific ways in which the plays acted on their audiences, then, I present the chronology of the theatrical season in relation to the political events of the time.

Bonapartism, as I have shown, combined a revolutionary populism with the promise of a strong leader and an active military.[58] The Bonapartists, like the *juste milieu* supporters of Louis-Philippe, occupied a position between the two political extremes in 1830—on the right were, the legitimists, who supported the deposed Bourbon monarchs, and on the left were the republicans, who advocated a form of democracy. Lacking political organization, however, the leaders of the Bonapartist faction threw in their lot with Louis-Philippe in the days following the Revolution of 1830, accepting positions in the new July Monarchy government and creating a *juste milieu* compromise coalition. The honeymoon was short-lived. By the winter of 1831, as it became increasingly clear that the July Monarchy government was a disappointment for the Bonapartists, offering stability

58. Hope for a Bonapartist restoration focused on Napoleon's descendants, especially his son, Napoleon II, otherwise known as the roi de Rome or the duc de Reichstadt, who was living in exile at the Austrian court. Following the young prince's death, the partisans of the Imperial family turned to Napoleon's nephew, Louis-Napoleon, who staged an unsuccessful coup in 1836 and then a successful one in 1851.

and security for the development of business, but not the kind of military glory or equality for the lower classes that had seemed possible in July, the Bonapartists shifted their allegiance away from the regime. Once again a party of opposition, they remained a threat to Louis Philippe throughout the rest of the July Monarchy.[59]

The Napoleon plays produced during the first months following the July Revolution reflected the alignment of the Bonapartist faction with the July Monarchy government. This first set of plays, produced from August to November, closely linked Napoleon with revolutionary ideals. In *La prise de la Bastille et le passage du Mont Saint-Bernard,* which opened at the Cirque-Olympique on August 31, 1830, the authors showed only an early battle from the Italian campaign against Austria, when Napoleon was still Bonaparte, a general fighting for the Republic, and joined it to a depiction of the storming of the Bastille. Napoleon's presence in this play was limited to a brief and silent appearance, late in the second act. In *Bonaparte, lieutenant d'artillerie, ou 1789 et 1800,* which premiered on October 9, 1830, at the Vaudeville, Napoleon disguises himself as a simple artillery officer to gauge public opinion, and attempts to reconcile the 18th Brumaire with the ideals of 1789. "After so many shocks and convulsions," Napoleon declares in the second act, "the Republic needs a rest: it will have it!"[60] The play implies that the Imperial interlude was a respite from the Revolution, offering the necessary release from Revolutionary intensity that will allow the work of Revolution to continue. In *Bonaparte à l'école de Brienne, ou le petit caporal, souvenir de 1783,* which opened on the same night at the Nouveautés, the future emperor is shown as a schoolboy, leading his fellow classmates in a snowball fight but also defending his teacher Morel (who turns out to be the father of Joséphine) when he is falsely accused of a crime. The future emperor is thus not only a warrior, but also a crusader for justice, a heroic defender of liberty, equality, and fraternity.

In these first plays, Bonaparte's actions are explicitly tied to the Revolution of 1789, and by extension to the Revolution of 1830, which appro-

---

59. As Marrinan explains, Louis-Philippe attempted to co-opt popular support for the Bonapartist legacy by appropriating Napoleon's image: "the July Monarchy attempted to tap this contemporary grassroots popularity by annexing the imagery of Napoleon and awarding him a prominent place in the iconography of official art," (*Painting Politics for Louis-Philippe,* 142). Commissioning paintings of Napoleon and his battles for the new museum of French history at Versailles and staging an elaborate spectacle for the return of Napoleon's remains in 1840, the government of Louis-Philippe attempted to claim the patriotic fervor that the image of the emperor commanded for its own, more banal form of bourgeois monarchy. Marrinan mentions the Napoleon plays of 1830–31 (145).

60. Xavier, Duvert, and St.-Laurent, *Bonaparte,* 45.

priated the terms of the prior revolution in its attempts to overthrow the Bourbon monarchs for a second time. The defense of egalitarianism, the hatred of oppression, the sense of justice that motivate Napoleon's battles in these plays all resonate with the ideals that the revolutionaries in 1830 borrowed from their fathers.[61] During the plays produced in the fall of 1830, identification with Napoleon intersects with the promotion of revolutionary identity in the present.

Over the winter, however, as the Bonapartists became dissatisfied with Louis Philippe, the content of the plays began to offer a different message. The Napoleon of these later, more elaborate spectacles was more inclusive, reaching out to viewers across the political spectrum by appealing to a series of emotions rather than to a specific set of political beliefs. Like the Bonapartist movement, which attracted opponents of the regime without proposing a concrete political platform, these plays sought to appeal to as broad a constituency as possible, proffering the image of Napoleon as a symbol of unity to a divided nation. In these plays, the image of the hero provides the basis for a national identity based not on politics but on patriotism.

These later plays, with titles that announce "Napoléon" rather than "Bonaparte," thus referring to the emperor rather than merely the general, proved less anxious to subordinate the Empire's glory to either the Revolution of 1789 or that of 1830. As the season progressed, the plays no longer focused on Revolutionary events but rather showed Napoleon as both military hero and suffering martyr. *Napoléon, Napoléon à Berlin, ou la redingote grise,* and *Napoléon, ou Schoenbrunn et Sainte-Hélène,* three more Boulevard productions that went up the same week in October, all depict later phases of Napoleon's career and represent his full military triumph. The two-act structure of *Napoléon, ou Schoenbrunn et Sainte-Hélène* contrasts Napoleon at the height of his glory following the Battle of Wagram in 1809 with his lonely death in exile in 1821. Lifted from Las Cases's *Mémorial de Sainte-Hélène,*[62] the scenes showing the great man's last hours portray him as a martyr at the hands of his British captors, a theme that was picked up by many of the later productions.

61. Other theaters at this time represented the Revolution of 1830 directly. The Vaudeville showed *27, 28, 29 juillet, tableau épisodique des trois journées* in August of 1830, and even the Théâtre français mounted a production of *Trois jours d'un grand peuple* in September.

62. The *Mémorial,* which combines the emperor's reminiscences, as dictated to the Count Émmanuel de Las Cases, with a description of his life in exile, was a big success when first published in 1823. By 1831, it had already gone through two editions and another was to follow in 1832. As I argue in Chapter 5, the *Mémorial* functions as a significant intertext in Stendhal's *Le rouge et le noir,* published in 1830, the same year as the Napoleon plays.

In these later plays, the figure of Napoleon ceases to promote identification with a specific set of political ideals, but rather comes to embody a transcendent image of national pride and suffering. These plays advance a much more diffuse sort of patriotism. Beginning in November, 1830, with the opening of *Quatorze ans de la vie de Napoléon, ou Berlin, Potsdam, Paris, Waterloo et Sainte-Hélène* at the Luxembourg, the theaters became more ambitious, staging not just Napoleon's victories, but his defeats as well. The Russian debacle and Waterloo now figured along with the early, victorious campaigns in Italy. *L'empereur,* staged at the Cirque-Olympique in December of 1830, contained five acts and eighteen sets *(tableaux),* ranging in time and place from the Rade de Toulon to the Battle of the Pyramids, from the entry into Madrid to the burning of Moscow and the disastrous crossing of the Beresina, from the coronation at Notre-Dame de Paris to the hero's martyred death. Dumas's *Napoléon* was not to be upstaged, however; it featured a startling twenty-three *tableaux*—each requiring an elaborate scenery change—and showed both victories and defeats. These later plays focused on the peripeties of Napoleon's biography, his dramatic rise and fall, but glossed over his affiliation—or lack thereof—with the Revolution, reflecting the way the Bonapartist political movement altered its own affiliations over the course of the July Revolution and its aftermath.

Both Jean Lucas-Dubreton and, more recently, Michael Marrinan have shown how the decade of the 1820s witnessed the formation of a Napoleonic cult in France.[63] The Restoration saw an outpouring of books and memoirs about Napoleon, most important, Las Cases's *Mémorial de Sainte-Hélène.* Another bestseller was Pierre-Jean Béranger's collection of songs extolling the emperor, which sold 11,000 copies in one week in 1821, the year of Napoleon's death.[64] As Marrinan explains, the contours of the Napoleonic myth became fixed in the public imagination not only by these written texts, but also by popular images, especially engravings. Focusing on his military victories, on his martyrdom at the hands of the British, these popular representations created an image of Napoleon that amounted to what Marrinan calls "a carefully groomed apologia."[65] Na-

---

63. In *La légende de Napoléon et les écrivains français du XIXe siècle* (Paris: Minard, 1967), Maurice Descotes describes the central role played by Napoleon in the works of major novelists from the period, including Stendhal, Hugo, and Balzac. On the cult of Napoleon in the nineteenth century, also see Jules Garsou, *Les créateurs de la légende napoléonienne* (Bruxelles: Hayez, 1899).

64. Marrinan, *Painting Politics for Louis-Philippe,* 142. On Béranger, see also Jules Garsou, *Béranger et la légende napoléonienne* (Bruxelles: P. Weissenbruch, 1897); Jean Lucas-Dubreton, *Béranger: La chanson, la politique, la société* (Paris: Hachette, 1934).

65. Marrinan, *Painting Politics for Louis-Philippe,* 144.

poleon's more nefarious political dealings, his lust for power and his willingness to sacrifice thousands to get it, were swept under the carpet in order to make the man an icon of national unity. It was this "carefully groomed" image, centered on military victories and martyrdom at the hands of the British, that the later Napoleon plays offered to a public disillusioned by the Revolution of 1830.

The depiction of Napoleon's illustrious battles encouraged audiences to unite in pride in his stunning victories. Indeed, many of the later plays offered little besides such military scenes. Dumas's play showed the battles of Toulon, Borodino, and Montereau, three of Napoleon's greatest military successes. Dumas's Napoleon repeatedly dismisses all danger, tossing off such memorable lines as "Don't worry, my children; the bullet that will kill me has not yet been forged."[66] Although a great many of the plays from the 1830–31 season invoked the battles that brought glory to France, no theater excelled at staging these victories like the Cirque-Olympique, which, thanks to its stable of trained horses, had made spectacular re-creations of battle scenes its specialty since the time of the Empire. In the production of *La République, l'Empire et les cent jours,* which premiered at the Cirque on October 13, 1832, and later traveled to the provinces, horses and all, the battles of Arcole and Marengo and the Passage of Mont Saint-Bernard were depicted. The play also showed the pacification of the Vendée and the meeting with the Russian emperor at Tilsitt, a scene depicted by one of Prévost's panoramas. In all these scenes, Napoleon's heroism takes center stage.[67] In this nearly silent pantomime (or *mimodrame* as these military re-creations were called), the re-creation of the battle allowed the audience to experience the thrill of victory. The play ends with an apotheosis scene, in which Napoleon is welcomed into heaven. Allegorical figures of victory lead the emperor toward immortality, where he joins his generals and eventually receives his son, the roi de Rome, at the "temple of glory."[68]

Similar apotheosis scenes appear in many other productions, but most elaborately in the Saint-Marcel theater's *Napoléon* of 1839, in which "heavenly spirits" appear with palm fronds and crowns "calling the hero

66. Alexandre Dumas *père, Napoléon Bonaparte, ou trente ans dans l'histoire de France* (1831; reprint, Paris: Calmann Lévy, 1894), 83.

67. This scene is typical: "Entrance of the generals.—Battle of Arcole.—After several charges, the French are pushed back; Bonaparte arrives, he sees hope for the army, but only on the other side of the bridge; addressing himself to the troops: Soldiers, he tells them, you are going to fight at Arcole, remember Lodi! He then takes up a flag and throws himself into the middle of the turmoil, followed by his soldiers who shout their rallying cry." Prosper [Auguste Le Poitevin de Saint-Alme], *La République, l'Empire et les 100 jours* (n.p., n.d.), 2.

68. Ibid., 11.

to his earthly resting place." As Napoleon is carried forward, "borne aloft on the clouds, surrounded by a shining light," a chorus sings: "Here, here is the immortal man / Here is our glorious sun! / Fall, fall doors of heaven, / Before the God of victory!"[69] As in a church, the audience unites together in worship, suppressing differences for the sake of communal adoration. In this *tableau*, Napoleon occupies the place of Christ, a theme that was elaborated in multiple ways in these productions.

In their depictions of victories and of the sanctification of the hero, these plays offered a vision of a united France to a public divided by politics in 1830. They also explicitly thematized reconciliation as a means of promoting unification. In 1830, the French were still recovering from the effects of a civil war. During the Revolution, thousands had lost their heads on the guillotine, as counterrevolutionary forces in the western province of the Vendée waged a guerrilla war and exiled nobles plotted to retake France with the help of invading foreign armies. Such political and ideological divisions were conveniently bridged in these dramas, which showed Napoleon forgiving his opponents—turning the other cheek as it were.

In Dumas's *Napoléon,* the future emperor grants a spy clemency, thus winning his undying devotion. The Porte Saint-Martin's production of *Napoléon, ou Schoenbrunn et Sainte-Hélène* had already depicted a similar (fictional) event two months before. In this play, Napoleon forgives a young German nationalist who attempts to assassinate him in Vienna at the end of the first act, which closes on a final *tableau* of the Austrian crowd cheering, "Vive l'Empereur!"[70] The Cirque's 1837 production of *Austerlitz* depicted a scene of Napoleon granting clemency to a would-be Italian assassin and was nearly suppressed by the July Monarchy censors, who were back on the alert following Fieschi's attempt to kill Louis Philippe (on the boulevard du Temple) in 1835. These plays staged a gesture of inclusion; they signaled to former opponents of the Empire—republicans and aristocrats alike—that despite their former opposition, all was now forgiven, that there was room for everyone in the temple devoted to Napoleon's memory.

Whereas depictions of patriotic fervor and forgiveness proved powerful weapons in the theatrical arsenal, perhaps the most effective means of promoting a new national identity lay in uniting against a common enemy. In

---

69. Théophile-Marion Dumersan and Antony Béraud, *Napoléon* (Paris: Dondey-Dupré, 1839?), 30.

70. In reality, the unrepentant would-be assassin was executed shortly after Napoleon left Vienna.

these plays, the villain's role fell to England, and particularly to Sir Hudson Lowe, the implacable officer dedicated to making Napoleon's life miserable in his final days of exile on Saint Helena. The second part of *Napoléon, ou Schoenbrunn et Sainte-Hélène* piles on the outrages against the emperor, most of which are taken directly out of Las Cases's *Mémorial*. Hudson Lowe forces him to live in a drafty house, to breathe bad air, and to pay for his own food. Lowe insults Napoleon repeatedly (he insists on calling him "General Bonaparte" instead of "Emperor"), attempts to confiscate his pens and paper to prevent him from writing his memoirs, and shoots one of his followers who has come to help him escape. At the end of the play, Napoleon's doctor Antomarchi tells the exiled emperor that he is dying not from cancer, but from captivity. Napoleon's only weapon of revenge is his memoir, which he vows will make future generations revile Hudson Lowe for his inhumanity—a self-fulfilling prophecy, given that the play, adapted largely from the *Mémorial de Sainte-Hélène*, enacts this very demonization. The death-scene *tableau* ends with Napoleon's loyal followers gathered around his corpse, pointing their fingers at Lowe, the author of their hero's destruction. Likewise, at the end of *L'empereur*, as Napoleon lies dying, his grand maréchal curses Hudson Lowe: "You made a study of how to wound Napoleon. . . . Shame on you, sir, shame on your government."[71] Small wonder, then, that the actor playing Lowe in Dumas's play, which reproduces many of the same elements (including the fictional shooting of the spy who comes to help Napoleon escape), was greeted by an angry mob at the stage door after the performance.

The ritualized reenactments of the clash between good and evil at the end of these plays are typical of the melodramatic form as it took shape in the period following the French Revolution.[72] Indeed, the last acts of the Napoleon plays can be read as mini-melodramas in which all the characteristics of the genre are present. Just as in traditional melodramas, the villain occupies a superior place in the social order (Lowe is the commander of the island), whereas the victim (Napoleon), who rightfully deserves to be elevated above the villain, occupies a lowly position. As in traditional melodramas, these plays end with the triumph of the victim over the villain, as Napoleon receives his due after death in an apotheosis *tableau*, such as the one at the end of *Napoléon, ou Schoenbrunn et Sainte-Hélène*.

71. Prosper, *L'empereur* (Paris: Barba, 1830), 53.

72. On the melodrama, see Peter Brooks, *The Melodramatic Imagination*, 2nd ed. (1976; reprint, New Haven: Yale University Press, 1995); Julia Przybos, *L'entreprise mélodramatique* (Paris: José Corti, 1987).

"The sky is dark, but the horizon clears, and we see, in the distance, like a promise of the future, the column of the place Vendôme, topped with a tricolor flag. A funeral carriage, bedecked with the national colors, is accompanied by the Parisian populace, who go to place the remains of the emperor on his immortal monument."[73] Forecasting what actually became reality only ten years later, in 1840, when Napoleon's body was exhumed from Saint Helena and brought to Les Invalides, this ending allows symbolic compensation for national suffering.

As Peter Brooks has argued, the Manichean terms of melodrama provided moral absolutes in a period that had surrendered the sacred foundations of God and king. Melodrama's stark oppositions between right and wrong, which Brooks terms the "logic of the excluded middle," allowed post-Revolutionary audiences to reaffirm moral truths in a post-sacred era.[74] The replacement of Christ by Napoleon, manifest in the representation of the emperor as suffering martyr, reflects the secularization of the sacred myth in these plays. Julia Przybos has described how the performance of melodrama serves a social function, promoting unity and fostering bonds of national cohesion in times of unrest: "The immense popularity of melodrama in anomic post-revolutionary France leads to the conclusion that individuals deprived of moral direction partake in the melodramatic ritual in order to achieve a sense of belonging to a community."[75] These theories help us to understand how the Napoleon plays use the melodramatic form to foster a sense of communal identity amid the political divisions of 1830; casting the Englishman Hudson Lowe as the villain and Napoleon as the victim, plays such as *Napoléon, ou Schoenbrunn et Sainte-Hélène, Napoleon Bonaparte,* and *L'empereur* encouraged the audience to unite in identification with Napoleon and to revile the foreign power that brought about his downfall and humiliation. By presenting the hero's eventual triumph over the foreign enemy, these plays encouraged audiences to enact a ritual of unification.

Le fils de l'homme

One of the most scandalous plays of the 1830–31 season, *Le fils de l'homme,* by Pillaud de Forges and Eugène Sue,[76] provides insights into the

---

73. Dupeuty et Régnier, *Napoléon, ou Schoenbrunn et Sainte-Hélène* (Paris: Barba, 1830), 83.

74. Brooks, *Melodramatic Imagination,* 15.

75. Julia Przybos, "Melodrama as a Social Ritual," *French Literature Series* 15 (1988): 93.

76. The published version of the play lists the author as Paul de Lussan, but a librarian's handwritten annotation states that this is a pseudonym for Pillaud de Forges and Eugène Sue.

way the plays themselves represented this process of historical identification. Sue, of course, went on to write the politically explosive *Les mystères
de Paris,* one of the best-selling books of the nineteenth century, and in
this earlier work he demonstrates the power of both texts and images to
capture the attention of a nation and its leaders. In its description of the effect of historical representation on the impressionable mind of Napoleon's
son, this play elaborates an optimal scenario for the reception of the entire
genre of Napoleon plays—indeed of all forms of spectacular history—by
French audiences in 1830. Sue's play allegorizes the process through which
spectacular images of the past helped promote a new identity for the
French nation.

Loosely based on an actual event, in which the patriotic poet Auguste
Barthélemy attempted to present a book about Napoleon to the emperor's
son, supposedly kept in ignorance of his father's glory by the imperial
court of Austria, *Le fils de l'homme* perpetuates a myth (promulgated by
Barthélemy himself in a poem also titled "Le fils de l'homme" from 1829)
that served Bonapartist political ambitions in the early years of the July
Monarchy.[77] During the Revolution of 1830, crowds had called for both
the deceased emperor and his exiled son (then age 19, and living with his
mother's family in Vienna). Indeed, hopes for a restoration of the roi de
Rome, a.k.a. the duc de Reichstadt or Napoleon II, as the boy was called,
did not fade until the boy's death from tuberculosis in 1832.[78] By falsely
portraying him as totally unaware of his origins[79] and hence of the history

---

Lecomte confirms this attribution (*Napoléon,* 302), as does Lucas-Dubreton (*Béranger,* 288).
Le fils de l'homme, souvenirs de 1824 (Paris: R. Riga, 1831).

77. In the poem "Le fils de l'homme" and in the historical notes published with it,
Barthélemy recounts how he was kept from seeing the duc de Reichstadt by the boy's tutor,
Dietrichstein, who reportedly told the poet that no foreigners and no foreign reading material were allowed into the boy's presence. Garsou, *Créateurs de la légende napoléonienne,*
38–50).

78. Bonapartists spoke of a "restoration" because the young duke had been officially (but
without effect) recognized as the emperor Napoléon II by the Chambre des Cent-Jours following Napoléon's second abdication on June 22, 1815. See "Napoléon II" in Michel
Mourre, *Dictionnaire d'histoire universelle* (Paris: Editions Universitaires, 1968), 1454.

79. Those in charge of the duke's education in Austria, under the direction of Metternich,
did in reality try to discourage the boy from dwelling on his father's glory, but their methods
were nowhere near so draconian or effective as those described in the play. Garsou, citing
Welschinger, declares that "Le duc de Reichstadt, on the contrary, received a brilliant education," (*Créateurs de la légende napoléonienne,* 40). Even critics in 1831 acknowledged that
this aspect of the play was pure fantasy: "It must be admitted [. . .] that the supposed ignorance, in which the son is kept, of his father's name and actions is an absurdity that demands
a certain gullibility [. . .]. The duc de Reichstadt, currently stationed at Brunn with his regiment, would doubtless laugh at his characterization on the Nouveautés's stage." Review of
Le fils de l'homme by Paul de Lussan, *Le cabinet de lecture,* January 4, 1831, 4.

of the preceding fifty years, the play thus provided a depiction less of the ignorance of the real Napoleon II than of the supposed historical amnesia of the French public following the Restoration's attempt to forget the past.

When the play was first produced at the Théâtre des Nouveautés on December 28, 1830, it touched a raw political nerve. Indeed, the play was so explosive that, as Krakovitch recounts, its initial production prompted the minister Montalivet to protest against the entire genre of Napoleon plays in the Chambre des Députés and to propose a new censorship law in 1831.[80] Subsequent requests to stage the play in 1836 and 1840 in Paris were denied by a ministerial decision, and a later revival in Boulogne-sur-mer was likewise forbidden because its message was considered too Bonapartist.[81] Although the play's scandal seemed to stem from its depiction of the threat of a Bonapartist pretender (even after Napoleon II was dead), its real threat lay in the power it ascribed to Napoleonic *representations*.

The action of the play takes place outside of Vienna, at one of the residences of the Austrian emperor, in 1824, three years after Napoleon's death. As the curtain rises, Werner, the conservator of the castle, nervously tells his daughter Mina that they are expecting a visit from the Duke of Reichstadt, Napoleon's son, and that she should give her tutor Georges the week off because the Duke must be prevented from encountering any strangers during his visit in order to keep him in ignorance of his origins. Georges arrives shortly after and promises Mina his love if she will agree to help him speak to the Duke. In an apostrophe, he reveals that he has been hiding his French nationality from Werner and Mina and that he has come to Vienna on a secret mission to bring the Duke a message from his departed father in the hope of one day restoring him to the French Imperial throne.

Mina agrees to hide him in a closet, where he overhears a discussion between the Abbé Zambini, the Duke's spiritual counselor, and Count Walterbruth, his tutor, about their efforts to keep the Duke in total ignorance of his true identity. "All that I was able to obtain," says the Count, "is the densest, most complete ignorance of history, and especially of contemporary history."[82] The Abbé, who is plotting to make the Duke into a priest, approves of the Count's efforts: "That's the most important thing: as for elevated and true ideas, it's easy to shape them" (14). The Duke, played by Virginie Déjazet (fresh from her triumph playing the boy's father in *Bona-*

80. Krakovitch, *Hugo censuré*, 119.
81. Ibid., 121.
82. De Lussan [De Forges; Sue], *Fils de l'homme*, 14. Subsequent quotations are cited in the text.

parte à l'école de Brienne at the same theater) then arrives and asks to be alone. A portrait of Romantic melancholy, the weak and consumptive young "boy" complains: "it seems to me that a veil is blocking my sight and hiding something from me that I don't understand . . . and as if my imagination wants to go farther, to penetrate these doubts, but then dissipates . . . and I find nothing . . . only an enormous void" (16).

The plight of the young Duke, wasting away with yearning for knowledge about his origins, can be read as a metaphor for the French nation searching for identity in the first decades of the nineteenth century. More specifically, it allegorizes the situation of the French theater-going public on the eve of the Revolution of 1830, deprived of any reference to Napoleon by the Restoration censors. Like the Restoration public, the Duke has gained a fleeting glimpse of the Man of Destiny in various publications that have slipped past his censors' watchful eyes—Georges managed to pass the Duke a volume of poetry he composed in honor of Napoleon one day while the Duke was out walking. Like the Restoration public, the Duke is aroused by this small taste of the Napoleonic legend. "Ah! this book," the Duke says, fondling the well-worn volume, "it's my most precious treasure! [. . .] what an interest Bonaparte holds for me. Bonaparte! . . . yet another word that awakens in me mysterious and vague notions" (17). The Restoration public had experienced a similar thrill from books and songs about the emperor during the 1820s, but still lacked the more concrete and "realistic" representation of the great man that only a spectacle could provide.

As the orchestra of the chateau strikes up the military tune "Victory Is ours!," that Georges has arranged for them to play, the Duke's heart starts to beat: "Yes, I've heard that tune somewhere before . . . long ago, and then, it reminds me of lavish festivals, of bright uniforms, of songs of victory . . . Yes, but where? at what time of my life? . . . Oh! who will dissipate these shadows that surround me?" [17] Once again, the Duke stands as an allegory for the French nation during the Restoration, able to recall only dimly the glorious events of the past. On cue, Georges emerges from his hiding place, reveals to the Duke the secret of his origins in the form of a brief history lesson summarizing Napoleon's rise and fall, and presents the Duke with a lock of the emperor's hair and a portrait. Just as the audiences of the Napoleon plays in 1830 were confronted not only with a historical narrative, but also with spectacular representations and simulacra of relics (the coat and the hat), all set to patriotic music, the Duke is presented with a spectacular form of the past. His reaction typifies how French audiences in 1830 were supposed to react to the Napoleon plays: in a burst of emotion, he recovers his memory and sense of self through the sight of this spectacle. Like the veterans who flocked to the various Napoleon plays to admire the resemblance between the actor and their hero, the Duke looks at the portrait and exclaims, "Oh! my father! . . . my father! . . . that forehead, those eyes . . . yes, they are his!. . . . Ah! I understand now . . . my memories are explained" (21). The visual realism of the historical representation thus serves as the catalyst for unlocking the mysteries of identity.

Restored to his past and thus to himself, the Duke gains the where-withal to challenge the authority of his jailors. Here his awakened self-determination figures the July Revolution's overthrow of the Restoration regime (represented by the Abbé and Count, church and aristocracy), whose attempt to obliterate the past is shown, through the allegory, to have been responsible for the weakness and melancholy of the French public. Once again, the Duke's challenge can be read not only as a symbol for the post-Revolutionary French quest for a new national image based on historical identification, but also as a specific allegory for the role of the theater in fostering such a project. Indeed, the terms of the Duke's reproaches to his "censors" bring to mind the Romantic rejection of the Classical theatrical model in their quest for a new *drame national*. Like Stendhal, he calls for a shift from Racine to Shakespeare:

> THE DUKE: Yes, a moment ago . . . I was dreaming of some historical points that didn't seem to me sufficiently explained.
>
> THE COUNT: Those must be points of ancient history . . . Greeks . . . Trojans.
>
> THE DUKE: No, it's modern history! *(The Count draws back.)* It's French history! *(The Count draws back again.)*
>
> (21–22)

Like the public described by Stendhal, the Duke thirsts for representations of his national history. He continues to challenge the Abbé and the Count to fill in the gaps in their version of history and increasingly puts them on the defensive as he reveals the full extent of his recently acquired knowledge by repeating the narrative of Napoleon's rise and fall recounted to him by Georges. "Sorry, my lord . . ." stammers the Abbé, "I must have been mistaken . . . there are so many different versions, I . . . but . . ." (22). The climax of the play comes when the Duke finally reveals that he is aware of his true identity as Napoleon's son. "All is lost!" whispers the Count, as the newly self-possessed heir to the imperial throne shows them "those unimpeachable proofs," the hair and the portrait, along with

Georges, who once again emerges from his hiding place to claim the Duke as France's long-awaited savior.

In the immediate aftermath of the July Revolution, when Bonapartism was still a viable political option and threat, this representation of the revivifying effects of national memory had dangerous political overtones that the authors of the play sagely sought to attenuate.[83] The play ends with a reversal, in which the young Duke renounces his dynastic ambitions, much as the Bonapartists would throw in their lot with the Orleanists after the July Revolution. As organ music plays in the background, Napoleon's son tells the stupefied Abbé and Count and the disappointed Georges that, like his father, "who would rather renounce the throne than ignite a civil war" (24), he will remain in exile and retires to the chapel to pray for his father as the curtain falls. Even though it stops short of realizing the full political potential of its Bonapartist message, this play shows how visual representations of Napoleon can serve as the basis for the restoration of the nation's spirit and the ground for the formation of a new identity in the aftermath of Revolutionary change. *Le fils de l'homme* shows how the Napoleon plays were supposed to function.

A New Waterloo?

Whereas *Le fils de l'homme* allegorizes the ideal effect of the Napoleon plays, revealing how images of the recent past can provide an identity to the post-Revolutionary generation, certain contemporary observers provide a quite different account of the effects of these spectacles on the French public of 1830. Indeed, to critics from across the political spectrum, the staging of the Napoleonic legend proved more alarming than edifying. In what follows, I examine the outpouring of criticism of the Napoleon plays in the popular press in order not only to gain insight into the scandal they created, but also to understand more generally the stakes of the spectacular past for the nineteenth-century French public. As the constant references to other forms of spectacle such as the wax display, phantasmagoria, and the panorama in these reviews attest, observers in the nineteenth century saw the Napoleon plays as linked to a larger cultural phenomenon, as part of a mode of historical representation that went beyond the walls of the theater. These reviews offer a critique of the entire project of spectacularizing the past, as well as a context for reading the

83. In 1829, Barthélemy was accused by the king's lawyer, Menjaud de Dammartin, of having produced the most "manifestly dangerous" work of the Restoration. Despite a vigorous defense, Barthélemy was condemned to three months in prison and a 1,000-franc fine. The work was ordered destroyed. Garsou, *Créateurs de la légende napoléonienne*, 50.

early Realist novels of Balzac and Stendhal that emerge at the same historical moment.

"Napoleon is a historical figure; there is no danger in presenting him for the public to see," reassured *Le Corsaire* in a review of Dumas's *Napoléon*. But to many critics, the two parts of this sentence stood in contradiction not conjunction; the visual representation of a historical figure such as Napoleon, offered nightly to the eyes of the public on stages all across Paris, raised a very real set of dangers that differed depending on the political positions of the viewer. Attempting to allay these fears, *Le Corsaire*'s words of comfort perceptively (though no doubt inadvertently) pointed to the heart of the matter, underlining the complicity between the Napoleon plays and the other forms of popular entertainment that were turning the past into a spectacle—"at the theater," the reviewer continued, Napoleon "is only one of Curtius's characters."[84]

Although some audiences might take pleasure in Curtius's display, for critics on the far right of the political spectrum, the so-called legitimist defenders of the Restoration monarchy, who were either aristocrats or their allies, the sight of the wax replicas of Revolutionary figures in Curtius's display were anything but reassuring. Although inanimate and immobile, these realistic representations brought to life very active fears of a return to the bad old days of the Revolution. Similarly, legitimists fantasized that the realistic representation of the Revolutionary period, and also of the Empire, on Parisian stages would reawaken dangerous impulses in the French public. In a review devoted to the first round of Napoleon plays in October of 1830 (*Napoléon à Berlin, Napoléon,* etc.), the anonymous critic for the legitimist daily *Gazette de France* attempted to interpret the dangerous political ramifications of the new genre of historical spectacles. "But what cannot be the object of any interpretation," the critic writes, "are the cries of *Long Live the Emperor!* that rang out in the hall when the Napoleon made his appearance, amid unanimous bravos."[85] The public's enthusiasm for the representation of the past aroused very real fears in the present: "To whom were these transports addressed?" the critic asks; and "were they memories or hopes?" Memory, it seems, had a way of ac-

---

84. "Théâtre royal de l'Odéon," review of *Napoléon Bonaparte* by Alexandre Dumas, *Le Corsaire,* January 14, 1831, 2. Only the representation of living persons on stage was still forbidden by law.

85. "Théâtres," review of *Napoléon à Berlin,* by Dumersan, and *Napoléon* by Régnier and Dupeuty, *Gazette de France,* October 23, 1830, 2. The *Gazette de France* was the leading newspaper of the legitimist right in the period. In 1831, it printed 12,400 copies. The major Parisian dailies together printed 61,000 copies of their papers in 1830 (this number rose to 81,493 by March of 1831). Claude Bellanger et al., eds., *Histoire générale de la presse française,* vol. 2 (Paris: Presses Universitaires de France, 1969), 100.

tualizing itself when evoked with a new type of realism in crowded public places.

As these threatening spectacles devoted to the great man continued to multiply across the stages of Paris, the *Gazette* prepared for battle and Dumas's play drew the heaviest fire. The right-wing newspaper's critics linked the horror of this play to the scandal of Romanticism itself. For these critics, Dumas's production merely exaggerated the corruptions of language and taste, the insult to traditional religious and political beliefs, that such Romantic dramas as *Hernani, Christine* and *Henri VII* had already effected in their depictions of bad or perverse monarchs and in their abandonment of the Classical style: "The *Napoléon* that we have been awaiting at the Odéon has finally arrived [. . .]. It's the strangest dramatic jumble that could ever emerge from the deranged brain of someone called a poet."[86] Dumas's *Napoléon* serves as a logical target for legitimist fury because of the author's Romantic pedigree, which helps the critic establish the connection between the Napoleon plays and the Romantic revolution.

"I'm sick of two things," the critic for the *Gazette* begins one review; "one is to have always to discuss the minor theaters; the other is so often to have to talk about Napoleon. Whose fault is that?"[87] Despite his great antipathy to the melodrama of the Boulevard, and his even greater antipathy to productions at the *grands théâtres* that pandered to the public by imitating the form and content of the Boulevard productions (Dumas's *Napoléon* at the Odéon being the prime example), the conservative critic nevertheless continued to discuss these plays repeatedly, if only to denounce them. Indeed, like Napoleon himself battling against the allies, he sees it as his duty to wage war on every front: "Since there are spectacles, and since they put on what passes for new plays, it is unfortunately the case, since the theater both echoes and propagates the most dangerous sort of ideas, that it must be opposed whenever the occasion presents itself."[88] His logic reveals the extent to which reactionary factions after 1830 saw the theater as capable not only of reflecting dangerous ideas, but of generating them. Like the censors, the critic seems to believe in the power of representation to lead to action: "It might very well be possible that the end result of the melodrama of popular riots will be to have us at-

86. "Théâtre de l'Odéon," review of *Napoléon Bonaparte* by Dumas, *Gazette de France,* January 14, 1831, 1.

87. "Théâtres," review of *Napoléon Bonaparte,* by Dumas, *Gazette de France,* January 24, 1831, 1.

88. "Théâtre de l'Odéon," review of *Médicis et Machiavel* by Jean-Baptiste Pellissier, *Gazette de France,* April 15, 1831, 2.

tacked even sooner by the people."[89] For reactionary critics, these plays were feared not so much as reenactments of the Revolution, but as rehearsals for the revolution yet to come.

For left-leaning critics during the July Monarchy, those who adhered to the tenets of the Revolution and advocated a republican form of government, however, the Napoleon plays generated a different kind of scandal. In their reviews of the first batch of plays, between October and December of 1830, which sought to ally the image of Napoleon with republican ideals, the critics for *Le National* offered only positive commentary.[90] One such critic rejoices in the new political liberty that allowed theaters to perform the formerly repressed subject matter of history: "For a long time," writes "A.R.," "theaters were forbidden to reproduce the great deeds and glorious life of the man whom reserve prevents us from naming, the greatest captain of modern times [. . .]. But they couldn't erase his memory by erasing his name."[91] Praising both the historical accuracy and the realism of the production, the left-leaning critic describes how *Napoléon, ou Schoenbrunn et Sainte-Hélène* at the Porte-Sainte-Martin presents its subject "with both taste and truth," and how the actor playing Napoleon (Gobert) "produced a great deal of illusion."[92] Another of *Le National*'s critics ("E.") waxes equally enthusiastic about the Cirque's production of *L'empereur*: "We merely want to attest to the success of the play [. . .] when such a fiction is as exact and as great as it could be, second only to reality itself, what else could you want, for heaven's sake?"[93] At the start of the theatrical season, when the plays echoed their own beliefs, these republican critics seem to believe in the virtues of the historical spectacle. A month later, however, they find much cause for complaint indeed.

Dumas's *Napoléon* was once again the proverbial straw that broke the camel's back, provoking a torrent of hostility toward the whole project of

89. "Théâtre de la Gaîté," review of *Favras, episode de 1789* by Merville [Pierre-François Camus] and Thomas Sauvage, *Gazette de France,* May 23, 1831, 1.
90. *Le National* was founded by Adolphe Thiers, Auguste Mignet, and Armand Carrel to oppose the Restoration government (the founders felt *Le Constitutionnel* had become too tame) and first appeared on January 3, 1830. During the July Revolution, the Restoration government seized its presses (on July 26, 1830). As the new regime of Louis-Philippe came to prove a disappointment to most on the left, *Le National* retained its opposition status. Roger Chartier and Henri-Jean Martin, eds., *Histoire de l'édition française* (Paris: Promodis, 1990), 174. One of the leading newspapers on the left, *Le National* printed 3,280 copies in 1831. Bellanger, *Histoire générale de la presse française,* 100.
91. A. R., "Théâtre de la Porte Saint-Martin," 1.
92. Ibid., 2.
93. E., "Théâtre du Cirque-Olympique," review of *L'empereur* by Prosper, *Le National,* December 13, 1830, 3.

staging the Empire that the critic "E." had so recently enthusiastically supported: "All of our theaters, all of our authors, major and minor [. . .] share an astonishing unanimity of affection for the *Mémorial de Sainte-Hélène,* a monotony of imperialism, if I may say so, that provides the public with the sole pleasure of watching Napoleon Bonaparte on his death bed at Saint Helena, dying three or four times a night, all week long, at three or four theaters at once."[94]

As in the *Gazette's* reviews, Dumas became the lightning rod for attacks on the phenomenon of the Napoleon plays in part because of his association with the Romantic movement. For *Le National's* critic ("E."), the Napoleon plays represented the most extreme form of the Romantic tendency to distort the past by presenting it realistically. In a review of Hugo's *Marion de Lorme,* which opened at the Porte Saint-Martin in August of 1831, the critic denounces the innovations that the Romantic dramatists had copied from the Boulevard productions (the historically accurate and detailed sets and costumes) that serve only to obscure history's true lessons. "Instead of the man's heart," the critic complains, "you show his breeches and his doublet." Such a visual treatment of history, the epitome of the spectacular mode of historical representation, amounts in the republican critic's eyes to fraud. "For a short while the public believed in your advertisements; but is there not also a public that believes in hair-growth tonic?"[95] the critic asks. Despite Hugo's attempt to ally Romanticism with liberal politics in the preface to *Hernani,* and despite the efforts of the early Napoleon plays to embody democratic ideals, the critic for *Le National* denounces the new form of historical theatrical vision as a betrayal of the Revolution.

For the left-leaning critic, the problem with the Napoleon plays, and with Dumas's play in particular, was the way these productions emptied the past of its revolutionary political content, reducing history to a mere image. His critique contrasted the superficiality of the existing plays with his fantasy of a play that would serve a progressive political function. Instead of showing Napoleon throwing snowballs with his school chums, prancing around with his hand in his vest, and dying a victim on Saint Helena, scenes that struck a chord with the public because paintings and engravings had made such images recognizable, a good historical drama should analyze the reasons for his rise and fall, reasons that went to the

---

94. E., "Théâtre de l'Odéon," review of *Napoléon Bonaparte* by Dumas, *Le National,* January 14, 1831, 1.

95. E., "Théâtre de la Porte Saint-Martin," review of *Marion de Lorme* by Hugo, *Le National,* August 15, 1831, 1.

heart of the social and political upheavals of the prior half century: "A Napoleon drama should embody the message [. . .] that a power born of liberty that does not base itself on liberty will always be precarious and about to fall."[96] For this critic, the real story of Napoleon—a story that the plays of the 1830–31 season neglected in favor of their spectacular *tableaux*—would depict how his ultimate downfall resulted from his betrayal of the ideals of the Revolution.

According to the republican critic, the lesson of the Empire, a lesson Napoleon learned only too late, was that "liberty should be the ultimate consequence of Napoleon's despotic will, the final ending to his conquests and enslavement of Europe." The representation of such a version of history would marshal the emotional energy aroused in the crowd by Napoleon's image for the cause of political progress: "To show Napoleon in this manner, at once great and guilty, would be true not only to the exigencies of the past, but also to the needs of the present; it would be a welcome counterweight to the authority that representations of a great man's memory hold over the crowd, which gets enflamed so quickly" (2). For the left-leaning critic, the Napoleon plays risked wasting revolutionary energy on useless nostalgia.

Le National blamed this corruption of Revolutionary history on the marketplace and on the greed of the theatrical producers who plundered the nation's annals to boost ticket sales. The critic saw through the producers' public relations smokescreens, deploring the degradation of Revolutionary principles that resulted from this exploitation of Napoleonic history:

> I won't even discuss those grotesque painters who show him preaching liberty
> and equality while wearing a lieutenant's uniform, set to music-hall tunes, or
> that turn him into a character in a comic opera, or that make him come on only
> at the end, to carry off a theatrical triumph in his bicorne hat, and make a mint
> with his riding boots, his frock coat, and his way of taking tobacco. (1)

The advertisements that the Odéon's producer placed in such journals as *La Revue de Paris* boasting of his expenditures to ensure the realism of his production provoked *Le National*'s critic to a righteous fury. Denouncing "the typical means used today to promote the commodification of the theater" in his review of Dumas's play, the critic lashes out at the commercialization of history: "Everything in this production can be reduced to a balance sheet and a bottom line. Authors and directors speculate on the rise that the month of July gave to the name of Napoleon, like

96. E., "Théâtre de l'Odéon," review of *Napoléon Bonaparte*, 1. Subsequent quotations are cited in the text.

a colonial merchant speculates on the price of sugar or coffee" (1). Such crass commercialism results in a leveling of the past, an emptying of the content of history, especially the political content, for the sake of pleasing the largest possible public. Who can doubt, the critic asks, that the unscrupulous directors and writers would be just as willing to depict the exile of Charles X at Holyrood as the exile of Napoleon at Saint Helena, if they thought the Bourbons would draw big crowds?

In his attack on Dumas's play, and on the other biographical dramas of 1830–31 that indiscriminately travesty Napoleon along with Charlotte Corday, Camille Desmoulins, and the comte de Mirabeau, the critic for *Le National* sketches an early nineteenth-century critique of the historical spectacle. His denunciation of the commodification of the past explicitly aligns the new historical theater with other familiar spectacles of history; "in general the whole thing can be reduced," he writes of the Napoleon plays, "to a long and scathing phantasmagoria; an astonishing spectacle, intended especially for the ears and for the eyes" (1). Like the phantasmagoria show, these plays aimed to portray the life of a historical figure and, with it, the age in which he or she lived, but actually reduced the past into a series of disconnected images. "Moreover, nothing could be less complete than these supposedly complete representations where they evoke a legendary period with a famous name, as if making a caricature," writes the critic of the Odéon's 1831 production of *Mirabeau,* another play that sought to depict history realistically by dividing it into a series of *tableaux.* "The biography of Mirabeau in six periods was treated almost exactly as Mr. Dumas treated the biography of Napoleon just a short time ago, in six acts and twenty-four *tableaux.*"[97]

Le National's reviews anticipate the analysis that Debord offered in *The Society of the Spectacle* of the social disintegration and individual alienation characteristic of a society dominated by images. "Images detached from every aspect of life flow together in a common stream in which the unity of life can no longer be reestablished," writes Debord. "Reality considered partially unfolds in its own general unity as a pseudo-world apart, solely as an object of contemplation."[98] Once separated for the sake of contemplation, the *tableaux* used to paint the life of Napoleon or Mirabeau seemed to the republican critic no longer to resemble the object they were supposed to represent. As the critic puts it: "next to the enormity of the actual lives, these biographies, thirty feet wide by fifteen long,

97. E., "Théâtre de l'Odéon," review of *Mirabeau* by M., *Le National,* November 6, 1831, 1.
98. Guy Debord, *La société du spectacle* (Paris: Gallimard, 1992), 15.

seem incredibly small, paltry, and false."[99] For the republican reviewer, these spectacular images deprive history not only of its dignity, but of its very humanity. One month after *Mirabeau,* the critic for *Le National* declared that this new type of theater had finally found its proper subject. In his review of the Cirque's production of *La vie d'un cheval* [The life of a horse] he writes: "Here is the biographical drama banished to the stable, which is where it belongs. It started with Napoleon, passed through Mirabeau, in order to arrive finally at one of Mr. Franconi's horses." Before we know it, he predicted, "the ass will have its drama."[100]

A somewhat different critique of the spectacular past emerges in the reviews of the *Journal des Débats.* A center-right publication during the 1830s, with strong ties to the July Monarchy government, this daily newspaper showed from the start a marked hostility to the phenomenon of the Napoleon plays. "Here is yet another Napoleon," writes a highly cynical critic in a review of the Cirque's *L'empereur,* "but I fear that Mr. Franconi's emperor mounted his horse a bit too late. His gray frock coat elicited only a moderate amount of enthusiasm; his bicorne hat caused only a dozen or so sensitive hearts to weep."[101] Mocking the costume devices employed to produce the image of Napoleon, the critic fails to be duped by the actor's impersonation: "when we saw a fat old man with burly shoulders and a banker's stomach arrive on stage, everyone winced" (2). Whereas *Le National* praised the exactitude of this production, the *Journal des Débats*'s cutting jab at the actor's girth deflates the theatrical illusion and, indeed, the entire project of the realistic staging of history: "Everyone knows, of course, that if [Napoleon] was the most ambitious thin man who ever lived, he was also the thinnest ambitious man; but since we also know that he expanded along with his empire, the illusion re-established itself bit by bit, and when he died on Saint Helena, he was just as presentable a Napoleon as any of the others" (2). Even while surrendering to the illusion, the critic subverts it, for a Napoleon "as presentable as any of the others" cannot be the man himself. The reference to the proliferation of Napoleons across the stages of Paris signals a refusal to accept the identity of this particular incarnation, on which the success of the historical representation depends.

Acknowledging the power of the spectacular staging of the past to move the audience in spite of its inevitable flaws ("And what to say about the

---

99. E., "Théâtre de l'Odéon," review of *Mirabeau,* 1.

100. "Cirque-Olympique," review of *La vie d'un cheval, Le National,* December 5, 1831, 3.

101. R., "Cirque-Olympique," review of *L'empereur,* by Prosper, *Journal des Débats,* December 9, 1830, 1. Subsequent quotations are cited in the text.

Crossing of the Beresina, except that such a spectacle is horrendous, even at the Cirque?" [2]), the critic ultimately finds the spectacle cold, unable to bring the past to life: "By showing you my magic lantern, I fear that, just as in some fable, I forgot one thing: to light the candle."[102] He concludes, "And here the candle is indispensable; all is spectacle, point-of-view, optics" (2). In other words, he implies, the spectacle attempts to show so much that the viewer sees nothing at all.

The critic's reference to a failed magic lantern links the Napoleon plays to the phantasmagoria show, as well as to the other forms of visual representation used by popular entertainments to depict the recent past. A later review pursues the analogy to contemporary forms of spectacle. "Have you ever gone to visit Curtius, or to one of his rivals?" the critic ("R") asks at the beginning of a review of *Benjamin Constant aux Champs-Elysées,* one of the biographical dramas of the 1830–31 season that shared the stage with the Napoleon plays. Here the wax display provides the model for the spectacular re-creation of the past and the deception that results from it: "When they pompously announce that behind this curtain you are going to see the great Frederick, the great Napoleon, or the great Voltaire, don't you feel a kind of respectful curiosity? But when they show you the great man decked out in dusty old rags, with a dazed look, his eyes frozen, his arms stiff, don't you feel a kind of mocking pity? That's exactly the effect that the new play at the Ambigu-Comique produced on me."[103] The viewer's disappointment when confronted with the spectacle lies in the discrepancy between the promise and the execution. The critic at once acknowledges the desire to see what lies behind the curtain, to see the past brought to life, and blames the representation for not living up to its inflated publicity, like the fat Napoleon at the Cirque. The critic pokes fun at the whole sorry spectacle, but behind his mirth lies a very serious critique of the dangers that proceed from such a deception—the result of these shabby imitations of the past is the viewer's shift in affect from "a respectful curiosity" to a "mocking pity" with regard to the nation's history. These spectacles, the critic suggests, undermine the very identity, the very cohesion, they purport to foster.

Unsurprisingly, Dumas's *Napoléon* drew the harshest criticism on this score, perhaps because the rhetoric surrounding it, Harel's advertising

---

102. The candle provided the light source that enabled the magic lantern to project images.

103. R., "Théâtre de l'Ambigu-Comique," review of *Benjamin Constant aux Champs-Elysées, Journal des Débats,* January 10, 1831, 1

campaign, had been the most inflated and the most misleading. Dumas was accused of showing contempt for the audience, for history, and for the theater itself: "Another bit of the author's scorn, this one aimed specifically at the principle and secrets of the dramatic art, consists in having attempted to stage events that are impossible to imitate materially in a theater which is forty feet square." To reproduce the attack on Toulon on a tiny stage, to offer a replica of the ship that brought Napoleon back from Elba made from cardboard, to re-create the mind-boggling spectacle of the Beresina with ten actors, for this critic, is to toy with history, to turn the past into a game, a mere plaything: "This shows, we must say, a kind of childlike confidence in the way it plays on the good faith of the spectators and trifles with their ignorant credulity." Dumas and the other authors and producers of Napoleon plays, who are no less guilty in the critic's eyes, make a mockery of the past: "These imperfect and terrible copies of an inimitable reality degenerate into actual parodies."[104] For the critic, this spectacle stages not the "terrible reality" of the past, but its decline into a shabby and derisory imitation.

The *Journal des Débats*'s legendary theater critic Jules Janin rarely wasted an opportunity to rail against the Napoleon plays and their parodying of the past in terms that remained remarkably consistent throughout his long career.[105] Reviewing a play from 1832 that treated the recent death of Napoleon's son, Janin complains of the theater's trivializing of a legend: "Poor great man! Poor unhappy child! Who would have thought that so much glory would end up there, and that the name of Bonaparte would be stuck on a theatrical poster?"[106] "Nothing but the Empire!" he writes in an 1845 review of yet another of the Cirque's imperial spectacles. "When at last will they leave him be, that poor emperor who has become the plaything of our shabby age?" In the 1845 attack on the Cirque, Janin makes the parallel with the various contemporary spectacles of history explicit, denouncing the way the "historical pattern cutters, hasty garbage collectors, insipid wordsmiths, furious declaimers, incompetent innovators" had not even waited for the emperor to die "before studying him

104. C. "Théâtre de l'Odéon," review of *Napoléon Bonaparte* by Dumas, *Journal des Débats,* January 13, 1831, 1.

105. In his memoirs recounting his twenty-five years as a theater critic, Jules Janin devotes a section to the phenomenon of *Les Bonaparte* of 1830, but without the same depth of reflection as the reviews at the time. *Histoire de la littérature dramatique* (Paris: Michel Lévy, 1855), 61.

106. Jules Janin, "Théâtre du Panthéon," review of *La Mort du Roi de Rome* by D'Ornoy [Alexandre Basset] *Journal des Débats,* September 3, 1832, 3.

against the floating walls of a magic lantern or all dolled-up in Curtius's style."[107] Like the reviewers for other papers, Janin used the wax display and the phantasmagoria show as convenient metaphors for denouncing the transformation of the recent past into tawdry entertainment.

Janin also sought out other, more visceral images to criticize the theater's commodification of history. In one review, he compares the French theater to a prodigal son "who squanders his father's fortune that he hasn't taken the trouble to earn,"[108] and in another he likens the creators of Napoleon plays to wild beasts attacking their prey: "We threw ourselves upon this history like wild dogs set upon the cadaver of a noble horse [...] each of us devoured him whole, the great man; each served him up whole in his drama."[109] According to Janin, the Napoleonic legend had been swallowed by the greedy writers and producers, ever hungry for new subject matter to pack in the crowds.

This glorious history, which could have supplied the material for a thousand years of epic poetry, like the house of Agamemnon, Janin writes, has now been travestied: "That whole unique and formidable historical period, that epoch that served humanity as a new starting point, that first dawn of a new creation [...] they laid their hands on all that [...] they blew on all that, and all that disappeared like straw blown by the wind, and all that is dead, and all that served to make an opening night, and nothing more."[110] The tragedy of these melodramas, according to Janin, is the loss of the past itself, which has forever been tainted by cheap and vulgar imitation: "A man falls!—Get your tickets at the box office, gentlemen, and for your money see the fallen hero."[111]

The result of the theatrical attempt to bring Napoleon back to life, Janin implies, was not to make the past more real but rather to make it less so: the spectacularization of the past ends in its destruction. Indeed, for Janin, the constant representation of Napoleon on the stages of Paris succeeded in substituting the counterfeit for the real. Describing the festivities surrounding the return of the emperor's remains to France in 1840, Janin comments on how the public reacted as if it were watching a play: "his coffin became a spectacle, and the crowd clapped its hands in the streets of

107. Jules Janin, "Théâtre du Cirque-Olympique," review of *L'Empire* by Laloue and Labrousse, *Journal des Débats,* February 17, 1845, 1.

108. Jules Janin, "Théâtre du Palais-Royal," review of *Le Camarade de lit* by Émile Vander Burch and Ferdinand Langlé, *Journal des Débats,* May 13, 1833.

109. Janin, "Théâtre du Panthéon," review of *La Mort du Roi de Rome,* September 3, 1832, 3.

110. Janin, "Théâtre du Palais-Royal," review of *Le Camarade de lit,* May 13, 1833, 2.

111. Janin, "Théâtre du Panthéon," review of *La Mort du Roi de Rome* September 3, 1832, 3.

Paris, as if it were attending some free performance at the Cirque-Olympique."[112] The spectacle had come to seem more real than reality itself. For Janin, the victim is not Napoleon or his memory, or even the poets of the future who will be unable to write epics because their sources will have been squandered. The real victim is the French nation, which is no longer capable of epic glory because it has betrayed its past: "In truth, for a people that drags onto every stage the names of its greatest men who are barely expired [. . .] alas! no glory is possible, no name is lasting, no tomb is respected."[113] Degraded by the hasty consumption of its history, the theatrical public forecloses on its future by spending its past. Such is their privilege; he concludes, "Shouldn't we leave that likeable nation free to gorge itself upon the emptiness and savor the trifles?"[114] The danger of the historical spectacle, for Janin, went beyond politics, beyond the fear or desire for another revolution, and straight to the center of post-Revolutionary French identity, built on historical identification, whose foundations turned out to be hollow.

The Napoleon plays crystallized a set of fears for critics in the 1830s. For Legitimists, these fears were largely political. Like the censors of the Restoration, reactionaries saw in the theatrical evocation of the Empire the threat of another and even more violent revolution. For republican and *juste-milieu* critics, however, the fears took on a more existential cast, touching on the very mechanisms of post-Revolutionary subjectivity. History itself, for these critics, became the defeated enemy in the spectacular re-creations of Napoleonic battles; unable really to make the past come to life, the highly wrought simulacra of these productions ultimately turned history into an object of parody or pity. The more realistic the sets and costumes, the greater the hype surrounding the effort at illusionistic representation, the more harshly did these critics condemn their failure. They saw the threat lying in the use that the public made of this degraded past: encouraged by the plays to identify with the figure of Napoleon, who seemed to reflect an image of a united and glorious France, audiences build their identity on shaky ground. Because the image that emerged from these plays, according to critics, was ultimately little more than a smokescreen, as insubstantial as bits of straw blown by the wind, to invoke Janin's memorable phrase, precisely because it offered nothing beyond an image. Spectacles that turned history into a series of *tableaux*,

112. Janin, "Théâtre du Cirque-Olympique," review of *L'Empire*, February 17, 1845, 1.

113. Janin, "Théâtre du Panthéon," review of *La Mort du Roi de Rome* September 3, 1832, 3.

114. Janin, "Théâtre du Cirque-Olympique," review of *L'Empire*, February 17, 1845, 1.

that substituted surface for depth, seemed to dazzle spectators with the illusion of a meaningful past, but, according to this critique, ended by duping their audiences with the tawdriness of a mere commodity.

As many of the critics made clear, this critique extended to the Romantic drama as a whole, marked by the desire to re-create the national past with what Stendhal called a "perfect illusion." The Napoleon plays brought the tendencies of the Romantic *drame national* to its logical conclusion, laying bare its assumptions and pointing up its limitations. The critical responses to these plays, lost to generations of theatrical historians along with the plays themselves, represent, moreover, a vital episode in the reception of Romanticism. Formulated at the very moment that Balzac and Stendhal were forging a new kind of novel that rejected Romantic historical assumptions, the critical response to the Napoleon plays reveals how the scandal that surrounded Romanticism had as much to do with politics, and specifically the politics of historical identification, as with poetics. Or rather it shows how the two are inextricably linked.

Chapter Four

Scott Comes to France

On November 1, 1826, readers of the *Journal de Paris* learned that fifteen ships had entered the port of Calais carrying 379 passengers "among whom could be seen the famous Sir Walter Scott making his way to Paris." The object of scrutiny from the moment he stepped off the boat, Scott remained in the public eye for his entire two-week stay in the French capital. Articles in the press commented on how little the historical novelist resembled his published portraits, while crowds of fans struggled to get a glimpse of the famous Scotsman for themselves.[1] Although the author who had published his first novels anonymously in order to keep his identity a secret pretended to shun the attention—Scott complained of his hordes of French admirers[2]—the degree of his displeasure caused some doubt in observers at the time. One account of his visit suggested that he disguised himself so well "that at the theater or while out walking, everyone recognizes and follows him."[3] But if Scott attracted all eyes, so too did his works; thanks to his innovations, the historical novel itself had become a spectacle.

1. A notice in *Le Globe* during Scott's visit to Paris commented: "Now is your chance to catch a glimpse of the illustrious novelist! [. . .] According to the portraits we had seen of Sir Walter Scott, we pictured him to look like someone from the Franche-Comté, well built, with a large belly, and a full and smiling face; ah, well! He is nothing like that." "Sir Walter Scott," *Le Globe,* November 4, 1826, 191.

2. John Sutherland, *The Life of Walter Scott: A Critical Biography* (Oxford: Blackwell, 1995), 310.

3. Le Bibliophile Jacob [Paul Lacroix], *Les soirées de Walter Scott à Paris* (Paris: Eugène Renduel, 1829), 18. In the introduction to this compendium of historical short fiction, Lacroix purports merely to have transcribed tales told by Scott during his visit to Paris. The stories were in fact written by Lacroix.

Scholars have long seen the arrival in France of Scott's works—if not of his person—as a vital moment in literary history. The two major early theorists of the historical novel, Louis Maigron and Georg Lukács, both point to ways in which Scott influenced the future development of French fiction, laying the groundwork for both Romanticism and Realism.[4] But although helpful in showing Scott's influence on authors later considered canonical, their studies overlook how Scott's novels intersected with larger trends in historical representation at the time of their initial publication. As I show, Scott's visual poetics made the Romantic historical novel complicit in the spectacular historical culture of early nineteenth-century France.

Unlike other historical spectacles, such as the panorama, illustrated historiography, or the plays about Napoleon, the novels of Scott and his French followers were not literally visual. But like the picturesque school of Romantic historiography that they influenced, Scott's novels attempted to cross the line between word and image. Through the introduction of a new technique of historical ekphrasis, a mode of literary description that encourages readers to form mental images of people, places, and things from the past, structured according to the logic of painting, Scott's novels simulated the process of looking at visual representations; contemporary critics described how Scott's novels made them feel as if they were seeing a painting, a wax display, or a panorama of the past. When illustrations eventually came to adorn Scottian historical novels, they thus did not so much supplement the fiction with a visual mode of representation as give physical form to the mental pictures already generated by the text.

The transformation of historical fiction into a visual medium meant significant changes both in the novel's form and in its function. The French historical novel, in its post-Scott incarnation, ceased to serve primarily as a guide to ethical conduct written by and for women and became instead a historical spectacle—a form of entertainment as well as a tool for the production of a new national identity. Moreover, in the hands of Scott and his French imitators of the 1820s, 1830s, and 1840s, the novel became a commodity to be consumed by readers of both genders. This chapter explores the nature of Scott's transformation of the historical novel in France, pro-

4. The classic studies of Scott's influence on the French novel are Louis Maigron, *Le roman historique à l'époque romantique: essai sur l'influence de Walter Scott* (1898; reprint, Geneva: Slatkine, 1970); Georg Lukács, *The Historical Novel,* trans. Hannah Mitchell and Stanley Mitchell (1937; Lincoln: University of Nebraska Press, 1983). A study of the internal evolution of the historical novel genre in the vein of Ferdinand Brunetière, Maigron's book does not attempt to link the problematics of literary history to larger historical forces, but otherwise contains many of the ideas that Lukács later developed.

viding insight into the literary history of the period as well as into the functioning of the spectacular past more generally.

The French Historical Novel before Scott

At the beginning of *The Historical Novel,* Lukács credits Walter Scott with the invention of a genre, stating flatly: "The historical novel arose at the beginning of the nineteenth century at about the time of Napoleon's collapse."[5] Yet when Scott's first novels came to France in the years following Napoleon's defeat at Waterloo, they did not arrive on virgin shores. As recent feminist scholarship has shown, the French historical novel had a long and distinguished history, and one associated primarily with a women's literary tradition.[6] To understand how Scott and his followers changed the historical novel, it is first necessary to look beyond the canon established by the male-dominated critical tradition to discover the ways in which historical fiction was written in France for over a century and a half before Scott's arrival. As I show, this female-oriented genre was explicitly un-spectacular.

For Madeleine de Scudéry, whose novels such as *Artamène ou le grand Cyrus* (1649), *Cléopâtre* (1648), *Clélie* (1656), and *Faramond* (1661) held seventeenth-century readers enthralled with their lengthy tales of amorous intrigues set in the past, history offered a believable setting for analyzing affairs of the heart. *La Princesse de Clèves* (1678) by Marie-Madeleine Pioche de la Vergne, comtesse de Lafayette, considered the first modern French novel because of its emphasis on the inner psychological states of its characters, takes place at the sixteenth-century court of Henri II. As Faith Beasley has argued, Lafayette and other seventeenth-century women novelists, such as Marie-Catherine-Hortense Desjardins, Madame de Villedieu, fictionalized the past as a way of writing women back into the historical record. By focusing on the secret history of behind-the-scenes romance and rivalry in which women played a leading role, these writers

---

5. Lukács, *Historical Novel,* 19.
6. On women and the origins of the historical novel, see Faith Beasley, *Revising Memory: Women's Fiction and Memoirs in Seventeenth-Century France* (New Brunswick: Rutgers University Press, 1990). In *Tender Geographies: Women and the Origins of the Novel in France* (New York: Columbia University Press, 1991), Joan DeJean offers an account of the origin of the French novel within a female literary tradition. DeJean, "Classical Reeducation: Decanonizing the Feminine," 22–36, and Nancy K. Miller, "Men's Reading, Women's Writing: Gender and the Rise of the Novel," 37–54, both in *Displacements: Women, Tradition, Literatures in French,* ed. Joan DeJean and Nancy K. Miller (Baltimore: Johns Hopkins University Press, 1991), speak to the question of women novelists and canon formation in France.

offered a corrective to the official male-authored historiography of the period that focused on the king and his battles.[7]

After falling out of favor in the eighteenth century, the historical novel was revived in the period immediately following the Revolution by a new group of women writers.[8] By 1816, when Scott's novels began to be translated into French, women such as Marie-Adèle Barthélemy-Hadot; Félicité de Choiseul-Meuse; Sophie Cottin; Marie Gacon-Dufour; Stéphanie-Félicité Ducrest de Saint-Albin, comtesse de Genlis; Augustine Gottis; Sophie de Maraise; Amélie Simons-Candeille; and Fanny Tercy had reawakened the French public's taste for historical fiction.[9] Their works went through multiple editions and received a great deal of critical commentary in the press of the period. Yet with the exception of Cottin and Genlis, who remain known to specialists, their names have largely disappeared from memory. Whereas Lafayette's place within the canon is secure largely because of her influence on nineteenth-century male novelists, the group of women historical novelists who immediately preceded Romanticism and Realism continue to be ignored even by most literary scholars of the period.[10] It was against this women's tradition, however, that Scott and his followers formulated a new set of conventions and codes to represent the past.[11]

7. Important studies of women and the practice of historiography include Natalie Zemon Davis, "Gender and Genre: Women as Historical Writers 1400–1820," in *Beyond Their Sex: Learned Women of the European Past*, ed. Patricia H. Labalme (New York: New York University Press, 1980), 153–82; Joan Wallach Scott, *Gender and the Politics of History* (New York: Columbia University Press, 1988); Bonnie G. Smith, *The Gender of History: Men, Women, and Historical Practice* (Cambridge, Mass.: Harvard University Press, 1998).

8. Unlike some of their descendents, critics contemporary with Scott recognized that women had inaugurated the genre of historical fiction: "Weren't they *the first* to trace such dramatic pictures of manners [. . .] costumes, fashions and prejudices of different periods?" asks one anonymous critic. "Romans," review of *Vanina Dornano* by Mme ***, *Gazette de France,* October 6, 1825, 2, emphasis added.

9. Each of these women published several novels and at least one that went through more than one edition. For the purposes of this study, I have limited my corpus to these more prolific writers. Many other women published historical novels during the Restoration, however. A comprehensive list would also include (but would not be limited to) Mlle Agier-Prévost, Félicité Bayle-Celnart, Louise Dauriat, Louise Désormery, Émilie Millon-Journel, Catherine Saint-Venant, and Mme Sartory (née de Wimpfren). Summaries of many of these women's novels can be found in Eusèbe Girault de Saint-Fargeau, *Revue des romans* (Paris: Firmin Didot frères, 1839).

10. Margaret Cohen's *The Sentimental Education of the Novel* (Princeton: Princeton University Press, 1999) treats many of these same women as authors of sentimental fiction.

11. My account of the male displacement of a prior female tradition of the historical novel parallels Cohen's account of the displacement of the sentimental novel by Realism.

The historical novels of the first two decades of the nineteenth century, almost all of which were written by women, typically center on an eponymous historical heroine.[12] Genlis's *La Duchesse de la Vallière* (1804), *Mme de Maintenon* (1806), *Mlle de Lafayette* (1813), and *Jeanne de France* (1816) fit this pattern, as do Cottin's *Mathilde* (1805), Barthélemy-Hadot's *Clothilde de Hapsbourg* (1817), Gottis's *Ermance de Beaufremont* (1818), and Simons-Candeille's *Bathilde, reine des Francs* (1814), among many others. Occasionally, however, the female character shares top billing with a more illustrious man, as in the case of Gottis's *François Premier et Madame de Chateaubriand* (1816). Although these heroines belong to diverse periods of history, the majority come from either the Middle Ages or the court of Louis XIV. With a few exceptions, they are French.

In the highly charged political atmosphere of the post-Revolutionary era, this focus on periods of Catholic and monarchical supremacy, such as the Middle Ages and the absolutist court of Louis XIV, might imply a conservative political affiliation. Yet, whereas all of these writers had witnessed the events of the Revolution firsthand,[13] it would not be accurate simply to ascribe to their choice of subject a political bias in the way that Chateaubriand's *Le génie du christianisme* (1802) explicitly sought to revive popular sentiment for Catholic and monarchist traditions through its celebration of the medieval past. Although many shared a taste for the Middle Ages, these women belonged to different classes and factions, and held differing political views.[14]

12. The few male historical novelists of the early nineteenth century follow this same pattern. Jean-Pierre de Brès, for example, published a novel titled *L'héroïne du quinzième siècle* (Paris: Léopold Collin, 1808) about Joan of Arc.

13. Genlis was born in 1746, Gacon-Dufour in 1753, Barthélemy-Hadot in 1763, Simons-Candeille in 1767, and Cottin in 1770.

14. Cottin married into a family of *emigré* nobles, and Gacon-Dufour had served as a *lectrice* in the court of Louis XVI. Genlis, an aristocrat (and mistress of Philippe-Égalité), viewed the Revolution favorably at first, but went into exile in 1791. Hated both by the Jacobins and the Royalists, she returned to France under the Consulate and received a pension under Napoleon, which the Restoration government later revoked. The husband of Barthélemy-Hadot, a schoolteacher, was president of his *comité révolutionnaire;* and Simons-Candeille, although also a commoner (she began her çareer as an actress), detested Napoleon and welcomed the Restoration. My biographical information on these writers derives from Alfred de Montferrand, ed., *Biographie des femmes auteurs contemporaines françaises* (Paris: Armand-Aubrée, 1839); Alexandre-Nicolas Pigoreau, *Petite bibliographie biographico-romancière* (Paris: Pigoreau, 1821). I also consulted general biographical dictionaries, including Jean-Pierre Lobies, ed., *Index Bio-Bibliographicus Notorum Hominum* (Osnabrück: Biblio Verlag, 1975); Joseph-François Michaud, *Biographie universelle ancienne et moderne*, new ed. (1811–12; reprint, Paris: A. Thoisnier Desplaces, 1843); Michel

If the political affiliations of these writers varied widely, their aesthetic affiliations were remarkably circumscribed. Indeed, the genre reflects a limited and highly consistent set of conventions and codes. In nearly all these novels, the historical characters, especially the female ones, face moral or ethical dilemmas, often involving an illicit love. In *Jeanne de France,* which tells the story of the plain-looking daughter of Louis XI and her unrequited feelings for her husband, the future Louis XII, Genlis describes the sacrifice of love to friendship, a common theme in the historical novels of this period. The unattractive but clear-headed Jeanne, who boasts not a single pretty feature except for her hands, realizes only after her marriage that her husband will never love her. Rather than importune her husband with feelings she knows he cannot reciprocate, she keeps her love for him a secret and retires into a convent, leaving him free to marry a more beautiful woman, Anne de Bretagne. Jeanne's struggle between sentiment and obligation is typical of the genre.

In her study of sentimental novels by women of this period, Margaret Cohen describes the "double-bind" facing many of the genre's female protagonists, who must choose between two moral imperatives or what she calls "conflicting duties." Individual freedom, associated with romantic or erotic love, clashes with societal values such as reason, the public good, and propriety.[15] In the historical novels of the period, authored by many of the same women who wrote sentimental novels set in the present, these struggles are attributed to more or less notable figures from the past and play out against famous historical events.

In Cottin's *Mathilde,* the eponymous heroine, an English princess, follows her brother, Richard the Lion-Hearted, on a crusade to the Holy Land, where she falls in love with her Muslim captor, Malek-Adhel, the brother of Saladin, the principal enemy of the crusaders. Amid the battles to retake Jerusalem, Mathilde must choose between following her heart and betraying her nation, religion, and family. Malek-Adhel faces a similar "double bind" expressed in starkly antinomic terms: "I admire the Christians and I shall fight them; I adore Mathilde and I am going to leave her, and if I can only obtain her hand at the price of a betrayal, I shall renounce her hand."[16] But if the male figure must also choose between duty and love, the focus remains on the female protagonist's difficult choice.

Prévost and Jean-Charles Roman d'Amat, eds., *Dictionnaire de biographie française* (Paris: Lethouzey et Aîné, 1951); Gustave Vapereau, ed., *Dictionnaire universel des contemporains* (Paris: Hachette, 1865).

15. Cohen, *Sentimental Education of the Novel,* 34.

16. Sophie Cottin, *Mathilde,* tome 8, vol. 2 of *Oeuvres complètes de Madame Cottin* (1805; reprint in collected volume, Paris: Ménard and Desenne, fils, 1824), 281.

Eventually Mathilde's Christian suitor, Lusignan, relieves Malek-Adhel of the burden of choosing by murdering him. Mathilde then takes the veil, remaining behind in the Holy Land to pray for her dead lover. Like the female protagonist in Genlis's *Jeanne de France,* Cottin's historical heroine resolves her struggle between self and society through the renunciation of both. The convent provides a space of mediation allowing the female character to remain true to her individual desires without acting on them.

Although many pre-Scott historical novels incorporate the moral dilemmas of sentimental fiction, many also make use of the macabre features of Gothic romance and Boulevard melodrama, including grim settings and stock characters. In Barthélemy-Hadot's *Les brigands anglais ou la bataille de Hastings* (1822) the beautiful Athénaïs, who has disguised herself as a man to accompany her husband on the Norman invasion of England in 1066, gets kidnapped by her husband's rival, the villainous Albert, who locks her in a deserted castle. Although Athénaïs escapes to reunite with her husband in a happy ending, the heroine of Gottis's *François Premier et Madame de Chateaubriand* lacks her good fortune; punished by her husband for succumbing to the seductions of the French king, the long-suffering Françoise is bled to death by her jealous husband and his evil doctor in a remote ancestral chateau. Genlis's *Le siège de La Rochelle ou le malheur et la conscience* (1808), one of the few novels from this period that remained in print into the late nineteenth century, also features bizarre murders, innocent women locked away in castles, and evil villains. In these works the historical heroine's virtue is put to the test. Her suffering either marks her innocence or compensates for her fall.

For Maigron and Lukács, these pre-Scott historical novels, both those from the seventeenth century and those from the early nineteenth, nearly all of which were written by women, do not qualify as genuine historical fiction because their sentimental plots might as well take place in the present as at any moment in the past. "What is lacking in the so-called historical novel before Sir Walter Scott," Lukács writes, "is precisely the specifically historical, that is, derivation of the individuality of characters from the historical peculiarity of their age."[17] In the hyperbolic rhetoric of Maigron, these novels "not only ignore history, they travesty it in the most grotesque and scandalous manner."[18] For Maigron, the past is travestied when these novels project the manners *(moeurs)* of their own time into the past. Mademoiselle de Scudéry's novels might take place in ancient Persia or Gaul, but the social structures they describe resemble seventeenth-

17. Lukács, *Historical Novel,* 19.
18. Maigron, *Roman historique à l'époque romantique,* 13.

century France. Maigron finds the novels produced by women in the early nineteenth century guilty of the same sin, denouncing them as an "insipid muddle"[19] and later as a "contagion"[20] infecting French literature with a false historicism.

In spite of Maigron's hysterical, and quite misogynistic, tone, his analysis of the form and function of the pre-Scott French historical novel contains a grain of truth. These works by women did in fact hold up the past as a mirror to the present and use history as a means of effecting moral change in contemporary society. As Maigron rightly observes, historical novels written by women before Scott employ history as a "veil" or "pretext." Indeed, the authors themselves describe setting their novels in the past primarily to teach a moral, rather than what Maigron or Lukács saw as a properly historical, lesson: "There is such a general prejudice [. . .] against the possibility of moral perfection," Genlis states in the preface to *Jeanne de France,* "that it must be presented with caution in a work of the imagination."[21] Novels of virtue, it seems, lose their impact when their characters are simply too good to be believed—unless the characters really existed. "One should search for these characters in history," Genlis writes, "because such perfection needs the authority of a famous and revered name in order not to be rejected as pure fantasy."[22] The prestige of history, according to Genlis, convinces readers of the truth of the fiction. The historical setting served, for these authors, as a guarantor of *vraisemblance,* as an anchor of believability, to help readers identify with the characters more readily and model their actions accordingly.

These novels valued the past not for its difference from the present, but for its similarity. Based on the assumption that matters of the heart remain constant in all times and places, the historical fictions from the early nineteenth century made use of history to teach a moral lesson. They asked the reader to engage actively with the ethical dilemmas faced by the historical characters, who despite their chronological distance from the reader, nevertheless shared her most basic concerns. This conception of history's role resembles that found in traditional historiography. During the ancien régime, one of the primary goals of history writing lay in offering up the past as a model of conduct for male readers. Originally written for the education of princes, historiography studied the actions of past rulers and great men for the lessons that might serve in the present. That most of

19. Ibid., 23.
20. Ibid., 27.
21. Stéphanie de Genlis, *Jeanne de France, nouvelle historique* (1816; reprint, Paris: Maradan, 1818), viii.
22. Ibid., viii.

these historical works focused on men comes as no surprise. Just as seventeenth-century women writing historical novels turned to the fictional realm to supplement the historical record with the actions and deeds of women, so too did the women of the early nineteenth century seek to offer an alternative to the male-focused historiography of their period, while maintaining history's function as exemplum.

In these novels, neglected women from the past take center stage to serve as models of conduct. In the foreword to *Agnès de France, ou le douzième siècle* (1821), Simons-Candeille first apologizes for presenting to her readers "yet another historical novel" and then goes on to describe how she chose her subject: "I thought of the twelfth century, when Agnès de France occupied such an interesting place, even if historians only name her in passing."[23] By focusing on female historical figures, on women who received only a glancing mention in conventional histories, these women novelists called into question the historiographic tradition, its pretensions to completeness as well as the universality of the values it imposed.

Unlike traditional male-authored historiography that extolled the virtues of the battlefield, such novels operated on a different terrain: "I want to prove," Simons-Candeille's narrator states in the opening sentence of *Agnès de France*, "that the power of friendship, like that of glory, can win out sometimes even over love itself."[24] These models of conduct instructed their readers not in matters of state but in matters of the heart, in private rather than public virtues. The elevation of friendship over not only glory, but also love, however, implied this genre's rejection not only of the values of traditional historiography, but also of popular novels of the eighteenth century destined for a female audience.[25]

With their focus on interior rather than exterior value, these novels made little attempt to evoke the materiality of the past through visual description. Indeed, there is little representation of the material world in most of the historical fiction authored by women in the period before Scott. When Maigron faults these novels for their lack of "local color," he takes for a defect what appears to less teleological eyes as a fundamentally different notion of the function of historical fiction. The absence of

23. Amélie Simons-Candeille, *Agnès de France, ou le douzième siècle, roman historique* (Paris: Maradan, 1821), vii.
24. Ibid., 1.
25. In *Popular Fiction before Richardson: Narrative Patterns, 1700–1739* (Oxford: Clarendon Press, 1969), John J. Richetti describes the emergence in England of a similar type of "pious" novel written by women for a female audience that sought to correct female reading habits formed by novels also written by women (211–61). See also Ina Ferris, *The Achievement of Literary Authority: Gender, History, and the Waverley Novels* (Ithaca: Cornell University Press, 1991), 53.

description in these novels should be read not as an insufficiency or lack but rather as part of an aesthetic and moral strategy that seeks to direct the reader's gaze away from the physical and toward the emotional states of the characters. Cohen describes a similar avoidance of description in sentimental novels by women authors in the same period who sought to focus readers' attention on interior conflict.[26]

Many of the early nineteenth-century historical novels thematized the absence of visual description on the level of plot and character. This is particularly true of the novels set in the seventeenth century, because the complex politics of appearance at Versailles during the reign of Louis XIV brought the dangers of the visual into sharp focus.[27] In the novels that take place at court (all royal courts, even those from the Middle Ages, resemble Versailles in these novels), and that depict the struggles of a woman to defend her virtue against the predations of a more powerful male character, usually the king (*La Duchesse de la Vallière, François Premier et Madame de Chateaubriand, Mademoiselle de Luynes*), the act of looking carries a negative connotation. As in Lafayette's foundational *La Princesse de Clèves,* which functions as an explicit intertext in several novels,[28] the moment at which the heroine becomes the object of the public gaze by appearing at court seals her doom.[29]

The virtue of the heroines at the beginning of many of these novels is demonstrated by their refusal to be seen looking. When the heroine of Gottis's *Ermance de Beaufremont* looks at the object of her forbidden desire, she directs her gaze to the man's soul rather than just his flesh: "For the first time she noticed his beauty. Until then she had paid no attention to those long eyelashes shielding his passionate looks, to those curls of black hair falling upon a forehead marked by both candor and courage!"[30]

---

26. Cohen, *Sentimental Education of the Novel,* 48–50. Cohen refers to the nondescriptive style of sentimental fiction by women writers as "a light touch," a phrase she takes from Alexander Pope.

27. Jean-Marie Apostolidès describes the spectacular nature of court life at Versailles in *Le roi-machine: spectacle et politique au temps de Louis XIV* (Paris: Minuit, 1981).

28. In Mme Sartory's *Mademoiselle de Luynes,* the characters read and discuss *La Princesse de Clèves.* The plot of Lafayette's novel is reflected in Sartory's, in which an innocent young French bride, forced to live with her husband's family in an Italian court, must defend herself against the advances of the rich and powerful Duke of Savoy. The male courtiers in *Mademoiselle de Luynes* deride the ending of *La Princesse de Clèves,* in which the heroine chooses solitude over love, for leaving the reader with "sad and unsatisfying impressions." *Mademoiselle de Luynes, nouvelle historique* (Paris: Rosa, 1817), 73.

29. Julia V. Douthwaite describes the stakes surrounding the "etiquette of sight" in Lafayette's novel in "Seeing and Being Seen: Visual Codes and Metaphors in *La Princesse de Clèves,*" in *Approaches to Teaching Lafayette's* The Princess of Clèves, ed. Faith E. Beasley and Katharine Ann Jensen (New York: MLA, 1998), 109–19.

30. Augustine Gottis, *Ermance de Beaufremont, Comtesse de Gatinois; Chronique du IXe siècle* (Paris: Eymery, 1818), 90.

When the innocent young Louise first sets eyes on the king's portrait in Genlis's *La Duchesse de la Vallière,* the spiritual likewise takes precedence over the physical: "she looked only at the expression of that physiognomy filled with sweetness and dignity; she searched for the soul of that face and believed in her own that she had found it!"[31] The rest of the novel describes Louise's vain efforts to avoid both seeing her lover and being seen by him, each of which could damage her virtue. Her struggle is made all the more difficult by the celebrity of her would-be lover, because the king's image proliferates across the kingdom: "she saw that cherished image in every form, in public monuments and squares, in the stores, and even the imprint on coins made it appear to her every day."[32] Gottis's *François Premier et Madame de Chateaubriand,* which tells essentially the same story but sets it in an earlier period, likewise shows the heroine fleeing the king's portrait and finding it, to her chagrin, even on the smallest coin in the realm. For these characters, and by implication for readers as well, the representation of outward appearance, as well as the act of looking at such representations, creates dangers for women. Virtue demands an avoidance of the spectacular.

According to Maigron, the seventeenth-century writers who avoided local color did not know any better, but the nineteenth-century novelists, nearly all of whom continued writing in the same style after Scott's arrival in France, had no such excuse. Maigron banishes these writers from the kingdom of the canon. Indeed, he puts the matter in just such cosmic— and visual—terms: "Mme de Genlis was fortunate enough to see the light, but was not enlightened."[33] It is tempting, however, to read Genlis's *Jeanne de France,* published in 1816, the very year that the first novel by Scott was translated into French, as a self-reflexive commentary on the refusal of local color, and of the visual more generally, in historical fiction authored by women.

This novel, as I have discussed, recounts the unrequited passion of Louis XI's daughter for her husband and ends with her magnanimous withdrawal into a convent so as not to serve as an obstacle to his passion for another woman. Right from the first sentence of the preface, Genlis directs the reader's gaze toward her heroine precisely because she is nothing to look at: "This historical novel offers a picture that has never before been drawn: by presenting a heroine to whom nature has not been kind, by describing the pain of a legitimate but hopeless love, a passion that even

31. Stéphanie de Genlis, *La Duchesse de La Vallière* (1804; reprint, Paris: Lecointe et Durey, 1823), 30.
32. Ibid., 81.
33. Maigron, *Roman historique à l'époque romantique,* 27.

virtue could not cure, I wanted to oppose moral and physical beauty."[34] Here spiritual qualities take precedence over surface appearances; the interior trumps the exterior.

As if to underscore the depreciation of outward appearance in the novel, Genlis avoids nearly all physical description; she describes Jeanne's excessive "sensitivity" and "goodness," but not even the color of her hair.[35] Complicit in the narrator's refusal to look, Jeanne goes out of her way to avoid being seen. At a ball thrown by her older sister, "The sad Jeanne was adorned as simply as always: she wore a completely shapeless dress in that most modest of shades to which she was so devoted, gray."[36] Jeanne's preference for gray might be seen as the negation of "color" in the Scottian sense, or instead as an affirmation of interior value that becomes the sign of her moral superiority. At the end of the novel, after seeing the ravishing portrait of her rival, Anne de Bretagne, she withdraws into a convent she has founded in which all the nuns wear gray. This decision, which signals her ultimate choice of friendship for her husband over love, and demonstrates the triumph of moral over physical beauty in the novel, is thus explicitly linked with the refusal of a poetics—and politics—of the spectacle.

The British Invasion

It is difficult today to imagine the scale of Scott's success in France during the 1820s. A decade after the first translation of one of his novels into French (*Guy Mannering* in 1816), Scott had become one of France's most popular writers, and he remained so for decades to come.[37] Scott's most popular novels went through roughly twice as many editions in the nine-

34. Genlis, *Jeanne de France*, p. vii.
35. Ibid., 5.
36. Ibid., 21.
37. According to Martyn Lyons, four translated works by Scott (*Ivanhoé, L'antiquaire, L'abbé,* and *Quentin Durward*) ranked among the top twenty French best-sellers between 1826 and 1830. Except for Béranger, Scott is the only contemporary writer on this list, and he is the only foreigner. (Other writers in the top twenty for the period 1826–1830 include Fénelon, La Fontaine, Voltaire, Racine, and Molière.) "Les best-sellers," in *Histoire de l'édition française: Le temps des éditeurs,* ed. Roger Chartier and Henri-Jean Martin (1985; reprint, Paris: Promodis, 1990), 415–23. As Lyons shows in another context, no fewer than twenty editions of Scott's complete works were published in France between 1820 and 1851. *Ivanhoe* alone went through twenty-eight editions with a total circulation of at least 60,000 copies by the beginning of the Second Empire. Lyons shows, moreover, that figures from reading rooms, the *cabinets de lecture,* indicate that Scott was France's most popular novelist of the 1820s; one such establishment offered 104 volumes by Scott (out of 3,000 total). This suggests a much larger public for Scott's works than even the print runs would indicate. "The Audience for Romanticism: Walter Scott in France, 1815–1851," *European History Quarterly* 14, no. 1 (January 1984): 27–28.

teenth century as did novels by Balzac or Stendhal.[38] And Scott left his mark on more than just literature—paintings by such Romantic artists as Delacroix, Delaroche, and Devéria all looked to the author of *Waverley* for their subject matter.[39] Clothing and furniture designers likewise sought inspiration in Scott. In the last years of the Restoration, fashionable ladies could be seen wearing "toques à la Walter Scott" in drawing-rooms decorated to look like a Scottish castle, and the duchesse de Berry gave masked balls in which guests dressed as characters from the Waverley novels.[40] "One can hardly conceive of that vogue which reached its peak in 1827," remarks Armand de Pontmartin of the craze for Scott; "it could be found in costumes, in fashion, in furniture, on signs for the stores and on posters for the theater."[41]

For contemporaries, the vogue for Scott's novels in the 1820s appeared not as the spontaneous generation of interest in a new genre, as scholars would lead us to believe, but rather as a struggle for market share within an existing and already popular generic category. To some, Scott's rise seemed to provide a welcome end to the dominance of women in the domain of the historical novel. Charles-Joseph Colnet's review in the rightwing *Gazette de France* of a translation of yet another of Scott's works (*Lettres de Paul à sa famille*) framed the Scottish author's popularity with the French public in terms of an implicit rivalry with the indigenous female tradition. Mocking the desperation of readers after waiting an entire month for a new work by Scott, the critic imagines the following scene at a bookstore:

> In order to dispel [his customers'] boredom, an officious bookseller vainly offered the freshest compositions of our attractive lady novelists; they rejected them disdainfully, and even rather testily.—This novel is by Mme de Gottis; it contains some very touching scenes.—We want Walter Scott, who touches us far more.—This story, by Mme de Choiseul-Meuse, is, we are

---

38. I derive my statistics from the *Catalogue général des livres imprimés de la Bibliothèque nationale* (Paris: Imprimerie Nationale, 1944).

39. "If one could still doubt the fame of Walter Scott, this year's *salon* would show to what extent he has occupied the imagination of our painters!" declared one reviewer of an edition of Scott's collected works. Review of *Oeuvres complètes*, by Scott, *Le Constitutionnel*, October 26, 1824, 3.

40. Émile Legouis, "La fortune littéraire de Walter Scott en France," *Études Anglaises* 24, no. 4 (1971): 493, cited in Lyons, "Audience for Romanticism," 26.

41. Armand de Pontmartin, *Mes mémoires*, vol. 2 (Paris: Lévy, 1885), 3, cited in Maigron, *Roman historique à l'époque romantique*, 121. Indeed, theatrical productions adapted from Scott's novels abounded in the 1820s and 1830s, as the Romantic historical drama reached its apogee: Pontmartin remarks how on a single evening in 1827 plays based on Scott's novels could be seen at three different theaters. Pontmartin was a critic for the *Revue des Deux Mondes*.

told, quite moral.—Once and for all, give us Walter Scott; we no longer want to read anything else. Mme de Genlis herself would have been power-less to attract them.[42]

In the competitive world of the nineteenth-century book trade, in which the freshest stock becomes quickly stale, French women novelists could not compete with the British import. According to the critic, one minute French women dominated the market, the next they appeared as has-beens. The critic's explanation for the shift in popular taste can be found in the terms that the hapless bookseller uses to market his wares: thanks to Scott, the qualities attributed to historical fiction authored by women, such as morality, no longer resonate with the reading public. What, then, did the British author offer in their place?

The answer has to do with the way Scott and his followers transformed the historical novel into a spectacle. While the pre-Scott historical novels by women eschewed the visual as part of an aesthetic and moral program to instruct readers in the dangers of appearances, Scott transformed history into something to see. For Scott and his followers, the essence of history inhered in external forms, in the very physiognomies that the women novelists refused to countenance. Although Lukács and others have argued that Scott's novels innovated in other areas, including the institution of the mediocre hero and a new conception of the process of historical change, these features are in fact subsidiary to the new novel's spectacular function.

As I have shown, the spectacular mode of historical representation, as exemplified by such popular entertainments as the panorama, consisted in making the past visual. But what does this mean for the novel? How can a verbal medium achieve effects similar to those produced by a visual medium? How can a novel *envision* the past? The key lies in the notion of ekphrasis, a rhetorical device that has come to refer to the description of a plastic form—usually a work of visual art—in a literary work, but that had a much broader definition in its earliest use. For the Greeks, *ekphrasis* referred to any attempt to conjure an image in words through descrip-tion.[43] The subject of ekphrastic description thus need not, according to

42. *Gazette de France*, June 17, 1822, 3.

43. According to Amy Golahny, in its original context in the discipline of rhetoric, the Greek verb *ekphrasein* meant "to report in detail." For more on definitions of ekphrasis, see Golahny, "Introduction: Ekphrasis in the Interarts Discourse" in *The Eye of the Poet: Stud-ies in the Reciprocity of the Visual and Literary Arts from the Renaissance to the Present,* ed. Amy Golahny (Lewisburg, PA: Bucknell University Press, 1996), 12.

Murray Krieger, be an art work but can be any visual form that is described in words. It can even be an image from the past.

In his theoretical discussion of the term and the concept, Krieger defines *ekphrasis* very generally as a "still moment" within a text, as an effort to halt the flow of narrative, to suspend argument or action, by indulging in description.[44] *Ekphrasis*, Krieger writes, includes "every attempt, within an art of words, to work toward the illusion that it is performing a task we usually associate with an art of natural signs."[45] Here Krieger points to what appears to be a fundamental difference between visual and verbal forms of representation. Whereas the visual generates meaning through "natural signs," signifers that serve as immediate substitutes for their referents, verbal forms of communications rely on words, which are an arbitrary, and hence supposedly less direct, form of signification. As W. J. T. Mitchell has argued, however, there is no essential semantic difference between words and pictures; both forms of communication serve a similar expressive function. Of course, as Mitchell recognizes, different media do set up different expectations in their audiences and do necessitate different representational strategies, but there is no reason to believe that words and images cannot achieve the same effects.[46]

When I say that Scott transformed the historical novel into a visual medium, then, I am placing his work in the long tradition of what Horace labeled *ut pictura poesis* (as in painting, so in poetry).[47] Instead of describing a work of art—a vase or a shield—Scott's novels create verbal images of the material world of the past. But like other forms of ekphrasis, his novels seek to collapse the distinction between the visual and the verbal by forcing words to act like natural signs. His words create images that, like pictures, point to certain preestablished configurations in a reader's visual memory. Of course, words will never function exactly like pictures; they will always require the added work of imagining, of translating the sign into a mental image. But the primary effect of Scott's fiction is to reduce

44. Murray Krieger, *Ekphrasis: The Illusion of the Natural Sign* (Baltimore: Johns Hopkins University Press, 1992), 6–9.

45. Krieger, *Ekphrasis*, 9.

46. In *Picture Theory* (Chicago: University of Chicago Press, 1994), W. J. T. Mitchell offers an account of ekphrasis that likens the barrier between the arts to the division between self and other.

47. For more on the way the nineteenth century generally, and British Romanticism in particular, redefined the relation between painting and literature, see Martin Meisel, *Realizations: Narrative, Pictorial, and Theatrical Arts in Nineteenth-Century England* (Princeton: Princeton University Press, 1983); Wendy Steiner, *Pictures of Romance: Form against Context in Painting and Literature* (Chicago: University of Chicago Press, 1988), 56–90.

this work to a minimum, to create such vivid mental images with words that the referent is immediately called to mind. Scott's verbal images function like visual ones; they make the reader see the past.

They achieve this effect through the accumulation of material detail. As Krieger has shown, descriptive passages constitute a "still moment" in the action of a story, pauses in the narrative that force the reader to form a mental image of places, people, and things. Scott's novels almost invariably begin (after an introduction locating the story in a precise historical moment) with a vivid description of a physical setting, including both natural and human-made elements. At the start of *Waverley* (1814), set during the eighteenth century, the hero journeys to Scotland and comes upon the castle of Tully-Veolan. The narrator observes that the roof of the castle "had some nondescript kind of projections, called bartizans";[48] that above the stables there were "granaries, called girnels, and other offices, to which there was access by outside stairs of heavy masonry";[49] and that the courtyard contained a fountain with a sculpture of a bear. The castle takes shape before the reader's gaze from side to side and from top to bottom. Such an ekphrastic *tour-de-force* could not have contrasted more greatly with the earlier tradition of French historical novels by women in which architectural details—even adjectives—were few and far between.

Human figures and their costumes in Scott receive the same kind of scrutiny. At the beginning of *Ivanhoe* (1819), a description of a medieval English forest, as detailed as a botany manual, precedes a description of two men. The first man's appearance harmonizes with the "gnarled" arms of the ancient oaks. "The eldest [. . .] had a stern, savage, and wild aspect."[50] His garment "was of the simplest form imaginable," consisting of a tanned animal skin reaching from throat to knees, "sandals, bound with thongs made of boar's hide," a "broad leathern belt, secured by a brass buckle" (11) from which dangled a knife and a ram's horn, and a brass ring around his neck indicating his status as a serf. The younger man wore a short jacket "of a bright purple hue" (12), a crimson cloak lined in yellow, and a hat from which bells dangled. Personality traits emerge only after, and as if *through,* descriptions of the physical. The "aspect" of the first, grimly costumed man, a serf, "was bent on the ground with an air of deep dejection" (13), like the tree next to which he stands, while that of the second, brightly clad fellow "indicated, as usual with his class, a sort

---

48. Walter Scott, *Waverley* (1814; reprint, London: Penguin Books, 1972), 78.
49. Ibid.
50. Walter Scott, *Ivanhoe* (1819; reprint, London: Penguin Books, 1984), 11. Subsequent quotations are cited in the text.

of vacant curiosity, and fidgety impatience of any posture of repose, together with the utmost self-satisfaction respecting his own situation and the appearance which he made" (13).

In addition to minute and detailed description, Scott relies on formal or structural analogies with visual forms of representation to achieve an ekphrastic effect. In *Ivanhoe,* the characters are referred to as "human figures" in a "landscape" (11), and in *Waverley* the narrator refers to the description of the castle as a "still life."[51] The link with a pictorial vocabulary is not accidental. Scott's elaborate descriptions of setting make use of the picturesque, a concept in aesthetic theory that refers to a verbal description of a place oriented according to the conventions of seventeenth- and eighteenth-century landscape painting.[52] Picturesque descriptions not only accumulate visual detail, but organize the elements composing the view according to a precise formal logic and unfold to the reader's "eye" in a specific and coherent manner. Although Scott's pictorial descriptions, such as those found in *Waverley* and *Ivanhoe,* strike the modern reader as commonplace, they led to a radical change in the aesthetics of the French novel during the 1820s, when French novelists began to copy his technique.[53]

Scott's novels, through their detailed descriptions organized according to formal properties associated with painting, seem to function in a manner akin to visual works of art. They turn readers into viewers, making the arbitrary signs of language act like the natural signs of painting in order to reduce to an absolute minimum the barrier that language poses between the subject (the reader/viewer) and the object (the past). And they seem to have achieved their goal, for French critics at the time repeatedly likened Scott's novels to painted canvases: "His pages speak as clearly to the mind as the most practiced paintbrush would to the eyes," announced one reviewer for the *Gazette de France,* adopting painterly terms that became a cliché in French writing about Scott.[54] "To paint a great historical period

51. Scott, *Waverley,* 79.
52. Andrew M. Ross discusses Scott and the picturesque in " 'Waverley' and the Picturesque," in *Scott and His Influence,* ed. J. H. Alexander and David Hewitt (Aberdeen: Association for Scottish Literary Studies, 1983), 99–108. Meisel argues that Scott's attempt to "picture" his subjects involved not only portraying their external features but also their habits, manners, and feelings (*Realizations,* 57).
53. Doris Kadish makes a similar point: "Sometime after Voltaire, and the older 'literature of ideas' he exemplifies, there emerged a newer 'literature of images' which increasingly contained description, notably the strikingly modern sort called landscape. Landscape was almost completely new when it emerged in the literature of images." *The Literature of Images: Narrative Landscape from Julie to Jane Eyre* (New Brunswick: Rutgers University Press, 1987), 1.
54. Ch. du R., "Variétés," review of *Les eaux de Saint-Ronan* by Scott, *Gazette de France,* January 20, 1824, 1.

truthfully," wrote another critic in an attempt to define Scott's method, "[. . .] that is what, since the appearance of Walter Scott's works, we call composing a historical novel."[55] In a review of Scott's *Quentin Durward,* Victor Hugo likewise metaphorically assimilates the new historical fiction to painting, comparing Scott's style to "a truthful paintbrush tracing a genuine likeness from a confusing shadow."[56] Hugo went on to produce one of the best-known historical novels of the first half of the nineteenth century, *Notre-Dame de Paris,* in which a vanished culture is evoked through a visual description of its architectural monuments.

Certain scholars have downplayed the importance of the pictorial elements in Scott's fiction. For ideological reasons, Lukács seeks to minimize the role of the visual as the harbinger of a new historicism in Scott's fiction, dismissing it as secondary to "deeper" historical concerns: "Scott never under-estimated the importance of picturesque, descriptive elements of this kind. Indeed, he used them so much that superficial critics have seen here the essence of his art. But for Scott the historical characterization of time and place, the historical 'here and now' is something much deeper. For him it means that certain crises in the personal destinies of a number of human beings coincide and interweave within the determining context of an historical crisis."[57] According to Lukács, Scott's importance lies not in visual description, but in the creation of a new kind of protagonist, the mediocre hero, who substitutes for the famous historical figures found at the center of previous historical novels. Lukács sees Scott as using this mediocre type to present the magnitude of world historical change in concrete, human terms: "Scott endeavours to portray the struggles and antagonisms of history by means of characters who, in their psychology and destiny, always represent social trends and historical forces."[58] Lukács's privileging of character served his political interest in casting Scott as a model for twentieth-century revolutionary writers, for whom the common man figured as an agent of historical change. It also served to depict Scott as a precursor to the French Realists, such as Balzac, who populated their fiction with middle-class characters, avatars of the new bourgeois capitalist order.

Maigron envisions Scott's singularity in a different manner. For Maigron, Scott's innovation has three main components. First, Scott

---

55. "Romans," review of *Les suisses sous Rodolphe de Hapsbourg* by Sophie d'Ordre, *Gazette de France,* June 14, 1827, 4.

56. Victor Hugo, "Critique littéraire," review of *Quentin Durward* by Scott, *La Muse Française* 1 (1823), 31.

57. Lukács, *Historical Novel,* 41.

58. Ibid., 34.

makes history of prime interest in itself, unlike the prior female practitioners of the historical novel genre in France, for whom the past functions only as an accessory to the romantic intrigue at the novel's core. Romance in Scott does not disappear entirely but becomes subordinate to the "historical element" that it serves to heighten.[59] Scott's second major innovation, according to Maigron, concerns the elevation of collective sentiments over those of the individual, which had dominated previously in the sentimental and historical novels authored by women. Like Lukács, Maigron mentions in this regard Scott's focus on minor or nonhistorical characters who function as types, incarnating the interests of their class or period, as well as the introduction of the people into the novel's realm.[60]

But for Maigron, Scott's most important innovation is the introduction of local color, defined as providing characters and locations with "as exact and as credible [*vraisemblable*] an expression as possible" of their era.[61] As I have shown, in the nineteenth century, local color became closely identified with Scott's descriptive process. When applied to the literary representation of exotic or historical subjects, *local color* refers to an attention paid to the characteristics that mark an object as the unique product of a time and place and conveys a sense of historical (or geographic) specificity. The description of distinctive places and costumes, of course, conveys a sense of local color, but reference to unusual turns of phrase or uncommon manners, which Andrew M. Ross has called the "colourful, striking, or singular,"[62] also achieves this effect. In Maigron's view, the attention that Scott pays to depicting both the appearance of a past age as well as its customs expresses a new kind of historicity notably absent from prior incarnations of the historical novel in France. Maigron, of course, had his own agenda, which included making Scott a predecessor of the French Romantics (and later Realists), for whom picturesque description played a central aesthetic role.

Maigron's privileging of the visual, including local color, in his account of Scott's innovation, despite its teleological intentions, comes closer to reflecting the way observers at the time viewed Scott's work. Balzac's biting

---

59. Maigron, *Roman historique à l'époque romantique*, 80–83.

60. More recent scholars have also highlighted these aspects of Scott's work. Ann Rigney, for example, describes Scott's "hybrid" mixing of fact and fiction, as well as the effort in Scott and Romantic historicism more generally to represent historical forces through individual perspectives. *Imperfect Histories: The Elusive Past and the Legacy of Romantic Historicism* (Ithaca: Cornell University Press, 2001), 13–58.

61. Maigron, *Roman historique à l'époque romantique*, 95.

62. Ross, "'Waverley' and the Picturesque," 100.

satire of the French publishing world of the 1820s in his novel *Illusions perdues* (1843) provides a case in point. Balzac's protagonist, Lucien de Rubempré, who is the author of a Scott-inspired historical novel, receives advice from the worldly critic Lousteau on how to write a work of criticism without having a genuine opinion. Fault the author, Lousteau tells him, for writing in the modern manner "in which everything is translated into images" and in which mere appearance counts more than philosophical concerns. "The novel *à la Walter Scott* is a genre and not a system," Lousteau proclaims, opposing Scott's "literature of images" to the eighteenth-century philosophical novel epitomized by Voltaire, Diderot, Sterne, and Lesage. Adopting an anti-Scott platform allows for the kind of provocative pronouncements that go over well with the readers of literary journals. "Movement is not life, painting is not ideas!"[63] the critic declares. Balzac mocks critical discourse in this passage, and as I show in the next chapter, his own relation to Scott's visual poetics was far more complicated than this summary dismissal suggests. But his playful description of a new "literature of images" reveals the degree to which Scott had become associated with a new type of visual description.

A sustained rendering of the appearance of people, places, and things first enters the French historical novel in the 1820s, when Scott's influence began to make itself felt.[64] For French writers, imitating Scott meant first and foremost producing a picture of the past. Readers today are familiar with the vivid descriptions of the monuments of medieval Paris in Hugo's *Notre-Dame de Paris,* but scores of historical novels published in the 1820s and 1830s featured a similar visual aesthetic. Literary historians have tended to reduce the number of Scott's French imitators to three novels in addition to Hugo's *Notre-Dame de Paris*: Alfred de Vigny's *Cinq-Mars* (1826), Prosper Mérimée's *Chronique du règne de Charles IX* (1829), and Balzac's *Les Chouans* (1829).[65] But if these four novels

63. Balzac, *Illusions perdues* (1843; reprint, Paris: Gallimard, 1974), 362.

64. In *The Art of French Fiction* (London: Hamish Hamilton, 1959), Martin Turnell describes the "new interest in material reality" (7) characterizing such nineteenth-century authors as Balzac and Stendhal and analyzes this shift in terms of language. In *Fiction and the Camera Eye: Visual Consciousness in Film and the Modern Novel* (Charlottesville: University of Virginia Press, 1976), Alan Spiegel argues that "visualized narrative" is consolidated in the fiction of Flaubert, particularly in *Madame Bovary* (1857), but also acknowledges that "certain early nineteenth-century novelists," including Scott and Balzac, pioneered in this direction (5). Christopher Prendergast examines the question of fictional reference from a semiological perspective in *The Order of Mimesis: Balzac, Stendhal, Nerval, Flaubert* (Cambridge, UK: Cambridge University Press, 1986).

65. Lukács follows Maigron's lead in focusing on these four novels as the prime representatives of the Romantic historical novel in France. Claude Duchet estimates, based on his

constitute the canon of French Romantic historical fiction today, they hardly suffice to demonstrate the extent to which the vogue for visual description of the past became widespread in the 1820s, 1830s, and 1840s. In this period, writers such as Alexandre-Pierre Barginet, Mathurin-Joseph Brisset, Gustave Delalance, Alexandre Dumas *père,* Paul de Kock, Paul Lacroix, Jean-Baptiste Mardelle, Théodore Muret, and Jean-Charles-Léonard Simonde de Sismondi rejected the home-grown sentimental tradition for a new mode of historical representation based on the visual.[66] A younger generation of women writers also followed this trend, including Laure Junot, duchesse d'Abrantès; Alexandrine-Sophie Goury de Champgrand, baronne de Bawr; Agathe-Pauline Caylac de Ceylan, comtesse de Bradi; Louise Désormery; Eugénie Foa; and Sophie Moser, baronne d'Ordre.

Although these novelists mostly wrote about French history rather than English, they followed Scott's formula quite closely. While focusing on a diverse array of periods, they exhibit a remarkable similarity in their modes of composition. Many open with a "landscape," a picturesque description of nature that turns the reader into an observer of a static scene. In the beginning of Barginet's *Le roi des montagnes* (1828), a typical French imitation of Scott, the gaze of a fictional observer is explicitly thematized as the narrator unveils a view of a valley in the Dauphiné region: "That countryside, nowadays so pleasant and fertile, but still bearing the traces of feudalism, merits the attention of the voyager who descends from our Alps. If the grand and noble scenes of the montains no longer excite his enthusiasm, his eye will nevertheless take pleasure in the long chains of green hills, as well as in those carefully cultivated valleys."[67] Here the narrator accesses the past—the novel takes place during the time of Louis XI—through a picturesque modern setting that bears the marks of prior ages. As in Scott's novels, the reader becomes a fictional voyager, through

---

study of prefaces, however, that between 1815 and 1832 approximately one-quarter to one-third of all novels published in France were historical, a figure he puts at between five and six hundred works. "L'illusion historique: l'enseignement des préfaces (1815–1832)," *Revue d'Histoire Littéraire de la France,* nos. 2–3 (March–June 1975): 252.

66. This list of Scott imitators is far from complete and contains only those writers whose works I have verified as containing a visual poetics. In her study of the historical novel genre, *Le passé recomposé: Le roman historique français du dix-neuvième siècle* (Paris: Hachette, 1996), Claudie Bernard provides a similar list of Scott imitators (although she only mentions men) (50).

67. Alexandre Barginet, *Le Roi des Montagnes, ou les compagnons du chêne, tradition dauphinoise du temps de Charles VIII* (Paris: Mame et Delaunay-Valée, 1828), 3.

time as well as space, and the visual descriptions of the landscape resemble those of travel writing, another popular genre during the Romantic period.[68]

Descriptions of costume and facial features play a vital role in the novels of Scott's French imitators. As in *Ivanhoe,* these works often present characters physically, and sartorially, before revealing personality traits or even names. In a great many of these novels, the reader first sees the protagonist on the road, and the identity of the anonymous voyager becomes a kind of mystery to be solved through the accumulation of visual clues. "In the year 1616, on an April day that shone with all the brightness of a beautiful spring sun," begins Delalance's *Le maréchal d'Ancre* (1832), "a voyager tranquilly traveled the road that leads from Meaux to the French capital."[69] First the narrator provides a description of the traveler's horse and then moves to a very detailed picture of his clothing—"a sky blue pair of breeches and matching doublet, adorned with braiding and sashes in black silk; extremely tight-fitting boots of soft leather."[70] Only later, and gradually, does the text reveal that his name is Léopold de Vrécourt and that he has come from Nancy to make his fortune in Paris. Many other Scott imitations begin with an almost identical scene, in which a mysterious voyager materializes before the reader's eyes.[71]

The repetition of this initial scene of visual introduction in so many of the French historical novels from the period suggests a commonality of purpose as well as method. These novels offer not only a fictionalized account of events from the past but a lesson in historical epistemology: they teach the reader how to look at history in a new way. In these works, as in Scott's novels, knowledge accrues through the eyes. The visual contains the key to resolving the narrative enigmas which in these works are also historical enigmas. In what is today probably the most widely read of the French novels influenced by Scott, Dumas *père*'s *Les trois mousquetaires* (1844), d'Artagnan's down-at-heels appearance at the start of the novel, while journeying from his home in Gascony to Paris on a broken-down horse, serves as a means of referencing the declining fortunes of his family

68. At the height of the Scott craze in France, Amédée Pichot, one of Scott's translators, published a *Voyage historique et littéraire en Angleterre et en Écosse* (Paris: Ladvocat et Charles Gosselin, 1825) and a *Vues pittoresques de l'Écosse* (Paris: Charles Glesselin et Lami-Denozan, 1826), with lithographic illustrations by François-Alexandre Pernot.

69. Gustave Delalance, *Le Maréchal d'Ancre* (Paris: Mme Charles Béchet, 1832), 3.

70. Ibid., 3.

71. These include Barginet's *La chemise sanglante* (1830), Mathurin-Joseph Brisset's *Les Templiers* (1837), Paul de Kock's *Le barbier de Paris* (1827), Eugénie Foa's *La juive* (1835), and Théodore Muret's *Mademoiselle de Montpensier* (1836).

and, by extension, the position of the disaffected provincial nobility under Richelieu.

Understanding the identity of the protagonist and the nature of his quest involves seeing him or her as a product of a particular time and place. Character and plot emerge from the concrete, material forms that only visual description, or local color, can provide. As I show in the next chapter, Balzac followed Scott's process closely in his Romantic historical novel *Les Chouans*. But he also adapted this technique to fictions about the present in his later Realist works, showing how characters belong to a specific moment based on what they wear and how they talk. It is important to realize, however, that this process is essentially historical in nature; as Lukács noted, the present of Realism (which is often actually the recent past) is really just another, less remote historical period.[72]

Visual description in historical fiction radically altered the way readers could imagine the past. First and foremost, the visual allows for the apprehension of the difference of the past on a concrete, material level. Showing the way people in different historical periods lived and dressed reveals a new kind of historicity, a narrative of change through the ages manifested not in the abstraction of dynasties or laws but in the forms of everyday life. Specific periods became associated not only with the king who reigned, as in the traditional compilation histories of the ancien régime, but as a succession of styles. Far more than mere decoration, the visual became a new way of depicting the process of history in accessible terms. This is what Balzac meant when he describes Scott's technique in an 1828 foreword to an early version of *Les Chouans*: "history becomes domestic beneath his brush."[73] As Balzac's well-chosen adjective shows, Scott's intricate descriptions of architecture made the past "domestic" both literally and metaphorically—by showing where and how people in the past lived, he made history human in scale, inhabitable.

Scott's novels, Balzac writes, help us "to understand a period better; he evokes its spirit and in a single scene expresses its genius and true face [*physionomie*]."[74] Not only does local color make historical change visible, as a series of differences in style, it also expresses the inner essence of a given period or culture—its "genius and true face." The theory of local color assumes that the inner essence of a culture manifests itself in its outward or surface appearances. Buildings and clothes make visible the spirit

72. "Balzac passes from the portrayal of *past history* to the portrayal of the *present as history*," (Lukács, *Historical Novel*, 83, emphasis in original).

73. Honoré de Balzac, *Les Chouans* (1829; reprint, Paris: Gallimard, 1972), 496.

74. Ibid.

of the people who produced them, the mentality of the people who lived in and wore them. Here lies the paradox of Scott's apparent superficiality: descriptions of outward appearance not only delight the reader with their ingenuity, but convey deeper historical truths. Unlike the women writers who preceded him, Scott emphasizes differences in character that make a time or place unique rather than the common emotional or spiritual essence of humanity in all times or places. As in the panorama or the Boulevard theater, visual details become the vehicle for communicating this sense of difference.

As I have shown, another important characteristic of spectacles such as the panorama was their ability to make viewers forget they were looking at a representation. Scott's visual poetics achieved something similar: "Few men have so well or so often endowed their pictures with reality as Walter Scott," affirms the author of a biographical sketch of Scott, published a decade after his death. This "viewer" describes seeing in Scott's fiction, "living beings [. . .] who walk, feel, breathe; we think we see their chest heave, or their lips tremble, or their eyes shine."[75] As in the wax displays of Curtius or the Napoleon plays, Scott's novels crossed the border between art and reality, producing an illusion of historical presence. Like the panorama, which gave viewers the feeling of being in the middle of a battle, Scott's novels, and those of his French imitators, achieved an effect of time travel. "Right from the start, you feel you have been transported to the old hôtel de Chaumont,"[76] comments a reviewer of Alfred de Vigny's *Cinq-Mars,* one of the most famous of the French novels to imitate Scott during the 1820s. "From the first page, he puts you in the middle of a historical period," writes a reviewer ("L.") of Scott. "He offers not invention, but something better: his imagination contains the truth, but a truth that has been captured alive, reproduced whole, not copied, but living."[77] Like other forms of popular spectacle, the historical novel sought to erase its status as representation.

The stunning specificity of the re-creation of the material aspect of the past in the novels of Scott and his French imitators helped create a new relation between the reader and the historical world described. Readers of earlier French historical novels had not felt transported to the past because the historical settings of these novels were merely a reflection of the present. If the past seemed less real in these earlier works, it was because it did

75. Michaud, *Biographie universelle ancienne et moderne,* vol. 38, p. 570.

76. Y., "Variétés," review of *Cinq-Mars* by Alfred de Vigny, *Gazette de France,* July 9, 1826, 3.

77. L., "Variétés," review of Scott's novels, *Journal des Débats,* September 28, 1822, 4.

not exist as a separate entity, as a coherent world apart from the world of the reader. Indeed, visual details in these novels would have distracted from the emphasis on the moral struggles facing the protagonist; the difference of the past was minimized in order to convey a sense of the universality of the sentimental dilemma at the center of the novel's intrigue. The reader of these earlier novels could share the protagonist's concerns in a way that negated the historical gap between them.

In the novels of Scott and his followers, however, the reader observed the protagonist from a distance, across a space dividing present from past, like the gap between the viewing platform and the canvas of the panorama. This barrier is one of the by-products of local color; by rendering the past as a distinct material entity, as a visibly real but different world, the new novel no longer confronted the reader with the same kind of moral dilemma. While the reader might still identify with the protagonist, the past ceased to function as an arena of ethical struggle in which protagonist and reader together engage in, and resolve, sentimental and social conflict. In the new type of novel, history became instead something to be seen but not touched. Indeed, the protagonists of these new novels are often themselves mere observers of historical events. Edward Waverley, the hero of Scott's first historical novel, joins in the efforts of his Scottish friends to return the Stuart monarchs to the throne, but it is not his struggle. He functions less as an active participant than as a passive lens through which the reader observes an exotic and vanished world.[78]

Astute readers at the time recognized this new feature in Scott's work. *Le Globe's* critic "F.," attempting to describe the Scottian mould that had produced so many French copies, cited as one of its chief features the introduction of a fictional (rather than historical) hero whose primary function is to look: "He would have preferred an unknown person, a sort of *spectator* with whom one might wander from one scene to another, through a variety of customs and events."[79] Whereas Lukács focused on

78. In *Le Chouan romanesque: Balzac, Barbey d'Aurevilly, Hugo* (Paris: Presses Universitaires de France, 1989), Claudie Bernard makes a similar observation in regard to later historical novels: "After 1848, however, the protagonist tends to be restricted to the position of a spectator" (32).

79. F., "Littérature," review of *Charles-le-Téméraire* by Scott, *Le Globe*, August 15, 1829, 515, emphasis added. *Le Globe*, founded in 1824 by Pierre Leroux, was one of the most significant literary journals of the era. Its critics generally approved of Romantic tendencies in the arts, including the novels of Walter Scott, and espoused liberal politics during the Restoration. After 1830, it became an organ of the Saint-Simonians (Claude Bellanger et al., eds., *Histoire générale de la press française*, vol. 2 [Paris: Presses Universitaires de France, 1969], 93). Jean-Jacques Goblot offers a comprehensive study of the paper's politics in *La jeune France libérale: Le Globe et son groupe littéraire, 1824–1830* (Paris: Plon, 1995).

the mediocre condition of the Scottian hero as the key element in the new brand of historical fiction, subsuming the role of description to that of characterization, the protagonist's *class* was secondary to his *function* as a model for a new kind of historical vision. In so many of the French historical novels produced in the Scottian mould, hero and reader wander through the landscape of history, "from one scene to another." Readers of this new historical fiction likewise find themselves transported to a past in which they look without being called on to act. Even when the protagonists do participate centrally and actively in events of the novel, as in the swashbuckling adventures of Dumas's *Les trois mousquetaires,* the reader remains in a passive role. The characters serve as a kind of optical instrument, allowing the reader to gaze on the otherness of the past.

As with the panorama and the other historical spectacles, however, the Scottian historical novel presented the past as the ground on which a new kind of national identity could be formed. To a large extent, this process depended on the appropriation of individual, regional histories into a unified national history. Katie Trumpener has argued that within the British context the Scottian historical novel, which she shows to be much less of an originator than Lukács and his followers have proclaimed,[80] offered a paradigmatic fiction of empire building by showing how regional cultural distinctiveness persists even after remote geographic regions surrender political autonomy. "As he enacts and explains the composition of Britain as an internal empire," Trumpener writes, "Scott [. . .] argues for the continued centrality of national identity as a component of imperial identity."[81] The French imitators of Scott adapted this model to the post-Revolutionary French cultural and political landscape, explaining—and enacting—the unification of France's regions into a unified national whole and thus completing the ideological work that both the Revolution and Napoleonic eras had begun through their policies of centralization and standardization.

Like the Waverley novels, which take place in Scotland, a country whose landscape and manners were relatively unknown even to the English reading public of the time, many imitators of Scott set their novels in remote French provinces with an exotic appeal. Novelists specialized in particular

---

80. Katie Trumpener writes that "most of the conceptual innovations attributed to Scott were in 1814 already established commonplaces of the British novel." *Bardic Nationalism: The Romantic Novel and the British Empire* (Princeton: Princeton University Press, 1997), 130.

81. Ibid., xiii.

regions. The comtesse de Bradi, for example, wrote several historical novels set in Corsica, the birthplace of her husband, a locale endowed with the double advantage of being both picturesque (unruly landscape and inhabitants) and topical (the birthplace of the recently defunct Napoleon, whom Bradi detested). In a frame narrative, set in the present, to Bradi's *Colonna, ou le beau seigneur* (1825), Charles d'Aunay, the putative author of the historical novel we are about to read, describes his ambition to follow in Scott's footsteps, to do for Corsica what the master did for his native Scotland, an ambition that the countess clearly shared: "I felt myself suddenly burning with the desire to celebrate my country, to describe its sites, to sketch its customs; I wanted to paint different characters, different periods."[82] Indeed, historical regionalism had become such a trend in France that in 1825 one anonymous reviewer complained, "Now it's the turn of those who ape the famous writer from Scotland [. . .] this one's editor calls him the Walter Scott of Picardy; that one's bookseller dubs him the Walter Scott of the Franche-Comté."[83] The taste for regional historical fiction continued despite such mockery. In the 1840s, Frédéric Soulié wrote a series of historical novels set in the Languedoc region, including *Le comte de Toulouse* (1840), which went through more than fifteen editions between 1840 and 1863.

Scott's novels provided France with a model for overcoming persistent regionalisms through the appropriation of local histories. Just as the Waverley novels celebrated the local culture of the Scottish Highlands, even while showing the inevitability of this region's surrender of political autonomy to the British empire, so too did the French regional historical novels enact the internal extension of a hegemonic model of French national identity. These novels celebrated local distinctiveness in a highly generic way—all France's regions have their history, but this history was standardized and homogenized according to the restricted formal techniques and structure of the Scottian novel. The novels of regional history were thus paradoxically almost identical. What emerges from the project of the Scottian historical novel in France is a unified national history composed of many parts, all equal in their distinctiveness and all made available to an ideal national (i.e., nonregional) French reader. The novels thus foreshadow the process of transforming "peasants into Frenchmen" that

82. Comtesse de Bradi, *Colonna, ou le beau seigneur, histoire corse du 10e siècle* (Paris: Chez l'Éditeur, 1825), 55–56.

83. R., "Variétés," review of *Le dernier des Beaumanoir* by Auguste-Hilarion de Kératy, *Journal des Débats*, December 18, 1825, 3.

Eugen Weber has described as taking place in the latter part of the nineteenth century.[84]

Many of the Scott-inspired historical novels, moreover, allegorized this process of standardization and unification through the depiction of a young man from the provinces who makes his way to Paris. These novels, including Dumas's *Les trois mousquetaires,* delighted in depicting the distinctiveness of this young man's clothing and dialect but also showed how the capital is composed of many such young men, each equal in his distinctiveness. While these novels served to document local particularities, often those that had vanished or were in the process of vanishing due to the centralizing and unifying policies of the Revolutionary and Napoleonic eras, they also aided in this vanishing process by subsuming the particular within a unified generic category of the historical novel and making this novel easily assimilable by an ideal national subject—the Parisian reader. The new historical novel thus produced a vision of a national history, composed of many individual parts, but unified in form and function, like post-Revolutionary France itself.

Novel Commodities

Walter Scott did more than change the style of the novel in France; he changed its status. Scott's impact was not only formal or epistemological or even ideological, but also social and material, altering the way the novel was produced and consumed in ways that continue to determine the way novels are read and written today. By making the historical novel a spectacle, he increased its commercial potential. Tracing this process allows us insight not only into the history of the novel, but also into the functioning of the spectacular past more generally. Understanding how Scott and his imitators capitalized on their creations provides a perspective on how enterprising entrepreneurs of other forms of historical spectacle saw the nature of their product and its appeal to particular audiences.

Gender once again provides perhaps the most significant lens through which to view these changes. Although women were hardly the sole readers of the novel before the nineteenth century, the novel was largely associated with women at a time when they authored a large percentage of French novels in a variety of genres. Novels by women of the seventeenth, eighteenth, and early nineteenth centuries—many of which, as I have shown, were historical—tend to center on a female protagonist and to

84. Eugen Weber, *Peasants into Frenchmen: The Modernization of Rural France, 1870–1914* (Stanford, CA: Stanford University Press, 1976).

raise social and ethical questions pertinent to a female reading public. Even male novelists during the ancien régime, such as Rousseau, who eclipsed their female contemporaries in the appreciation of subsequent literary historians, often centered their novels around women.

By the 1830s the situation had changed dramatically. Although Balzac was still accused of pandering to a female clientele by exploring the intricacies of adultery and passion, his works hardly reflect the woman's point of view that had defined the novel in its earlier manifestations.[85] Certainly a new conception of the novel's virility made itself felt during the nineteenth century as the *Bildungsroman* (almost exclusively focused on the education of a male protagonist) came to overshadow the novel of female sensibility.[86] Flaubert, despite his famed identification with his character Emma Bovary, distanced himself from her in part through the act of novel writing, cast in his *Correspondance* as a heroic and manly labor.[87] These stereotypes, of course, reflect not the real social conditions of novelistic production in the period (as Margaret Cohen has shown, a great many women continued to write novels after Balzac) but a shift in perception confirmed by subsequent literary historians who largely excluded women from the nineteenth-century canon.[88]

---

85. In *Scenes of Seduction: Prostitution, Hysteria, and Reading Difference in Nineteenth-Century France* (New York: Columbia University Press, 1994), Jann Matlock characterizes Balzac's reputation among contemporary critics as "the 'lady's man' of July Monarchy literature" (166). Catherine Nesci describes the dynamics of Balzac's representation of women in *La femme mode d'emploi: Balzac, de la* Physiologie du mariage *à* La Comédie humaine (Lexington, KY: French Forum, 1992).

86. In *The Male Malady: Fictions of Impotence in the French Romantic Novel* (New Brunswick: Rutgers University Press, 1993), Margaret Waller shows how male power is often deployed through weakness in the Romantic novel. She locates the shift toward androcentrism in French fiction as early as the 1802 publication of Chateaubriand's *René* (29).

87. Flaubert wrote to Louise Colet on September 12, 1853, during the composition of *Madame Bovary*: "I spent four hours without being able to write a *single* sentence [. . .] What horrible labor! [Quel atroce travail!]" Gustave Flaubert, *Correspondance*, ed. Jean Bruneau, vol. 2 (Paris: Gallimard, 1980), 428, emphasis in original.

88. Germaine de Staël and George Sand, alone among nineteenth-century women novelists, can claim a secure place in the canon of nineteenth-century French literature. In *George Sand and Idealism* (New York: Columbia University Press, 1993), Naomi Schor describes how Sand's canonizing has, however, involved the exclusion of a significant portion of her oeuvre. Linda Orr notes that Staël's historiographic texts, including the *Considérations sur la Révolution française*, are dismissed in many accounts of the historiographic literature of the period as mere biography (because Staël's father was Necker). "Outspoken Women and the Rightful Daughter of the Revolution: Madame de Staël's *Considérations sur la Révolution française*," in *Rebel Daughters: Women and the French Revolution*, ed. Sara E. Melzer and Leslie W. Rabine (New York: Oxford University Press, 1992), 121–36. Cohen offers a significant corrective to traditional histories of nineteenth-century literature in *Sentimental Education of the Novel* by recovering the tradition of women writing sentimental and social fiction.

Scott played an important role in effecting this shift in perception of the novel's gender affiliation. Ina Ferris has argued similarly about Scott's impact on the English novel: whereas by 1800, the English novel was largely associated with women readers and women writers, both in its "popular" and "proper" forms, the Scottian historical novel offered a "compelling alternative" and a male "release" from this feminized space.[89] With their "serious" subject matter and claims of objectivity and accuracy, Scott's historical novels "allow male subjectivity to enter into a female genre without losing its masculine purchase on truth and fact."[90] The supposed rigor of the new historical novel, in which romance was relegated to the background, made the novel safe for male production and consumption.

A survey of the reception of Scott and his imitators in the French press reveals that the historical novel did indeed lose its associations with women once the spectacular style came to dominate. "Ten years ago a serious man would hide in order to read a novel; today, as long as you aren't a Jansenist, you no longer have to be secretive about such reading," wrote an anonymous critic in a review of Scott's *Legend of Montrose* in 1826.[91] As this review makes clear, men had been reading novels all along; but because of the feminine point of view of such works, the sentimental intrigues aimed at an implied female reader, men had been reading in secret. Thanks to Scott, the novel no longer appeared to pose a threat to masculinity.

Scott endowed the novel with the gravity, *le sérieux,* of a supposedly more realistic history. "For two centuries the novel has been harvesting the field of history," wrote a critic for the *Journal des Débats* in 1825. For this critic, women novelists who had mixed "the fables of their imagination" with the "realities of history" could not be read by serious-minded people (i.e., men), "from which derives that hereditary disfavor that weighs both on Mme de Scudéry and Mme de Genlis." Unlike his female predecessors, Scott used the past to teach historical rather than moral lessons, and in the process raised the status of the novel in the eyes of (male) critics. "Finally a man came along who was able to elevate the novel to the dignified level of history," declared the critic for the *Débats.*[92] In a review

89. Ferris, *Achievement of Literary Authority,* 91. In England, however, where women such as Jane Austen, the Brontës, and George Eliot were associated with the prestige of Realism and remain an integral part of the canon, the eclipse of the feminine was not as total as it was in France. Ferris's thesis is thus perhaps even more applicable to the French context.

90. Ibid., 88.

91. "Littérature étrangère," review of *Legend of Montrose* by Scott, *Le Globe,* August 8, 1826, 524.

92. L. S., "Théâtre de Vaudeville," review of *L'exilé, vaudeville imité des Puritains d'Écosse* by Achille Dartois et al., *Journal des Débats,* July 17, 1825, 1.

of James Fenimore Cooper's historical novels set in America, which were cast in the mould of Scott, *Le Globe's* critic stated baldly: "We rejoice that these works are novels, because we regard the novel as the most reasonable and most fruitful [*féconde*] literary form."[93] Thanks to Scott and his imitators, by the mid-1820s the historical novel had come to seem preferable even to historiography as a tool for learning about the past.

By removing the need to identify with a female protagonist and offering up the past instead as an object of contemplation, Scott enabled the novel to reach a wider readership. In its new form, the historical novel seemed to appeal to both men and women. Recalling the literary tastes of his youth, Pontmartin, an *homme de lettres* of the later nineteenth century, describes how Scott attracted readers of both sexes: "Female readers with poetic, lyric, and romantic pretensions preferred Lord Byron; but serious men, sensible women, and mothers looking for honest reading for their sons and daughters opted for Walter Scott."[94] Sensible (rather than sensitive) women, as well as serious men, according to this observer, were able to identify with the male protagonist of the new novel. For a certain public, at least, Scott did not so much masculinize the novel as popularize it.

As I have shown, moreover, writers of both genders produced the new Scott-inspired historical fiction. Whereas Alexandrine-Sophie de Bawr's *Le novice* (1830), in which a young monk in the fourteenth century leaves his cloistered life of study to become a soldier, centers on male characters and particularly male concerns (indeed, not a single female character appears in the first two volumes of the novel), other women who wrote in the wake of Scott combined local color with more feminocentric features, including typically romantic plots revolving around women. Despite being a protégée of Madame de Genlis, Bradi placed her writing under the sign of Scott; whereas Genlis dedicated *Le siège de la Rochelle* to her, Bradi in turn dedicates her second Corsican novel, *Colonna, ou le beau seigneur,* centered on a female character and a romantic intrigue, to the Scotsman.[95]

Scott's novels appealed to "serious" readers because of their historical rigor, but this was not their sole attraction. Like the popular spectacles of the era, the new historical novels of the 1820s combined informative subject matter with a capacity for entertainment. From the beginning of the

93. F. A. S., "États-Unis, Littérature américaine," review of James Fenimore Cooper's novels, *Le Globe,* June 19, 1827, 174.
94. Pontmartin, *Mes mémoires,* 2–3.
95. The dedication reads: "To the writer compared to Tacitus, to Ariosto, to Cervantes; to the writer who will always respect religion, manners, and ill fortune; to the creative genius of the nineteenth century: TO SIR WALTER-SCOTT." Bradi, *Colonna, ou le beau seigneur, histoire Corse du 10e siècle* (Paris: Chez l'Editeur, 1825).

nineteenth century, spectacles such as the wax display and the panorama had managed both to educate and to entertain. Scott's novels pulled off the same feat. "What makes Scott so popular," declared a review by the critic Jean-Marie-Napoléon-Désiré Nisard of a "popular edition" of Scott's novels from 1830, "is that he appeals to two classes of readers [. . .] the broader public as well as educated people."[96] According to Nisard, there was something for everyone in Scott; common readers could enjoy the picturesque surface of the text and skip over the historical asides and didactic digressions that delighted those with more ambitious intellectual agendas.

Whereas Scott's own novels were often seen by critics as fusing intellectual seriousness with entertainment value, those of his French followers were denounced for minimizing the former in favor of the latter. Even Mérimée's *Chronique du temps de Charles IX,* considered by both Maigron and Lukács as one of the most worthy of the Scott imitations, was seen by certain nineteenth-century critics as pandering to the popular taste for spectacle. "It is decidedly to the 16th century that we address, of late, our need for strong emotions and for novel spectacles," declares one review in the left-leaning *Le Constitutionnel,* in which the critic likens Mérimée's novel to a costume ball or a historical drama. According to this critic, such "spectacles" emphasize the exterior features of the past, the superficial details of costume and architecture, but lack the degree of historical accuracy that had at least been present in Scott. "If you want to be deliciously moved, if you want to abandon yourself for a few hours to some ravishing scenes, read this story [histoire], and regard the rest merely as some exterior paintings the truth of which matters little."[97] In this novel and the dozens of others like it, history becomes a "scene," not unlike the décor of a theater. In order to be "moved," the reader must only "look" at the past as a "painting."

Coinciding with the expansion of the reading public in the early nineteenth century and the commercialization of the book trade, Scott's success helped make the novel into a form of popular entertainment for broad segments of the population. During the 1820s and 1830s, publishers such as Charles Gosselin began selling Scott's novels in relatively cheap, serialized installments, which were also made available in the *cabinets de lec-*

---

96. Jean-Marie-Napoléon-Désiré Nisard, "Variétés," review of Scott's novels, *Journal des Débats,* January 6, 1830, 2, cited in Lyons, "Audience for Romanticism," 32.

97. Armand Carrel, "1572," review of *Chronique du temps de Charles IX* by Prosper Mérimée, *Le Constitutionnel,* April 9, 1829, 5. *Le Constitutionnel* was the leading organ of the liberal opposition during the Restoration.

ture. Gosselin later estimated that he produced almost 1,500,000 volumes of Scott. By 1848, Charpentier began publishing pocket-size editions of single Scott novels, which sold for as little as 3.5 francs each. According to Martyn Lyons, whose social history of Scott's reception provides key insights as well as valuable statistics, "Scott played a vital role in the formation of a mass literary audience in France, crossing barriers of class and education, and helping to make the novel an article of everyday consumption for families all over France."[98] Scott's influence reached beyond Paris to the provinces; during the Restoration, the provincial *cabinets de lecture,* like their Parisian contemporaries, carried a large number of Scott volumes. According to Lyons, Scott's success was instrumental in forging a truly national literary culture in France.

Scott made the novel a hot commodity. Like other forms of historical spectacle, Scott's novels sought to engage the largest possible clientele in order to make a profit. And as in the panorama, the illustrated histories, and the Boulevard theater, the visual provided the key to their success.[99] In 1826, a luxurious new edition of Scott's complete novels was vigorously marketed by Gosselin. A prospectus for the new edition appeared along with the Christmas issue of the *Journal des Débats* so that readers could place their orders for the traditional New Year's gift (*étrennes*). "This is an ingenious idea," declared the *Débat's* critic "V"; "it provides the opportunity to offer as a gift the entire collection of the Works of Walter Scott; this is the nicest gift one could give."[100] This edition, which supplemented the visuality of Scott's prose with actual images, made history into an object of exchange.[101] Adorned with thirty maps and seventy-five copper-plate il-

98. Lyons, "Audience for Romanticism," 28–32.

99. Lukács describes how by the end of the nineteenth century, Scott's novels "slip from the hands of the educated" to become popular as gifts to one's nieces and nephews for birthdays and confirmations (*Historical Novel,* 182). For Lukács the reduction of Scott's works to the status of gift signifies the passing of the era of the Classical historical novel; he overlooks the degree to which Scott's novels had already served a similar commercial function during their heyday in the 1820s.

100. V., "Variétés," review of *Oeuvres complètes* by Scott, *Journal des Débats,* December 25, 1826, 4.

101. The 72 volumes of the set were sold in installments of three volumes. Initial subscribers paid 12 francs for an installment, so 4 francs for a volume, which included the engravings and maps. Collectors could pay 25 francs for engravings made *avant la lettre,* i.e., images printed before the addition of text (title, artists' names, etc.); later subscribers paid 15 francs (5 francs a volume) and 30 francs for engravings *avant la lettre.* Each volume of this set of Scott's works thus cost about the same as earlier editions of female novelists containing engravings. An illustrated edition of Gottis's *François Premier et Madame de Chateaubriand,* published by Eymery in 1818, cost 5 francs.

FIGURE 4.1   Engraving after Alexandre-Joseph Desenne, "Waverley porte des consolations à Flora Mac-Ivor," in *Oeuvres complètes de Sir Walter Scott* (1826), vol. 13, chap. 68, p. 86. Image courtesy of the Bibliothèque nationale de France, Paris.

lustrations by "the best French and English artists,"[102] it was marketed to a new clientele, a readership whose interest required the added allure of the visual to be awakened (fig. 4.1). As one advertisement put it, "We trust that thanks to our historical notes, drawings, and maps, readers of Sir Walter Scott, and especially the ladies, to whom this edition is particularly aimed, will find in the works of that author a new source of interest and instruction."[103] This advertisement reverses earlier stereotypes. Whereas previous historical novels had addressed themselves to women precisely by

102. V., "Variétés," review of *Oeuvres complètes,* 4.
103. "Annonces Générales," advertisement for *Oeuvres complètes de Walter Scott, Le Constitutionnel,* March 20, 1826, 5, emphasis in original.

refusing the visual, here it is through the visual that the new historical novel markets itself explicitly to both genders.

The commercialization of Scott and his imitators becomes an object of satire in Balzac's *Illusions perdues*. In this Realist *Bildungsroman,* the protagonist Lucien de Rubempré writes *L'archer de Charles IX,* a Romantic historical novel "in the manner of Walter Scott," in order to secure both fame and "enough money" to repay a debt to his family.[104] Descriptions of the novel within the novel almost always revolve around calculations of its profitability: "After having read the first pages of *L'archer de Charles IX,*" Lucien fantasizes, "booksellers will open their cash registers and ask:— How much do you want for it?"[105] The novelistic codes instituted by Scott resonate for Lucien less as a means of accessing a distant past than as a means of ensuring a successful future.

Scott's own commercial success could have served as the model for Lucien's financial daydreams. Indeed, biographies of Scott from the 1820s devote a great deal of attention to the monetary value of his work, entering into surprisingly specific financial detail *à la Balzac.* In a *Notice sur Walter Scott et ses écrits,* Amédée Pichot (one of Scott's primary French translators and imitators) boasts that "Sir Walter Scott enriches himself without ruining his booksellers. The manuscript of the *Prison d'Edimbourg* was bought for 4000 liv. sterling, which is to say 100,000 French francs."[106] These biographies, as well as obituaries published after Scott's death in 1832, inevitably narrate the writer's financial peripeties, including his near ruin due to the collapse of his publishing house and his heroic return to prosperity through his literary labors.

Critics occasionally mocked the rapidity with which Scott responded to the public's demand for his work: "One can bet that he begins a novel without knowing how he will finish it."[107] They nevertheless acknowledged that new market realities necessitated new literary strategies: "Even in literature, it can't be forgotten that consumption determines production,"[108] writes the critic for the *Journal des Débats* in a review of Scott's *Les eaux de Saint-Ronan.* In a period when the literary marketplace was solidifying the autonomy of authorship as an institution, Scott demonstrated to ambitious young men such as Lucien de Rubempré, and to some women as well, how the historical novel offered a viable (if hazardous) path to career

104. Balzac, *Illusions perdues,* 142.
105. Ibid. 161.
106. Amédée Pichot, *Notice sur Sir Walter Scott et ses écrits* (Paris: Ladvocat, 1821), 37.
107. T. L., "Variétés," review of *Les eaux de Saint-Ronan* by Scott, *Journal des Débats,* 3.
108. Ibid.

success. In his rise to riches through literary labors, Scott served as a model for the Balzacian hero and for a host of spectacle entrepreneurs: he made history look like easy money.

The French Historical Novel after Scott

Scholars tend to agree that if the historical novel did not decline in popularity, it did decline in quality sometime after Scott's death in 1832, although the reasons for this decline remain the subject of debate. Lukács sees a degradation culminating in the production of "an historical novel which drops to the level of light entertainment" by neglecting political concerns in favor of "an adventurous or emptily antiquarian" exoticism.[109] The novels of Dumas *père* represent the adventure pole, whereas Flaubert's *Salammbô* (1862) fits the antiquarian label. Lukács traces the motivation for the exoticism of Flaubert to the traumatizing experience of the Revolution of 1848, in which the brutal repression of the workers spelled the end of the bourgeoisie's claim to embody universal values. Flaubert and others looked back to the past as an escape from the "ugliness and sordid triviality of their capitalist present," and stylized and idealized history "out of romantic protest" (183). As Lukács recounts, Flaubert had sought refuge from the banality of nineteenth century life by observing it in minute detail in *Madame Bovary* (1857), but in *Salammbô* he applied this systematic mode of description to ancient Carthage, creating a "picturesque, decorative, grandiose, gorgeous, cruel and exotic world" (186) that in Lukács's view is profoundly uninteresting. The problem for Lukács is that the characters in Flaubert's historical novel reflected not the genuine historical forces of their age, as Scott's characters did, but rather the subjective mental state of their creator.

More recently scholars such as Claude Duchet and Thomas Gretton have dated the historical novel's decline to the Revolution of 1830 rather than that of 1848. Duchet argues that the past ceased to serve as an important battleground for debates over bourgeois ideology once the July Revolution confirmed the bourgeoisie's triumph: "the conquests of July made the old problematic outdated; the historical novel loses, along with its political mission, its principal raison d'être, which until that point had masked its constitutional flaws, the extent of its uncertainties, and the weakness of its position as a genre."[110] Focusing on the

109. Lukács, *Historical Novel*, 183. Subsequent quotations are cited in the text.
110. Duchet, "Illusion historique," 263.

work of forgotten novelist Théophile Dinocourt, one of the most prolific historical novelists of the period, Gretton argues that the post-1830
historical novel sagged under the weight of clichéd characters and story
structure, becoming merely a vehicle for the propagation of a national
mythology.[111]

Gretton is correct in his description of the progressive emptying of political content from the French historical novel, but the process is not as
neatly circumscribed by the July Revolution as he would have it.
Dinocourt's historical *romans-à-thèse*, which had courageously argued
against aristocratic and ecclesiastical privilege during the reactionary years
of the Restoration, were reissued in revised editions *after* 1830. Moreover,
Dinocourt's equivalent on the right, the vicomte Victor d'Arlincourt, really came into his own only after the July Revolution, publishing a spate of
novels in the 1830s in which attacks against Louis-Philippe's bourgeois
monarchy were lightly veiled in historical allegory.

The change in the French historical novel after Scott's death had less to
do with a reduction in its political content than with an exaggeration of its
spectacular aspects. During the July Monarchy, the historical novel became even more visual and more commodified. To be sure, this represented less of a dramatic change from the practice of the novel during
Scott's lifetime than a heightening of certain features he had introduced
into novelistic practice in France. The historical novels of the 1830s and
1840s—by the likes of Frédéric Soulié and Eugène Sue, who were also
known for their nonhistorical, social novels, as well as Dumas *père*,
known for his Romantic historical dramas—carried the spectacle to an extreme.

Indeed, the marketing campaigns undertaken on behalf of these novels,
testimony to the genre's increasing commercialization during the July
Monarchy, vaunted their capacity to depict the past in visual terms. An
1837 advertisement for one of Soulié's historical novels set in the Languedoc region began with a reference to the work's commercial potential:
"Here is a book whose success can scarcely be doubted." Attempting to
arouse mimetic desire for a book coveted by one and all, the advertisement
ascribed the collection's desirability to its visibility: the Languedoc is the
"province with the greatest legacy of famous events and illustrious personages, remarkable for its *picturesque* manners and for the changes these

111. Thomas Gretton, "La Politique dans le roman historique des années 1820–1840:
L'exemple de Théophile Dinocourt," *Revue d'Histoire Littéraire de la France*, nos. 2–3
(March–June 1975): 373–88.

have undergone."[112] Soulié's novels promised to combine the depiction of colorful manners with a representation of the "dominant passions of each era." Uniting a minute attention to the details of costume and clothing with a lurid fascination for the grotesque and bizarre, these novels represent the culmination, but also the undoing, of the Scottian trajectory.

In Soulié's *Le comte de Toulouse* (1840), one of the post-Scott historical novels that Maigron cites as a cut above its contemporaries and one of the most successful historical novels of the period, Scott's visual technique reaches its extreme end point. Like so many of its predecessors, the novel opens on the road, as two men make their way home from the Crusades. The first is a young knight, the Count Albert de Saussac, who receives the physical description readers had come to expect of the spectacular historical novel: "Along with his light armour, he was enveloped in a scarlet cloak upon which was sewn a white cross; he wore a helmet without a visor."[113] This description of the knight's clothing provides the historical information necessary to identify him as a crusader and is immediately followed by a description of his facial features: "His features were handsome, but rather too pronounced. Beneath the vast projection of his forehead were buried large black eyes shaded by long brown lashes" (9). The exaggerated nature of the young knight's features, their overly accentuated aspect, and particularly the giant eyes standing out in the enormous face, at once stand as a kind of metaphor for Soulié's visual style and foreshadow the significance of facial features in the story to come.

The young knight Albert, accompanied by a buffoonish slave named Goldery, eagerly anticipates returning to his family's castle following his long absence. Coming upon a ruin in the vicinity of his old home, he finds a hideously disfigured old man whose wounds are described in gory detail: "Monstrosity and disgust! His nose cut off, his upper lip cut off, his ears cut off, his tongue torn out" (15). By forcing the reader to contemplate the old man's facial mutilation, Soulié signals the degree to which the post-Scott historical novel has departed from the historical novels written by women, with their demure aversion to looking and avoidance of description of any kind.

Indeed, the detailed description of the old man's *lack* of facial features— the bloody spectacle of their severance that renders him unrecognizable— carries to the limit Scott's visual technique. Scott's historical epistemology

---

112. Advertisement found in the front of Mortonval [Alexandre Fursy Guesdon], *Charles de Navarre et le clerc de Catalogne* (Paris: Ambroise Dupont, 1837), emphasis added.

113. Frédéric Soulié, *Le comte de Toulouse* (Paris: Charles Gosselin, 1840), 9. Subsequent quotations are cited in the text.

based on appearance here gives way to a blinding sort of horror that denies the kind of knowledge the visual promises to provide. Whereas in
Scott visual description underpins historical knowledge, providing the key
to understanding the narrative and historical enigmas posed by the fiction,
in Soulié's novel the material world is rendered so grotesque as to impede
recognition. Soulié dares the reader to look away. Whereas the historical
novels by women from the early years in the century had kept their characters' faces hidden to focus attention on interior struggles and the Scottian novel had exposed its characters' countenances as the basis for a new,
visual mode of historical understanding, Soulié's novel pushes the logic of
physiognomy to the point where it ceases to function.

Eventually the mangled man, through an elaborate pantomime, reveals
himself to be young Albert's father and manages to communicate, despite
his missing tongue, that a marauding band of Crusaders, led by the evil
Baudouin de Toulouse, have laid waste to the ancestral manse and perpetrated horrors upon the family. The father, the text now reveals, got off
lightly compared to what the Crusaders did to Albert's sister, whose gang
rape and murder is recounted first by the father in pantomime and then
summarized by the narrator in excruciating detail. The rest of the novel
describes Albert's attempt to avenge his family and to "wreak upon them
and their families the destruction and outrage that they had perpetrated in
Provence" (30). Albert does not dwell on his misery or mourn his sister;
there is no effort to interiorize or psychologize his suffering: "He merely
calculated his chances of inflicting the same degree of evil he had received"
(30). Setting off for Toulouse, accompanied by his father who covers his
face with a hood to shield others from the horror, Albert pursues
vengeance. Although the rest of the plot, marked by various reversals of
fortune, unfolds in conventional fashion, the novel remains haunted by the
spectre of the father's hidden face—the sign of the historical novel shielding itself and the reader from the spectacle's grotesque extreme.

Not all of Soulié's historical novels are quite so dark. I now turn to a
short novel about Napoleon that Soulié wrote for children in 1838. Entitled *La lanterne magique*, the work casts light on the historical novel's
transformation into a spectacle in nineteenth-century France as well as on
its function as a tool for promoting a new national identity.[114] A foreword
accompanying the volume describes its pedagogic purpose. Lamenting the

114. In Chapter 2, I mention this novel as an example of an illustrated historical text that
uses wood engraving. Laurent Mannoni discusses Soulié's *La lanterne magique* as an example of the renewed fascination with the image of Napoleon during the Romantic period in
" 'Son ombre descend parmi nous . . . ' Napoléon et la Grande Armée des jeux d'optique," in
Napoléon et le cinéma, ed. Jean-Pierre Mattei (Ajaccio: Alain Piazzola, 1998), 18.

fact that children know more about ancient Greece and Rome than about the glories of France's own Empire, the editor-narrator describes the need for a novelized version of recent history accessible to young audiences: "Thus it is useful for the young to educate themselves concerning the great events of the nineteenth century; for them to learn to admire and to venerate the great men to whom France owed its place as the greatest of nations."[115] Like contemporary forms of illustrated historiography, Soulié's novel turns to the image as a means of communicating its patriotic message to a young audience: "*La lanterne magique* presents the history of the emperor and of the empire in a picturesque style, designed to strike the imagination" (vii). Just as in the histories I describe in chapter 2, the "picturesque" carries both a literal and figurative meaning. The story is told in highly imagistic language, full of visual description and spicy slang, but is also supplemented by actual images. Anticipating the illustrated histories of Napoleon by Jacques de Norvins and Paul-Mathieu Laurent de l'Ardèche by a year, Soulié's novel makes elaborate use of wood-engraved vignettes by Charles-Émile Jacque. Like those illustrated histories, it takes advantage of the new technique of wood engraving to incorporate the image onto the same page as text. Unlike those illustrated histories, however, it thematizes the images, incorporating them into the diagesis.

The story takes place in 1822, the year after Napoleon's death, in an unnamed provincial town. A dozen members of the local gentry, including the unidentified narrator and several retired military officers, gather at a party given by Madame Bénard, a *Parisienne* "given to mockery and royalism" (2) who bears antipathy toward Napoleon because her father and two brothers died in the Wars of the Empire. Just as they are about to put the children to bed, the company hears the shouts of two itinerant entertainers advertising a magic lantern show. The children can hardly contain their enthusiasm: "'Ah! Do you hear?' One of the children said. 'It's the magic lantern; papa, let's see the magic lantern!'." (4) Ceding to the children's wishes, the party settles in for what they expect to be a puerile entertainment entitled "Monsieur le soleil et madame la lune." As I explain in Chapter 1, the magic lantern made use of an internal lighting source (a candle) to project images painted on glass slides onto a wall or a screen (like a slide projector), and was used in the phantasmagoria show, beginning during the Directory, to represent historical and literary personages.

As the two entertainers prepare their show, however, they spy the ribbon of the Legion of Honor belonging to several of the former military of-

115. Frédéric Soulié, *La lanterne magique: Histoire de Napoléon* (Paris: Alphonse Henriot, 1838), vi. Subsequent quotations are cited in the text.

ficers among the company and mutter to each other, "These are good people. It's all right" (7). Believing they are safely among Bonapartists and that they therefore run no risk from the Restoration authorities who banned all reference to the emperor ("During that period, the face of the emperor was still a forbidden image that one showed in secret" [12]), they replace the slides of "monsieur le soleil" with images of Napoleon. They then proceed to recount the rise and fall of the great man as a series of commentaries on the images they project: "Attention, ladies and gentlemen, you are going to see what you will see. Here is the army of the Italian campaign," they declare as they show the first image (18). The wood-engraved illustrations representing the magic lantern's images are incorporated into the narrative as slides, which we see as the characters see them (fig. 4.2).

Through their highly biased narrative glorifying the emperor, the proprietors of the magic lantern eventually betray themselves as Imperial army veterans. The company hangs on their every word as they describe Napoleon's brilliant victories and his tragic defeat at Waterloo. The images, which rely on the conventional tropes of Napoleonic representation discussed in Chapter 3, such as the distinctive hat and coat, serve to glorify the great man. "Here he is after becoming First Consul," one of the veterans declares as he shows a slide of the emperor as a young man (fig. 4.3); "he already has the bicorne hat [*petit chapeau*]." But while the narrative serves to inculcate the children of the house into the cult of the hero, the images provide an even more immediate form of representation, a direct link with the emperor and his glory: "Let's now talk about Napoleon on that fateful day. I saw him; I was next to him, I reproduced him on this glass as he appeared to me during that infernal battle between him and the world" (95). Eventually even Mme Bénard, the royalist, is won over by the sound and sight of the Napoleonic legend.

When the last image appears, representing Napoleon's tomb at Saint-Helena, the candle suddenly goes out. Left in darkness, the company hears the murmuring of the servants and the children who have sunk to their knees and begun to pray for—or perhaps to—the martyred hero. The text thus describes the role of visual representation in the formation of the Napoleonic cult during the Restoration, but it also serves to bolster such patriotic nostalgia for the July Monarchy reading—and viewing—public.

Whereas Scott's novels and those of his French imitators offer metaphorical visions of the past analogous to the representations found in the panorama and other historical entertainments, Soulié's novel becomes literally visual. In *La lanterne magique,* the optical technologies that made a new kind of visual history possible not only serve as a structuring

je te donne l'armée d'Italie.—Fameux, qu'il
se dit. — Attention, messieurs, mesdames,
vous allez voir ce que vous allez voir.

Voilà l'armée d'Italie; le cadeau n'est pas
supérieur. Un tas de blancs-becs que nous
étions, avec des pantalons où il ne restait
pas de quoi faire une culotte courte, des

FIGURE 4.2   Engraving after Charles-Émile Jacque in F. Soulié, *La Lanterne Magique* (1838), p. 18. Image courtesy of the Bibliothèque nationale de France, Paris.

Le voilà devenu premier consul, il a déjà
son petit chapeau, les cheveux à la **Titus**,
porte des bas de soie et des souliers à bou-
cles; il a fait fortune.

FIGURE 4.3   Engraving after Charles-Émile Jacque in F. Soulié, *La Lanterne Magique*
(1838), p. 11. Image courtesy of the Bibliothèque nationale de France, Paris.

metaphor for the narrative but also provide the means for a new kind of visual representation. The stated goal of the novel, as of so many of the historical spectacles of the time, is to combine "instruction with amusement" (viii) and, in the process, to arouse patriotic sentiment. The actual result of such spectacular representations, as I show in the chapters that follow, however, remained a subject of debate for acute observers at the time.

Chapter Five

Balzac's Spectacular Revolution

As Honoré de Balzac set off to research details about the Breton countryside for his historical novel *Les Chouans* (1829), about the Counterrevolutionary uprising of the 1790s, it seems he saw himself embarking on a career as a French Walter Scott.[1] In the initial preface Balzac wrote for the work in 1828, a fictional authorial persona named Victor Morillon looks to Scott as a model: "A novel by Sir Walter Scott fell into the hands of M. Victor Morillon, and he was delighted by it, having fully shared in the secrets of its composition."[2] The novel described by this preface is promised to be the first in a series by Morillon that would apply Scott's technique of painting the picturesque details "of landscapes, costumes, and real people" to the "generous, melodious, cheerful, and warlike" (495) history of France. Such a project corresponds to Balzac's own ambition of producing a series of Romantic historical novels devoted to French history.

This ambition was never realized. In 1830, just a year after the publication of *Les Chouans*, Balzac began publishing fiction set in the present, or in the not too distant past of the Restoration, that later scholars labeled Realist and that formed the bulk of *La comédie humaine*. The classic theorists of the historical novel, Louis Maigron and Georg Lukács, have min-

---

1. *Les Chouans* was the first novel Honoré de Balzac published under his own name. His previous pseudonymous literary production was also composed almost entirely of Romantic historical fiction. The style of works such as *L'héritière de Birague* (1822) and *Falthurne* (1823) is reminiscent of Walter Scott, even if at times it verges on parody or pastiche.

2. Honoré de Balzac, *Les Chouans* (1829; reprint, Paris: Gallimard, 1972), 496. Subsequent quotations are cited in the text.

imized the importance of Balzac's shift from past to present, defining Balzacian Realism as the continuation of Scottian Romanticism. According to Lukács, Balzac's Realist novels are essentially historical because they reveal an understanding of how the past affects the manners and morals of contemporary life.[3] For Maigron, the Balzacian Realist novel is simply "the novel of Walter Scott emptied of its archaic substance and filled with modern material."[4] In this chapter, I argue that despite certain commonalities between his Romanticism and Realism, Balzac's shift from writing about the past to writing about the present did indeed signify a turning point, not only for literary history, but also for the history of historical representation. What gets left out of traditional accounts of the neat filiation between Romanticism and Realism is the way that Balzac's post-1830 fictions call into question the spectacular forms of history that dominated the popular imagination of his time and that had given shape to his own work as recently as 1829.

In order to make my case, I look at Balzac's fictions before and after 1830 in relation to the events of that year. I show that the shift in his subject matter and style from *Les Chouans* to such texts as *Adieu* (1830) and *Le colonel Chabert* (1832) relates not only to the events of the July Revolution, as many scholars have suggested, but also to contemporary developments in historical representation—in his early Realist texts, Balzac offers a critique of the spectacular past. Written at the very moment that Romantic dramas could be seen all over Paris, that Scott's novels were at their peak of popularity, and that the panorama was about to stage a comeback, Balzac's early Realist fictions could not have been more different from these forms of historical representation. Balzac's early Realism, I suggest, can best be defined not as a history of the present, as Lukács and others would have it, or as an aesthetic of verisimilitude, as other scholars have advanced, but rather as a rejection of the way Romanticism viewed the past.

The Novel as Spectacle: *Les Chouans*

Balzac's pre-1830 historical novel, *Les Chouans,* follows Scott's formula quite closely.[5] Like Scott's *Waverley* (1814), set in the mid-eighteenth cen-

3. In *The Historical Novel*, trans. Hannah Mitchell and Stanley Mitchell (1937; Lincoln: University of Nebraska Press, 1983), Georg Lukács writes, "This continuation of the historical novel, in the sense of a consciously historical conception of the present, is the great achievement of [. . .] Balzac" (81).

4. Louis Maigron, *Le roman historique à l'époque romantique: Essai sur l'influence de Walter Scott* (1898; reprint, Paris: Librairie ancienne H. Champion, 1912), 232.

5. The original title of the work was *Le dernier Chouan ou la Bretagne en 1800* when it was published in 1829. The second edition, in 1834, appeared as *Les Chouans ou la Bre-*

tury, in which the ousted Stuart monarch attempts to recruit the support of the disaffected Scottish clansmen for his bid to reclaim the throne of Great Britain, *Les Chouans* recounts the efforts of the Breton peasants to fight against the army of the Republic in the hope of restoring the Bourbon monarchy. Like Scott's Highlanders (or like James Fenimore Cooper's Mohicans, to whom they are explicitly compared[6]), the rebel Chouans remain steeped in ancient traditions and superstitions, and use their superior knowledge of the land to wage a guerrilla war. These crafty but ignorant peasants are led by a young nobleman, the marquis Alphonse de Montauran, who adopts the *nom de guerre* "Le Gars," meaning "boy" but also signifying strength and virility in the local Breton dialect. The plot centers around the tempestuous and ultimately tragic love affair between Montauran and Marie de Verneuil, a Mata Hari–esque spy sent by Napoleon's minister of police, Fouché, to ensnare the rebel leader. Marie attempts to abandon her mission when she falls in love with Le Gars, but is manipulated into betraying him into the hands of Hulot, the Republican commander, by Fouché's dangerous disciple, the master spy Corentin.

Like Scott, Balzac keeps real historical figures (such as Napoleon or Fouché) conveniently offstage, centering his drama on characters of his own invention. These characters nevertheless represent what Lukács calls historical types. Montauran signifies the last incarnation of the chivalric breed, Marie the Revolutionary woman thrust into the tempest of historical events, Hulot the exemplar of the Revolution's universal message fighting against local backwardness and superstition, and Corentin the crafty and self-interested manipulator who flourished in the nineteenth century.[7] For Lukács, the ability "to portray the struggles and antagonisms of history by means of characters who, in their psychology and destiny, always represent social trends and historical forces"[8] represents one of Balzac's most important legacies from Scott, who had sought to give a human face to history by embodying social and political struggles in individual characters.

---

tagne en 1799, and it was under this title that the work entered into *La comédie humaine* (in vol. 13). I refer to the novel here by its second and definitive title.

6. Balzac writes, "Patriarchal simplicity and heroic virtues combine to render the inhabitants of these countries poorer in intellectual contrivances than the Mohicans and Redskins of North America, but just as great, just as sly, just as hard as they are" (*Chouans*, 39). James Fenimore Cooper's *The Last of the Mohicans* was first published in 1826.

7. For later examples of Corentin's role as master spy in Balzac's *La comédie humaine*, see *Une ténébreuse affaire* (1843) and *Splendeurs et misères des courtisanes* (1847). In *La Cousine Bette* (1847–48), a retired Hulot causes the downfall of his family through his erotomania.

8. Lukács, *Historical Novel*, 34.

Even more than the four principal figures, the minor characters in *Les Chouans* reflect the spirit of their time: the superstitious Breton peasants (with colorful nicknames like Marche-à-terre) who are manipulated by the nobles and clergy into fighting against the Republic; the dissolute Breton nobles who serve the cause of the Bourbons in the hope of material gain; and, on the other side, the resilient *Bleus,* the soldiers of the Republic driven by the force of their belief in the ideals of the Revolution. "This novel is devised entirely in the spirit of Scott," Lukács concludes, "even if at times Balzac surpasses his master in [. . .] showing the hopelessness of the counter-revolutionary uprising precisely in terms of this social and human contrast between the contending classes on both sides."[9]

Balzac's fidelity to Scott's technique is most apparent, however, on the surface of the text, in the extraordinary attention paid to describing the Breton landscape and its inhabitants. In *Les Chouans,* as in Scott's historical fiction, the past becomes a spectacle; through elaborate descriptions, the external features of a vanished past world seem to materialize before the reader's eyes. Far from the center of modernizing France, with inhabitants who still retained at the time of the Revolution a strong link to ancient traditions, Brittany provided the ideal homegrown picturesque subject for nineteenth-century French readers who had delighted in Scott's evocation of the Scottish Highlanders in *Waverley* and of the Norman and Saxon chieftains in *Ivanhoe. Les Chouans* exploits its setting for maximum effect, with long passages devoted to the unusual clothing of the local peasants—which featured a sort of cloak made from animal hide—as well as to the topographical features of the rugged, mountainous landscape.

These descriptions, however, are not merely decorative. Just as they serve to situate the plot in a recognizable time and place, they also locate the novel itself in the contemporary debate over modes of historical representation. As I show in Chapter 4, during the 1820s Scott's legion of French imitators transformed the historical novel from a genre dominated by women, centering on sentimental or ethical conflict, into a kind of spectacle, in which description of the material world of the past made history into an object to be viewed and consumed. Both this transformation and the critical debate to which it gave rise are thematized explicitly in the very first paragraph of Balzac's novel, as the narrator explains his motivation for describing the distinctive appearance of the motley crew of Breton conscripts marching toward Mayenne: "This detachment [. . .] offered a collection of such bizarre costumes and a grouping of individuals belonging to such diverse localities and professions, that it will not be unhelpful to

9. Ibid., 82.

describe their characteristic differences to give this story the bright colors to which such a high price is attached these days; although, according to certain critics, it takes away from the painting of sentiments" (21). Right from the start, Balzac's text aligns itself with the new brand of historical representation that sought to reanimate the past through visual description rather than with the earlier mode of sentimental historical fiction written by women, which denied the visual. This self-conscious and partisan affirmation of what might be termed the politics of local color puts the novel squarely on the side of the spectacle, signaling an affinity not only with the Scott-inspired Romantic historical novel, but also with other forms of historical representation that made the past visual in a more literal manner. *Les Chouans* theorizes the act of historical representation while engaging in it, laying bare the epistemological and aesthetic implications of the processes it employs to reconstruct a vision of the past.

Les Chouans, moreover, abounds in references to the kinds of historical entertainments that delighted crowds in the early decades of the nineteenth century with new optical technologies. Throughout *Les Chouans,* the Breton peasant fighters rise up like ghosts at Robertson's phantasmagoria show to frighten the Parisian characters at the center of the story. At the beginning of the novel, as the column of Republican soldiers makes its way toward Mayenne, the appearance of one of the Chouan rebels is explicitly analogized to the popular spectacle: "The two poor soldiers had made it halfway up the slope when Marche-à-terre showed his hideous face. He aimed so carefully at the two Bleus that he finished them off with a single shot, and they rolled heavily into the ditch. Hardly had his big head revealed itself when the barrels of thirty guns were raised; but like a *phantasmagorical figure,* he had disappeared behind the deadly tufts of broom" (59, emphasis added). Here the text relies on its readers' familiarity with the phantasmagoria to give a sense of the uncanny speed with which the rebels appear and disappear, and of the fear they inspire in the Republican army. The Chouans, however, are not the only phantasmagorical figures in the novel. Marie likewise appears to Montauran as a vision straight out of the phantasmagoria, which projected images of historical figures onto screens or clouds of smoke: "The marquis rose, turned his head, and remained frozen upon seeing, as if in a cloud, the face of Mlle de Verneuil" (270). Even the landscape itself is described as a "fantasmagorie" (292) because of its otherworldly shadows and fog.

In *Les Chouans,* popular historical spectacles provide a constant source of metaphor, an ever-present pool of allusions for referencing the past. When the corrupt nobles in Montauran's entourage cast aspersions on Marie's ancestry and morals, the young marquis's anger takes a spectacular form: "A terrifying rage broke out on this angry and ruddy face, which took on the complexion of wax" (226). Had the marquis de Montauran existed, he very well might have been put on display in Curtius's wax display. The panorama also makes several explicit appearances within the novel. When Mlle de Verneuil looks out over the Breton countryside, searching for a sign that her lover will come, the object of her gaze resembles the spectacle that delighted spectators at the time with its 360–degree view: "Marie herself draped the curtains around the window from which the eyes took in a rich panorama" (305). The year in which the action of the novel takes place, 1799, was the same year in which the panorama made its first appearance in France.

The novel's network of spectacular imagery thus indexes the process by which historical representation took a new form around the time of the Revolution. Balzac's text references the wide array of entertainments that constituted the spectacular past. But how do these references to contemporary spectacles function within the text? And what do they say about the novel's relation to the past? The answer cuts to the heart of what I see as the difference between Balzac's Romanticism and his Realism. For, whereas Balzac's later Realist fictions, such as *Adieu* and *Le Colonel Chabert*, also reference contemporary forms of spectacular entertainment, they do so in order to establish their difference from them. In the Romantic historical novel *Les Chouans,* on the other hand, the popular historical spectacles provide analogies for the text's own spectacular vision.

By describing its historical characters as phantasmagorical figures or as wax sculptures and its landscape descriptions as panoramas, *Les Chouans* reveals its complicity with these forms of entertainment on both an extra-diagetic and a diagetic level. On an extra-diagetic level, references to the spectacles help the reader envision the past in a manner analogous to popular forms of entertainment. Like the spectacles, and like the fictions of Walter Scott, Balzac's novel conjures an image of history. It presents the past through its external material forms, such as the clothing that the Breton peasants wear or the unique features of the landscape. The key to the novel's historical representation lies in the details that take shape through the evocative verbal descriptions of Balzac's prose. Of course, unlike the popular spectacles, the novel can never provide an image of the past in the literal sense. By referring to spectacles such as the panorama, however, the novel bridges the gap between the verbal and the visual through analogy. It relies on readers' familiarity with the literal images of the panorama to help the figurative images of the novel materialize in their imagination.[10]

---

10. For a discussion of the relation between pictural and textual panoramas, and for a specific analysis of the panoramic writing of Émile Zola, see Olivier Lumbroso, "Passage des

The popular entertainments, however, also provide a model for historical vision *within* the novel. They provide an epistemological template that
structures the way characters perceive events as they unfold. In this way,
the novel reveals an even deeper complicity with the spectacles of popular
culture because it affirms the power of vision to resolve historical enigmas.
In the novel's opening scene, a brigade of Republican soldiers marches
from Fougères to Mayenne, leading a band of Breton conscripts. As the
troops stop to admire the view along the way, the narrator also stops to
watch them watching the landscape: "these young men, whom the defense
of the homeland had snatched away, like so many others, from distinguished studies, and in whom the war had not yet extinguished the feeling
for the arts, were stunned at the spectacle which presented itself to their
eyes" (30). With its extended view of the horizon, the spectacle that unfolds before the recruits offers a panoramic view of the countryside.[11]

"From the summit of the Pèlerine the great valley of Couësnon appeared to the eyes of the voyager [. . .]. From there, the officers discovered, spread out before them, that basin remarkable as much for the
prodigious fertility of its soil as for the variety of its sights" (30–31). The
picturesque description that follows resembles the language of the brochures that visitors to the panorama used to guide their visit, evoking the
viewer's fixed gaze as a stable reference as it names points of interest in the
field of vision. But if the soldiers' view of the valley seems at first like a
panorama, it comes to resemble even more closely Daguerre's diorama,
which made use of special lighting effects to give the impression of atmospheric changes in a landscape—"Just then, the view of the country was lit
up by one of those fleeting flashes which nature employs to heighten its
stunning creations" (31)—and occasionally placed actual objects, such as
sculptures of animals, in the foreground—"Some livestock brought that
already dramatic scene to life" (33).

By assimilating the reader's vision to that of the characters, the presen-
tation of the landscape through the language of the spectacle allows readers to form a mental image through association with other panoramas and
dioramas they have seen. But the panoramic description also serves to
highlight differences among the characters, offering a contrast between
two different styles of viewing. Whereas the soldiers view the landscape as
Romantic "dilettanti" (30), savoring the aesthetic pleasure the view af-

Panoramas (poétique et fonctions des vues panoramiques dans *Les Rougon-Macquart*)," *Littérature* 116 (1999): 17–47.

11. In *Le Chouan romanesque: Balzac, Barbey d'Aurevilly, Hugo* (Paris: Presses Universitaires de France, 1989), Claudie Bernard notes how the topography of *Les Chouans* is mediated by references to painting and optics (84–85).

fords "beneath a feigned desire to examine the military positions in that beautiful countryside" (33), Hulot, their commander, looks with the eyes of a trained officer, "One of those military men who, in the face of impending danger, does not let himself be distracted by the charms of the landscape" (33). These two modes of viewing correspond, as I discuss in chapter 1, to the two functions attributed to the panorama in the early nineteenth century—"to delight and to educate"—when it was considered both a form of entertainment and a pedagogical tool.

Hulot ignores the former function in favor of the latter, overlooking the beauties of the valley in order to search for rebels hiding in the underbrush. When a Chouan appears, Hulot scans the region for others like him: "the commander's eyes roamed from the man to the landscape, from the landscape to the detachment, from the detachment to the steep embankment of the road" (36). His fears are certainly justified. As the narrator makes clear, the peaceful valley hides secret dangers: "In those days, the flowering hedges of those beautiful valleys hid invisible aggressors. Each field was a fortress, each tree a trap" (42). The contrast in viewing styles between Hulot and his soldiers provides a lesson in looking; whereas the soldiers see beauty, colored by the projections of their own artistic temperaments, Hulot sees the reality of the situation. Making use of his elevated position to dominate the landscape with his gaze, Hulot asserts his control over the scene and over events.

Hulot's manner of looking, modeled on the panorama, provides a paradigm for the way knowledge is gained and power asserted in the novel. Each of the principal characters/combatants struggles to gain a panoramic view of the surrounding landscape, to see the dangers lurking therein and thereby to gain the upper hand in the war. Corentin, deceived by Marie as to the location of her secret rendezvous with Le Gars, climbs to an elevated point in order to see whether Hulot's men have a chance of capturing their man: "Corentin, certain of having delivered the fate of the leader of the Chouans into the hands of his most implacable enemies, hurried to the Promenade in order to get a better view of the whole of Hulot's military positions" (387). Searching for signs of her lover, Marie seeks out the same point in order to gain a better perspective on the valley below: "She admired the huge segment of the great valley of Couësnon that stretched out before her eyes from the summit of the Pèlerine to the plateau through which the Vitré road passed" (263). If at first the beauty of the scene overwhelms her and prevents her from pursuing her mission, as it did the young soldiers in Hulot's regiment—"the magnificence of the spectacle momentarily silenced her passions" (263)—her sense of purpose returns when she spies the object of her quest: "The senseless hope that had brought her to the Promenade was miraculously realized. Through the furze and the broom that cross on the facing peaks, she thought she made out, despite the goatskin covering them, several of the Vivetière partygoers, among whom she recognized Le Gars, whose slightest movements stood out against the soft light of the setting sun" (264). Marie's panoramic vision allows her to distinguish Le Gars beneath his disguise; it provides her with a means to access the truth of his identity.

The historical entertainments of the early nineteenth century, such as the panorama, I have argued, provided a valuable service to post-Revolutionary subjects, presenting a vision of the past as the ground for individual, class, and national identities that had been rendered precarious by the rapid pace of historical change. Balzac's Romantic historical novel dramatizes and ratifies this process whereby identities are assured through the agency of vision. At the beginning of the novel, uncertainty hovers over the identities of the characters. Nearly all the soldiers in the novel on both sides have one or more *noms de guerre* meant to protect their true identity—Le Gars, Marche-à-terre, Pille-Miche, Galope-Chopine, Beaupied—fulfilling a need for anonymity that the war has imposed, but also opening a rift within the text in which the characters are always someone other than whom they are presented to be. To compound this confusing state of affairs, the principal characters adopt a string of aliases as they hide their real identities from the reader and from one another. The rebel leader Montauran (a.k.a. Le Gars) presents himself as "the citizen du Gua-Saint-Cyr," a graduate of the École Polytechnique, on his way to a posting with the Republican army, in order to avoid being recognized by Marie, Corentin, and Hulot. The leading female Chouan, who goes by Mme du Gua but whose true identity remains something of a mystery throughout the novel, poses as his mother. Neither "mother" nor "son" believes that Marie de Verneuil is truly the aristocrat she pretends to be until late in the novel when she reveals herself as the *fille naturelle* of a nobleman (and the widow of Danton!). Marie herself seems unsure whether she is a Chouan or a Republican, whether she will betray Montauran or love him.

The confusions brought about by this fracturing of identity provide the plot with its motor. Nearly all the reversals in the action derive from the attempts of the two lovers to unravel the web of obfuscation and deceit they have woven around their true selves and inner desires. This confusion of character at the core of the text, a direct product of upheavals caused by the Revolution, stands as an allegory for the identity crisis that the Revolution provoked within French society as a whole, as a symbol of the way recent historical events had undermined traditions that had formerly provided the basis for a supposedly stable sense of self. Within the novel, these confusions are resolved by the characters through the act of looking. Balzac's text, like the panorama, advances vision as the solution to the Revolution's identity crisis.

Just as the panorama offered visual perspectives from which new post-Revolutionary identities could be formed, so too do the characters within the novel gain knowledge about themselves and others by looking. *Les Chouans* abounds in stolen looks and furtive glances, in penetrating gazes and pregnant regards that seek to peer behind the characters' masks. While vision might be said to provide an epistemological model in many nineteenth-century French Realist novels, and particularly those by Balzac, the specificity of this text resides in the way it mobilizes the eyes in an undercover war fought between adversaries hiding behind a series of camouflages and false fronts.[12] Although hardly a form of entertainment, this war of vision points to the ways in which the text affirms the epistemological model on which the spectacular past relied.

An example of this battle of the gaze plays itself out during the initial meeting between the principal antagonists at an inn, when Le Gars tries to pass himself off as a *Bleu*. Not fooled by his Republican uniform, Marie sees right through him: "With a single look, Mlle de Verneuil was able to distinguish beneath that dark suit the elegant form and the distinctive characteristics that indicate noble birth" (121). Gifted with superior sight, she unmasks the rebel leader, penetrating his true identity as a noble even while revealing to the reader, through the movement of her eyes, *her* true identity as a spy: "To see all of that in the blink of an eye, to come to life with the desire to please, to incline her head languidly, to smile coquettishly, to throw one of those velvety looks that can revive a heart dead to love; to veil her long black eyes beneath large lids whose lush and curved lashes sketched a brown line against her cheek [. . .] this whole trick was accomplished in less time than it has taken to describe it" (122). Marie employs her eyes as a secret weapon, but the other combatants come equally armed. Le Gars and Corentin face off a moment later in a silent duel: "The two young men looked at each other for a moment like two young cocks ready to fight, and this look hatched an everlasting hatred between them" (123). Here once again, their competing gazes reveal their

12. On Balzac and vision, see among many others, Andrea Goulet, "Tomber dans le phénomène: Balzac's Optics of Narration," *French Forum* 26, no. 3 (2001): 43–70; Dorothy Kelly, *Telling Glances: Voyeurism in the French Novel* (New Brunswick, N.J.: Rutgers University Press, 1992); and Maurice Samuels, "L'érotique de l'histoire: *La Vendetta* et l'image de Napoléon au XIXe siècle" in *L'érotique balzacienne*, ed. Lucienne Frappier-Mazur and Jean-Marie Roulin (Paris: Sédès, 2001), 105–16.

real selves: "As much as the blue eye of the soldier was frank, the green eye of Corentin betrayed malice and deception" (123).

Just as the characters perceive the truth about one another by looking carefully, so do their eyes offer up insights into their identities to the reader, to whose own powers of visualization the descriptive mode of narration appeals. Corentin turns his gaze on Mme du Gua, in disguise as the mother of Le Gars, but not before she in turn scrutinizes him, made suspicious by his remarks in defense of Marie's claim to be an aristocrat: "The strange woman [. . .] retreated several steps in order to examine that unexpected interlocutor; she fastened upon him her black eyes full of that bright shrewdness so common in women [. . .]. At the same time Corentin, who was studying that lady on the sly, relieved her of all the pleasures of maternity in order to bestow upon her those of love" (125–26). Finally, to complete the circle, Marie looks at Corentin looking at Mme du Gua and Le Gars: "The guests were about to sit down, when Mlle de Verneuil perceived Corentin, who kept scrutinizing the two strangers, to be rather unsettled by her gaze" (131). She then shoots him a "steady and scornful look," signaling that his manner of looking risks exposing them as spies, but it is too late; in this battle of the eyes, everyone has seen everyone else for what he or she is. The act of looking provides both the characters and the reader with the tools to penetrate the confusion of identity and power in the novel.

Or so it seems at the start. At the end of the novel, vision fails to maintain its status as guarantor of truth. When Marie leaves her makeshift residence in the town of Fougères to attend a ball thrown by Le Gars for his fellow Chouan rebels at the town of St. James, she discovers that the nature of a guerrilla war cannot be understood from a panoramic perspective but only from down below, in the thick of the underbrush, where the Chouan rebels have innumerable hiding places from which to ambush the soldiers of the Republic. The panorama has less to offer than does up-close contact: "Mlle de Verneuil understood at last the war of the Chouans. Taking these roads she was better able to appreciate the state of the countryside which, seen from an elevated point, had seemed so ravishing to her; but which, when seen from within, revealed both its dangers and its inextricable difficulties" (321). As she discovers while moving amid the vegetation, the low walls, and innumerable enclosures that characterize the Breton countryside, "five hundred men can defy the troops of an entire kingdom" (324).

This realization comes as part of a transformation within Marie's character, as she begins to observe more closely, from down below, the life of the Chouan rebels. Continuing on her way toward St. James, she comes across a Catholic religious ceremony, illegal during the Revolution, and held secretly in a clearing in the woods. Marie watches this "most astonishing of spectacles" (326) as if contemplating one of Daguerre's dioramas of a cathedral interior. "Mlle de Verneuil was struck with admiration" (327) by the mass, but she does not participate. Here once again, the perspective provided by the spectacle fails to provide access to a higher truth. Marie remains shut out, barred by her spectatorship from taking part in a ceremony that allows the Breton peasants, including her own maid and companion Francine, to affirm an identity with something beyond themselves.

In the novel's final, climactic sequence, Marie waits impatiently for Le Gars to come for her at Fougères. Tricked by a forged letter, a ruse engineered by Corentin, into believing Le Gars has no feelings for her, she betrays the secret of his visit to the Republicans. Corentin and Hulot set a trap for Le Gars, but a dense layer of fog prevents them from perceiving his arrival: "The fog and the night thus wrapped in terrifying shadows the place where the drama [. . .] was to play out" (441). Here, for once, vision is actually blocked. Corentin finds himself unable to achieve the kind of superior, all-seeing control of the situation on which he bases his power over others and over events.[13]

Still blinded by rage at her lover's supposed perfidy, Marie too loses the ability to see clearly: "like a person asleep, no object appeared to her in its true form or color" (448). Like Corentin, she finds herself cut off from her principal source of knowledge and power. When Le Gars eventually arrives, with a priest and witnesses to celebrate a clandestine marriage ceremony, she gradually understands how wrongly she has estimated him, and the magnitude of her own betrayal looms large as she remembers the ambush she has helped Corentin and Hulot to set. For the first time in the novel, Marie prays fervently; confessing to a priest, she asks for God's help or for death. This faith in what cannot be seen marks a significant transition for Marie, bringing her beyond the barrier that the visual relation to the world imposed during her contemplation of the religious ceremony in the woods.

13. In *The Literature of Images: Narrative Landscape from* Julie *to* Jane Eyre (New Brunswick: Rutgers University Press, 1987), Doris Kadish points to the importance within *Les Chouans* of "perceptual screens such as darkness and fog," and reads them as a metaphor for the characters' political confusion (124–25). Kadish also discusses the function of landscape within the novel in "Landscape, Ideology, and Plot in Balzac's *Les Chouans*," *Nineteenth-Century French Studies* 12, no. 4 (Summer–Fall 1984): 43–57.

The role of vision as a barrier against truth is symbolized at the end of the novel by the bulls-eye window at the top of Marie's house in Fougères, now surrounded by Republican troops. Providing a panoramic view of the surrounding countryside, the window also serves as the one means of escape from Corentin's trap. To pass through this window is to relinquish the comfortable distance that the spectacle provides; it is to have faith in something beyond the visual, to risk entering the landscape once and for all. "Never will I be able to pass through there" (460), declares Montauran in fright at the crucial moment. Eventually he does make it through, followed by Marie who has donned his clothes to act as a decoy. Her noble sacrifice, however, fails to facilitate her lover's escape: unable to see because of the fog, the *Bleus* shoot both Marie and Montauran. Vision thus proves fallible, and even deadly, but trust in something beyond the visible—call it faith or love—offers the possibility of salvation.

Despite the death of the lovers, the novel ends on an uplifting note of reconciliation, as Le Gars, before dying, asks his enemy Hulot to write to his brother in London, instructing him never to bear arms against France even while retaining his devotion to the king. Just as the two lovers are united in death, so too do the two sides in the Revolutionary struggle vow to resolve their differences without violence. The confusion engendered by the fog thus leads to a more far-sighted ending to the conflict than any of the characters was able to envision previously. Both Hulot and Le Gars look beyond the present, full of disguise and ruse, and toward a future in which peace can be achieved through trust and faith in the humanity and innate nobility of the adversary.

Like Marie's discovery of faith in God, this willingness to trust the other at his word signals a departure from spectacularity, a newfound belief in something that cannot be seen. Yet even while valorizing this belief, the vestige of a more chivalrous past, the novel acknowledges that the future will remain under the spectacle's sway. Corentin, the man of the nineteenth century and one of the supreme geniuses of *La comédie humaine,* mocks Hulot's gesture of reconciliation. "Here is yet another of those honest people who will never make his fortune" (463), he says to himself, in a quintessentially Balzacian curse.

The fog at the end of *Les Chouans* registers not only the characters' increasing disenchantment with the regime of vision, but the novel's as well. By casting suspicion on the power of sight, *Les Chouans* questions its own method of representing the past through (verbal) images, through descriptions of material forms (of clothing or landscape) that take shape in the mind's eye. The obscuring of vision figures the text's self-critique, its suspicion of the very means that had grounded its mode of representation up to that point. The technique of the Romantic historical novel as inherited from Scott, which invited the reader to gaze on a vividly rendered past world, comes to seem an obstacle to historical truth rather than its precondition. This transition within *Les Chouans* announces the transition within Balzac's oeuvre that was about to take place; although still highly visual, Balzac's Realist texts abandoned the past in favor of a new type of writing about the present. As I show, this new Realist fiction pursued the critique of Romanticism's visual mode of historical representation that *Les Chouans* began, but without its redemptive ending.

Farewell to the Spectacle: *Adieu* and the Emergence of Realism

Already in 1829, Balzac's Romantic historical fiction betrayed doubts over vision as a way of knowing the past and, by extension, over the entire project of spectacular historical representation. The doubts that end *Les Chouans* become the focal point of *Adieu*. First published in the journal *La Mode* in May and June of 1830, *Adieu* was one of the first works to enter *La comédie humaine*. Despite its founding status, however, *Adieu* figured only as a minor text in the Balzacian canon until the mid-1970s, when poststructuralist theorists began to consider it crucial for understanding the nature of nineteenth-century French Realism. Before exploring how various scholars saw *Adieu* as both epitomizing and thematizing a certain Realist poetics, and how their different views of the text's relation to Realism elicited a vituperative debate, I will first recapitulate the story.

Adieu opens in the French countryside during the summer of 1819, four years into the Restoration of the Bourbon monarchy. Philippe de Sucy, a Napoleonic officer recently returned from captivity in Siberia, goes hunting with his friend, the marquis d'Albon. They come upon the ruins of an old monastery, a picturesque landscape, and notice what seems like a ghost frolicking in the park. Upon closer inspection they see that it is not a ghost at all, but a beautiful woman who appears insane—endlessly repeating, but without seeming to understand what she says, a single word, "adieu." Philippe takes a closer look, realizes that she is his former lover, and faints.

Later, d'Albon returns to the monastery and meets the madwoman's uncle, a doctor who explains that his niece, the countess Stéphanie de Vandières, lost her mind while accompanying her husband on the ill-fated

Russian campaign of 1812. In the second section of the text, entitled "The Crossing of the Beresina," the doctor describes the notorious military disaster in which the French, on their retreat from Moscow, were forced to burn the only bridge across the Beresina river to prevent the Russians from giving chase, leaving a large portion of their freezing, starving, and exhausted army on the far bank to face certain slaughter or capture. Just as the bridge goes up in flames, Philippe arrives at the icy riverbank, dragging Stéphanie as well as her husband, the General, both more dead than alive. Two places remain in a raft, and Philippe magnanimously surrenders them to his lover and her husband, but the General falls overboard and is decapitated by a block of ice, just as they reach the other side. Parted forever from Philippe, Stéphanie calls out a miserable "adieu" to her lover, who remains on the far bank.

Back in the present time of narration, the doctor tells how his niece lost her mind at that fatal moment and was used sexually by the retreating army until he found her, by chance, after her escape from a mental hospital in Strasbourg in 1816. The third and final part of the story, entitled "The Cure," recounts Philippe's attempt to restore his former lover to sanity. Reduced to an animal-like state, and only able to utter the word "adieu," the countess ignores all reminders of her former life. Unable to make Stéphanie recognize him during his frequent visits to the monastery over the next few months, Philippe finally resorts to drastic measures. Returning to his estate, he orders the construction of an exact replica of the Beresina at the moment of their separation, hoping that the sight of the scene will shock Stéphanie back to reality. A river is dug, peasants are costumed as soldiers, a bridge is built and burned. In January 1820, as snow covers the scene just as it did that tragic day in Russia, he returns to the monastery. With the help of the doctor, Philippe drugs the Countess, blindfolds her, and brings her to his estate. The blindfold removed, the madwoman contemplates the scene with horror and is momentarily restored to sanity. She recognizes Philippe, says a final (now lucid) "adieu," and falls dead in his arms. Ten years later, Philippe commits suicide.

Adieu marks a transition in Balzac's oeuvre. Whereas the prior year he had published *Les Chouans,* a Romantic historical novel set completely during the Revolutionary wars, after 1830 he embarked on the Realist fictions, set in the present (i.e., after the Revolution and Empire), that form *La comédie humaine. Adieu* bridges the gap: there is still a historical narrative, but it is sandwiched between two sections set in the "present" of the Restoration. Although the Napoleonic historical section stands on its own as a coherent narrative, and may have been conceived independently of the fiction that surrounds it,[14] the text incorporates this historical sequence into the larger structure as an analepsis or flashback, with a clearly delineated scene of enunciation, so as not to disrupt the temporal consistency of the frame.

In other words, the narrative in *Adieu* takes place completely between 1819 and 1820 (with the exception of the last paragraph which takes place ten years later, hence in the very year of the story's publication, 1830). The historical section, set in 1812, is technically a *story* told in 1819.[15] I insist on the temporal consistency of *Adieu* to show the extent to which it departs from the Romantic historical project of *Les Chouans*, despite the fact that more than a third of the text is given over to a historical narrative. By emphasizing the constructed nature of the historical narrative, its status as representation, *Adieu* prevents readers from entering completely into the past, from losing themselves in contemplation of the historical landscape.

The text also signals its departure from a Romantic vision of the past through parody. At the start of the story, Philippe epitomizes the plight of a certain type of hero common in Romantic fiction: young, rich, and aristocratic, he suffers from a rather grandiose melancholy brought about by the trauma of the past. "Ah! my poor d'Albon, if like me you had spent six years in the depths of Siberia. . . . Leaving his thought unfinished he raised his eyes to heaven, as if his misfortune were a secret between himself and God."[16] Like Chateaubriand's René, whose troubled past likewise inspires an inner torment, Philippe tempts his interlocutor (and the reader) with a history that he at first withholds:[17] "One day, my friend," he tells d'Albon, "I will tell you the story of my life. But I can't right now" (148). The story nevertheless begins to emerge just moments later, in spite of Philippe's resistance, when the two friends come upon the ruined monastery, home to

14. In his introduction to the Pléiade edition of *Adieu,* Moïse Le Yaouanc suggests separate sources for the Beresina section and questions whether Balzac originally intended to join it to the story about a woman's madness. Le Yaouanc, introduction to *Adieu,* in Balzac, *La comédie humaine,* vol. 10 (Paris: Gallimard, 1979), 965.

15. As Le Yaouanc points out, this incorporation of the historical section into the frame narrative leads to certain inconsistencies: how does Stéphanie's uncle, the narrator of the Beresina episode, obtain such accurate information, down to the smallest details of Philippe's reactions and emotions, without having been there or met Philippe?

16. Balzac, *Adieu,* in *Le Colonel Chabert suivi de trois nouvelles* (Paris: Gallimard, 1974), 146. Subsequent quotations are cited in the text.

17. Chateaubriand's *René* (1802; reprint, Paris: Gallimard Folio, 1971) begins with a very similar scene of difficult memories evoked during a hunt and a hero who defers their painful narration (141). In *The Male Malady: Fictions of Impotence in the French Romantic Novel* (New Brunswick: Rutgers University Press, 1993), Margaret Waller refers to the "timeworn convention" of the hero's secretiveness (38).

the mad Stéphanie, a ghost out of Philippe's past and the key to his suffering.

Circled by ancient oaks, with its "antique and black" iron gate, its park full of grottoes and terraces, this property is described as the apotheosis of the kind of Gothic historical landscape favored by Romantic painters, novelists, and historians: "The structures of art had been united with the most *picturesque* effects of nature [. . .]. Brown, green, yellow, and red mosses spread their *romantic* colors on the trees, on the benches, on the roofs, and on the stones" (150, emphasis added). The clichéd tone of this description, its use of catchwords such as "picturesque" and "romantic," invites readers not to conjure up the image of any such real location they might have seen but rather to associate the description with other representations—that is, with Romantic art. By categorizing the type of effect the scene inspires, by naming it, the text signals its own distance from the sublime nature of such representations.

Readers, moreover, see the ruin through the far more prosaic, or should I say realistic, eyes of d'Albon: "What disorder!" (151) he exclaims. A moment later, d'Albon himself makes the connection with the fiction of romance, "It's the palace of Sleeping Beauty" (151), and then finally, in the true spirit of nineteenth-century materialism, he looks at the scene with the eyes of a real-estate broker: "To whom then can it belong?" (151). Alluding to the sale of properties confiscated from the clergy during the Revolution, d'Albon's final question robs the setting of its Romantic aura by situating it firmly in the post-Revolutionary present.

As opposed to *Les Chouans,* which offers historical vistas for the contemplation and edification of its characters and readers, *Adieu* undercuts the picturesque effect of the landscape by filtering it through the modern discourses of hygiene, literary history, and land speculation. Philippe, however, remains oblivious to d'Albon's irreverences and continues to function as a proper Romantic hero, propelled by the sight of the monastery and its inhabitants toward a crisis of memory. Recognizing Stéphanie, his former love, in the madwoman frolicking amid the ruins, he struggles between revulsion and fascination at this vision of his past: "When the colonel opened his eyes, he turned them toward the meadow where the unknown woman ran about screaming, and let out a faint but horrified exclamation; then he closed his eyes once again with a gesture begging his friend to tear him away from this spectacle" (159). The focus on visual perception, the thematizing of Philippe's act of looking, and the naming of the scene as a "spectacle"—all call to mind the techniques of the Romantic historical novel, but the text undercuts the effect of these techniques through its irony.

In his introduction to the Gallimard-Folio reedition of the work in 1974, Pierre Gascar also emphasizes the distance the text establishes from the Romantic historical tradition. Gascar and Patrick Berthier, who wrote the notes for the volume, single out for praise the middle section of the text, which describes the horror and suffering of the Beresina episode with what they label as a "realism without precedent in literary history."[18] According to Gascar, the originality of the war scenes in *Adieu* lies in their departure from conventional accounts of the Napoleonic epic that tended to mythologize or idealize. With his graphic images of the soldiers of the Grande Armée, haggard, half dead from the cold, straggling toward the frozen river, Balzac "strikes at the myth of military grandeur, involuntarily no doubt, a blow the repercussions of which went far beyond the post-Napoleonic era."[19] For Gascar, Balzac's Realism involves a rejection of the Romanticized accounts of the war that preceded it and sets the tone for a new mode of writing about history, grounded not in myth but in reality.[20]

In a landmark work of feminist-deconstructionist criticism published a year later in *Diacritics,* Shoshana Felman took Gascar and Berthier to task, transforming Balzac's text itself into a battlefield in the critical war over the politics and poetics of Realism. By focusing exclusively on the historical flashback in the middle section of the story, Felman argues, the two French male scholars overlook the female character and her concerns, thus reproducing the narcissistic blindness of the male protagonist. And by doing so, they miss the way the ending of the story undermines the model of Realism that the middle seems to embody.

For Felman, Stéphanie's meaningless "adieu" signals a refusal to attach the sign to its referent, the linguistic process on which, she argues, Realist historical narrative depends. Philippe's reconstruction of the Beresina river succeeds in restoring the identity of the sign, in putting an end to Stéphanie's madness, but only by dealing a fatal blow both to the woman and to the text: Philippe's effort to restore Stéphanie to a "realistic" conception of the world brings about her death and the end of the story. "Through this paradoxical and disconcerting ending," Felman writes, "the text subverts and dislocates the logic of representation which it has

18. Pierre Gascar, preface to Balzac, *Le Colonel Chabert suivi de trois nouvelles* (Paris: Gallimard, 1974), 9.

19. Ibid., 10–11.

20. This is not, of course, to underestimate the enormous prestige that the myth of Napoleon retains throughout *La comédie humaine.* As Pierre Barbéris has shown, Balzac often contrasts Napoleon's "dynamism" with the banal, bourgeois present: "He is the image—deformed, undoubtedly, by the war and tyranny, but real, perceptible—of the potential of a purely human world, a once free world that has wound up with Guizot." *Mythes balzaciens* (Paris: Armand Colin, 1972), 232.

dramatized through Philippe's endeavor and his failure."[21] The text thus signifies its "impotence" to control what Felman calls "its own linguistic difference" or to represent the reality of history with "identity or truth."[22] *Adieu,* according to Felman, thus shows not the triumph of Realism, as the male scholars would have it, but its undoing by the female character and her madness.

The debate over *Adieu* produced a great deal of acrimony, with Felman accusing the French scholars of an "allegorical act of murder"[23] and Gascar and Berthier denouncing her spirit of "intolerance."[24] The clash certainly reflected the spirit of its time, testifying to the stakes of the feminist and deconstructionist challenge to the scholarly establishment in the 1970s. It also reflects the way certain outmoded critical concepts survive even the most bitter academic feuds. Although Felman and the French scholars disagree over the text's position vis-à-vis the poetics of Realism, they share a similar notion of what this term connotes. Both sides see Realism as a process of assigning signs to referents. More recent scholars, however, have problematized this traditional definition, grounding their description of Realist literary codes in the material practices that governed representational possibilities at the time Realist texts were written.[25] This later approach allows us to see how both the traditional and deconstructionist readings of *Adieu* overlook a crucial way in which the text intersects with its historical context. Situated historically, Balzac's text offers a commentary, or critique, of the way new, visually realistic forms of history were changing the face of the past in the post-Revolutionary period.

As I have indicated, the climax of the story occurs when Colonel Philippe de Sucy attempts a radical cure of his insane former lover by transforming his estate into an exact replica of the Beresina River in Russia where they had been parted and where she had gone mad. To achieve

21. Shoshana Felman, "Women and Madness: The Critical Phallacy," *Diacritics* 5, no. 4 (1975): 9.

22. Ibid., 10.

23. Ibid.

24. Sandy Petrey analyzes the debate over *Adieu* in "Balzac's Empire: History, Insanity, and the Realist Text," in *Historical Criticism and the Challenge of Theory,* ed. Janet Levarie Smarr (Urbana: University of Illinois Press, 1993), 29.

25. Exemplary definitions of *literary Realism* in relation to other contemporary discourses can be found in Jann Matlock, "Censoring the Realist Gaze," *Spectacles of Realism,* ed. Margaret Cohen and Christopher Prendergast (Minneapolis: University of Minneapolis Press, 1995), 32; Sharon Marcus, *Apartment Stories: City and Home in Nineteenth-Century Paris and London* (Berkeley: University of California Press, 1999), p 9. For my purposes, Petrey also provides a useful definition of Realism in his article on *Adieu*: "Insofar as the realist text has any generic specificity whatsoever, it derives from history's presence throughout its narratives." "Balzac's Empire," 33.

his re-creation that he hopes will shock Stéphanie back to reason, Philippe assembles a veritable army of craftsmen and laborers, aiming to create a perfect copy of the historical scene:

> The Colonel assembled workers to dig a canal which represented that devouring river where France's treasures, Napoleon and his army, were lost. Aided by his memories, Philippe succeeded in copying on his estate the riverbank where General Éblé had constructed his bridges [. . .]. He ravaged his grounds in order to perfect the illusion on which his last hope depended. He ordered uniforms and tattered costumes to clothe several hundred peasants. He erected sheds, bivouacs, batteries that he burned. *In the end, he overlooked nothing that could reproduce that most horrible of all scenes, and he attained his goal.* Sometime early in December, when snow had covered the ground with a thick white blanket, he recognized the Beresina. So dreadfully true was that false Russia that several of his comrades in arms recognized the scene of their former miseries. (203–4, emphasis added)

As Felman points out, the description of Philippe's "Realist" triumph ("he overlooked nothing that could reproduce that most horrible of all scenes, and he attained his goal") mirrors the terms Gascar uses to praise the war scenes in the middle section of the story. Yet, if one can, along with Felman, read the description of Philippe's historical reconstruction as a *mise-en-abyme* for the novella in which it figures, one can also read it as a comment on the way French spectacle entrepreneurs and theatrical producers were staging just such realistic historical representations at the time.[26]

The year the text was published, 1830, represented a kind of culmination or apotheosis of the spectacular past—the transformation of history into a visual commodity. As I show in chapter 3, twenty-nine new plays about Napoleon and the empire opened in Paris after the July Revolution, once it was no longer forbidden to mention the emperor's name on stage. Featuring actors who looked like the emperor (including a woman, Virginie Déjazet, who played Napoleon as a schoolboy) and who copied his characteristic gestures and tics, these productions carried Romanticism's

---

26. In his introduction to the Pléiade edition of *Adieu*, Le Yaouanc suggests several possible sources for Philippe's therapeutic reconstruction of the Beresina, including the efforts of Esquirol, a pioneer of early French psychiatry, to cure melancholia through "the effect of frightening, of dread"(cited in Le Yaouanc, introduction to *Adieu*, 968). To Le Yaouanc's list of sources, I add the efforts of the alienist Philippe Pinel to cure mental patients, including those suffering from emotional trauma associated with the Napoleonic Wars, through theatrical stagings; see Jan Goldstein, *Console and Classify* (Cambridge: Cambridge University Press, 1987), 84–87. A literary source might be found in Uncle Toby's efforts to reconstruct the Battle of Namur on his lawn in Laurence Sterne's *The Life and Opinions of Tristram Shandy, Gentleman* (1759–1767), one of Balzac's favorite novels. I thank Marshall Brown for this reference.

interest in historical realism to an extreme. Throughout 1830, moreover, Charles Langlois, the great *panoramiste,* was hard at work on the *Panorama de Navarin,* which would open in January 1831.[27] The first new panorama in almost a decade, Langlois's naval spectacle depicted a recent French victory over Turkish forces and placed the viewer on a real battle-ship purchased after the battle and transformed into a viewing platform.

Contemporary reviewers fell over themselves to heap praise on Langlois's new panorama, delighting in the "terrible truth"[28] of his picture. "Masts, ropes, cannons, megaphones, compasses, telescopes, the captain's cabin, the meeting room, nothing is lacking on this vessel," reported the reviewer for the legitimist *Gazette de France,* delighting in the scrupulous fidelity to detail.[29] The republican journal *Le National* likewise praised the "remarkable exactitude" of the panorama, describing it as "so strikingly true" that a member of the Scipion's crew would have no problem recognizing the ship on which he served: "This spectacle, so new and so interesting, will exert a powerful attraction on all French hearts, sensitive as they are to glory."[30] For viewers at the time, Langlois's representation of the celebrated battle had quite literally made French history come alive.

Amid all this enthusiasm, Balzac refused to be carried away. In a series of articles on Parisian political and cultural life that he wrote for *Le Voleur* in the months following the July Revolution, the author consistently registered his dislike for the newly triumphant and seemingly omnipresent spectacular mode of historical representation. "I went to see Virginie Déjazet playing Napoleon. What a joke!" he wrote on October 18, 1830, accusing "these napoleonized representations [*ces représentations napoléonisées*]" of prostituting the emperor's memory "in order to give one and all a piece of the great man in small change."[31] In later months, other voices critical of the Napoleon plays were heard, but Balzac was one of the first to accuse these plays of transforming history into a degraded, visual commodity: "In a week, we have had our fill of Napoleon, and in

27. The first announcement for the *Panorama de Navarin* appears in *Le Corsaire* on March 23, 1830. Vanessa Schwartz discusses the technological innovations of this panorama in *Spectacular Realities: Early Mass Culture in Fin-de-Siècle Paris* (Berkeley: University of California Press, 1998), 154.

28. Auguste Jal, "La Bataille Navarin," review of *Panorama de Navarain* by Charles Langlois, *L'Artiste* (1831): 26.

29. "Nouvelles des théâtres," review of *Panorama de Navarin* by Langlois, *Gazette de France,* May 1, 1831, 1.

30. "Panorama de Navarin," review of *Panorama de Navarin* by Langlois, *Le National,* January 21, 1831, 3.

31. The articles from *Le Voleur* are collected as the *Lettres sur Paris* in the Pléiade edition of Balzac's *Oeuvres diverses,* vol. 2 (Paris: Gallimard, 1996), 867–981.

another week, even the July Revolution will be seen on screens and prints, and you'll blow your nose with the storming of the Hôtel de Ville."[32] For Balzac, the proliferation of historical images ends by cheapening the past itself and by alienating the viewer from crucial moments in modern history. In another article, Balzac criticized the *Panorama de Navarin* for its "mechanical charlatanism,"[33] deflating the historical illusion that had so captivated other critics by exposing its special effects as mere gimmicks.[34] Despite his professed conservatism, Balzac's critique seems to mirror what I show in chapter 3 to be the way more left-leaning critics denounced the Napoleon plays in 1830, as well to anticipate the later fulminations of Adorno against the "culture industry." That Balzac finds fault with these spectacles should, however, come as no surprise because less than a year previously he had provided a startling critique of the spectacularization of history in *Adieu*.

If, as Felman points out, the language used to describe Philippe's reconstruction of the Beresina has much in common with Gascar's description of Balzac's own literary reconstruction of the event, it bears an even closer resemblance to the discourse surrounding the historical spectacles of its era. Just as the critic for *Le Journal des Arts* raved about the "striking truth" of Prévost's *Panorama de Wagram* in 1810,[35] and critics praised the "terrible truth" of Langlois's *Panorama de Navarin* in 1831, the narrator of *Adieu* says of Philippe's creation, "so dreadfully true was that false Russia that several of his comrades in arms recognized the scene of their former miseries" (204). Balzac's text thus inserts itself in the discourse surrounding the spectacular past by making use of its clichés.

Philippe's "false Russia" has more in common with the historical spectacles than mere rhetoric, however. Sandy Petrey rightly calls him a "Griffith or von Stroheim *avant la lettre*,"[36] but Philippe was also very much a man of his time. The means Philippe uses to achieve his illusion of historical reality are exactly those of the theatrical producers of his era—histori-

32. Ibid., 881.

33. Ibid., 954. This was the only negative review of the *Panorama de Navarin* that I have found in more than a dozen periodicals surveyed for the period 1830–1848.

34. When Balzac denounces the "charlatanism" of the panorama, he echoes the language used by Enlightenment rationalists to denounce the visual fakery and legerdemain associated with both con men and the Catholic Church, especially the educational philosophy of the Jesuits. Barbara Maria Stafford describes how, for these critics, "the potential for fraud lurked in any demonstration in which the performer created the illusion of eyewitnessing without informing the beholder how the action was done." *Artful Science: Enlightenment Entertainment and the Eclipse of Visual Education* (Cambridge: MIT Press, 1994), 79.

35. "Variétés," review of *Panorama de Wagram* by Pierre Prévost, *Journal des Arts, des Sciences, de Littérature et de Politique,* August 5, 1810, 179.

36. Petrey, "Balzac's Empire," 27.

cally accurate costumes and props, right down to the construction of a fake river (which had already been attempted for the production of Pix-erécourt's *Tékéli* in 1814). François-Antoine Harel's assembly of a prover-bial cast of thousands for his production of Dumas's *Napoléon* in January of 1831 calls to mind Philippe's huge casting call for a very similar pro-duction. And Harel's production did in fact feature a re-creation of the crossing of the Beresina. Balzac did not forecast the future; rather, both *Adieu* and the Napoleon plays of the 1830–31 season responded to the ever-increasing tendency toward spectacularly realistic historical represen-tations that defined the Romantic movement in the preceding decade. Philippe fulfills what I describe in chapter 3 to be Stendhal's and Hugo's longing for theatrical representations that would re-create the past with a "perfect illusion"—the psychodrama depicted in *Adieu* is really the ulti-mate *drame romantique*. The text even labels it as such, referring in the last paragraph to Philippe's suicide as the "final scene of a *drama* that had begun in 1812" (209, emphasis added).

Philippe borrows optical techniques not only from the theater, but also from the panorama. Drugging Stéphanie with opium and carrying her to the scene blindfolded, he achieves the same disorienting effect as the dark staircase that visitors were forced to pass through before entering onto the panorama's viewing platform. As with the panorama, Philippe's spectacle succeeds in fooling Stéphanie's senses by denying her any point of refer-ence with the world outside the illusion. Placed in the middle of the repre-sentation, everything she sees is part of the scene: "The Countess jumped out of the car, ran with a delirious anguish to the snowy spot, saw the burned bivouacs, and the fatal raft that was thrown into a frozen Beresina. Major Philippe was there, waving his saber at the multitude. Madame de Vandières let out a cry that froze all hearts, and stood before the colonel, who was quivering. She drew back, looking vaguely at first at this strange picture" (206). The text likens Stéphanie's act of looking at the three-dimensional scene to the act of looking at a picture, establishing another connection with the two-dimensional panorama. Stéphanie's stupefied re-sponse even seems to echo the amazement of critics in front of the can-vases of Prévost and Langlois.

The panorama, as I argued in chapter 1, served an ideological function for its post-Revolutionary public. Like the other historical spectacles of the time, the panorama provided perspectives through which new individ-ual, class, and national identities could be assumed by viewers after the Revolution and Napoleonic Wars. Allowing privileged spectators to see and hence to know the historical events and figures that had affected their lives powerfully but indirectly, the historical spectacles gave the illusion of control over a mysterious past, restoring to viewers a sense of agency and subjectivity. The effect on Stéphanie of the spectacular reconstruction of the Beresina dramatizes this process but also points to its dangers.

Like the Restoration public, Stéphanie suffers from an identity crisis brought on by recent historical events. Dislodged from the moorings of her past persona by the horrible episode in Russia, she has ceased to resemble herself. As Philippe laments, after she gobbles up some sugar like a greedy animal, "When she was a woman [. . .] she didn't like sweet things" (196). The historical trauma has severed her *identity* with her prior being.[37] And just as the historical spectacles proposed to restore lost identities through historical representation, so too does Philippe's representation of the Beresina restore Stéphanie's memory of her past life.[38]

As her gaze passes from the historical scene to Philippe, who hovers nervously nearby, she recognizes him for the first time, transforming, in an instant, from animal back to human: "For an instant as fast as a flash of lightning, her eyes had the lucidity lacking intelligence that we admire in the bright eye of birds; then she passed her hand over her face with the lively expression [*l'expression vive*] of a thinking person, she contemplated this living memory [*ce souvenir vivant*], this past life [*cette vie passée*] translated before her, turned her head quickly [*vivement*] toward Philippe and *saw him* [le vit]" (206, emphasis in original). The text plays on the homonymic equivalency between *vit* (the simple past tense of *voir*) and *vie* (life), variations of which it repeats four times in a single sentence, to emphasize the extent to which Stéphanie's resuscitation is linked to her vision of the historical representation.

But while bringing her back to life, her gaze turns Philippe into a *tableau*. Here the dangers that the spectacle poses begin to emerge, for what is shown is its contaminating effect. In a remarkable instance of metonymy, the frozen artificiality of the representation passes to its creator, to Philippe, who becomes part of the scene, part of what Stéphanie sees. This vision reawakens her memory and restores her powers of recognition along with her prior identity—"Stéphanie, cried the colonel / Oh!

37. Felman likewise places Stéphanie's identity crisis at the center of the story, but sees it less as an allegory for the historical situation than for the mystery of "woman." The repeated questions "She? Who?" which the two hunters pose in the opening scene, according to Felman, "situate from the start the textual problematic within a systematic search for the nature of feminine identity." "Women and Madness," 7.

38. In *Psychoanalysis and Storytelling* (Cambridge: Blackwell Publishers, 1994), Peter Brooks reads *Adieu* as a dramatization of the dynamics of transference in the process of psychoanalysis, as well as in the act of narration itself (70).

it's Philippe, said the poor countess" (207)—but in the process turns her into a spectacle: "She collapsed into the trembling arms that the colonel held out to her, and the embrace of the two lovers terrified the spectators" (207). The spectacle is spreading; now Stéphanie, the original spectator, is viewed by the peasant-actors who form part of the scene. The spectacle becomes the spectator, as Stéphanie freezes into non-life before the eyes of the onlookers.

A moment later, she dies in Philippe's arms: "All of a sudden her tears dried, she cadaverized [*elle se cadavérisa*] as if lightning had touched her" (207). The text leaves the cause of her death vague. Petrey suggests that Stéphanie dies of shame when she remembers the sexual degradation she suffered at the hands of the retreating French army after becoming insane. But I suggest that she dies as a martyr to the spectacle, for her death occurs in the blink of an eye and in the act of looking. As Petrey points out, the text invents the phrase "se cadavérisa" to convey the rapidity and reflexivity of the event.[39] Blaming the spectacle, moreover, allows us to see how Philippe also dies as its victim. At first, he makes an attempt to break free from the fatal vision of the false Beresina and his dead lover: "Monsieur de Sucy took several steps to tear himself away from this spectacle" (208). Ultimately, however, he remains under its spell, unable to move forward, frozen. His own story stops there, as suicide beckons.[40]

The danger of the historical spectacle, *Adieu* makes us see, lies in the tricks it plays on the identity of the viewer. On the one hand, it posits history as the ground for the formation of subjectivity: Stéphanie recovers the identity she lost on the banks of the Beresina through the sight of the spectacle. But at the same time the spectacle undermines that identity by forcing the viewer into a position of paralyzing passivity. By encouraging the public to consume the past and by making that past more real than life, the text tells us, the new visual forms of history have robbed post-Revolutionary French culture of the very identity such spectacles hoped to foster. The remarkable image of Philippe and Stéphanie being looked at by the figures of their past—the spectators become the spectacle—stands as the text's diagnosis of the way new forms of historical representation, under the guise of reawakening public memory, and of cementing a collective social identity based on a narrative of a shared past, undermined that

39. Petrey, "Balzac's Empire," 38.
40. By setting the ending of the story in 1830, Balzac makes it topical, thus perhaps also further establishing a connection with the historical spectacles that were so pervasive when the story was published.

society's possibility for continuing the narrative into the future. For what hope for continuing forward, politically or socially, the text asks, exists for a society fixated on the spectacle of its past?

Karl Marx made a similar diagnosis in *The Eighteenth Brumaire of Louis-Bonaparte* (1852). For Marx, the failure of the Revolution of 1848 stemmed from the backward glancing of the revolutionaries, their troping of the first Revolution. Rather than "draw its poetry from the past,"[41] rather than mould its discourse on the bourgeois Revolution, the social revolution of the nineteenth century, according to Marx, needed to look to the future, tailoring its discourse to the problems facing the emerging proletariat class. But the forms of the past held the revolutionaries in sway: "Men make their own history," he famously writes,

> but they do not make it just as they please [. . .]. The tradition of all the dead generations weighs like a nightmare on the brain of the living. And just when they seem engaged in revolutionizing themselves and things, in creating something that has never yet existed, precisely in such periods of revolutionary crisis they anxiously conjure up the spirits of the past to their service and borrow from them names, battle cries and costumes in order to present the new scene of world history in this time-honoured disguise and this borrowed language [. . .] the Revolution of 1848 knew nothing better to do than to parody, now 1789, now the revolutionary tradition of 1793 to 1795.[42]

The references to costumes and borrowed language in this passage provide an apt characterization of the way nineteenth-century historical representations of the Revolution and Empire exerted a nefarious hold over nineteenth-century revolutionaries. "Hegel remarks somewhere that all facts and personages of great importance in world history occur, as it were, twice. He forgot to add: the first time as tragedy, the second as farce."[43] Marx's theatrical metaphor signals how history was increasingly perceived as a spectacle by astute mid-century observers and the extent to which the spectacular view of the past was identified as the major obstacle blocking historical progress. *Adieu* makes a similar observation as early as 1830.

As Richard Terdiman has remarked, Alexis de Tocqueville, who participated in the early stages of the Revolution of 1848, expressed his frustration with that revolution's outcome in similarly theatrical terms in his *Sou-*

41. Karl Marx, *The Eighteenth Brumaire of Louis Bonaparte* (1852; reprint, New York: International Publishers, 1963), 18.
42. Ibid., 15.
43. Ibid.

venirs of 1850, complaining of the way his fellow revolutionaries "performed the French Revolution rather than continuing it. . . . We sought without success to warm ourselves at our fathers' passions; we imitated their gestures and their poses as we had seen them in the theater. . . . It all seemed a vile tragedy staged by a provincial troupe."[44] According to Terdiman, this failure of authenticity in 1848, coming as it did in the middle of a century that had begun to deify originality, had a profoundly alienating effect on the generation of 1848, revealing the extent to which all action was already an imitation, a representation. *Adieu* shows that not even this sense of alienation was original to the generation of 1848, however, because the perception of history's spectacular nature had already been registered by the generation of 1830.

Returning now to the middle section of the story, to the historical narrative of the Beresina episode, it becomes clear that the act of witnessing events is already analogized to the act of looking at popular entertainments. When the general in charge of the evacuation of the French troops across the river considers his course of action, "he began to contemplate the spectacle presented by the camp" (166). Here, as later when Stéphanie encounters Philippe's representation of the scene, the reader views the event at a distance, mediated through the gaze of the characters and through the language of spectacle. When a group of freezing soldiers attacks the carriage carrying the half-dead Stéphanie and her husband, the general, and dons the countess's clothes to keep warm, the result has a theatrical appearance: "The young countess looked at this spectacle twice and remained silent" (174). As Philippe oversees the construction of the raft that will carry Stéphanie and her husband across the river, she once again watches as if attending a theatrical event, cut off from the action and passive in the face of danger: "The young countess, seated next to her husband, contemplated this spectacle with the regret of being able to contribute nothing to the work" (185–86). After the raft's completion, Philippe watches in horror as the soldiers fail to leave a place for him and his charges: "he shuddered when he saw the crowded embarkation and the men pressing together like spectators in the stalls of a theater" (186).

Distanced from events as they unfold, the characters in Balzac's text look rather than act. This section of the story thus eerily foreshadows the passivity and alienation generated by Philippe's historical representation at the story's end. It also reveals what some critics take to be the spectacu-

---

44. Alexis de Tocqueville, cited in Richard Terdiman, "Class Struggles in France," in *A New History of French Literature,* ed. Denis Hollier (Cambridge: Harvard University Press, 1989), 705–6.

lar past's deeper danger: by transforming historical events into objects of vision even as they take place, spectacles undermine the impetus to action. From a Marxist perspective, such spectacles might be seen to serve the interests of the ruling class; by turning people into viewers of Revolutionary or Imperial history, historical entertainments seem to eliminate the danger of future revolution. As Debord put it well over a century later, "The more we watch, the less we live."[45] *Adieu* exposes the mechanism of this process.

Balzac's novella, however, did not have the last word on the spectacle. On August 3, 1835, a theatrical adaptation of the story by E. Téaulon, entitled *La folle de la Bérésina*, opened at the théâtre du Palais-Royal. The new version was a musical, with songs by the *chef d'orchestre* at the Palais-Royal. This was not, however, the only change from page to stage. Although the second act of *La folle de la Bérésina*, like the original story, depicts the attempt of Colonel Falbert (the new name for Philippe de Sucy) to restore his lover Julie (Stéphanie) de Vandières to reason by reconstructing the battlefield on which she lost her sanity, the theatrical version, after literally staging the spectacle, does away with the tragic ending. Julie faints when she sees the scene, but then wakes up with her reason and health intact. After a moment's hesitation in which she remembers her dead husband, she vows to live happily ever after: "Ah! poor Vandières," she intones sadly, "dead . . . over there . . . before my eyes . . . in the torrent . . . (with dignity) Colonel Falbert . . . one more year for the memory of the general . . . and the rest of my life . . . for you!"[46] The representation thus succeeds in the mission it set out to accomplish: the madwoman is restored to reason, and to her lover, by the sight of the spectacle. Memory is kept under control—allowed for, but confined within limits set by the characters themselves. In the theatrical version, the critique of the visually realistic historical entertainments found in *Adieu* gives way to an affirmation of their redemptive power, both for the characters on stage and for the members of the audience, some of whom might have been veterans, who confront the spectacle along with Julie.

As Patrick Berthier points out, for reviewers in the popular press at the time, the lavish Beresina set, created by none other than Cicéri, the famous designer of sets for the Opéra and for the great Romantic dramas, literally dominated the play. One critic remarked that the "second act is by M. Eugène Cicéri alone. It's for the décor of M. Eugène Cicéri that the second act was constructed."[47] By turning a story that condemns the spectacle into an

---

45. Guy Debord, *La société du spectacle* (Paris: Gallimard, 1992), 31.
46. Emmanuel Théaulon [de Lambert], *La folle de la Bérésina* (Paris: Barba, 1835), 37.
47. "Théâtres," review of *La folle de la Bérésina* by Théaulon, *Revue de Paris*, August 10, 1835, 141, cited in Patrick Berthier, "'Adieu au théâtre'," *L'année balzacienne* (1987): 52.

actual spectacle, by literalizing its dominant metaphor, the production transforms condemnation into celebration. This recuperation of Balzac's critique by its very object testifies to the threat that *Adieu* posed as well as to the spectacle's crafty resilience.

In my reading of *Adieu*, then, Philippe incarnates the nineteenth-century impulse to bring the past to life through realistic representation. His heroic but misguided attempt to re-create the scene of his "former miseries" as a means of curing his lover of the trauma inflicted by history focuses our attention on the dangers inherent in the kinds of historical spectacles that proliferated in the post-Revolutionary period. The drive toward a spectacular vision of the past did not confine itself to popular entertainments, however; it formed an essential part of the Romantic movement more generally.

Philippe's obsession with the recent past and his drive to represent it with a visual accuracy identify him as a Romantic historian. Born in 1789, Philippe is not only literally a child of the Revolution, but he is also part of the same generation as the writers who began their historical careers around 1820: Barante was born in 1782, Guizot in 1787, and Thierry in 1795. It is tempting, I think, to see the disastrous effects of Philippe's historical vision as a prescient allegory for the way the Revolution of 1830 was about to propel Romantic historians such as Thiers and Guizot to positions of authority in the new government of Louis-Philippe, the citizen-king, and for the way their ministry would prove a spectacular disappointment to the cause of liberty and progress that their histories had seemed to advocate.

If Philippe is the historian, then Stéphanie represents the French people, duped and done in by nineteenth-century forms of history that promised a cure for the traumas of the Revolution, as well as a foundation on which to construct a solid identity. Not wanting to overlook her specificity as a woman, however, and thus fall victim to Felman's critique, I also point out that women fared particularly badly at the hands of this new history. Not only did Romantic historians such as Michelet at times demonize women, blaming them paradoxically both for the Terror and for the Counterrevolution, but they also excluded women from their rapidly professionalizing ranks.[48] Their voices silenced and their characters maligned, nineteenth-century French women had much in common with Stéphanie de Vandières. Balzac's female spectator thus epitomizes the particular oppression experi-

---

48. For an example of the negative portrayal of women in Romantic historiography, see Jules Michelet's 1854 *Les femmes de la Révolution,* vol. 16 of *Oeuvres complètes* (Paris: Flammarion, 1980). Bonnie G. Smith describes the exclusion of women from the historical profession in the nineteenth century in *The Gender of History: Men, Women and Historical Practice* (Cambridge: Harvard University Press, 1998)

enced by women in relation to the historical practices of the day—forced to become spectators of historical events rather than creators of either the events themselves or their representation, women were all the more susceptible to the spectacle's dangers.[49] The only character in *Adieu* to escape unscathed is the marquis d'Albon, who from the beginning casts an ironic glance on Philippe's Romantic obsession with the past and who takes no part in the reconstruction of the Beresina. D'Albon might therefore be seen to figure the Realist novelist, who lives to tell the tale.

The Spectacular Spectre: *Le Colonel Chabert*

Another of Balzac's key early Realist fictions, *Le Colonel Chabert,* published two years after *Adieu* in 1832, pursues the critique of the historical spectacle. Like *Adieu, Le Colonel Chabert* takes place in Restoration Paris, a few years following the return to power of the Bourbons in 1815. As I note in the Introduction, the story opens in the office of the lawyer Derville, into which walks an old, broken-down man who claims to be the Colonel Chabert, an officer reported killed during the Napoleonic Wars.

The clerks in the office laugh in the old man's face, but Derville listens in fascination as the old man tells of having been wounded and left for dead on the battlefield of Eylau, having emerged from a pit of corpses, and having slowly recovered his memory and health while staying with some Prussian peasants near the site of the battle. The colonel describes making his way back to Paris, just after Napoleon's defeat at Waterloo, only to discover that his troubles have just begun: his wife, believing him dead, has used his sizable estate to engineer a new marriage to a prominent member of the Restoration government, the count de Ferraud. Unwilling to accept that her former husband has returned from the dead, which would invalidate her new marriage, threaten her social position, and cast the legitimacy of her two children by Ferraud into question, the countess refuses to acknowledge Chabert's claim to be himself. Like Stéphanie in *Adieu,* the old colonel thus finds himself without an identity as a result of the trauma of war and Revolution, but unlike the madwoman, he attempts to assert his rights through legal channels and appeals to Derville to help him take his wife to court.

Derville takes the case. Masterfully manipulating the countess de Ferraud, also his client, by raising the threat of a scandal that would permit her husband to further his ambitions for a peerage by repudiating her,

---

49. Not all women were victims to the spectacle, of course. See chapter 1 for a discussion of how some women may have turned the spectacles to their own advantage.

Derville convinces her to negotiate with Chabert in order to hush up the whole affair. After a fruitless confrontation in Derville's office, the countess brings Chabert to her country estate and prevails upon him to remain "dead," to renounce his claims to his former identity in exchange for a fixed sum. When the old colonel overhears her pledge to send him to the mental hospital, however, his pride revolts. He refuses to participate in her scheme and vows to disappear, leaving her free to remain the countess de Ferraud. As in *Adieu,* the story ends ten years later, around 1830, when Derville spots Chabert on a visit to Bicêtre, the hospital-poorhouse. Old, alone, and broken, Chabert no longer claims to be anyone at all.

Adieu and *Le Colonel Chabert* share many features. Both contain historical analepses that recount episodes from the Napoleonic Wars as part of a larger narrative set in the present of the Restoration. Both stories describe the difficult return of a victim of these Wars, and both center on the effort to restore that victim's identity, which the trauma of war has robbed. *Le Colonel Chabert* and *Adieu* have thus unsurprisingly found themselves grouped together by Balzac scholars. The preface by Pierre Gascar that provoked Felman's wrath is actually to an edition that includes both works.[50] In it, Gascar points to several of their common themes: "It is significant that *Le Colonel Chabert* and *Adieu* are stories about the living dead, about ghosts [*revenants*], characters who escaped by accident (if not by a miracle) from an adventure or drama which, at the moment Balzac wrote, belonged to a time that people hoped was past, but whose prolonged last echoes continued to trouble or annoy."[51] In the reading suggested by Gascar, *Le Colonel Chabert* and *Adieu* both serve as allegories for the way the repressed memory of the Revolution and its imperial aftermath threatened the Restoration's efforts to turn back the clock, to forget the past. The image of Chabert emerging from a pit of dead bodies on the battlefield of Eylau gives the lie to Louis XVIII's proclamation that "the abyss of Revolutions was closed,"[52] cited later in the novel, in the course of Derville's meditation on the countess's precarious conjugal politics. The degree to which the Revolutionary abyss was still very much open would, of course, have been all too apparent to readers of *Le Colonel Chabert* when it first appeared in *L'Artiste,* one of the new Romantic journals to emerge after the Revolution of 1830.[53]

---

50. The edition also includes two other war stories, *El verdugo* and *Le réquisitionnaire.*
51. Gascar, preface to Balzac, 7–8.
52. Balzac, "Le Colonel Chabert," in *Le Colonel Chabert suivi de trois nouvelles* (Paris: Gallimard, 1974), 79. Subsequent quotations are cited in the text.
53. The first issue of *L'Artiste* appeared on February 6, 1831. An early version of *Le Colonel Chabert,* entitled *La transaction* (meaning "deal" or "compromise"), was published

For Gascar, Chabert's return to Restoration Paris as a ghost haunting the fragile marriage of his former wife, like Stéphanie's own ghostlike appearance at the ruined monastery, figures the return of the repressed content of history. The eventual destruction of both spectres, following Gascar's logic, spells the desire of Balzac to forget the historical trauma of Revolution and Empire once and for all. Balzac, of course, professed himself a monarchist and a Catholic, even though he criticized the Restoration government for its cowardice and ineptitude. According to Gascar, in *Adieu* and *Le Colonel Chabert,* he thus puts his fiction in service of his politics, enacting on a symbolic level, by killing Stéphanie and committing Chabert to Bicêtre, what Restoration society could not quite achieve in reality. "An enterprise of historical liquidation," writes Gascar of these stories, "Balzac feels only aversion for the adventure of the Revolution and the epic of the Empire. Like a large part of France in 1830, he attempts to turn the bloody pages of History."[54]

To understand these stories as allegories for the way the past haunted the Restoration is certainly plausible and helps show a vital way in which the literature of the post-Revolutionary period functioned in relation to its time. Yet, while taking into account the general historical dynamic of the period in which the texts were written, such a reading overlooks some key elements of the texts' historical specificity. I have already shown how both *Les Chouans* and *Adieu* make reference to the kinds of historical spectacles that had become popular at the time and how *Adieu* diagnoses the dangers that these spectacles had unleashed on the post-Revolutionary populace. *Le Colonel Chabert* offers what might be an even more damning condemnation of the spectacular past.[55]

What actually haunts this story? Is Chabert's ghostly presence only an allegory for the past itself, or could it also be read as an allegory for the way new forms of representing the past, the new spectacular modes of historical representation, were turning history into a kind of spectre? Through the figure of Chabert, Balzac's novella reveals what history looked like in 1832, but also problematizes the very notion that history had become something to see.

---

in *L'Artiste* on February 19 and 26, and on March 5 and 12, 1832. Balzac's text acquired its definitive title when it entered tome 10 of *La comédie humaine* in 1844, although "La transaction" remains the title for the middle section of the story.

54. Gascar, preface to Balzac, 18.

55. In "The Reality of Representation: Between Marx and Balzac," *Critical Inquiry* 14, no. 3 (Spring 1998): 448–68, Sandy Petrey reads *Le Colonel Chabert* in the context of Marx's *The Eighteenth Brumaire of Louis Bonaparte,* showing how the two texts undermine the opposition that would privilege the economic over the ideological. Petrey discusses how identity is shown to be a performance in both works.

When Chabert first goes to the lawyer Derville for help proving his identity, the lawyer finds himself listening to the old man's story more with his eyes than his ears. "Listening to his client express himself with a perfect lucidity and recount facts that seemed so plausible, although strange, the young lawyer put down his files, placed his left elbow on the table, put his head in his hand, and stared intently at the colonel" (41). Ultimately Derville decides to advance Chabert the money to live on while he proceeds with his case because of the colonel's bearing and attitude, his appearance, or rather, his *performance*. As the lawyer puts it to his head clerk after Chabert has taken his money and gone: "I just heard a story that possibly will cost me twenty-five louis. If I am robbed, I won't regret my money, for I will have seen the most skilled actor of our age" (58). What makes Derville such an extraordinary lawyer, and what makes *Le Colonel Chabert* such an extraordinary text, lies precisely here, in the understanding that in the world of post-Revolutionary France, good actors made the best clients because history had become a spectacle.

Like *Les Chouans* and *Adieu, Le Colonel Chabert* abounds in references to contemporary spectacles. The first reference occurs rather stunningly at the very opening of the text, when Chabert first arrives at the lawyer's office, looking for Derville. "Monsieur, is your boss visible?" (27) the old man asks the lawyer's clerks, ironically paying homage to the spectacular regime that will contain and eventually destroy him. Unable to obtain a response, he vows to return, but once out the door his comically disheveled appearance provokes the clerks to wager over his identity. The stakes of the bet, as I discuss at the beginning of this book, prove to be none other than a spectacle: "Ah! I'll bet everyone tickets to a spectacle that he was not a soldier," (31) offers the lawyer's clerk, Godeschal. When the other clerks press him on which theater they will go to should he lose the bet, Godeschal defines the spectacle as a thing one sees for money. This includes, he points out, cheap forms of entertainment such as the Curtius wax display.

Aside from saving Godeschal quite a few francs, this argument over the nature of the spectacle, on the surface a rather bizarre digression in a story about a man returning from the war, foreshadows the network of spectacular images and allusions used to portray Chabert. It is precisely as a figure in Curtius's wax display that he is identified when Derville first sees him a few pages later: "Colonel Chabert was as perfectly still as a wax figure in Curtius's display where Godeschal had wanted to bring his comrades" (37). The narrator goes on to describe the emaciated body, the hollow eyes, the waxlike, cadaverous texture of the colonel's skin that render the lawyer speechless: "The young lawyer remained stupefied for a moment when he caught sight of the peculiar client waiting for him in the shadows" (37). Just as in the passage already cited, when, after hearing Chabert's testimony, Derville calls him "the most skilled actor of our age," here once again Chabert is rendered as a spectacle, "a thing one sees," and Derville as the spectator-customer, who hands over money for the privilege of looking. Godeschal's definition of the spectacle thus theorizes the mechanism by which Chabert's story—which incarnates the history of the Revolution and the Napoleonic Wars—is represented to Derville, the man of the nineteenth century, eager for knowledge about the past and ready to pay to see it.

Published two years after *Adieu, Le Colonel Chabert* bears witness to the explosion of the historical spectacle into Parisian popular culture following the Revolution of 1830. As I show in chapter 3, by 1832, reviews harshly critical of the Napoleon plays could be read in much of the press. Through its inquiry into what constitutes a spectacle and by likening its main character to a popular entertainment, Balzac's novel thus inscribes itself in a debate over the spectacularization of history in nineteenth-century French culture. The stakes could not have been higher, for what lay in the balance was the degree to which the past could serve as a stable referent, as a firm basis for the formation of subjectivity, in the post-Revolutionary period.

Chabert, the man attempting to reclaim his name, learns that in post-Revolutionary France, historical truth is beside the point. In a world where history has become a thing one pays to see, appearances count more than facts. Derville, the crafty lawyer, knows this from the beginning and is willing to bet his money that they can force Chabert's wife, now the Countess de Ferraud, to negotiate, but only provided that she does not *see* Chabert. When he brings the two of them together at his office, he arranges for them to be in separate rooms to spare the countess's nerves, he tells her, but really to prevent her from witnessing the degree to which her husband both does and does not look like himself.

For the occasion, Chabert has disguised himself as himself; that is, he has dressed as an old Napoleonic officer is supposed to look: "Seeing him, passersby would have easily recognized in him one of those handsome wrecks of our old army" (91). Wearing the "red ribbon of the officers of the *Légion d'honneur*" (90), he conforms to the expectations generated by representations. "These old soldiers," the narrator tells us, "are nothing but paintings and books" (91), making reference to the kinds of illustrated histories of Napoleon that, like their theatrical counterparts, delighted viewers at the time. Chabert's costume is good enough to convince even the skeptical clerks in Derville's office: "Ha!" one of them cries, "who wants to bet a spectacle that Chabert is a general, and a decorated one at that?" (91).

But as Derville realizes, even this perfect illusion of Colonel Chabert will not be enough to win the case. When, unable to restrain himself, Chabert bursts into the room in which his wife is sitting, she denies his existence outright, even while recognizing him as her husband. Derville later rebukes his client: "Ah! well, colonel, wasn't I right to beg you not to come? I am now certain of your identity. When you showed yourself, the countess made a movement whose meaning was not equivocal. But you lost your case, your wife knows that you are unrecognizable [*méconnaissable*]!" (96) Chabert comes to learn the lesson—which Derville and the Countess, described repeatedly as a good actress, have already mastered— that in a spectacular world, appearances count both for everything and nothing. When reality is indistinguishable from its counterfeit and the historical referent has been forever replaced by its representation, the truth of the past is ultimately unknowable, *méconnaissable*. The spectacle has so colored visions of the past that the signs of real suffering—Chabert's cadaverous complexion—serve only to make him look fake, to increase his resemblance to a figure in a wax display.

At the end of the story, Derville sees his client once again, while taking his clerk Godeschal on a tour of Bicêtre, the hospital-poorhouse. This sad locale is revealed to be the scene of enunciation for the story that has gone before, as Derville, provoked by Godeschal's curiosity, recounts the sad history of Chabert. A few days later they return to visit the old colonel, who has renounced all claims to his identity once and for all: "Not Chabert! not Chabert!" he yells at the two lawyers, "my name is Hyacinthe [. . .]. I am no longer a man, I am the number 164" (118). Yet even as the old soldier voluntarily adopts the nonidentity of a bureaucratic number, his old self resurfaces, briefly, when the lawyer and his former clerk give the old man some money for tobacco before heading back to Paris: "he thanked them with a stupid look, saying: 'Brave troops!' He stood at attention, pretended to aim a gun, and shouted while smiling: 'Fire both barrels! Long live Napoleon!'" (119) The old soldier emerges to enact one last Napoleonic representation.

True to form, Derville at first looks at the madhouse as a piece of scenery and sees Chabert as a character on stage: "Derville took his *lorgnon*, looked at the poor chap, let out a startled gasp, and said:— That old man, my friend, is a poem, or, as the Romantics say, a drama" (117). Like the Napoleon plays themselves, Chabert has become the grotesque end point of the trend toward spectacular representation called for by Stendhal and Hugo. But when Derville recognizes the old and abandoned colonel as his former client, even he, the master of appearances, the director of Chabert's performance as himself, cannot bear the sight. Listing to Godeschal all the horrors he has witnessed—"I can't tell you everything I have seen" (120)—Derville renounces the spectacle and the city that propagates it once and for all: "You are going to know such pretty things; as for me, I am gong to live in the country with my wife. Paris horrifies me" (121).

This asylum ending suggests one more intertextual reference. A few months before the initial publication of *Le Colonel Chabert* in *L'Artiste*, Balzac published another short story, entitled "Les proscrits: Esquisse historique" in *La Revue de Paris*.[56] Set in 1308, this work epitomizes the kind of Romantic historical fiction that seeks to evoke the past through visual details and that characterizes much of Balzac's literary output prior to 1830. In this same number of *La Revue de Paris*, however, there is another article that may have provided Balzac with the inspiration for the ending of *Le Colonel Chabert*. Entitled simply "Bicêtre," this article, by a medical doctor named Eus. Corbin, contains a detailed overview of the hospital/poorhouse, from an architectural description of its buildings to an analysis of its therapeutic methods, based largely around the "moral treatment" of Philippe Pinel.

According to Corbin, the madness of the inmates of Bicêtre derives from a variety of causes, but the largest number are what he calls "crazed with ambition." Included in this category are a number of men who claim to have had (or to continue to have) a special relationship with Napoleon. One man, dressed in rags that reflect a certain faded grandeur, begs, in tears, to be taken away, claiming that Napoleon has demanded his services. Corbin analyzes this mania: "But the emperor is the one who occupies him the most. Formerly he was, or so he says, in charge of Josephine's candles, and the name of his former master, repeated often since the events of July, has become his sole preoccupation."[57] Corbin may have intended this description as a reference to the bald way in which Louis-Philippe and his followers co-opted the political support of the Bonapartists during the July Days, appropriating the ex-emperor's popularity for their own pacifist, pro-business regime.

Corbin then reveals that the cause of the man's madness has less to do with the political machinations of the regime, than with the effect of historical *representation*: "What is more there are those who went crazy following the July Days, among them an old soldier, wounded at Waterloo,

---

56. Balzac, "Les proscrits: Esquisse historique," *La Revue de Paris*, 26 (1831): 12–51.
57. Eus. Corbin, "Bicêtre," *La Revue de Paris* 26 (1831): 215.

who roughly sketches the outline of the hat and coat of the great man on the wall, and who cries in front of the picture like he cried when seeing his portraits on the Boulevard, and in watching those dramatized Napoleons, the emotions of which drove him to Bicêtre."[58] Here the man weeps in front of a crude drawing of the emperor, but this image is merely a feeble copy of the full-blown portraits of Napoleon that appeared on Boulevard stages following the Revolution of 1830. Corbin blames the "emotions" caused by these theatrical productions for the man's mental disturbance in what amounts to one of the clearest denunciations of the historical spectacle and its dangerous effects encountered so far. Ultimately, however, the ability to claim this inmate as a source for the old colonel in Balzac's text matters less than the insights the article provides into how the spectacle entered the phantasmatic space of post-Revolutionary France. By ending Chabert's story in Bicêtre, Balzac's text incorprates the terms of a critique of the historical spectacle that circulated through the medical, journalistic, and political discourses of the time.

WRITTEN shortly after *Les Chouans,* and shortly before the novels about the post-Revolutionary present that form the bulk of *La comédie humaine, Adieu* and *Le Colonel Chabert* represent an important turning point not just for their author, but for the nineteenth-century French novel. Like the old colonel, gazed at through a *lorgnon* at the end of *Le Colonel Chabert,* history was viewed at a distance by the authors referred to as Realist. After 1830, Realist texts by Balzac, like those of Stendhal, invoked the history of the Revolution and Empire and thus perhaps benefited from its vogue as a subject, but they did so only indirectly. In these works, history appears not as a spectacle to be consumed by the reader/viewer, but as the object of obsession, mediated by representation, that leads the protagonists astray.

Instead of inviting the reader into the space of the past, the early Realist novels of Balzac, like those of Stendhal, remain firmly grounded in the present. Through the example of their characters, these novels show history to be the unknowable and unreal, an obstacle both to the formation of identity and to the hope of political progress. At the moment of its emergence, then, the French Realist novel seemed to have realized that the proliferation of counterfeit representations in nineteenth-century culture had made history "unrecognizable" and thus unable to serve as the ground for identity or as the basis for fiction. In all of these works, and this is ultimately a description of Realism at the time of its emergence in

58. Ibid., 217.

1830, the Romantic obsession with history is at once incorporated and banished, allowing the novel, if not to propose an alternative to history for the formation of subjectivity, at least to stake out an oppositional space, the space of critique, in which modernity's relation to the past is continually called into question.

Chapter Six

Stendhal's Historical Role

Stendhal was obsessed with history.[1] Unlike Balzac, his junior by sixteen years, Stendhal actually participated in the great modern epic: attached to Napoleon's army, he witnessed the conquest of Berlin and Vienna as well as the devastating disaster of the Beresina. What existed as mere myth for Balzac had been a reality for the older writer, and, like Balzac, Stendhal attempted throughout his *oeuvre* to analyze the legacy of this poetic past for the more prosaic present.[2] Both writers, moreover, saw their fiction as an essentially historical enterprise. Just as Balzac called *La comédie humaine* a "history of manners,"[3] Stendhal subtitled *Le rouge et le noir* (1830), "A Chronicle of 1830"[4] and described it as a historical novel about the present. "One day this novel will paint bygone days, like those of Walter Scott,"[5] he declared in a preparatory sketch for the book.

1. Stendhal was the pseudonym of Henri Beyle (1783–1842).
2. Whereas Balzac referred to Napoleon frequently in his novels, Stendhal actually wrote two biographies of the emperor, the *Vie de Napoléon* (1818) and the *Mémoires sur Napoléon* (1837).
3. In the 1842 "Avant-propos" to the *La comédie humaine*, Balzac described his intention to "write the history forgotten by so many historians, that of manners." *La Comédie humaine,* vol. 1 (Paris: Gallimard, 1976), 11.
4. On the title page of the original edition, the subtitle read, "A Chronicle of the Nineteenth Century." Priscilla Parkhurst Ferguson describes how subsequent editors alternated between the two versions in "The Specters of Revolution; or, Politics at the Concert," in *Approaches to Teaching Stendhal's* The Red and the Black, ed. Dean de la Motte and Stirling Haig (New York: MLA, 1999), 24.
5. From Stendhal's "projet d'article sur *Le rouge et le noir,*" sent to the Count Salvagnoli, cited in Maurice Bardèche, *Stendhal romancier* (Paris: Éditions de la Table Ronde, 1947), 192.

Scholars have long seen the presence of the past in the fiction of both authors as the key to their Realist style. Along with the serious treatment of everyday reality, it is the "embedding of random persons and events in the general course of contemporary history, the fluid historical background" in Balzac and Stendhal that provides, according to Erich Auerbach, "the foundations of modern realism."[6] Although Stendhal would set *Le rouge et le noir* in the very year of its composition, 1830, the novel's contemporaneity bears the stamp of the past. "The present" of Realist novels, Auerbach notes, "is something in the process of resulting from history." The characters and atmosphere in both Balzac and Stendhal, "contemporary as they may be, are always represented as phenomena sprung from historical events and forces."[7] In *Reading for the Plot*, Peter Brooks likewise sees the "historical perspective" as the dominant feature of Stendhal's fictional universe[8] and examines its workings on a narrative level, showing how the past, represented as a model of "paternity and authority," provides the plot of *Le rouge et le noir* with its principal motor.[9] For Brooks, the Realist novel, epitomized by Stendhal's *Le rouge et le noir*, struggles with history's power to determine both the actions of the characters and the action of the story.

But how, exactly, does history function within the novel? In *Le rouge et le noir*, the past takes many forms, but in particular it figures as a kind of spectacle: the characters play roles inherited from the script of history in a manner akin to actual performances of Romantic historical dramas that the characters both see and discuss. In this chapter, *Le rouge et le noir* emerges as a parody of the historical spectacles that are thematized within the novel. I argue that *Le rouge et le noir*, like Stendhal's later novel, *La chartreuse de Parme* (1839), is everywhere penetrated not only by the *effect* of history but by the *form* history took in early nineteenth-century France and that the mode of the representation of these two novels, their form, takes shape in opposition to the historical conventions of the culture. Not merely a commentary on the influence of the past on the present, or on the ways in which history determines action, the novels of Stendhal,

6. Erich Auerbach, *Mimesis*, trans. Willard R. Trask (1953; reprint, Princeton: Princeton University Press, 1974), 491.

7. Ibid., 481.

8. "Stendhal's novels are inescapably pervaded by a historical perspective that provides an interpretive framework for all actions, ambitions, self-conceptions, and desires." Peter Brooks, *Reading for the Plot* (Cambridge: Harvard University Press, 1984), 62.

9. "And the nineteenth-century novel as a genre seems to be inseparable from the conflict of movement and resistance, revolution and restoration, and from the issues of authority and paternity, which provide not only the matter of the novel but also its structuring force, the dynamic that shapes its plot." Ibid., 65.

like those of Balzac, describe the material ways in which the post-Revolutionary period sought to make history real but ended by making it unreal, an exercise in collective delusion. Stendhal's Realism provides a vivid critique of Romanticism's effort to visualize the past—an effort, ironically, that Stendhal had helped to articulate.

Napoleon's Reflection

Le rouge et le noir recounts the rise and fall of Julien Sorel. The son of a humble miller, with appealing looks and prodigious talents matched only by his still more prodigious ambition, Julien begins his upward climb by serving as tutor to the children of M. de Rênal, the mayor of the small provincial town of Verrières—and by seducing his wife. Realizing that his best path to advancement lies in the priesthood, Julien spends some time in a monastery in Besançon, professing religious convictions he does not feel, before finally making his way to Paris. Once there, he nearly succeeds in overcoming his lowly origins by marrying the haughty daughter of his aristocratic patron, the marquis de la Mole. On the verge of success, with a noble title and a commission as an officer, Julien throws everything away by shooting his former lover, Mme de Rênal, who has exposed him as a hypocritical intriguer. Despite the heroic efforts of Mathilde de la Mole and a repentant Mme de Rênal, Julien perishes on the scaffold.

Inspired by the real-life story of the crime and punishment of one Antoine Berthet, the son of a provincial artisan who was guillotined on February 27, 1828, Stendhal composed the novel in the months preceding the July Revolution. By transforming Antoine into Julien, Stendhal created a portrait of the youth of his age, frustrated by the stifling political atmosphere and narrowed opportunities of Restoration society, in which the only hope for social advancement lay in professing obedience to church and king. For this generation, the memory of the recent Revolutionary and Imperial past seemed like a paradise lost—a time of freedom and possibility, when a military career allowed young men to overcome the accident of a lowly birth. No figure incarnated the glamour of the past like Napoleon, who haunts the novel from start to finish, providing Julien with both a prototype of social mobility and a reminder of all that the Restoration has banished from its stultifying *salons*.

Julien's investment in Napoleonic history marks him as a man of his age. As I have described in the preceding chapters, the French were obsessed with Napoleonic history in the early nineteenth century. Hungry for details about the great man, the post-Revolutionary public devoured historical representations of the Napoleonic period in all forms. Parisians, of course, could sample the wax display, the phantasmagoria show, the panorama, the diorama, and Boulevard theatricals, all of which catered to the popular demand for imperial history. Although some of these spectacles could be seen beyond Paris, provincials such as Julien Sorel had to resort mostly to more traditional forms of historical representation to learn about Napoleon—such as books, oral history, and popular prints. Stendhal's novel provides a catalog of these historical sources, surrounding its protagonist with a proliferation of Napoleonic representations.

Julien emerges quite literally as a product of this historical fascination. Indeed, the extent to which Julien's identity is bound up with representations of Napoleon is thematized from the very start of the novel. When Julien first appears, he is perched on a rafter reading a book that proves so engrossing that his father must resort to a stick to get his attention. The blow that sends Julien forward to meet his destiny knocks his book into the river below: "Passing by, he looked sadly at the stream into which his book had fallen; it was the one he loved best of all, the *Mémorial de Sainte-Hélène*."[10] A huge bestseller in the 1820s, the *Mémorial* comprises Napoleon's memoirs in exile as dictated to the count de Las Cases, as well as an account of his mistreatment at the hands of his British captors.[11] Although the narrator of *Le rouge et le noir* does not make the parallels between Napoleon's martyrdom and Julien's mistreatment at the hands of his abusive family explicit, the reader familiar with the tone of the *Mémorial* clearly infers the extent to which Julien's fascination with the book is based on identification with its suffering hero.

When the narcissistic young man stares into the stream carrying his book away, we can only imagine that he sees Napoleon's image staring back. Indeed, the description of Julien that follows the drowning of his book seems almost a portrait of the emperor as a young man, right down to the diminutive proportions and classical countenance: "He was a small young man, eighteen or nineteen years old, frail-looking, with irregular but delicate features, and an aquiline nose" (39). Although Napoleon became rather bloated in later life—his girth expanding like the empire itself—representations of the future great man as a youth reveal that he possessed the same characteristics as Julien.[12]

    10. Stendhal, *Le rouge et le noir* (1830; reprint, Paris: Flammarion, 1964), 39. Subsequent quotations are cited in the text.

    11. First published in 1823, the *Mémorial* had already gone through two editions by 1831 and another was to follow in 1832. As I discuss in chapter 2, its reprinting in 1842 by Bourdin with images by Nicolas-Toussaint Charlet is one of the period's best examples of Romantic book illustration.

    12. For an example of Napoleon as a (thin) young man with delicate features and an aquiline nose, see the famous painting by Antoine-Jean Gros, *Bonaparte au pont d'Arcole*, as well as other sketches by Gros of the future emperor. Judith Dolkart discusses Napoleon's

Julien acquires knowledge of the imperial past through books such as the *Mémorial* and the *Bulletins de la Grande Armée,* as well as through the oral history of an old surgeon-major, but one of his main means of accessing Napoleonic history is visual. Julien is fascinated by the emperor's image and hides a portrait of Napoleon in the mattress of his bed during his stay with the legitimist Rênal family in order to dissimulate his potentially compromising admiration for the usurping monarch. Kept in a "black and shiny" (81) carton, the portrait of Napoleon becomes a kind of fetish object for Julien, substituting for the romantic attachment he does not feel for Mme de Rênal, despite his efforts to seduce her. Sent by Julien to remove the portrait when it is at risk of being discovered by a hostile servant, Mme de Rênal quite rightly sees the image as her rival for Julien's affection, although she little suspects that it depicts a great man rather than a beautiful woman. In the description of Julien's preference for historical images over actual human relations, the text begins to reveal its critique of the spectacular past.

This critique centers on the theater. The year the novel was written and published, 1830, was the year that the Romantic historical drama triumphed on Parisian stages. Hugo's *Hernani* staged its scandalous premiere in February of that year, and August saw the first of the twenty-nine plays about Napoleon that would dominate Parisian theaters for an entire season. As I show in chapter 3, Hugo's drama and the Napoleon plays attempted to capture the look of the past with a hitherto unknown degree of material specificity. Enormous sums were spent on historically accurate costumes and sumptuous sets for these productions. These plays brought the theater in line with popular entertainments such as the panorama— they turned the past into a spectacle.

Stendhal, as I show in chapter 3, was instrumental in paving the way for these productions. His Romantic theatrical manifesto, *Racine et Shakespeare,* calls for a radical realism in the staging of the past. Arguing against Classical theater's sacrifice of historical accuracy to the unities of time, place, and action, Stendhal's treatise points to the post-Revolutionary desire to see the past represented with a "perfect illusion." Such an illusion, he suggests, was necessary to convince viewers of the reality of the representation and thereby encourage them to identify with the characters and actions depicted on stage. New post-Revolutionary identities could be procured, Stendhal's treatise implies, through this process of identification with a visually realistic representation.

image and imperial portraiture in her dissertation-in-progress at the University of Pennsylvania, "Dressing the Part: Artists, Allegiance, and Costume during the French Revolution and Empire."

The author of *Racine et Shakespeare* could rightly claim to have invented not only the Romantic historical drama, but also its logical culmination—the Napoleon plays. Indeed, the second version of his *Racine et Shakespeare,* from 1825, ends with an outline for a play about Napoleon, "Le retour de l'Île d'Elbe" [The Return from the Isle of Elba], which resembles very closely the actual plays that appeared in 1830. And Stendhal did not fail to boast of his foresightedness; on March 1, 1831, six years after the publication of his treatise, he wrote to Virginie Ancelot in regard to Dumas's *Napoléon Bonaparte,* the *summum* of the Napoleon spectacles: "Have you seen the *Napoleon* at the Odéon? I predicted in 1826 that such a drama would be put on, and before ten years were out the political circumstances were right for it to be performed. And to think that my genius goes unrecognized."[13] By the time of the success of *Hernani* and the Napoleon plays in 1830–31, however, the theater no longer appeared to Stendhal as the best way to represent the past.

This moment of triumph for Stendhal's theatrical vision corresponds paradoxically to a shift in the writer's literary ambitions. As Michel Crouzet has shown, around 1830 Stendhal abandoned earlier dreams of writing successful plays and devoted himself to the less glamorous (and less lucrative) genre of the novel.[14] Stendhal's shift in genre was accompanied, moreover, by a shift in his outlook on the historical spectacle. This shift can be gauged through a change in Stendhal's attitude toward that other harbinger of the spectacular past, the novels of Walter Scott. Whereas in his Romantic theatrical manifesto, *Racine et Shakespeare,* Stendhal had looked to Scott's visual descriptions as a model for the new kind of historical theater he was advocating,[15] in February of 1830, he published an article entitled "Walter Scott et *La Princesse de Clèves,*" in which he put a question to the novel: "Should the novelist describe the dress worn by the various characters, the landscape around them and their physiognomy, or would he do better to depict the passions and sentiments

13. Stendhal, "À Madame Virginie Ancelot," in *Correspondance générale,* ed. Vittorio Del Litto et al. (Paris: Champion, 1999), 54, cited in Jean Lucas-Dubreton, *Le culte de Napoléon* (Paris: Albin Michel, 1960), 289.

14. In *Le roman stendhalien*: La chartreuse de Parme (Orléans: Paradigme, 1996), Michel Crouzet describes the author's shift from theater to the novel: "there was a slow modification of his objectives, and Stendhal only 'theorized' the ascension of the novel as the genre of modernity after 1830, after having accomplished it. In 1829 he proclaimed, 'the golden age of dramatic literature is coming to an end' " (239).

15. "What is the literary work that has had the greatest success in France in the last ten years? The novels of Walter Scott. What are the novels of Walter Scott? Romantic tragedy mixed with long descriptions." Stendhal, *Racine et Shakespeare* (1823; reprint, Paris: L'harmattan, 1993), 6.

which agitate their souls?"[16] Stendhal's query, coming at the height of the Scott craze in France as well as the very moment of the battle over *Hernani*, marks a significant departure for the author of *Racine et Shakespeare*—a rejection of the goal of re-creating the materiality of the past that put him, characteristically, at odds with his contemporaries.

In this article, Stendhal comes out *against* the visual descriptions of Scott and in favor of the sentimental poetics of Madame de Lafayette and the very unfashionable tradition of female-oriented historical fiction. "My reflections will not be welcome," he acknowledges. "An immense body of men of letters finds it in its own interest to praise Sir Walter Scott to the skies, together with his method of composition."[17] Ever mindful of historical trends and the need to oppose them, Stendhal thus turns against the Scottian system at the very moment of its apotheosis in 1830—and surely to no little extent *because* of this apotheosis. This article signals the extent to which Stendhal had become deeply suspicious of the visual representation of the past characteristic of Romanticism, and indeed of the entire spectacular historical project, by the time he wrote *Le rouge et le noir*.

Despite his desire to produce a novel that would one day become a work of Scott-like historical fiction, Stendhal saw his novel serving a very different function in the new political and cultural climate of 1830. To Stendhal, the spectacular representation of the past that he saw as the goal of the Romantic historical drama seemed no longer to serve as a radical way to re-invigorate a stagnant culture but rather had become a new kind of cultural orthodoxy. In *Le rouge et le noir*, the Romantic *drame historique* appears as the object of parody and critique. The project of re-creating the past with a "perfect illusion" is shown to be just that—an illusion, and a dangerous one at that. The shift within Stendhal's oeuvre from theater to the novel and from Romanticism to Realism involves a rejection of the historical spectacle. *Le rouge et le noir* both performs and thematizes this shift.[18]

16. Translated by Geoffrey Strickland in John O. Hayden, *Scott: The Critical Heritage* (New York: Barnes and Noble, 1970), 318–21. Stendhal's article originally appeared anonymously in *Le National*, February 19, 1830, 3–4.

17. Stendhal in Hayden, *Scott*, 318.

18. In *Sur Stendhal* (Paris: Messidor/Éditions sociales, 1982), Pierre Barbéris recounts how in 1836 Stendhal noted in the margin of a copy of *Le rouge et le noir*, "I consider the novel as the comedy [*la comédie*] of the nineteenth century." Barbéris explains that for Stendhal, comedy in the theater, long based on the ridicule of bourgeois *moeurs*, was no longer possible once the audience was composed of the bourgeoisie. The novel henceforth became the space in which such social critique could best be expressed. Barbéris also notes perceptively that "the theater is never very far from *Le rouge* and one easily detects theatrical scenarios in the scenes and dialogues of any given chapter" (94). In *The Melodramatic Imagination* (New York: Columbia University Press, 1985), Peter Brooks likewise describes the

Novel Theatrics

Many scholars have remarked that Stendhal's "Chronicle of 1830" makes no mention of the July Revolution.[19] But even though the political revolution of 1830 is notably absent from *Le rouge et le noir,* the year's revolution in theatrical representation is very much present. The novel refers to both Hugo's *Hernani* and Casimir Delavigne's *Marino Faliero,* which premièred at the Porte Saint-Martin Theater in 1829, the two most talked-about Romantic historical dramas prior to Dumas's *Napoléon.* The invocation of these popular theatrical productions does more, however, than anchor Stendhal's text in the cultural calendar of the time or provide it with the trappings of contemporaneity; it provides a vital intertextual connection between the novel and the new modes of spectacular represen-tation that dominated the popular historical imagination in 1830. As I will show, the characters in *Le rouge et le noir* structure their relation to the past according to the Romantic theatrical model, whereas the novel itself structures its own relation to the past *against* this model.

The reference to *Hernani* occurs mid-way through the text, after Julien has come to Paris and begun his rise to fortune as the secretary to the mar-quis de la Mole. In order to ingratiate himself with a conservative *académicien* among the marquis's retinue, Julien feigns dislike of Hugo's play: "he shared in his fury over the success of *Hernani*" (338). *Hernani* functions as an important intertext for *Le rouge et le noir* for a number of reasons. Peter Brooks has argued that the emphasis in Hugo's play on the power of the paternal figure foregrounds the oedipal crisis facing the post-Revolutionary generation, struggling against the "gerontocracy" of the Restoration, and thus mirrors Julien's struggle (against his father and against patriarchal Restoration society) in *Le rouge et le noir.*[20] The refer-ence to *Hernani* also serves, however, as a reflection on what it means to take the past as a model, and hence as a means of reflecting on the entire project of spectacular historical representation.

---

connection between popular theatrical forms and nineteenth-century Realist fiction, al-though he describes Stendhal as "one of the least melodramatic of authors" (91).

19. In *Reading for the Plot,* Brooks suggests an interpretation of the ending of the novel as an allegory for the absent revolution: "Is the guillotine that executes Julien, the 'peasant in revolt' as he has called himself at his trial, a displaced figure for 'les Trois Glorieuses,' a rev-olution notable for having made no use of the guillotine? Is the catastrophic ending of *Le rouge et le noir* a displaced and inverted version of the revolution that should have been?" (66).

20. Peter Brooks, "An Oedipal Crisis," in *A New History of French Literature,* ed. Denis Hollier (Cambridge: Harvard University Press, 1989), 649–56.

Set in 1519, Hugo's play, with elaborately realistic sets created by the legendary designer Eugène Cicéri, did more than just represent the past with a new material specificity; it also thematized the nature of the Romantic desire to learn from the past, to draw on history for the formation of individual and national identities in the present. Act 4 of *Hernani* takes place at the tomb of Charlemagne and shows Don Carlos, the king of Spain and aspirant to the crown of the Holy Roman Empire, seeking wisdom from the past: "Who will advise me? Charlemagne! it's you! [. . .] Speak, and do not leave your frightened son in darkness, / For your tomb is no doubt full of light!"[21] But just as Don Carlos attempts to base his present actions on the authority of a historical "father," so too does the bandit Hernani, who seeks vengeance for his own father who was put to death by the (actual) father of Don Carlos. "The king! the king!" Hernani cries; "My father/Died on the scaffold, condemned by his. / But, although much time has passed since that ancient event, / For the shade of the departed king, for his son, for his widow, / For all his kin, my hatred is still fresh!"[22] Hernani's evocation of his father's death on the scaffold not only resonates as an allusion to the authority of history in general, as is the case with Don Carlos's prayer at the tomb of Charlemagne, but also as a transposed reference to a specific history—for a post-Revolutionary audience, the "scaffold" referred to by Hernani might also invoke the recent horrors of the Revolution.

The bandit's oath of vengeance figures the post-Revolutionary generation's obsession with the legacy of the past. It symbolizes the extent to which the generation of 1830 remained locked in a struggle to work through the trauma of the Revolution and the degree to which post-Revolutionary identity was defined by this history. Through the struggles of the two historically minded sons, *Hernani* showed audiences in 1830 how the past could serve as a model for the formation of identity in the present. The play's triumph spelled a victory for the Romantic model of historical representation and paved the way for the Napoleon plays, with their promotion of a national identity based on worship of a historical hero. The reference to the "scaffold" in *Hernani* might thus also be seen as an allusion to the scaffolding of the theater, the artifice through which the past, including the recent past of the Revolution, was represented to the French populace in 1830.

21. Victor Hugo, *Hernani*, in *Théâtre complet* (1830; reprint, Paris: Gallimard, 1963), 1265–66.
22. Ibid., 1164.

Within *Le rouge et le noir, Hernani* stands for this Romantic historical project, which the Realist novel incorporates in order to critique. The other Romantic historical drama mentioned in the novel, *Marino Faliero,* serves a similar function. The reference to *Marino Faliero* comes midway through the text, when Julien, now a secretary to the wealthy and powerful marquis, receives a compliment from the Count Altamira, a political conspirator, who has sought refuge in France from a death sentence in his native Spain. "You haven't got that French flightiness, you understand the principle of *utility*" (334), the count tells Julien, who is much gratified at being distinguished as superior to the insipid nobles who figure in the salon of the Hôtel de la Mole. The narrator then comments, "It happened that, just the night before last, Julien had seen *Marino Faliero,* a tragedy by Casimir Delavigne" (334).

Delavigne's play, set in 1355, describes a conspiracy led by Israël Bertuccio, a "plebeian," against the patrician oligarchy of Venice. According to contemporary newspaper accounts, audiences present at performances of the play at the Porte Saint-Martin theater, located in a working-class section of Paris, applauded when Israël affirmed with pride his plebeian origins in his initial confrontation with the Venetian doge. Julien clearly shares their enthusiasm, as evidenced by his reflections following the performance: "Doesn't Israël Bertuccio have more character than all those noble Venetians? our rebellious plebeian said to himself" (334). Julien identifies with Israël, making common cause with the struggle to overcome a lowly station through violent means. He makes the analogy between the historical drama and his present situation and thus figures as the ideal audience for Romantic historical theater, basing his identity on a representation of the past.

Reactionary commentators at the time feared exactly this kind of response to Delavigne's drama, which became a lightning rod for right-wing criticism of the Romantic historical project. Conservative critics imagined that audiences would attempt to enact the kinds of violent actions they saw represented on stage. As the critic in the *Gazette de France* put it in his account of the première of Delavigne's play, "Whom should we blame if the theaters have been put at the disposal of the revolutionary faction, if every day they threaten the social order with a total subversion? Already they have been made into a school of massacres, and yesterday all sorts of aristocrats were turned over to the brutal frenzy of a pit [*parterre*] full of workers." For the conservative critic, the theatrical representation of a conspiratorial subversion from the past acts on viewers in the present, instructing them in the ways of political protest. According to the critic from the *Gazette de France,* Delavigne's drama is "less a dramatic work than a political vehicle meant to direct the popular masses in the direction of revolution."[23]

Le rouge et le noir depicts the play's effects in an exactly similar manner: Julien, "our rebellious plebeian," does indeed formulate seditious thoughts following the play by drawing a parallel between Venetian history and what he hopes will be his own situation: "A conspiracy wiped out all the titles given by social whim," states the narrator of *Le rouge et le noir* in a commentary that typically reflects the sentiments of the protagonist without being directly attributed to him; "Then, a man immediately received the rank conferred by his attitude in the face of death" (334). In its representation of the effect of *Marino Faliero* on Julien Sorel, the novel illustrates how the Romantic vision of history was supposed to function for the nineteenth-century observer. The degree to which the novel also parodies Romantic historical discourse, as well as the fantasmatic role assigned to the new Romantic historical theater of the period by nervous partisans of the established order, however, becomes increasingly apparent as the novel continues.

Unlike the "frenzied" workers making up the *parterre* of the Porte Saint-Martin, Julien knows how to keep his enthusiasm to himself. In the passage concerning *Hernani,* which comes a few pages after the mention of *Marino Faliero,* Julien appropriates the hysterical rhetoric of the *Gazette's* critic to win the confidence of the reactionary academician:

> They were getting up from the table. I must not let my academician get away, Julien told himself. He approached him as they were entering the garden, adopted a sweet and submissive attitude, and shared in his fury over the success of *Hernani.*
> —If only we were still in the age of *lettres de cachet! . . .* he said.
> —Then he would never have dared, cried the academician with a gesture worthy of Talma. (338)

Julien's feigned scorn for *Hernani* reveals his artifice. Threatening Hugo with a *lettre de cachet,* imprisonment without trial, he acts the part of an ultraroyalist who looks backward to the good old days of absolutism. What makes Julien so convincing in his hypocrisy is the very theatricality of his performance; not only does he know how to act his part, but by performing his hatred of *Hernani* he mimics the dramatic demeanor of the academician who renders his own reactionary opinion with a gesture worthy of the legendary tragic actor Talma. Julien succeeds in the Hôtel de la

<hr/>

23. "Théâtre de la Porte Saint-Martin," review of *Marino Faliero,* by Casimir Delavigne, *Gazette de France,* June 2, 1829, 1.

Mole—that is, in the world of Restoration France—precisely because he realizes that all the world's a stage.

Scholars have long singled out hypocrisy as the key element in Julien's character. Forever feigning feelings and acting emotions, Julien masters the art of dissimulation necessary to succeed in Restoration France, learning to play the part of a legitimist and espousing the most vile hatred of Napoleon or adopting, on occasion, the "sad role of rebellious plebeian" (341). As Peter Brooks points out, the Greek word *hypokrites* means "a player of roles," and a long French tradition associates this figure with the theater itself. Indeed, Julien refers to that famous theatrical hypocrite, Molière's Tartuffe, as one of his role models.[24] Ironically, then, for a character who pretends to abhor the theater, Julien appears repeatedly in the novel as an actor playing a part.

Although Julien at times acts like a Revolutionary rabble-rouser, the role he really longs to play is Napoleon. Throughout the text, but especially during his initial exploits in Verrières, Julien explicitly patterns his behavior on that of his hero, turning to the Napoleonic model for guidance in everything from business decisions to courtship. When Julien almost accepts the offer made by his friend Fouqué to join him in the timber trade, thus renouncing his ambitions for greater glory, he sternly rebukes himself by referencing his ultimate authority: "Alas! perhaps I have lacked character, I would have made a bad Napoleonic soldier" (105). Instead of settling for a secure but mediocre existence, he plots his conquest of Mme de Rênal—"he devised for himself a very detailed battle plan" (106)—and comically adapts his course of action from Napoleon's accounts of famous battles.

Like an actor in one of the many Napoleon plays that were entertaining audiences in 1830, when the novel was published, Julien reenacts the life of the great man. His own life becomes a representation of Napoleon's, although reproduced on a smaller scale—shrunk down to fit his provincial stage, just as critics of the Napoleon plays complained that the life of the great had been cut down to fit inside a theater. His love affair, for example, mimics the great man's military exploits in miniature. Each small caress or stolen glance in his courtship becomes for Julien a "victory" in the "combat" against Mme de Rênal's virtue. And he rewards himself for each skirmish with the pleasure of studying his hero: "he had done *his duty, and a heroic duty*," the narrator comments in language italicized to indicate its origin in historical accounts of the Empire; "Filled with happiness at this thought, he locked himself in his room, and devoted himself

24. See Brooks, *Reading for the Plot*, 71.

with renewed pleasure to reading about the exploits of his hero" (79). Playing the part of Napoleon motivates Julien to vanquish not only Mme de Rênal, but her husband as well: "By thinking of Napoleon's victories, he had seen something new in his own. Yes, I won a battle, he said to himself, but I have to press my advantage. I have to crush the arrogance of that proud gentleman while he is retreating. That's pure Napoleon" (91). The Napoleonic model encourages Julien to act in an artificial manner, to pursue a glorious destiny in spite of his native timidity.

By living his life as if acting in a Napoleon play, Julien loses sight of his own ideas and emotions. Lacking true passion for Mme de Rênal at the beginning of the novel, he perceives his seduction as a duty, as a necessary obligation in his struggle for self-advancement. "Have I lived up to everything I owe to myself," he asks during an interlude between skirmishes with his mistress. "Have I played my role well?" (112). The narrator repeats the metaphor of role-playing throughout his description of Julien's contrived courtship: "That day, he found more happiness in the presence of his friend because he wasn't thinking constantly of playing a role" (115). And just a few lines later, the narrator describes Mme de Rênal's blissful ignorance of Julien's staged emotions: "If she had perceived his efforts to play a role, that sad discovery would have made her forever miserable" (115). In *Le rouge et le noir,* Julien loses himself while acting a part from the past.

The novel thus portrays the very model of theatrical identification that Stendhal had called for in *Racine et Shakespeare* and enacts the Napoleon plays he had predicted would enflame audiences at some future moment. As I have shown, the Napoleon plays, like other forms of historical spectacle, were supposed to offer up an image of history as the ground on which new identities might be formed in the post-Revolutionary era. Audiences divided by class and politics in 1830 were meant to unite through identification with the historical figures depicted in these productions, conjured in as visually realistic a manner as possible. Julien's role-playing reveals the dangerous underside of this process. What emerges from Julien's Napoleonic representation is not only an indictment of his inauthenticity, but a critique of the spectacular past.

Playing at History

Julien is not the only character in the novel to transform his life into a historical spectacle. Immediately following the references to *Hernani* and *Marino Faliero,* the text produces another historical drama in which Mathilde de la Mole stars as a figure from her ancestral annals. The intertextual proximity to real examples of historical theater encourages the reader to see Mathilde's production as yet another parody of the Romantic historical project, revelatory of the absurdity—and danger—of acting a part from the past. Like Julien, Mathilde too eagerly models herself on a vision of history and in the process makes a mess of her life in the present.

Immediately after their interchange over *Hernani*, Julien asks the academician why Mathilde de la Mole, the daughter of the marquis, has dressed in mourning and acted even more imperiously at the daily meal than usual: "What! you're a member of the household, said the academician, stopping short, and you don't know about her folly?" (338). Taunting Julien with his ignorance, the pompous academic prolongs the mystery by alluding to the date: "Today is the 30th of April!" (338). Julien fails to make the connection: "What link could there be between ruling a household, wearing a black dress, and the 30th of April? he wondered" (339). The older man, thrilled to discover "a virgin ear," provides Julien with a history lesson: on April 30, 1574, Boniface de la Mole, ancestor to the family of Julien's patron, "the best-looking young man of his age" (339), and the lover of Queen Marguerite de Navarre, had his head cut off on the place de Grève for having attempted to rescue his friends held in prison by Marie de Médicis. Fascinated by this tragic story, and especially by the legend that Marguerite de Navarre had carried her lover's head from the scene of execution and buried it in a chapel on the hill of Montmartre, Mathilde de la Mole commemorates the event on its anniversary. She dons mourning, calls her family members by names evoking the historical characters, and chastises them for not participating in her elaborately ritualized form of remembrance. Dressed in a costume, following a script, Mathilde quite literally performs the past.

Mathilde can conceive of passion solely in historical terms: "She only gave the name of love to that heroic sentiment encountered in France during the age of Henri III and Bassompierre" (348). Tinged by nostalgia for the bygone era of the Wars of Religion, the period that provides the setting for *Hernani* as well as for many of the other Romantic historical dramas, Mathilde's romantic scenarios unfold as epigones, as reproductions never quite as vivid as the original.[25] "What a pity for me that there is not a true court like that of Catherine de Médicis or Louis XIII!" she laments. "I feel myself to be at the level of all that is most great and daring" (348). Unable to transport herself back in time, Mathilde settles for transforming her

25. Plays taking place in the sixteenth century were common in the Romantic repertoire. Dumas's *Henri III et sa cour* opened at the Comédie-Française in 1829, and Lucien Arnault's *Catherine de Médicis aux États de Blois* ran at the Odéon later the same year.

surroundings into an elaborate theatrical fantasy—with unfortunate consequences both for herself and for her unwitting co-stars.

Chapter XIX, entitled "The Comic Opera," begins with Mathilde's musings on the certainty of an upcoming revolution, and particularly on the part she will assign herself in its production: "Preoccupied with the future and with the unique *role* she hoped to play, Mathilde soon came to regret the dry and metaphysical discussions she often had with Julien" (395, emphasis added). The interest she takes in Julien's arid conversation derives from the comparisons he makes between the necessity of a future revolution and the lessons of the past, which Mathilde refers to admiringly as "his ideas about the resemblance of the events that are about to swoop down upon us and the Revolution of 1688 in England" (395).[26] Bored with playing the timid victim like her fellow nobles who live in perpetual fear of the future, Mathilde resolves to embrace the coming revolution as long as she and Julien can star in it.

Here, once again, she envisions her future role based on the script of the past: "If there is a revolution, why wouldn't Julien Sorel play the role of Roland, and I that of Mme Roland?" (396) she asks herself. Once her mind's eye dresses Julien in period costume, he ceases to be her father's secretary, an "inferior being," (394) but takes on the heroic prestige of the great men he resembles. His gauche manners become dramatic gestures worthy of the great actors of the Comédie-Française: "She looked at Julien, and found a charming grace in his slightest actions" (396). Mathilde's erotic fascination with Julien derives from her ability to dramatize, to transform her world into the kind of historical spectacle she applauds on stage. For Mathilde, life and theater commingle, and her box at the Italiens provides the ideal space for indulging her passion: "During the entire first act of the opera, Mathilde dreamed of the man she loved with all the rapture of the most raw passion" (397). Just as Mathilde makes real life into a theatrical production, the theater provides her with the dream space in which emotional attachments can be fantasized into existence.

Julien, meanwhile, sees Mathilde as a supporting actress in his Napoleon play. If Madame de Rênal is his Joséphine, the older woman who oversees his rise to fame, then Mathilde is Marie-Louise, the daughter of a powerful man, whose conquest provides prestige and position.[27] The

26. Victor Hugo's reading drama *Cromwell* (1827) had recently made explicit not only the link between the two revolutions but also between this period in English history and the aesthetics of the new Romantic drama.

27. Napoleon's divorce and remarriage figured in many of the staged biographies of his life and even became the subject of a light opera—Gabriel [Jules-Joseph-Gabriel de Lurieu]

courtship of Julien and Mathilde, moreover, reads like a parody of the melodramatic intrigues that constituted the plot of so many of the era's historical productions, including the Napoleon plays. When Mathilde slips Julien a letter instructing him to climb up a ladder to her bedroom window at one o'clock in the morning, he suspects treachery (the chapter in which the action unfolds is titled "Is It a Plot?") because the whole scenario seems so contrived, so artificial. Because her father and brother are absent almost continuously, leaving them ample time to talk, why the need for a secret nighttime rendezvous? The answer contains one of the keys to the novel's critique: the Romantic model of historical identification has been carried so far that neither of the characters is capable of experiencing emotion in the absence of the spectacle.

Eventually Julien gets into the spirit of the liaison by participating in its theatrical character. In a letter that he sends to his friend Fouqué, to be opened "in case of an accident" (374), Julien exaggerates the dangers he faces, imagining cloaks and daggers everywhere. He succeeds in scaring himself: "Moved by his own tale like a *dramatic author,* Julien became truly scared when he entered the dining room" (375, emphasis added). Through the force of his own dramatic style, he nearly convinces himself of the reality of his passion: "He looked at Mlle de la Mole in order to read her family's plans in her eyes; she was pale, and resembled a figure out of the Middle Ages. Never had he found her so grand, she was truly beautiful and imposing. He almost fell in love with her" (375). The problem with Julien's amorous desire, like Mathilde's, is that it requires historical mediation for arousal.

After their passion takes carnal form, both Julien and Mathilde give way to feelings of regret and revulsion. Once their love ceases to exist as pure fantasy, as historical role playing, it seems to them ugly and base. Julien resolves to make himself scarce (planning a much delayed trip to the Languedoc), and Mathilde expresses disgust with both him and herself: "I'm horrified at having given myself to the first person who came along" (387), she tells Julien in a quip aimed at quelling his pretensions to greatness. This disparaging remark has the unintended effect of reviving their flagging romance. Outraged by Mathilde's expression of scorn, Julien draws a sword as if to kill her, like the prideful Israël Bertuccio in *Marino Faliero,* but immediately perceives the ridiculousness of his gesture: "The idea of the marquis de La Mole, his benefactor, presented itself starkly to Julien. I would kill his daughter! he said to himself, how horrible! He

---

and Ferdinand Delaboullaye's *Joséphine ou le retour de Wagram,* with music by Adolphe Adam, which opened on December 2, 1830 at the Opéra-Comique.

made as if to toss away the sword." Momentarily able to perceive the absurd theatricality of his gesture, however, Julien recoils in horror: "Surely,
he thought, she will burst out laughing at the sight of this melodramatic
gesture" (387).

Pretending to examine the sword for a spot of rust in order to dissemble
his motive for having drawn it, he feigns nonchalance. Not knowing
Mathilde as well as he thinks he does, however, Julien fails to see that it is
precisely such a coup de theatre—and the more melodramatic the better—
that Mathilde needs to regain the passion she has lost through its realization. As if watching from the erotic space of her *loge* at the Italiens, she is
transfixed by Julien's self-conscious performance with the sword: "This
whole movement, drawn out at the end, lasted for a good minute; Mlle de
La Mole watched him with astonishment. So I was on the verge of being
killed by my lover! she said to herself [. . .] That idea transported her to
the finest moments of the period of Charles IX and of Henri III" (387).
Julien's gesture with the sword proves highly erotic to both parties; Julien
becomes attractive once again to Mathilde, as does she to him, because his
action transforms her into the audience of a historical drama: "She stood
motionless before Julien who had just replaced the sword. She looked at
him with eyes no longer full of hate. It must be said that she was truly se-
ductive at that moment" (388). For Julien and Mathilde, the sword is neither just a sword, nor a phallic substitute, but rather a prop allowing the
lovers to reinstate the distance or mediation (both theatrical and historical) necessary for their erotic fulfillment.[28]

Although both Julien and Mathilde conduct their romantic escapades as
if acting in a *drame romantique,* they do not always follow the same
script. Indeed, the comedy of their coupling derives from the fact that they
often seem to be rehearsing different plays altogether. Whereas Mathilde
imagines herself re-creating the sixteenth century (and Hugo's *Hernani* or
Dumas's *Henri III et sa cour* would have provided her with a great part),
Julien joins the ranks of the famous actors Lemaître, Déjazet, and Gobert
by playing Napoleon or, given his occasional sympathy for the Terror,
seems to be acting a role in the production of *Robespierre,* which also
graced the stage of the Ambigu-Comique in 1830. Considering the fluency
with which actors at the time passed between different productions and
different historical periods—Gobert, acclaimed as the best of the Napoleon impersonators in 1830, had scored a triumph the year before as Israël

28. Such a separation between the subject and his or her object of desire is described by
René Girard in *Mensonge romantique et vérité romanesque* (Paris: Grasset, 1961). Girard
makes multiple references to *Le rouge et le noir.*

Bertuccio in Delavigne's *Marino Faliero*—it comes as no surprise that Mathilde and Julien occasionally find themselves on the same page, as in the sword scene. But, as Mathilde realizes, the dissonance in their repertoires accounts for the continual misunderstandings that prevent them from forging a genuine bond: "The Wars of the League were France's heroic period, she told him one day, her eyes shining with spirit and enthusiasm. A man would fight to get something he desired, or for the good of his party, and not just to win a dull cross like in the time of your emperor. You must admit that there was less selfishness and pettiness. I like that century" (342). For Mathilde, the distance that separates her from Julien is less a barrier of class or position than a difference in historical periods. Despite Julien's efforts to play the role of a legitimist, she sees him as just another banal Napoleon impersonator.

Julien's perpetual fear of exposing his admiration for Napoleon complicates matters. Unlike Mathilde, he cannot freely act the part he would like to play, although the extent to which Julien's love of Napoleon is a secret to nobody—and certainly not to Mathilde—suggests that he is not a very good actor. Julien maintains a pretense of legitimism, but without ever being able to enter into Mathilde's fantasies of the Wars of the League or the court of Marie de Médicis. For Julien, Mathilde's bond with history, seen as more authentic than his own because its roots lie in genealogy, erects a barrier between them: "That is the immense advantage that they have over us, Julien said to himself when he was alone in the garden. The history of their ancestors raises them above vulgar concerns" (342). Although Mathilde manages eventually to raise Julien to her level, to incorporate him into her historical drama, their relationship remains a performance throughout the novel. The spectacle thus blocks genuine intimacy, erecting a barrier between the lovers through its mediation of their passion.

The Spectacle's Dangers

Through the role-playing of Julien and Mathilde, the novel critiques the effects of the spectacularization of history on nineteenth-century French culture. In addition to preventing the development of a genuine romantic relationship between them, the Romantic theatricality also has disastrous implications for the formation of their individual subjectivities. What becomes of the self, the novel asks, if it is formed by imitating historical characters and if these historical characters are known primarily through the medium of images? As in Balzac's *Adieu*, published the same year as *Le rouge et le noir*, the dramatic re-creation of the past paralyzes its onlookers, freezing them into a mortal passivity. Stéphanie de Vandières takes one look at the elaborate reconstruction of the Beresina river her lover Philippe has staged in order to help her recover her reason—and drops dead. Balzac's text represents the historical spectacle as that which frustrates action and prevents forward movement, putting a premature end not only to the characters but also to the text itself.

Le rouge et le noir shows a different aspect of the spectacle's danger. Instead of paralyzing onlookers and inhibiting movement, the historical dramas enacted in Stendhal's novel motivate their spectators to make absurd and meaningless gestures. Marx says something similar about the reasons for the failure of the Revolution of 1848: by remaining fixated on the "tragedy" of past revolutions, the proletariat remained blind to the exigencies of their own time, turning their actions into "farce."[29] I have already shown how Julien's farcical attempt to seek vengeance for a perceived slight with the aid of a sword resembles a "melodramatic gesture" (387) and becomes an immediate source of embarrassment to him (albeit a perverse turn-on for Mathilde). Julien's attack on Mme de Rênal at the end of the novel likewise represents the kind of absurd melodramatic action motivated by having seen one too many plays.

At the time of this unprecedented act of physical violence, Julien has just succeeded in fulfilling his wildest ambitions. With Mathilde in love with Julien and pregnant by him, her father eventually consents to a marriage that will elevate Julien to a noble position. The marquis de la Mole solves the problem of Julien's lowly origins by obtaining for him a new name and title—le chevalier Julien Sorel de la Vernaye—as well as a respectable commission in the army. Julien rejoices: "my novel is finished" (491), he declares. But the theatrical impinges on the literary; a coup de theatre disrupts the happy ending of Julien's story.

Mme de Rênal, under the influence of a strict priest, writes to the marquis to denounce Julien as a hypocritical intriguer. Julien immediately goes to Verrières, buys some pistols, and fires two shots at his former lover in the town's church, wounding but not killing her. Bound to reverse in a single blow all the advantages he has painfully acquired, Julien's attempt at murder has seemed to many scholars *invraisemblable,* out of character, "disturbingly unmotivated," to borrow D. A. Miller's formulation, by what has gone before.[30] Indeed, the novel thematizes its own *invraisem-*

---

29. See the opening of Karl Marx's *The Eighteenth Brumaire of Louis-Bonaparte* (1852; reprint, New York: International Publishers, 1963) and my discussion of it in relation to Balzac's *Adieu* in chapter 5.

30. D. A. Miller, *Narrative and Its Discontents: Problems of Closure in the Traditional Novel* (Princeton: Princeton University Press, 1981), 199–200. Also see Sandy Petrey's dis-

blance: "This Julien is an odd creature; his action is inexplicable," (508) reflects the Abbé de Frilair, one of the powerful provincial notables. In fact, the narrator does not give a full account of what goes on in Julien's head as he pulls the trigger—a contrast to the usual practice of thoroughly revealing Julien's motives through a combination of omniscient commentary and indirect discourse. By contrast, here the text presents only action, devoid of explanation: "he fired his pistol at her and missed; he fired a second time and she fell" (497).

This scene, which brings the novel to a climax, leading to the denouement of Julien's trial and execution, must figure in any interpretation of the novel, although it has posed problems for generations of readers. For Miller, the shooting represents the "text's own foul play," the moment in which the novel calls into question the very possibility of explaining human action and hence of interpretation itself.[31] "The interpretation of Julien's crime, however, necessarily stands in the position of keystone to any interpretation of the novel," Miller explains, because it represents Julien's most "spectacular and consequential act of self-definition."[32] Miller sees in the multitude of possible explanations for the shooting a sign of the novel's resistance to closure, both its renunciation of plot and its prolongation of it. Peter Brooks begins his own narratological interpretation of the enigmatic crime scene by first proposing a "rational," which is to say psychologically motivated, explanation. The shooting, Brooks proposes, represents Julien's attempt to commit suicide out of guilt for his transgressions: "This portrait of Julien has a certain truth, not only because it offers an interpretation that an unsympathetic reader might well adopt but also because it corresponds to Julien's occasional portrayals of himself as the monster. If we were looking for psychological explanations, could we not say that Julien, in attempting to kill Mme de Rênal, is seeking to kill the monster, to eradicate the person who has preserved and transmitted the monster image of himself?"[33] Brooks then goes on to offer what he refers to as a "perverse" reading of the ending, in which an attempt to make sense of Julien's psychology gives way to an interest in how the text comments on its own narrative processes. For Brooks, the shoot-

---

cussion of Julien's apparently unmotivated gesture in *Realism and Revolution: Balzac, Stendhal, Zola, and the Performances of History* (Ithaca: Cornell University Press, 1988), 123.

31. Miller, *Narrative and Its Discontents*, 217.

32. Ibid. Miller rejects Gérard Genette's reading of the crime as an "ellipsis of intention" a signifier without a signified, deliberately unmotivated, and hence a "great action" worthy of a Sartrean existentialist hero. In Miller's reading, meaning is not so much absent as deferred. See Gérard Genette, "Vraisemblance et motivation," *Figures II* (Paris: Seuil, 1969), 77.

33. Brooks, *Reading for the Plot*, 81.

ing of Mme de Rênal represents not the character punishing himself for having transgressed social conventions but rather Stendhal punishing Julien for having attempted to direct his own destiny—or to use Brooks's terminology, for having had a plot. "To frame Julien's novel within his own novel—to continue beyond the end of Julien's novel and take it to pieces—is Stendhal's way of having a plot and punishing it, of writing a novel and then chopping its head off."[34] According to Brooks, Stendhal encloses his "conventional" novel, Julien's novel, in which the protagonist has a happy ending, within a larger structure that censures this kind of text and the desires that drive it.

The ending of the novel, however, can be read not only as a self-conscious reflection on its own status as narrative, but also as a commentary on its relation to contemporary forms of historical representation, particularly the Romantic historical drama. If Julien is seen less as the "author of his own text," as Brooks has it, and more as an actor playing a role—that is, if the ending is seen not as a novel within (or around) a novel but as a spectacle within a novel—then the enigma of the shooting of Mme de Rênal begins to resolve itself. While avoiding the attribution of easy psychological explanations, such a theatrical reading also avoids viewing the novel as merely preoccupied with its own narrative processes by showing how it engages with contemporary discourses besides the novelistic.

The scene of the shooting begins with Julien's journey to Verrières. Upon arriving in the village, Julien's first move is to acquire the props necessary for his production—guns, which he attempts to buy from a local arms dealer—but he has difficulty making his desires known: "Julien had a hard time making him understand that he wanted a pair of pistols" (496). Endowed with a tremendous capacity for language—able to memorize and recite at will the entire New Testament in Latin—Julien finds himself struck with a sudden aphasia, unable to express even the simplest request. The melodrama, of course, was originally a wordless form of theater, in which actors, playing types, drew from a stock of gestures to convey the meaning of their actions. The remainder of the scene proceeds as an authentic melodrama—as a pantomime, complete with set decoration and sound effects.

The ringing of the church bells gives the cue to start: "The *three chimes* [*trois coups*] rang out; this is a well known signal in the villages of France that, after the various morning bells, announces that mass is about to begin" (496). Despite the narrator's interjection of a religious explanation for the presence of the bells, the *"trois coups,"* italicized as if to justify an

34. Ibid., 85.

alternate meaning, also resonate as the traditional raps announcing the start of a (profane) theatrical production. To complete the theatrical image, the narrator has even decked the set in a red velvet curtain: "All the upper windows of the building were draped in crimson curtains" (496). Julien, playing the melodramatic villain and costumed appropriately with pistols in hand, enters stage left. He comes up behind Mme de Rênal, sees her bow her head in prayer, and shoots. The curtain falls on the chapter here. The next chapter opens with a farcical chase, as the frightened parishioners prevent Julien's getaway: "A woman who tried to flee more quickly than the others pushed him rudely and he fell" (497). His feet caught in a chair, Julien tries to reach his pistols, but eventually submits to a "policeman in full uniform" (497), a costumed Keystone cop, who escorts him to prison. No one utters a word.

The pistol shot in the church at Verrières cannot help but call to mind the famous narratorial intervention from several chapters earlier concerning the presence of politics in a novel: "Politics in the middle of affairs of the imagination are like a pistol shot in the middle of a concert" (419). Stendhal later employed a nearly identical formula in *La chartreuse de Parme*.[35] But while opening the scene to a political reading, this phrase also reinforces the spectacular character of the shooting. Julien's attack on Mme de Rênal in the church is above all a representation—a repetition or performance rather than a spontaneous action. Scholars have had difficulty reconciling Julien's motivations with the rationality demanded of a Realist character because they have failed to see the extent to which Julien acts not out of an original or individual impetus but in imitation of historical and theatrical models. This, however, is precisely what makes him exemplary of the Realist protagonist. Julien has been so conditioned by the spectacular culture of his era, and is so accustomed to model his actions on other representations, that he stages his movements rather than acting for his own benefit or in his own interest.

Le rouge et le noir reveals the dangers of living life as a Romantic historical drama. It shows the fatal error of attempting to ground identity on a representation of the past. No matter how realistic the reconstruction, how elaborate the scenery, or how convincing the portrayal, the result is an emptying of the spectating self. Julien's robotic pantomime in the church figures the absurdist horror of a subjectivity mediated by Boulevard theater. And in this Julien is absolutely emblematic of his age, be-

---

35. "Politics in a literary work is like a pistol shot in the middle of a concert, something boorish but which cannot be ignored." *La chartreuse de Parme* (1839; reprint, Paris: Flammarion, 1964), 419.

cause, as the novel seems to know all too well, the popularity of the Romantic drama with its vision of the past was reaching a frenzied height in 1830. Perhaps, then, the shooting scene allegorizes not the missing July Revolution but the cultural event that accompanied it—the culmination of history's transformation into spectacle.

Beyond the Spectacle

The pistol shots, while bringing Julien's spectacular performance to a climax, paradoxically allow him to escape from the spectacle's grip. The sound of the shots shatters Julien's delusions. For the remainder of the novel, he shuns the spectacle, preferring isolation over performance, authenticity over hypocrisy. In fact, Julien wrestles with an impulse to authenticity throughout the novel. Like many of Stendhal's heroes, Julien finds himself torn between public and private selves. He vaunts his ability to perform roles, whether playing Tartuffe in legitimist society or reciting the New Testament by heart before rapt onlookers, but all the while seeks refuge from the public's gaze.

Julien's schizophrenic attitude toward isolation, his desire to be at once the center of attention and "far from the eyes of men" (74), is represented by an ambivalence toward actual theatrical performances. On his first day in Paris, he finds himself both attracted and repelled by the spectacle: "In the evening, Julien hesitated a long time before entering the theater [*avant d'entrer au spectacle*], as he had strange ideas about this place of perdition" (268). Julien's "strange ideas" about the spectacle, his "hesitation" in the French sense of wavering, of being unable to decide, summarizes the dichotomy of his attitude toward the public gaze throughout the novel, as well as the novel's own ambiguous relationship to the culture of spectacle that it both incorporates and critiques. Julien's "de-liberation" on the threshold of the theater, which comes at the geographical center of the novel, midway both in terms of plot and page number, might be seen as the novel's vanishing point—the moment at which the various lines of perspective come together and at which the novel exposes the limits of its system of representation. Unsure whether to enter and thereby submit to the hypocrisy of role playing or remain outside in the antisocial space of isolation, Julien's hesitation makes the reader wonder to what extent the protagonist and the novel that encompasses him will be implicated in the spectacle's logic. Julien's indecision foreshadows the dilemma of the novel's ending. As the theatricality of the shooting scene reflects, the spectacle does indeed prove to be a "place of perdition" for Julien, leading to

256 The Spectacular Past

his beheading, but it also proves a means toward a certain liberation from the spectacle—if not ultimately for Julien, then perhaps for the text.

The final chapters of the novel, those that follow the shooting, recount Julien's efforts to overcome the spectacle's effects, to leave the theater he has entered despite his better judgment. In prison, Julien finds the isolation he has craved since the beginning of the novel, the antidote to the spectacular regime of his culture, and the hope for a new grounding for his fragile sense of identity.[36] For the first time in his life, Julien finds a sense of peace while waiting for his trial: "The following day, there was an interrogation, after which they left him alone for several days. His soul was calm" (503). Part of Julien's tranquility derives from the materiality of his surroundings; the prison pleases him because of its antiquity: "He judged the architecture to be from the beginning of the fourteenth century; he admired its grace and its whimsy. Through a small opening between two walls at the back of a deep courtyard, he had a sliver of a superb view" (503). This detail of the prison architecture, the small "view" afforded by a gap in the walls and Julien's admiration for it despite the gloom of his prospects, deserves to be remarked upon, because it provides a hint of an alternative to the theatrical mode of historical representation in the novel.

In the prison, Julien finds himself surrounded by the reality of history rather than its representation. The stones of the prison possess the solidity of actual relics from the past rather than the flimsiness of reproductions created to give a sense of local color. And most important, perhaps, the prison does not separate itself from the world of the present. Whereas the theater (or the panorama) depended for its illusion of historical reality on the isolation of the viewing subject from all points of reference with the outside world, the prison offers a "sliver of a superb view" through a courtyard, allowing Julien to retain his sense of perspective between interior and exterior, past and present. In the prison, Julien views the present quite literally through the frame of the past, but without illusion (or delusion).

The authenticity of the prison's architecture inspires a corresponding need within Julien for simple and genuine human interaction—something to which he has seemed oblivious up to this point. Simplicity, however, has never formed part of Mathilde's repertoire. One morning Julien is awakened in his prison cell by the arrival of a visitor. At first he fears his

---

36. Victor Brombert likewise notes that Julien attains freedom and lucidity while locked in prison. Interestingly, Brombert shows how the isolation of prison is often associated for Stendhal with a "panoramic" vision derived from topographic elevation. See Brombert, "Stendhal et 'les douceurs de la prison,'" in *La Prison romantique* (Paris: José Corti, 1975), 67–92.

detested father has come and imagines the theatrical scenario such a visit will provoke—"Ah! good God, he thought, this must be my father. What a disagreeable scene!" (509). Instead of the old man, however, Julien sees an even more spectacular figure: "Just then, a woman dressed in peasant garb threw herself into his arms. He barely recognized her. It was Mlle de la Mole" (509). Mathilde has costumed herself for a full-scale production worthy of the Boulevard and demands that Julien play his role in return.[37] Of course, the play is a Romantic historical drama in which the past will be re-created with a "perfect illusion": "She examined her lover and found him to be beyond what she had imagined. It seemed to her that it was Boniface de la Mole come back to life, but even more heroic" (511). Just like the actors in Romantic historical dramas, Julien appears to Mathilde as a copy that is better—that is, more artful—than the original.

Mathilde sets about stage-managing the entire town, transforming the local notables into supporting actors to be directed according to her will, and turning the townspeople into her admiring fans. For the first time, however, Julien finds himself unwilling or unable to act the part demanded of him. With his newfound peace of mind, he sees through Mathilde's brilliant performance or, rather, sees it for what it is—a role played in front of a public: "Julien thought himself unworthy of so much devotion. To tell the truth he was tired of heroism. He would have been more susceptible to a tenderness that was simple, naïve or even timid, whereas on the contrary, Mathilde's haughty spirit always needed an audience and *other people*" (516, italics in original). This is the closest the novel comes to making the terms of its critique of the historical spectacle explicit. The narrator exposes Mathilde, the epitome of her culture's tendency to perform the past, as incapable of authenticity. Her concerns and emotions prove mere histrionics because she must have an audience to experience them: "In the middle of all her anguish, all her fears for the life of her lover, whom she did not want to outlive, she had a secret need to impress the public with the excess of her love and the sublimity of her undertakings" (517). Julien experiences Mathilde's love as worthless because it is always mediated by the spectacle. She is an empty vessel, a mere performer, devoid of genuine identity.

Throughout the ordeal of his trial, Julien attempts to resist the tendency toward spectacularization forced on him not only by Mathilde but also by

37. Note that the false name Mathilde has chosen for herself in order to gain access to Julien's cell is Mme Michelet. Although in 1830, Jules Michelet was known primarily only for his *Précis de l'histoire moderne* (1827), it is tempting to hear in Mathilde's pseudonym a reference to the rise of Romantic historiography.

society at large. Julien refuses to speak on his own behalf at first in an effort to avoid becoming the object of public scrutiny: "My lawyer will
speak, and that is enough, he said to Mathilde. As it is, I will be exposed
as a spectacle [exposé en spectacle] for too long to my enemies" (526).
Julien's unwillingness to be "exposed as a spectacle" sets him in diametric
opposition to Mathilde, for whom actions have no meaning if they are not
performed in public. For Mathilde, the key to Julien's salvation lies in
pleasing the audience; they must both become actors or he will lose his
head: "They want to see you humiliated, it is only too true," she tells him.
"My presence in Besançon and the spectacle of my pain have aroused the
sympathy of the women; your pretty face will do the rest" (527). Deep
down, of course, she craves the opportunity to perform her own emotions
and sees Julien's trial as the perfect stage.

Julien, on the other hand, seems rather surprised at the degree to which
the courtroom resembles a theater, with crowds bursting through the
doors as if at a particularly exciting premiere:

> But soon all his attention was absorbed by the dozen or so pretty women
> who, situated opposite the box of the accused, filled the three boxes above
> the judges and the jury. Turning toward the audience [le public], he saw that
> the circular platform that presides above the amphitheatre was filled with
> women: most were young and seemed to him quite pretty; their eyes were
> shining and full of concern. In the rest of the room, the crowd was enor-
> mous; they were bursting down the doors, and the guards couldn't keep
> them quiet. (527)

Julien looks out at the crowd like a nervous actor on opening night.
Through his eyes, the reader sees the swarm of young and pretty women
making up this *public,* and is aware of what they have come to see.

Mathilde's initial assumption that Julien's good looks and charming
manner will seduce the female spectators proves accurate. She fails to fore-
see, however, that the jury members, all of them male, have not come to
admire Julien but rather to play their own role in the unfolding tragedy.
Valenod, the chief jurist, a parvenu like Julien who has likewise risen from
obscure origins to the ranks of the nobility, seeks Julien's punishment in
order to cover his own tracks. By censuring in Julien what he himself has
accomplished, he legitimates his own path to success. By denying the very
possibility of social advancement, he pretends that his own position was
acquired naturally, as if through birth. Such a stance is the very essence of
hypocrisy and Valenod appears ready for this role: "The little door to the
jury room opened. The baron de Valenod advanced with a serious and
theatrical step, followed by the jury" (531, emphasis added). Like

Mathilde and the townspeople who have transformed themselves into spectators, Valenod seems willing to play his part in an elaborately choreographed representation. And his theatrical bearing spells doom for Julien, for the spectacular culture demands the tragic ending of a Romantic historical drama. Unable to imagine an authentic present reality, the actors in the novel have recourse to a preexisting script, reenacting the kinds of productions (*Hernani* and *Marino Faliero* or the plays about Napoleon) that always result in the death of the hero.

Following his sentencing, Julien begins to understand the nature of the spectacle and to see the inevitability of his own role in it. In a conversation with Mathilde, who continues to plot his release, he offers the following ironic justification for seeing Mme de Rênal, whom he has now come to love with a hitherto unknown depth of passion: "the visits of Mme de Rênal will help the lawyer from Paris charged with obtaining my pardon to make his case; he will depict the murderer honored by the attentions of his victim. This might have an effect, and perhaps one day you will see me as the subject of some melodrama, etc., etc." (552). Julien's cynical prediction of the way in which the spectacle will recuperate everything, transforming even the truest love into such a stale rehashing of trite emotions that it can be summarized with a double "etc.," offers an apt characterization of the register in which Mathilde and the other characters in the novel function. It also calls to mind Stendhal's own co-opting of the story of Antoine Berthet for *Le rouge et le noir*, begging the question of whether the novel that is nearly finished is in fact the very melodrama imagined with such disgust by Julien. Melodramas, however, are usually devoid of this type of self-reflexive irony and seldom call attention to their own mechanism. Perhaps, then, Julien's commentary represents the moment at which the character and the novel assert their independence from the theatrical conventions of the culture. Julien analyzes the spectacle from the outside rather than consenting to play its victim.

All tenderness and devotion, Mme de Rênal has come to signify for Julien the very opposite of Mathilde, the very opposite of the spectacle. The extent of her authenticity is ironically illustrated by her willingness to play a theatrical role by throwing herself at the feet of the king to beg for Julien's release. Whereas Mathilde would have derived unimaginable satisfaction from such a scene-stealing gesture, Mme de Rênal can imagine no worse fate: "She had made the sacrifice of separating from Julien and after such an effort, the unpleasantness of making a spectacle of herself [*le désagrément de se donner en spectacle*], which formerly would have appeared to her worse than death itself, seemed like nothing to her" (554). Mme de Rênal's moral superiority, in other words, derives from her readiness to become a spectacle for Julien's sake in spite of her repugnance for such publicity.

Julien's own moral heroism at the end of the novel derives from his refusal to allow her to make such a gesture in spite of the fact that his life hangs in the balance. "I will cease to see you, I will bar you from my prison, cried Julien, and the next day I will certainly kill myself in despair, if you do not swear to take no action that will make us into a public spectacle" (554). For the post-trial Julien, as for Mme de Rênal, the spectacle represents a fate worse than death. Rather than let his story be turned into a shoddy melodrama, he would rather do anything, even deny himself the pleasure of his lover's company or die. "Let's hide ourselves," (554) he tells her, preferring a death in privacy than a life in the public eye. His refusal to play a role is categorical, leading him to resist the suggestion, made by an opportunistic priest, to convert "with show [*avec éclat*]," (553) which is to say to make a public spectacle of his conversion, in a bid to win the clemency of the authorities. Julien denounces the priest as an agent of the spectacular culture that threatens to destroy his soul as it destroys his body: "With show! repeated Julien. Ah! I have caught even you, father, play-acting [*jouant la comédie*] like a missionary" (553). At the end of the novel, Julien steps outside of the spectacle to become a critic, taxing the cast members for their bad performances.

In the process, he voices the novel's critique of the spectacle even while becoming its victim. Julien dies because he acted a part and because those who surrounded him insist on acting one as well, but he manages to escape from the theatrical imperative in the act of dying, even though the guillotine that kills him could be a prop in a Revolutionary drama: "Everything happened simply, properly, and without the slightest affectation on his part" (555). On his way to the guillotine, Julien ceases to play a role; he becomes, for the first time, himself. The narrator appropriately switches metaphoric registers, from the spectacular to the literary, to signal the lack of theatricality in Julien's comportment: "Never had that head been so poetic as at the moment it was about to fall" (554). The actual event of the execution, moreover, is elided, as if to hide it from the reader's eyes, to make it as unspectacular as possible.[38]

---

38. In an article originally published in *La Nouvelle Revue de Paris* in 1864, Hippolyte Taine likewise saw the scene of Julien's execution as a refusal of the spectacle: "The novel is the story of Julien, and Julien winds up being guillotined; but Beyle would have been horrified to write like the author of a melodrama; he was too well bred to lead us to the foot of the scaffold and show us the dripping blood; this spectacle, according to him, is made for butchers." Taine, *Nouveaux essais de critique et d'histoire* (Paris: Hachette, 1905), 226.

Just as the critique of the spectacle voiced in Balzac's *Adieu* was co-opted by the theatrical staging of the story, Julien fails to escape completely from the spectacular culture that surrounds him. Realizing his fear that his story will become "the subject of some melodrama," Mathilde appropriates Julien's mortal remains for her elaborately staged funereal performance. The final *tableau* of the novel begins with Mathilde's dramatic entrance into the room housing Julien's decapitated body. "I want to see him," (555) she tells Julien's loyal friend Fouqué, signaling her allegiance to the spectacular regime. While Fouqué averts his gaze, Mathilde parts the curtain covering the corpse, all the while thinking of her historic models: "The memory of Boniface de la Mole and of Marguerite de Navarre no doubt gave her a superhuman courage" (556). Julien's death gives Mathilde the role of a lifetime, the role she was born to play. Finally she can reenact the sublime gesture of the legendary queen, carrying her lover's head on her lap to its final resting place. The producer and director of the scene, as well as its star, Mathilde supplies the lights, the costumes, and an audience:

> Arriving thus at the uppermost point of one of the high mountains of the Jura, in the middle of the night, in that little cave magnificently illuminated with an infinite number of candles, twenty priests celebrated the service of the dead. All the inhabitants of the little mountain villages through which the convoy crossed had followed it, attracted by the singularity of that strange ceremony.
> Mathilde appeared in the middle of them in long mourning attire, and, at the end of the service, threw them several thousand five-franc pieces. (556)

Even going so far as to bribe the spectators—paid applauders, the claque, were typical of the show-business culture of the time—Mathilde ensures that her final performance is a smashing success.[39]

Mathilde appropriates Julien's story for her historical drama and uses his body as a prop, but the novel itself establishes a definite distance from the spectacular conventions of the culture. This distance is, in part, generated by irony. As I have shown, Julien embodies the voice of the critic by describing how Mathilde's need to perform prevents her from providing genuine human compassion. The text ends with her representation of a historical drama, her reenactment of Marguerite de Navarre burying the head of her lover Boniface de la Mole, but thanks in part to Julien's criti-

---

39. Here once again, the ending mimics *Adieu*—local peasants are incorporated into the historical spectacle as an audience for the aristocratic actors.

cal commentary, this scene is viewed with suspicion by readers—an audience prepared to see through her method acting. Mathilde's final dramatic gesture, her triumphant climax, thus becomes a horrifying commentary on the effect of the historical spectacle on nineteenth-century French culture. Julien, pushed to commit a senseless crime by blindly following a script, dies so that Mathilde might have her moment in the spotlight. Like the ending of Billy Wilder's *Sunset Boulevard,* in which the aging actress played by Gloria Swanson announces that she is "ready for her close-up" despite the fact that nobody is watching, Mathilde's theatrics prove empty—or worse, fatal. Just as Wilder's film captures the pathos of a heroine who lives her life as a Hollywood film, Stendhal's novel analyzes the danger of turning self and world into a Romantic historical drama.

As I argued in chapter 4, the Romantic historical novel as inherited from Scott and as it emerged in its classic form in France in the late 1820s was complicit with contemporary forms of spectacle in presenting the past as a visual entertainment. Just as Balzac's *Les Chouans* analogizes its mode of viewing history to the panorama, showing how historical knowledge accrues through unfolding vistas, Hugo's *Notre-Dame de Paris* (1831) begins with a theatrical performance, equating the novelistic re-creation of the past to the dramatic. Both novels beckon the reader toward an illusionistic space in which a visual representation of history substitutes for reality.

Like the spectacles of popular culture, the Romantic historical novel convinces its "viewers"/readers to suspend disbelief, to enter into the illusion of the past. History is offered as a foundation for knowledge about the world and the self, as a stable ground on which subjectivity can and should be formed. *Le rouge et le noir* offers just the opposite. Instead of entering the world of the past with the characters, the reader watches, firmly anchored in the present, as the characters enter by themselves, and to their peril. The classic Romantic historical novel presents the past as a drama; the Realist novel brings us backstage—the *échafaudage* visible, the illusion never taking hold. Rather than re-creating the past as a play, *Le rouge et le noir* offers us insight into the mechanics of such a production, its motivation, and its devastating effect on both actors and viewers.[40]

---

40. My point parallels Girard's distinction between the romantic (*romantique*) and the novelistic (*romanesque*). For Girard, works falling into the former category passively reflect mediated desire, whereas those in the latter "reveal" it (*Mensonge romantique et vérité romanesque,* 25). Like Girard's categories, my opposition between the Romantic and the Realist does not seek to provide fixed, positivist labels for literary works so much as to explore a tension between two ways of looking at the past in the nineteenth century.

Spectacular States

Stendhal's later novel, *La chartreuse de Parme,* likewise foregrounds this tension between Romanticism and Realism, between the re-creation of a distant past and the ironic critique of the desires motivating such a re-creation. At first glance, *La chartreuse de Parme* reads like a classic Romantic historical novel: "*La Chartreuse* could be a historical novel," acknowledges Michel Crouzet, "in the manner of Scott or of Manzoni."[41] Thanks to the near absence of the trappings of modern nineteenth-century culture in the novel, the reader could be forgiven for thinking it takes place during the Middle Ages. Whereas *Le rouge et le noir* begins with a description of the effect of modern capitalism on the provincial town of Verrières, assaulting readers with the sound of a mechanized nail factory,[42] the economy of *La chartreuse de Parme* seems to operate according to the feudal system; all the characters are either nobles living off the revenue of their estates or peasants who serve them as lackeys. Yet, despite what Crouzet labels the "passéiste" tone of the novel, Stendhal has taken pains to set it in the recognizable present of the post-Napoleonic era with multiple references to contemporary politics.

Like Julien, Fabrice del Dongo, the hero of *La chartreuse de Parme,* is obsessed with Napoleonic history from his earliest youth, and learns about this past through visual media: "You know that I had, in my lovely apartment in the Dugnani palace, prints of the battles won by Napoleon," Fabrice's aunt Gina explains; "My nephew learned to read by reading the legends on these engravings."[43] Historical illustration thus serves Fabrice as a kind of ur-text, a primary template on which his vision of the world will be formed. Given such an education, it comes as little surprise that Fabrice attempts to forge his identity on the Napoleonic battlefield. Unfortunately for him, however, this battlefield turns out to be not the sites of such victories as Marengo or Austerlitz, but Waterloo, and instead of serving as a stable ground from which to confront the world, it provides little more than a source of confusion.

Unlike a historical engraving or a panorama, which offer a clear if fictitious perspective from which to gain knowledge of the historical event, Fabrice's position in the thick of things fails to teach him a lesson. Despite

41. Michel Crouzet, preface to Stendhal, *La chartreuse de Parme* (Paris: Flammarion, 1964), 25.

42. "Hardly did one enter the town before being stunned by the din of a noisy and terrible looking machine" (Stendhal, *Le rouge et le noir,* 24).

43. Stendhal, *La chartreuse de Parme,* 116. Subsequent quotations are cited in the text.

his best intentions and eagerness to learn, "he understood nothing at all" (77). His sight continually blocked by smoke or distracted by officers attempting to steal his horse, Fabrice never gets a clear view of his hero, Napoleon. Indeed, he is never really sure whether he was at Waterloo at all. As Gina explains his confusion later in the novel, "He was still a child, despite his seventeen years; his big worry was knowing whether he had really been at the battle, and if the answer were *yes,* if he could say he had fought, not having attacked a single battery or enemy column" (301). History in *La chartreuse de Parme* quite resolutely fails to provide a foundation for the hero's identity; as unstable as a cloud of smoke fired from a musket, the past hovers over Fabrice and the other characters in the novel, obscuring both sight and insight.

In *La chartreuse de Parme,* the obsession with the past that drives the characters of *Le rouge et le noir* to acts of folly takes on a collective and political dimension, extending to the entire court of the fictionalized Parma. This critique of the spectacular past takes shape most clearly in the character of Prince Ernest IV, who turns his entire state into a giant Romantic historical drama. Whereas Mathilde de la Mole finds her best role in the sixteenth century and Julien Sorel and Fabrice del Dongo in the Revolutionary and Imperial periods, the prince in *La chartreuse de Parme* shows a marked preference for *le grand siècle,* seeking to model his every move, indeed his very being, on the Sun King.

Such historical performing is recognized and criticized by Gina, the Duchess Sanseverina, a pitiless onlooker and occasional participant in the ritualized reenactment of history at Parma: "The duchess found that at certain times the prince's imitation of Louis XIV was a bit too pronounced; for example, in his way of smiling graciously with his head thrown back" (136). Reflected not only in physical gestures, but in political ones as well, the obsession with history that reigns in Parma nearly leads the state to ruin. The political intrigue at the center of the plot, the rivalry between Mosca and Rassi that eventually lands Fabrice in prison, derives from this misguided effort to copy Louis XIV. As Count Mosca explains: "But in a moment of boredom and anger, and also a bit in imitation of Louis XIV having beheaded some hero of the Fronde who had been found living quietly and peacefully on an estate near Versailles, fifty years after the Fronde, Ernest IV one day had two liberals hung" (137). An effort to copy history leads the prince to the misguided execution of two opponents of his regime. The prince never conquers his fear of reprisal inspired by his dramatic action and remains as a result a slave to his ministers, who must quite literally check under his bed for vengeful liberals before he can go to sleep at night. Possessing the style of Louis XIV without the substance, and seeking to translate his gestures into a quite different historical milieu, the Parmesan prince turns himself and his court into a mere performance, an historical illusion, and suffers the consequences on a nightly basis.

Like *Le rouge et le noir*, *La chartreuse de Parme* is thus not a historical novel, but an indictment of the present's desire to look and act historical. Through the example of Fabrice and the court of Parma, the novel reveals the absurdity, as well as the danger, of looking to the past as a model. This indictment extends, of course, to Restoration-era France (for which Parma is a thinly veiled substitute) and its effort to turn back the clock, to reenact the absolutist ancien régime. As I have shown, French culture kept looking backward after the July Revolution ended the reactionary Restoration: 1830 brought the tendency toward historical performance not to a conclusion but to a climax. The critique offered by *Le rouge et le noir* and *La chartreuse de Parme* is thus aimed not only at Restoration politics but at modernity itself and at the spectacularization of the past that marks it. These realist novels expose the historical obsession of the nineteenth century as a Romantic delusion, as incapable of providing a basis for the formation of either individual or national identity. The prince of Parma's fear of assassins hiding under the bed thus serves as a perfect Realist metaphor for the problem of modernity's relation to history—despite all efforts to create the illusion of a bygone era, the threat of the present always lurks just below the surface.

Conclusion

Toward the end of Abel Gance's silent film *Napoléon* (1927), the young General Bonaparte stops at the Convention before heading off on the Italian campaign. He has come to the deserted building alone in order to seek inspiration. He does not, however, remain alone for long; the ghosts of Danton, Marat, Robespierre, and Saint-Just appear to the future hero, exhorting him to be true to the ideals of the Revolution and to spread its message to foreign lands. In this phantasmagoric scene, just as the future emperor affirms his connection to France's Revolutionary history, so too does the cinema, which emerged in the dense entertainment culture of nineteenth-century France, acknowledge the legacy of its own spectacular past.

The phantasmagoria is not the only pre-cinematic technology that I have discussed in this book to haunt Gance's *Napoléon*. The film quite obviously harkens back to the Napoleon plays that stunned audiences in 1830 with their realistic sets, lavish costumes, and actors who imitated the emperor. Gance's historical epic seems to place itself self-consciously in the lineage of the panorama through its use of "Polyvision" split-screen technology, in which three different images provide a panoramic perspective on Napoleon's famous battles. And the film enacts many of the same *tableaux* found both in the Napoleon plays and in the illustrated histories of the emperor from the 1830s and 1840s.[1] It adapts many of the formal

---

1. One example is the famous snowball fight scene that opens the film, a version of which had been featured in *Bonaparte à l'école de Brienne, ou le petit caporal, souvenirs de 1783*, the Napoleon play starring Virginie Déjazet in 1830. Images of the snowball fight also ap-

techniques of these illustrated histories as well, relying on the processes of cutaway, insert, and close-up that they pioneered to produce a total—and realistic—vision of the past. Indeed, silent cinema as a whole harnessed word and image in much the same way as these illustrated editions to engage multiple senses and faculties of perception simultaneously.

Gance's film not only borrows from its spectacular predecessors many of their formal and thematic components, but also shares in their ideological affiliations. Like the panoramas, illustrated histories, and plays about the emperor, Gance's film celebrates a certain vision of Napoleon. Mythifying the man as the heroic defender of democratic ideals and the vehicle for their worldwide dissemination, it conveniently excludes the more sinister aspects of his legacy. Ending with the Italian campaign allows the film to avoid the entire question of the Empire, when Napoleon's dictatorial tendencies emerged in full force. As I have shown, popular forms of history glorifying Napoleon aligned themselves with potentially dangerous political forces during the nineteenth century, when a return to Bonapartist dictatorship remained a very real threat (and one that became a reality during the Second Empire). In 1927, when demagoguery and dictatorship were again very much at issue following Benito Mussolini's rise to power and Adolf Hitler's failed *putsch,* such a vision of the past was hardly less dangerous.

Gance's film acts as a bridge between the historical entertainments of the nineteenth century and the cinematic spectacles of our own time. It reveals the extent to which the issues attending the inception of modernity's historical imagination continued to mark its later manifestations. Viewed from the other side of the twentieth century, an era in which the image triumphed, along with modern forms of popular dictatorship, the spectacular past of the nineteenth century takes on new relevance. Although, as I have shown, popular forms of visual history helped the bourgeois individual assert a new, post-Revolutionary identity, they may also have contributed to modernity's darker side, in which the individual surrendered that identity to irrational passions and hero worship. The propaganda machines of twentieth-century mass culture proved particularly adept at using the image as an instrument of manipulation.

For certain nineteenth-century observers, however, the dangers of the spectacular past were less political than existential. The early Realist

---

pear in A.V. Arnault's *Vie politique et militaire de Napoléon* (1822) and Laurent de l'Ardèche's *Histoire de l'empereur Napoléon* (1839), two of the illustrated histories I discuss in chapter 2. In "L'image de Napoléon au cinéma, son jeu et sa gestuelle," *Napoléon et le cinéma,* ed. Jean-Pierre Mattei (Ajaccio: Alain Piazzola, 1998), Vanina Angelini notes that early films about Napoleon "faithfully reconstruct famous painted or engraved works" (38).

fiction of Balzac and Stendhal denounced the negative impact of Romantic historical spectacles on individual and collective identities. As I have shown, the protagonists of these works become victims of historical illusions. Rather than offering the heroes of these fictions a platform on which to act in the present, Romantic historical spectacles provide a false and ultimately destructive sense of the past, a negative model leading these characters astray. Realist novels show modern spectators to be so captivated by the surface charms of the historical image that they wind up transfixed, paralyzed, and unable to participate in the events of the present.

Gustave Flaubert says something similar in his analysis of the Revolution of 1848, *L'éducation sentimentale* (1869), a late Realist masterpiece. Like its Balzacian and Stendhalian predecessors, Flaubert's novel critiques the alienation produced by the modern historical imagination. The novel's protagonist, Frédéric Moreau, who dreams of becoming a historical novelist in the style of Walter Scott, misses the climax of the Revolution of 1848 while on a historical sightseeing trip to Fontainebleau. Frédéric's historical tourism perfectly captures both the dream of the historical spectacle and its nightmare: the historical spectacle might provide Frédéric with a safe alibi, a comfortable remove from history's turmoil, but it also prevents him from living in the present, from participating in the most important event of his own time.

The Realist critique of the historical spectacle tends toward pessimism. In Balzac and Stendhal, as also in Flaubert, spectacular forms of history undo the subjectivity of the protagonists, undermining identity and evacuating the self of the originality that could lead to positive engagement in the present. Colonel Chabert winds up in the poorhouse, his name surrendered for a number; Philippe de Sucy and Stéphanie de Vandières die as a result of the spectacle, as does Julien Sorel. Frédéric Moreau survives, but in a reduced state, his life a record of emptiness and missed opportunity. Realist novels show the dangers of the Romantic historical spectacle, all the horrible fates that befall its victims, but fail to suggest an alternative way of relating to the past. These novels denounce the transformation of history into a visual commodity, but seem to point to the inevitability of this transformation.

Postmodern theorists have updated this critique. I have described how Guy Debord lambasted the society of the spectacle in the 1960s, denouncing how images mediate social relations under capitalism, and lamenting the passivity and alienation that both produces such a state and is produced by it. Debord's spectacularized subject resembles Flaubert's antihero in his inability to act or to perceive the reality of his alienation. More recently, Umberto Eco has written compellingly and not without humor of the "hyperreal" simulations of wax displays, historical theme parks, and local history museums in the United States. His analysis of the American desire to see simulations of history—the Oval Office reproduced in exact detail at the Lyndon B. Johnson Library in Austin, Texas—comes even closer than Debord's text to providing a twentieth-century version of the critique I have described in this book. Eco sees the American obsession with "the real thing" giving way to a fascination with the "absolute fake," with dangerous consequences for the American sense of history.[2] Attuned to the pleasures procured from such spectacles of past, Eco nevertheless denounces the historical distortions that result from such a blurring of reality and illusion, as well as the negative effects on the spectating subject. Allegories of "consumer society," these spectacles are places of "total passivity," according to Eco.[3]

For Jean Baudrillard, the danger inherent in the historical "simulations" of cinema lies in the way they rob history of meaning. This meaning consists of the belief in the possibility of narrative to structure human experience, which Baudrillard describes as a "myth" underpinning the heroic age of both history and the novel—the nineteenth century. The attempt to re-create history with an absolute visual realism—which Baudrillard calls "this negative and implacable fidelity to the materiality of the past"— leads to the "disappearance" of history as a structuring force and its replacement by "the archive," by which he means the mere object or detail from the past divorced from any connection to the kind of myth that gives history its power.[4] Baudrillard sees this process as equivalent to the loss of God for the individual subject: "Photography and cinema contributed in large part to the secularization of history, to fixing it in its visible, 'objective' form at the expense of the myths that once traversed it."[5] The result, according to the French theorist, is an impoverishment of the spectating self, because history loses its ability to provide the ground for a meaningful individual existence.

Baudrillard's condemnations of historical simulation seem to apply exclusively to the recent products of Hollywood, just as Eco sees the hyper-

2. Umberto Eco, *Travels in Hyperreality*, trans. William Weaver (1973; New York: Harcourt Brace Jovanovich, 1983), 8.

3. Ibid., 48.

4. Jean Baudrillard, *Simulacra and Simulation*, trans. Sheila Faria Glaser (1981; Ann Arbor: University of Michigan Press, 1994), 47.

5. Ibid., 48.

real re-creation of history as a particularly American obsession.[6] I have shown in this book, however, that even if the United States has produced the latest and most spectacular examples of the spectacular past, the phenomenon traces its roots back to France in the period following the Revolution, the period Baudrillard nostalgically proclaims to be the heroic period of narrative and myth. Ironically, therefore, these postmodern critiques of the emptying out of history by spectacle reproduce the same gesture of historical evacuation they denounce. By reducing the phenomenon of the spectacular past to a contemporary and American problematic, the European critics overlook the specific social and political factors that produced it, as well as those that have made it an ongoing part of our historical imagination. Although the hyperbole of such theories might help us to comprehend the implications of the spectacular past for our own time, I have described its history, which might help put it into a larger perspective.

The spectacular past forms an essential part of the history of modernity as it took shape in France in the nineteenth century. A product of the Revolution, the spectacular mode of historical representation emerged as a response to the demands that the new era placed on historical understanding. The Revolution created modernity, I have argued, by shaking the present loose from its mooring in the past. Through the consumption of popular and visually realistic forms of history, particularly those depicting the Revolution and Napoleonic Wars, bourgeois spectators were able to envision the process of historical change that had created their new subject positions. The point of view offered by the historical spectacles may have been a distortion or an illusion, as critics claimed, but such an illusion was distinctly modern in its attempt to ground a new identity in relation to an elusive vision of the past. Today we are no longer obsessed with the image of Napoleon—thematically, Gance's film seems more like a testament to the historical culture that preceded it than a sign of things to come. But spectacles of history continue to shape us because modernity must ever define itself in relation to an image of the past.

6. Eco acknowledges the existence of European wax museums, but sees them as marginal compared with their American counterparts: "Paris has only one, as do London, Amsterdam, and Milan, and they are negligible features in the urban landscape, on side streets. Here they are on the main tourist route [. . .]. The whole of the United States is spangled with wax museums" (*Travels in Hyperreality*, 12). I would point out that the Musée Grévin in Paris is on the boulevard Montmartre, hardly a side street.

APPENDIX
Plays about Napoleon and the Empire in 1830–1831

Date of Premiere	Title	Author(s)	Theater
Aug. 31, 1830	La prise de la Bastille et le passage du Mont Saint-Bernard	Villemot, Nézel	Cirque-Olympique
Oct. 9, 1830	Bonaparte, lieutenant d'artillerie, ou 1789 et 1800	Saintine, Duvert, Saint-Laurent	Vaudeville
Oct. 9, 1830	Bonaparte à l'ecole de Brienne, ou le petit caporal, souvenir de 1783	Gabriel, Villeneuve, Masson	Nouveautés
Oct. 14, 1830	Napoléon	Anicet Bourgeois, Cornu	Ambigu Comique
Oct. 15, 1830	Napoléon à Berlin, ou la redingote grise	Dumersan, Dupin	?
Oct. 20, 1830	Napoléon, ou Schoenbrunn et Sainte-Hélène	Dupeuty, Régnier-Destourbets	Porte St.-Martin
Oct. 22, 1830	Napoléon à Brienne	Dupontchartrain	Comte
Oct. 27, 1830	Le cocher de Napoléon	Sauvage	Gaîté
Oct. 30, 1830	Napoléon ou la vie d'un grand homme	Lamerlière	(Lyon)
Nov. 2, 1830	Napoléon en Égypte, ou la Bataille des Pyramides	Queriau	(Lyon)
Nov. 17, 1830	Napoléon en Paradis	Simonnin, B. Antier, Nézel	Gaîté

Nov. 23, 1830	*Quatorze ans de la vie de Napoléon, ou Berlin, Potsdam, Paris, Waterloo et Sainte-Hélène*	Clairville aîné	Luxembourg
Dec. 2, 1830	*Joséphine ou le retour de Wagram*	Gabriel, Delaboullaye	Opéra-Comique
Dec. 6, 1830	*L'empereur*	Saint-Alme, Laloue, Franconi	Cirque-Olympique
Dec. 1830	*Napoléon, ou Berlin, Paris et Sainte-Hélène*	Ch. Desnoyer	Belleville
Dec. 28, 1830	*Le fils de l'homme*	P. de Lussan (Sue, De Forges)	Nouveautés
Jan. 1, 1831	*Napoléon aux Tuileries*	Dumersan	Belleville
Jan. 10, 1831	*Napoléon Bonaparte*	Dumas	Odéon
Jan. 13, 1831	*Malmaison et Sainte-Hélène*	Pixerécourt, Ducange, Sauvage	Gaîté
Jan. 22, 1831	*Le maréchal Brune, ou la Terreur de 1815*	Dupeuty, Fontan	Porte St.-Martin
Jan. 28, 1831	*L'entrevue, ou les deux impératrices*	de Villeneuve, Masson, Saintine	Vaudeville
Feb. 12, 1831	*Joachim Murat*	B. Antier, Nézel, Decomberousse	Ambigu-Comique
Feb. 17, 1831	*L'Impératrice Joséphine*	?	Luxembourg
Feb. 23, 1831	*Malet, ou la conspiration de 1812*	de Chavanges, Nézel	?
May 14, 1831	*Le grenadier de Wagram*	H. Lefebvre, Saint-Amand	Ambigu-Comique
Aug. 20, 1831	*Le grenadier de l'Île d'Elbe*	Anicet Bourgeois, Cornu	Folies-Dramatiques
1831	*L'île d'Elbe, ou le soldat de la Vieille Garde*	Belfort-Delvaux	(Grasse)

Index

Debord, Guy, *La société du spectacle*,
12–14, 59–60, 144, 222, 268–269
Déjazet, Virginie, 120, 135, 215
DeJean, Joan, 153n.6
Delacroix, Eugène, 64
Delaistre, Jean-Alexandre-François, 121
Delalance, Gustave, *Le maréchal d'Ancre*,
172
Delaroche, Paul, 64; 87–89, 101
Delavigne, Casimir, *Marino Faliero*,
240–243
Delécluze, Étienne-Jean, 48n.98
Descotes, Maurice, 129n.63
Desmoulins, Camille, 21, 25
Diderot, Denis, 124–125
Dinocourt, Théophile, 187
Diorama: effects, 48; location, 48; subjects:
churches, 49; July Revolution, 49; Napo-
leon's tomb, 49–50, 56. *See also* Da-
guerre, Louis-Jacques-Mandé
Doane, Mary Ann, 37, 39
Dolkart, Judith, 236n.12
Douthwaite, Julia V., 160n.29
Drame national, 109–117, 150
Duchet, Claude, 170n.65, 186
Dulaure, Jacques-Antoine, *Nouvelle de-
scription des curiosités de Paris*, 20; *His-
toire de Paris et de ses monuments*,
97n.78
Dumas, Alexandre, *père*, 3, 186
—Works: *Christine*, 115, 140; *Napoléon
Bonaparte*, 120–123, 129–131, 133,
140–144, 146–147, 217, 238; *Les trois
mousquetaires*, 172, 176, 178

Eco, Umberto, 269–270
Elisabeth, Madame, 21
El Nouty, Hassan, 115n.25
Empereur, L' (Saint-Alme, Laloue, Fran-
coni), 122–123, 129, 133, 141, 145
Encyclopédie, 36, 65
Engraving: metal, 67–68; wood, 15, 67–79,
96, 101–102, 105, 190–193
Enlightenment, 36; art criticism, 24. *See
also* Pedagogy
Entertainment. *See* Spectacles (of history)
Ekphrasis, 14–15, 152, 164–166

Felman, Shoshana, 212–214
Feminism, 10
Ferguson, Priscilla, 43n.81, 233n.4
Ferris, Ina, 180
Festivals, 40
Fiesci, Joseph-Marie, 131
Flâneur, 43
Flaubert, Gustave, 14, trial 9–10
—Works: *Bouvard et Pécuchet*, 5, 9n.24;

Correspondance, 179; *L'éducation senti-
mentale*, 3n.4, 268; *Madame Bovary*, 10,
9n.24, 186; *Salammbô*, 186
Folle de la Bérésina, La (E. Théaulon),
222–223
Fontaine, Jean-Michel-Denis, 31
Foucault, Michel, 6n.18,
Fournel, Victor, 21–22
Franconi. *See* Cirque-Olympique
Franco-Prussian War, 104–105
Franklin, Benjamin, 20
Fried, Michael, 124–125
Friedland, Paul, 116n.28
Freud, Sigmund, 23n.19
Fulton, Robert, 31, 46
Furne, Charles, 74n.28

Gaehtgens, Thomas W., 86n.52
Gaillard, Gabriel-Henri, 110
Galperin, William, 11n.37
Gance, Abel, 266–267, 270
Garsou, Jules, 129n.63, 134n.79
Gascar, Pierre, 2n.2, 212–213, 225–226
Gautier, Théophile, 5
Gazette de France, La 55, 63, 83–86,
139–141,
Général, Le, 118
Genlis, Stéphanie-Félicité Ducrest de Saint-
Albin, comtesse de: *La Duchesse de la
Vallière*, 155, 161; *Jeanne de France*,
155–156, 158, 161–162; *Mlle de
Lafayette*, 155; Mme de Maintenon,
155; *Le siège de La Rochelle*, 157,
181
Genette, Gérard, 252n.32
Géorama, 48
Girard, Henri, 65n.6, 68n.17
Girard, René, 249n.28, 262n.40
Girodet, Anne-Louis, 50
Globe, Le, 175
Gobert, 120, 141, 249–250
Golahny, Amy, 164n.43
Goldstein, Jan, 214n.26
Gosselin, Charles, 182–183
Gossman, Lionel, 4n.11, 63n.2
Gothic, 157
Gottis, Augustine, *Ermance de Beaufre-
mont*, 155, 160; *François Premier et
Madame de Chateaubriand*, 155, 157,
161, 183n.101
Goulet, Andrea, 204n.12
Green, Nicholas, 59n.132
Gretton, Thomas, 186–187
Gros, Antoine-Jean, 50, 236n.12
Guizot, François, 4, 82, 223
Gunning, Tom, 36n.63
Gusman, Pierre, 68n.17